Open
Systems
Interconnection

Open Systems Interconnection

Gary Dickson
Alan Lloyd

Prentice Hall

New York   London   Toronto   Sydney   Tokyo   Singapore

Acquisitions Editor: Andrew Binnie.
Production Editor: Fiona Marcar.
Cover design: Patrick Myles and Norman Baptista.

Printed in Australia by Impact Printing, Brunswick, Victoria.

    3 4 5 96 95 94 93 92

ISBN 0 13 640111 2.

National Library of Australia
Cataloguing-in-Publication Data

Dickson, Gary.
    Open systems interconnection.

    Bibliography.
    Includes index.
    ISBN 0 13 640111 2.

    1. Computer network protocols. I. Lloyd, Alan.
    II. Title.

004.62

Library of Congress
Cataloging-in-Publication Data

Dickson, Gary.
    Open systems interconnection / Gary Dickson,
    Alan Lloyd.

    p.   cm.
    Includes bibliographical reference and index.
    ISBN 0-13-640111-2

    1. Computer networks -- standards. 2. Computer
    network protocols. I. Lloyd, Alan. II. Title.

TK5105.5.D53	1991	91-42066
004.6'2--dc20		CIP

Prentice Hall, Inc., *Englewood Cliffs, New Jersey*
Prentice Hall Canada, Inc., *Toronto*
Prentice Hall Hispanoamericana, SA, *Mexico*
Prentice Hall of India Private Ltd, *New Delhi*
Prentice Hall International, Inc., *London*
Prentice Hall of Japan, Inc., *Tokyo*
Prentice Hall of Southeast Asia Pty Ltd, *Singapore*
Editora Prentice Hall do Brasil Ltda, *Rio de Janeiro*

 PRENTICE HALL

A division of Simon & Schuster

Contents

Part 3 — Standards for Information Exchange

Part 4 — Standards for Distributed Applications

Part 5 — Document Handling Standards

Part 6 — OSI Distributed Systems

Appendices

Preface

Who should read this book? Open Systems Interconnection (OSI) is a central part of the future of the information technology industry, but reading the standards is boring and it is difficult to get the full picture because the information is dispersed over so many documents. This book provides a broad, systematic, up to date coverage of the international standards that constitute OSI. It brings together, in the one volume, a comprehensive summary of all of the main standards, but it does more than just paraphrase them. Where of benefit, it gives the background information and rationale behind the formulation of the standards. Abstract concepts in OSI are explained, where possible, by drawing analogies with real life.

The book is designed to appeal to a variety of readers. It does not cover the basics of data communications, and readers will need some prior knowledge of communications principles and technology. If you do not know basically what packet switching is, then study an introductory text first. However, the book is designed to help those with little background in OSI to:

- clarify any misunderstandings about OSI;

- comprehend the fundamental concepts and the broad picture of open networking;

- perceive the major issues in procurement of conformant OSI systems;

- develop the skills necessary for further study of the standards themselves; and,

- gain some insight into future industry trends.

How to use the book The structure of the book is designed so that introductory material accompanies the technical details. The book is divided into seven parts. Part 1 contains three introductory chapters. Chapter 1 gives the rationale behind OSI while Chapter 2 explains fundamental technical concepts. Chapter 3 introduces object oriented concepts that are prerequisite background for the technical aspects in Parts 3 and 4. Parts 2 and 3 deal with the seven layers of the OSI model — the first chapter in each part is an overview. Part 4 includes chapters for each major OSI application standard — each chapter commences with an introductory section. Part 5 covers standards for document handling, and Part 6 deals with systems integration, functional standards, conformance testing and procurement matters.

To gain insights into the impact of OSI on the industry, managers and technology planners would benefit by reading the introductory material identified above, skipping some of the technical details and reading selected chapters from Part 6. Depending on their background, technical professionals may be able to skim the introductory material to select technical chapters for study. Combined with another text on basic data communications, this book would also be suitable for undergraduate or postgraduate instruction.

Some chapters include questions or examples. These may be used for reinforcement or to extend the concepts discussed in the text. As such, the questions should be treated as an integral part of the book for a complete treatment. A comprehensive glossary and a list of the standards are included in the appendices to help locate topics of interest or for future reference.

Where new terms or concepts first appear, their definitions appear in italics. The margins are used for subheadings and also to highlight definitions.

Currency and status

Most of the standards covered in this book are reasonably stable and the information contained herein is believed to be accurate and up to date at the time of writing. Nonetheless, the standards are the subject of on-going review and interpretation, and changes will no doubt have occurred in the time since this book was written. It is recommended that the appropriate standards bodies be consulted to obtain the latest versions before any work on OSI is commenced. Likewise, some commentary is given on functional standards and this is also subject to change.

The examples of the benefits of standards quoted in Chapter 1 should be regarded as anecdotal, and comments about the future prospects of OSI and further developments are the authors' considered opinions, rather than commitments from any standards body.

For brevity and clarity, some simplifications have been made in the description of the OSI standards. In particular, a notation called ASN.1 is used for the definitions of the format of some Application Layer protocols. The ASN.1 definitions in this book are an abridged form and the standards should be used if a complete definition is required.

Acknow-ledgements

Part of this book has been developed from an OSI training course that is presented by one of the authors in Australia and South East Asia. The base material for the course was prepared by J. Breen, D. Rowe and A. Lloyd. It was revised and expanded by G. Smith, T. Winsemius and R. Harvey who built upon their practical experience with OSI. The course has been presented as a professional seminar since 1988 by G. Dickson who has continued to expand and refine it. The course notes have been extensively supplemented and transformed into this book by the authors who are grateful for the earlier contributions by their colleagues.

The support of the various reviewers is also gratefully acknowledged. In particular, Dr Warwick Ford suggested many improvements and clarifications that have been incorporated in the final text.

The authors are indebted to their many friends and colleagues in the standards committees and the industry who have worked long and hard to bring OSI to fruition.

Trademarks and the names of various products have been used in an editorial fashion to help clarify certain concepts and to give more realistic examples. Such use does not refer to actual products and no infringement of the rights of any trademark owner is intended.

Part 1 – Introduction

1 Why OSI?

1.1 THE INFORMATION AGE

It is now a cliche to say that industrialized nations have entered the Information Age. In an industrial society, the strategic resource is capital. In our new post-industrial society, the strategic resource is information. To an increasing extent, the economy is based on a resource that is continually growing as mankind accumulates knowledge. For an enterprise to benefit from this resource, direct and ready access to the growing amount of information about the enterprise and its environment is essential.

To underline the importance of this change in society, studies indicate that about 70% of labor costs are spent on information work — handling and exchanging information within companies or between organizations. It may be formal communication such as orders, invoices, financial transactions or technical data, or informal personal conversation. Estimates of the total amount of time spent on communication activities range from 50 to 90% of the available work time. To put it simply, the majority of the workforce goes to work not to make things, but to communicate.

Business information systems

For better or worse, our society is increasingly dependent on computers to help in our work. The relentless advance of technology, by providing improved performance at decreasing cost, has spurred the proliferation of computers in our workplaces and homes. Business is evolving rapidly, creating an increasing need to interconnect computers for faster access to broad sources of information and for improved business systems. Computers in different companies or different computers within one company need to be interconnected for the exchange of technical data for computer integrated manufacturing systems, trading documents such as orders, invoices, shipping data and other types of business transactions, and correspondence. Just like the human workforce that goes to work to communicate, information systems can no longer afford to be centralized monolithic computers that communicate with others by hard-copy print-out sent through the post for rekeying at the other end.

These increasing requirements for interdepartment and intercompany communications transcend the capabilities of existing proprietary information systems in two ways:

- Existing systems were designed to support data flow up and down the hierarchy of an organization, e.g. from executive, to management and then to staff levels in a company, rather than horizontally across organizational boundaries.

- They required the costly creation and maintenance of telecommunications plant separate from and in addition to the telephone service.

Along with the increasing number of computers in an organization, there is an increasing variety of devices from multiple vendors resulting from three factors:

- independent purchasing of computers by users in organizations;

- the inability of a single vendor to meet the requirements for mixed or specialized capabilities; and,

- purchasing policies designed to encourage competitive procurements.

Computer networking

We take for granted the ability of such information tools as the telephone and facsimile machine to provide virtually instant communications to any location around the globe at a low cost. But how well can computers communicate? The basic technology to send information between computers has been developing for some time. Unfortunately, however, many incompatible communications systems have been developed by computer vendors, limiting global information exchange, and giving rise to an electronic "Tower of Babel".

If this limiting factor could be removed, the need to send information between the growing number of computers would make computer communications as ubiquitous as telephone conversations. The desirable features for such a solution (see Figure 1.1) would include:

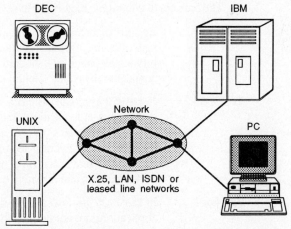

Figure 1.1   OSI – any to any information exchange independent of vendor and network

- cost effective communication;

- flexibility to support different organizational architectures;

- independence of vendor;

- global coverage;

- open to all parties who agree to communicate; and,

- integration with other telecommunications services.

The telephone network owes its success to the use of international standards to avoid potential incompatibilities in what is the world's largest multi-vendor information system. Likewise, many people now believe that the ultimate solution for global computer communications lies in the use of international standards.

1.2 WHY STANDARDS?

Multi-vendor networking

Why is international standardization crucial to solve these limitations of proprietary networks? Although multi-vendor networks can be constructed without international standards, their implementors face many difficulties.

Unfortunately, there has been a proliferation of languages (or protocols) for computer communications. The proprietary protocols used by the various computer vendors are incompatible. Consequently, an enterprise's work tools and repositories of business information have very restricted ability to exchange information with computers from different suppliers. Sometimes, even computers from the same supplier have problems exchanging information.

The barriers to communication occur at several levels:

1st level   Because of technical incompatibilities, different types of networks are difficult to interconnect. This is like a private telephone switchboard (PABX) that is unable to connect to the public telephone network.

2nd level   Even if they could connect, computers are unable to strike up a conversation, because vendors have used different "languages" or proprietary protocols. Consider the difficulties at your place of work if the sales people spoke only French; accounts, only German; engineering, only Japanese; and research, only Swahili.

3rd level   Because of the lower level difficulties, most existing applications are not designed to operate in a distributed environment. Overcoming the other two barriers does not turn existing centralized applications into distributed systems. Much application development is still required to take advantage of the improved communications capability.

Vendor lock-in   The differences in proprietary communication protocols stem from:

- the idiosyncratic nature of the protocol designers and their perception of market requirements;

- absence of user demand for conformance to standards; and,

- a corporate desire for product differentiation.

The exploitation of these incompatibilities by vendors has been a controversial backdrop to the push for the development of standards. By increasing a customer's investment in a proprietary network, it becomes more difficult for the customer to purchase products from a competing vendor because of the need to maintain compatibility with the incumbent network.

Gateways   The use of protocol conversion gateways to overcome communication incompatibilities has been used as an interim solution for the exchange of data in multi-vendor networks. However, gateways are inadequate in the long term (see Figure 1.2). Often it is impossible to find a complete mapping between functions in different proprietary networks. As more services are offered through gateways, more conversions are required and more limitations become evident. Furthermore, the number of different types of gateways required for any to any conversion increases with the square of the number of different protocols being used.

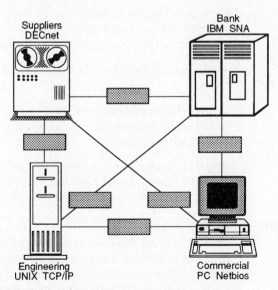

Figure 1.2   Gateways are not a viable alternative to OSI.

The number of gateways (*G*) required for the interconnection of *N* different systems is:

$$G = \frac{N^2 - N}{2}$$

Clearly, a common, standardized language for computer communications can provide faster, cheaper and more accurate business communications than gateways, and avoid the problems of supporting a myriad set of protocols and a complex maze of conversions.

Standards   By definition, the sender and receiver of any communication must co-operate for effective information transfer, and, in the long run, international standards are the most cost effective way of achieving the co-operation necessary for global computer communications. In order to break down vendor lock in, and to enable a global communications network to be established without unfair advantage to any supplier, the standards are generally based on new internationally agreed protocols. Each computer must directly implement the protocols sanctioned by the standards committees in order to participate in Open Systems Interconnection (OSI). In some cases, OSI protocols will replace the need for proprietary protocols, but for most systems OSI will co-exist with existing proprietary protocols for some time to come.

Only the widespread use of international standards will realize the benefits of distributed systems, and create a multi-vendor market place which increases the choice available to the user and suppresses costs because of increased competition.

1.2.1 Benefits of Improved Communications

There is a widespread belief that the long term benefits of standards outweigh the resources required to implement them. Is this assumption justifiable for OSI? A quantitative answer cannot be given here because:

- the analysis depends on the circumstances of individual organizations; and,

- to maximize the benefits of standardization, OSI is usually introduced in conjunction with other standards and so the effects of OSI alone are difficult to isolate.

Nonetheless, products that implement the OSI standards, and related standards for data interchange, first became available in the late 1980's, and some qualitative reports of benefits are discussed below.

Lower costs   The use of standards allows sharing of such network resources as transmission facilities, network equipment and people. Some organizations have had to develop and maintain separate networks for each vendor represented in their information system. Standards allow simpler networks and eliminate costly duplication. Furthermore, in the long term, increased competition between suppliers for a more uniform market will result in lower prices. Some specific examples include:

- Kodak is committed to OSI and related standards with an objective to slash corporate communications costs by 50% over 5 years.

- The British Government has achieved a 20% savings in annual network equipment and transmission costs by installing a national X.25 network with OSI applications shared between four departments.

Improved productivity

Improvements in network implementation, application development and change management have been reported when OSI is used together with other standards for data formats:

- During the late 1980's, BHP, an Australian steel manufacturer, spent $1 million (Australian) per year on software development and additional equipment to overcome incompatibilities between the various components of an automated process control system in one steel plant alone. BHP has implemented the OSI standards for Manufacturing Automation Protocol (MAP) in several plants to avoid these costs and to focus its resources on steel making, rather than software development.

- Hughes aircraft pioneered the use of standards to enable the interoperation of otherwise incompatible computer-aided design and manufacturing (CAD/CAM) systems. With 240 possible combinations of different hardware and software, interconnection of the systems was not possible before the introduction of standards. A common data format and an OSI network were introduced by Hughes engineers in the late 1980's. This allows the electronic exchange of engineering and graphic design data between various locations. In 1987, 18 to 24 staff months were required to implement the standards by Hughes to effect interoperability between two different vendors. As the standards are implemented by the vendors, this effort dropped to 2 to 3 months in 1990, and is expected to be minimal in the middle of the decade.

Strategic benefits

The main benefits of OSI occur when it is used to create new distributed applications. OSI should be viewed as an enabling tool for advanced applications that can give an enterprise an important competitive advantage.

- In the automotive industry, a US$2,000 reduction in the price of each standard model car is estimated by the use of advanced information technology in manufacturing and administration.

- Standards for the electronic exchange of orders, invoices and other trading documents (known as Electronic Data Interchange or EDI) are being rapidly implemented in many industry sectors to lower costs and for improved inventory management. In the consumer retail industry, it has been shown that the cost for handling a paper invoice is approximately $20, whereas an electronic version costs 20c.

Penalty of in-compatibility
Over the coming years, the trading blocs in Europe and North America will become increasingly dependent on OSI for business data communications. The European Community in particular views OSI as crucial to the operation of a single European market after 1992.

Other countries will be disadvantaged if they do not also follow these standards. To remain competitive, business and public sector computer systems must also use OSI to improve efficiency and facilitate trade. Companies that do not conform to the business communications standards of their customers will find that they lose business to competitors able to exchange orders and other information electronically.

1.3 WHAT IS OSI?

Open Systems Interconnection (OSI) is a collection of international standards for computer communications that have been developed to support distributed processing systems. The foundation standard is the Reference Model. The OSI Reference Model has the distinction of being widely written and talked about, but it is also widely misunderstood even by communications professionals.

The OSI model, with its seven layers, is well and truly embedded in the lore of the computer industry and there are a growing number of implementations. As a framework for analyzing network concepts it is powerful. As a set of architectural concepts it is having an effect on networks that is increasing daily. The concepts of OSI are spreading beyond the confines of the computer industry to encompass standards development in related areas of information technology, such as the telecommunications industry and manufacturing automation.

At its most basic, the Reference Model is an architecture for the development of standards. The purpose of the architecture and the standards is to enable processing systems to communicate easily with others. This is the distinction between "open" systems and "closed" systems that do not need to communicate outside their own community of similar types of systems.

Open systems?
Throughout the information technology industry, however, the term "open systems" has taken on a much broader but loosely defined meaning. The wider concept of open systems is usually (but not necessarily) associated with the UNIX operating system and typically means:

- vendor independence; and,

- software portability.

The open systems concept is gradually embracing such standards as:

- POSIX (Portable Operating System Interface);

- OSI;

- SQL (Structured Query Language); and

- new developments such as X Windows.

Although OSI is a prerequisite for standardized distributed "open systems", it is not confined to it. OSI can be used for communications between any computers that implement the standards, regardless of operating system.

A common misconception about OSI is that it is a particular product with certain performance constraints, limitations, etc. It is most definitely **not** a product, although there are products emerging, both within proprietary networks and as portable protocol "stack" implementations, that conform to sets of standards within the OSI environment.

Introduction to OSI

The OSI model is structured to overcome the three barriers to communications mentioned in Section 1.2. The broad functions of the layers are illustrated in Figure 1.3 and described below:

- The lower three layers (Physical, Data Link and Network layers) standardize network interfaces and the linking of multiple networks to provide a path across them. The lower layer standards end the isolation caused by technical incompatibilities of proprietary networks. In most cases, OSI generally adopts or models existing standards in this area, e.g. High level Data Link Control (HDLC); X.25 for

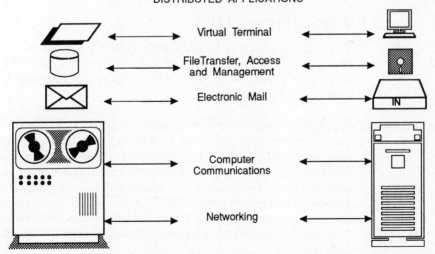

DISTRIBUTED APPLICATIONS

Virtual Terminal

FileTransfer, Access and Management

Electronic Mail

Computer Communications

Networking

Figure 1.3   OSI – standard protocols for network access, computer dialogues and a variety of distributed applications

packet switched data networks; and the Institute of Electrical and Electronics Engineers (IEEE) standards for Local Area Networks (LANs). The specific contribution of OSI is the definition of a global addressing scheme in the Network Layer, and associated protocols to convey the address. The scheme has the capacity to identify unambiguously every computer independently of the network it is attached to.

- OSI defines new protocols specifically for the next three layers (Transport, Session and Presentation). By implementing these layers in all open systems, OSI provides a common "language" to overcome the second barrier to computer communications. These layers provide uniform ways to control the flow of data, to co-ordinate the communicating applications and to encode the information exchanged between the computer systems.

- Standards for the Application Layer cover a wide range of distributed applications. By providing a base functionality for the exchange of messages, files, transactions, etc., the OSI standards enable the creation of new distributed systems that were previously impractical.

Interoperate   To underline the sweeping change to past ways of interconnecting computer systems, the OSI committees have added new words to the standards lexicon. *Interoperate* and *interwork* mean the achievement of proper and effective communication or linking between different application programs and data despite the fact that these may be on different systems from different manufacturers, connected remotely by some transmission medium or network. Ultimately, global "interoperability" depends on widespread conformance to the OSI standards.

1.3.1 A Brief History of OSI

To put OSI in its correct historical perspective it is appropriate to look briefly at the history of computer networking. Figure 1.4 illustrates the progression of networking, and Table 1.1 (page 12) summarizes the evolution of the standards.

Early networks The earliest computer networks consisted of a few, slow, teletype terminals operating over slow lines. As networks grew larger, techniques were introduced to enable expensive lines to be shared between several terminals, through the use of cluster controllers and polled protocols on multi-drop lines. By the early 1970's, most mainframe manufacturers had introduced front end processors (FEPs) to manage the communication lines and in some cases were able to have more than one mainframe participating in the network. There were two major characteristics of these early networks:

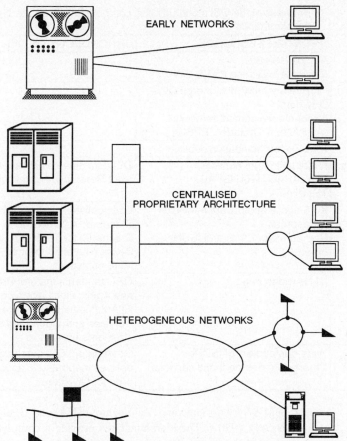

EARLY NETWORKS

CENTRALISED
PROPRIETARY ARCHITECTURE

HETEROGENEOUS NETWORKS

Figure 1.4   Progressive development of distributed, multi-vendor networks

- Apart from the lines and modems, there was virtually no use of standard components and techniques. Every manufacturer used its own protocols for lines, message formats, etc. In many cases manufacturers used different protocols for different terminal types.

- The communications systems were constructed specifically for the applications, e.g. time sharing, teleprocessing, remote batch. Consequently it was common to find important aspects of the line control and network management being left to the application software.

The Topsy-like growth of the early communications network facilities made it difficult for a terminal to switch between different applications. It was often very difficult to interconnect two mainframes of the same manufacture, and well nigh impossible to achieve this with different mainframes.

To support the interconnection of the various components of their networks, vendors developed proprietary communications architectures,

Table 1.1   Progress of the OSI standards and comparison with related
developments

PERIOD	NETWORK EVOLUTION	CHRONOLOGY OF OSI
1960's	Ad hoc RS-232. Message switching (SITA, SWIFT).	–
Early 1970's	Proprietary networks emerge (SNA, DECnet). Experimental shared networks (ARPANET, Cyclades, EPSS).	–
1976	X.25 Recommendation published.	–
Late 1970's	First public X.25 networks (DATAPAC, TRANSPAC, TELENET).	OSI committee established in ISO. Draft Reference Model published in 1979.
1983/84	X.25 public and private networks widespread. Standards for LANs and ISDNs emerge.	OSI published as International Standard. X.25 revised to comply. Standards for Transport and Session layers published. X.400 MHS published.
1988	LANs widespread.	OSI standards mature. Presentation and Application Layers complete. FTAM (file handling), Directory Services and Virtual Terminal standards emerge.
1990's	Wide deployment of ISDNs. Emergence of broadband services.	Government OSI purchasing policies mandated. Range of OSI products available.

e.g. IBM's Systems Network Architecture (SNA) and Digital's DECnet in the early 1970's. These architectures provide a complete computer communications answer for an organization using one vendor's equipment. However, it is difficult to integrate equipment from other vendors to create a multi-vendor network.

Shared networks

During the late 1960's and early 1970's a number of networks were built to serve communities of users. These networks set out to provide a degree of communication between different computer systems, initially by message switching, i.e. moving complete long messages from node to node through the network, and later by packet switching, i.e. the transmission of smaller (e.g. 100 byte) messages. Eventually packet switching became the dominant technique as it lent itself to the support of many applications (remote terminal log-in, file transfer, printing) and removed the need for the networks to be concerned with application issues.

The early networks demonstrated the need to specify a "standard" interface for computers connecting to the network. This allowed the network resources to be shared by equipment from different vendors. In the early networks these interfaces were unique and usually consisted of a synchronous line protocol and a message format for the addressing, etc.

An early shared network was the one developed by SITA, which is responsible for the communications of the international airlines. Other major networks include the large experimental ARPANET funded by the US Defense Department's Advanced Research Projects Agency (ARPA), the British Post Office's Experimental Packet Switched Service (EPSS), the Cyclades network developed by a French research agency, and the European Informatics Network (EIN). Australia made a pioneering effort with the Australian Post Office's Common User Data Network (CUDN) that saw limited commercial operation in the 1970's. A more successful early Australian network was CSIRONET that was developed by the Commonwealth Scientific and Industrial Research Organization (CSIRO).

The move to X.25

While the early network developments and trials were under way, a study group of CCITT (International Telegraph and Telephone Consultative Committee, the standards body of the telecommunications carriers) was examining the scope and application of possible future standards for public networks. By 1972, it had settled on packet switching as an appropriate technique and the new High level Data Link Control (HDLC) as the standard line protocol. This public packet switched network standard, X.25, was ready in its preliminary form for the 1976 CCITT Plenary Session. Some early public network developments based on the X.25 interface were already under way at that time. The DATAPAC network in Canada and the TRANSPAC network in France were early implementations, followed by the TELENET and TYMNET networks in the USA. Australia's public X.25 network, AUSTPAC, entered commercial operation in 1983.

X.25 has a world wide acceptance, with large public networks in most major countries, and it is supported by all computer and communications vendors. The arrival of X.25, with its standard computer interface, opened up the potential for many computer systems to interconnect. X.25 provides basic capability to exchange packets of information between computers regardless of location. It does not apply to all the other issues of addressing applications, data encoding, logging on, file transfer, terminal formats, checkpoints, etc. that are essential for computer interworking.

Standardization of X.25 did not impede the development of new network technology and subsequent standards for LANs and Integrated Services Digital Networks (ISDNs) have evolved in more recent years. Modern networks often incorporate components from many vendors, with a mixture of network types, requiring a new technological order for their interconnection.

Early OSI work

By the late 1970's, the pressure to establish some standards that could go beyond the basics of X.25, and achieve true interworking between computer systems was growing. The International Organization for Standardization (ISO) Technical Committee on Data Processing, TC 97, responded by forming a new subcommittee, on "Open Systems Interconnection". The term "open" was chosen to emphasize the fact that by conforming with the (eventual) international standards, a system would be capable of interacting with all other systems obeying the same standards throughout the world. The committee was chaired by Charles Bachman, an early pioneer of database systems, who was then with Honeywell.

Layered model   An early consensus was reached on the use of a layered architecture which would meet most requirements, with the potential of being expanded later. Within 18 months the draft Reference Model had been completed and passed to TC 97, along with recommendations for work to begin on an initial set of standard protocols. TC 97 adopted the recommendations, with the result that the Reference Model has set the framework and agenda for most of the development of communications standards over the past decade.

The Reference Model itself went through the review and voting procedures of ISO, receiving Draft Proposal (DP) and Draft International Standard (DIS) status in 1980 and 1982 respectively. In 1983 it became an International Standard: ISO 7498. Additions have since been made in the form of addenda and additional parts to the standard to extend its coverage.

In 1984, the Reference Model received important recognition from the CCITT Rapporteur's Group on Public Data Network Services, with the result that it was formally adopted by CCITT as Recommendation X.200. Also by now, standards were in place for the Transport and Session layers, X.25 was revised to meet the requirements for the Network Layer, and the X.400 standards for Message Handling Systems (MHS) were first available. 1984 was an important milestone for OSI because the shape of the standards was finally taking form. However, it was not until about 1988 that the remaining gaps were filled in to provide a complete set of standards for all of the seven layers. Other major application standards also appeared at this time. Work is continuing in the standards committees today to add new standards and increase the functionality of the old.

Major support from purchasers and vendors emerged to mark the late 1980's and early 1990's as the transition from standards to products. All major vendors now **recommend** OSI for multi-vendor networking and most are replacing their proprietary architectures with OSI.

1.4 THE STANDARDS PROCESS

Role of standards   Data communications is an area of the computer industry that makes very extensive use of formal standards. This comes about because the basic task of communications is to facilitate the interworking of many different components, and a high degree of compatibility is required between them all. Standards are needed in communications because:

- there are many different groups of people involved — users, equipment suppliers, telecommunications authorities;

- there are many different components — hardware and software, private and common carrier; and,

- there are many different places where a working agreement is needed between two components — physical interfaces, electrical interfaces, protocols, etc.

Standards used in communications have mainly been developed either by the suppliers of major components (*de facto* standards), or by formal standards bodies representing industry groups on a national or international basis. The OSI standards fall into the later category.

1.4.1 Standards Bodies

Who's who in standards? The development of the OSI standards is performed by experts volunteered by companies and organizations with interests in the work, as either users or vendors. The work is organized into a committee structure, and the outcomes are closely scrutinized to ensure that the standards have the widest possible international approval. The standards are the result of extensive collaboration between a number of international bodies headquartered in Geneva:

ISO The International Organization for Standardization is a voluntary organization whose members represent users, vendors, governments, carriers and the scientific community.

IEC The International Electrotechnical Commission is a voluntary organization concerned with electrical standards.

CCITT The International Telegraph and Telephone Consultative Committee is part of the International Telecommunication Union (ITU), an agency of the United Nations. It makes *Recommendations* for international telecommunications among participating governments and carriers.

ISO/IEC ISO and IEC have formed a joint technical committee (JTC 1) that merges overlapping work in the two bodies. This merger of interests took place in the late 1980's. Previously, OSI work was performed by ISO Technical Committee 97 (TC 97). The work is divided into a number of sub-committees, the main ones covered in this book being:

- SC 6 — the lower four layers;

- SC 18 — text and office systems; and,

- SC 21 — OSI architecture, upper layers, database and open distributed processing.

The members of ISO are the national standards bodies of each country. These bodies set national standards in their own right, for example:

- AFNOR (France)

- ANSI (American National Standards Institute)

- BSI (British Standards Institute)

- DIN (Germany)

- JSI (Japan)

- Standards Australia.

ISO is the vehicle for international collaboration on standards. National member bodies nominate experts to participate in the ISO committee meetings and have the right to vote on the progression of standards. ISO also maintains liaison with the other standards bodies.

The creation of a standard is an involved process that may take several years. Each standard goes through a number of phases. Each phase is subject to a ballot by voting members to determine whether the standard progresses to the next phase, or requires further work. The phases are known as:

CD   Committee Draft (previously called Draft Proposal or DP). This is a working document under active development in a committee.

DIS   Draft International Standard. This reflects basic technical agreement on the standard but it is still subject to change.

IS   International Standard. The standard is stable and ready for implementation.

The standards are given numbers to distinguish them from others in the ISO series. To refer to a particular standard, both the phase and standard number are used, e.g. ISO/IEC DIS 10026 (for brevity, such a standard is referred to as DIS 10026 in this book). Multi-part standards may also have the part number appended. If it is necessary to amend a standard, addenda are produced and these are referenced in a similar fashion.

CCITT   The members of the CCITT are the Post, Telephone and Telegraph (PTT) administrations or the governments of member nations. The CCITT operates in a 4 year cycle, or Study Period, terminated by a Plenary Assembly. The Plenary Assembly approves the Recommendations developed during the study period and determines the work program for the next period. Accelerated approval processes allow the publication of important Recommendations in mid-term. The work is divided into Study Groups. The main Study Groups covered in this book are:

SG VII   Public Data Networks, OSI, X-series (e.g. X.25, X.400)

SG XVII   Data Transmission, V-series (e.g. V.24, V.28)

SG XVIII   Integrated Services Digital Networks, I-series (e.g. I.431)

The CCITT and ISO/IEC have co-operated to produce the OSI standards. In most cases, the respective sub-committees work jointly to produce common texts for standards where they have mutual interests. In some areas, where the two bodies have different perspectives (i.e. that of carrier and of user), they produce standards that are technically aligned. Where relevant, references to both CCITT and ISO/IEC standards are given in this book.

Industry bodies
    Other multinational standards organizations also have played a major role in the formulation of OSI, often by supplying proposals for, or first drafts of, new standards. Some of the industry bodies include:

ECMA   European Computer Manufacturers' Association. The source of considerable input to ISO and CCITT on OSI.

EIA   Electronic Industries Association. Formulates technical standards and represents the industry in the USA. Origin of the RS-232 standard.

IEEE   Institute of Electrical and Electronics Engineers (USA). Recently responsible for the IEEE 802 series of standards for LANs.

In summary, the OSI standards are the culmination of literally hundreds of thousands of man-years of work by international experts with backing from major companies and governments. Their implementation reflects a growing maturity of the information technology industry. The industry can now capitalize on the innovation of the past 20 years to deliver more cost effective networking products for general use and to foster creativity in new distributed applications.

1.4.2 Functional Standards

From standard to product
    The ultimate goal of OSI is to allow the exchange of information, trade documents and business transactions with an indefinite number of partners in multi-vendor networks. The global interoperability of distributed applications demands unprecedented uniformity and compatibility of products from competing vendors. To achieve this, the vendors need two things:

- Motivation to develop conforming products. In other words, purchasers have a responsibility to express correctly their requirements for OSI conformance in terms of the standards.

- A way of testing and certifying products to avoid costly incompatibilities between different vendors' products.

The standards for OSI are a very comprehensive set of protocol definitions covering almost all conceivable applications and networking environments. However, the base OSI standards are not precise enough to guarantee compatible implementations of OSI. They are intended as generic specifications and they allow considerable latitude in terms of options, subsets and parameter ranges to allow flexibility for implementors.

For instance, if there is no technical reason to define the length of a particular parameter, the standard will leave it undefined. However, for practical reasons, implementors must put constraints on the range of parameter lengths and values, and select options from the standards appropriate to their application and network requirements. If implementors took arbitrary choices, there would be little chance that similar choices would be made by all, and so a low probability that different systems would fully interwork.

So a further step of functional standardization is necessary to achieve compatibility. A functional standard, also called a profile, is an agreement between implementors, or a specification by purchasers, of the details chosen for compatibility of different products. In effect, a profile is a selection of subsets of the OSI standards chosen on the basis of their network and application needs and taking product availability into account. The base standards remain unchanged as the definitive specification of OSI — the profiles will grow to reflect increasing product capabilities.

Who's who in profiles?

Profiles have generally been developed by industry groups, rather than the formal standards bodies. This division allows the standards bodies to focus on the base standards, while expediting the creation of profiles by people working closely with OSI products. A number of groups have created their own profiles. The most well known and widely implemented profiles are:

MAP/TOP   Manufacturing Automation Protocol/Technical Office Protocol. MAP was instigated by General Motors to facilitate the interconnection of process controllers and robots in a manufacturing environment. TOP was initially developed by Boeing to help automate the exchange of technical information and design drawings. MAP and TOP are closely aligned. MAP/TOP specifies a number of application profiles, and specific subsets of each of the lower layers to support those applications. Their many adherents have formed the worldwide MAP/TOP Users Federation.

GOSIP Government OSI Profile. Many governments have specified OSI profiles to be used for government procurement of information systems. The UK and US governments were the first to do so, and most other governments have selected compatible profiles. (Other governments also use different terms; e.g. the Canadian equivalent to GOSIP is called COSAC.) The profiles were selected to facilitate interworking between government systems, but are generally suitable for other administrative or service organizations.

A number of other organizations have been prominent in the development of profiles. The various initiatives in this area are described in Chapter 25.

ISP To avoid duplication and regional divergence of profiles, a co-ordinating group, called the Feeder's Forum, has been established. The objective is to "harmonize" the outputs of the contributing groups and to submit finalized profiles to ISO for publication as *International Standardized Profiles (ISP)*.

A profile is a set of one or (usually) more OSI standards with the identification of selected subsets, options and parameters necessary for accomplishing a particular function (e.g. transferring mail messages). The upper three layers are usually specified as a group called an Application profile. The lower four layers are specified together as a Transport profile. Initial profiles specify only restricted subsets of the standards, reflecting the fact that early products have limited capabilities. Other profiles represent increased functionality corresponding to more comprehensive implementations of the standards.

The numbering scheme for ISPs uses a three letter acronym, which identifies a particular group of the standards, followed by a number to identify a particular ISP; e.g. AHM 11 is an Application profile for message handling, number 11. A different identification scheme is used in GOSIP. Eventually, it is expected that the profiles in the various GOSIP publications will be replaced when appropriate ISPs are available.

1.4.3 OSI Conformance

There are a number of aspects to consider when evaluating claims of conformance to OSI:

* conformance clauses in the base standards;

* profile requirements; and,

* testing.

Appropriate parts of the base standards for each layer contain conformance clauses specifying the cardinal subsets that constitute a valid implementation of the standard. These are broad requirements only and are not sufficient for interoperability. In order to acquire products which will successfully interoperate, it is not sufficient to specify that the product shall interwork with some other vendor's system using an OSI standard. For instance, both parties may implement some obscure profile or there may be some errors which are not revealed by that particular combination of products. This of course would make it difficult to communicate with other parties.

Profiles

A software or equipment vendor would normally develop a product to conform to an internationally recognized profile. For confidence that different products will interwork and will be widely available, purchasers should also explicitly specify their needs in terms of an international profile. Such profiles clearly define the mandatory services and capabilities provided to end users and prescribe the behavior necessary for successful interoperability of conforming products. (This does not exclude the possibility that products may also be developed to suit particular customer requirements or applications.)

The crucial point is that purchasers must put the onus on vendors to achieve conformance with the standards, **and** also with defined profiles.

Testing

Testing is a way of measuring the degree of conformance of a product to a specific profile. Indeed, it is not possible to test for conformance to the base standard because that is too open ended. Standards and procedures are being established to give vendors and users confidence that products conform to the appropriate OSI standards and profiles. The implementation of testing systems usually lags behind the publication of the standard, and testers may not be available for some time after the first products. Nevertheless, conformance testing is now well established for the main OSI standards. The details of the conformance testing process are covered in Chapter 26, but the significance of this is far reaching — profiles and conformance testing represent a new way of purchasing information systems. For the first time, purchasers have a method of unambiguously defining their requirements in terms of international standards and have the ability independently to verify claims of conformance.

By consistently insisting on conformance to internationally recognized profiles in procurement specifications, users can be confident that compatible products will supplied. To evaluate offered products, purchasers should request evidence that the product has satisfactorily passed appropriate tests (where available) to demonstrate conformance to the requested profile.

2 The OSI Reference Model

2.1 BASIC CONCEPTS

Organization Ambitious projects, requiring the co-operation of large numbers of people, require a very clear, systematic approach. The organization of the development and documentation of the OSI standards produced a succession of documents at increasing levels of detail. The Reference Model is the foundation standard, defining the overall guidelines, basic concepts and terminology used in all of the standards under the OSI umbrella. This chapter introduces the modeling concepts of the Reference Model that will be applied in all of the subsequent chapters of the book. Some of the concepts are explained only at an abstract level in this chapter but concrete examples appear in subsequent chapters.

The Reference Model is ISO 7498 and CCITT X.200. It is published in four parts:

Basic Refer-   Covered in this chapter of the book.
ence Model

Security   Security is not covered as a topic in this book, although
Architecture   security aspects of certain standards are discussed, and the status of standards work in this area is mentioned in Section 24.3, page 416.

Naming and   Aspects of this topic are covered in the chapters on the
Addressing   Network Layer (Chapter 7), Internetworking (Chapter 8), and Directory Services (Chapter 16).

Management   Covered in Chapter 19 on Systems Management.
Framework

Purpose   Basically, the Reference Model defines the concepts used to partition the communications between computers into a number of layers (similar to the modularization of software), and broadly allocates functions to each layer. Typically, there are several standards stemming from the Reference Model covering the details of each layer. The Reference Model provided a common basis for co-operation between separate teams of people working in standards committees on different parts of the project. As such, the Reference Model is a very conceptual document that specifies the overall architecture for OSI, but it contains nothing concrete that could be implemented as a product. It is a standard for standards writers! Vendors' claims of "compliance to the Reference Model" are meaningless.

2.1.1 The Reference Model

Computers and networks participating in OSI communications may be modeled as shown in Figure 2.1, which is an example of two systems communicating via some intermediate network. The communications component of the computers is divided into seven layers with the names shown; the network implements only the lower three.

Open system   In the Reference Model, an *open system* represents that part of a computer system that implements the OSI standards to provide communications. However, the term has become hackneyed and has acquired a wider meaning. For the purposes of this book, the more specific term *OSI end system* (or simply, end system) is used to denote the open systems attached to and communicating across a network.

End system   OSI specifies only the external behavior of systems, irrespective of how they are implemented. In practice, an end system may encompass a spectrum of configurations. At one end of the range, an end system is an individual computer, workstation or personal computer that implements OSI standards. This is regarded as the ideal, as no conversions are required for communication with other OSI end systems. Even where an end system is a discrete piece of equipment, it is typically made up of several printed circuit cards interconnected via a proprietary communications bus. By admitting proprietary interconnection of components, the concept of an end system can be extended to include, for example:

- mainframe architectures comprising central processors, front ends and proprietary terminal communications; and,

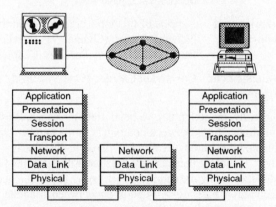

Figure 2.1   The layered Reference Model – each end system (computer or work-station) implements all seven layers; intermediate nodes (routers or packet switches) implement the lower three layers.

- Local Area Networks (LANs) that use proprietary communications for local interactions and file sharing, and a gateway for OSI communications to external systems.

Subnetwork

The term "network" also suffers from semantic overload. When spelt with all lower case letters, network refers generically to networking aspects of end systems and intermediate systems. When spelt with an initial capital N (i.e. "Network"), it refers to the overall data transfer service provided by the OSI Network Layer. The term *subnetwork* is used to identify a single, real, physical communications network (such as an X.25 packet switching network or a LAN).

Intermediate system

The various nodes in the subnetwork (e.g. packet switches, routers) are termed *intermediate systems* in OSI. The distinction between end system and intermediate system is a logical one. Although some physical configurations may correspond to a discrete end system or intermediate system, some products combine the functions of both.

2.1.2 The Layering Concept

Central to the modeling of open systems is the layering concept. Layering is a structuring technique which enables a complex task, such as the interconnection of open systems, to be viewed as a succession of layers. Each layer deals with a particular aspect of the networking problem, and performs a specific set of functions which enhance those performed by the lower layers. Ultimately the highest layer is able to provide the services required, say, to run distributed applications.

Layering divides a problem into smaller pieces, thus making the overall solution more achievable, and the systems involved more easily maintained. Another major objective of layering is to enable independence between layers. By defining only the services provided by each layer, and not how they are carried out, changes can be made in layers, or layers can be developed by different people. This gives OSI scope to accommodate innovation and incorporate improved technology when available for a particular layer, without major disturbance to adjacent layers.

Notation

When describing layers in a generic sense, the following notation is used to distinguish between adjacent layers:

- (N)-layer denotes the layer being described;

- (N+1)-layer is the layer above it; and,

- (N−1)-layer is the one below.

This notation also applies to other concepts, e.g. (N)-protocol. When referring to a specific layer, the generic notation is replaced by the layer's abbreviated name, e.g. S-protocol for the Session Layer.

Why seven layers?   ISO agreed on a number of principles to be considered for defining the specific set of layers in the OSI architecture, and applied these principles to come up with the seven layers of the OSI architecture. The principles considered are listed in Table 2.1.

Table 2.1   Principles used in selecting OSI layers

Do not create so many layers as to make difficult the system engineering task of describing and integrating these layers.

Create a boundary at a point where the service description can be small and the number of interactions across the boundary is minimized.

Create separate layers to handle functions that are manifestly different in the process performed or the technology involved.

Collect similar functions into the same layer.

Select boundaries at points that past experience has demonstrated to be successful.

Create a layer of easily localized functions so that the layer can be totally redesigned and its protocols changed in a major way to take advantage of new advances in architectural, hardware, or software technology without changing the services and interfaces with the adjacent layers.

Create a boundary where it may be useful at some point in time to have the corresponding interface standardized.

Create a layer when there is a need for a different level of abstraction in the handling of data, e.g. morphology, syntax, semantics.

Create for each layer interfaces with its upper and lower layer only.

Create further subgrouping and organization of functions to form sublayers within a layer in cases where distinct communication services need it.

Create, where needed, two or more sublayers with a common, and therefore minimum, functionality to allow interface operation with adjacent layers.

Allow bypassing of sublayers.

2.1.3 The Seven Layers

Before discussing other modeling concepts, each layer is briefly described for initial familiarization (see Figure 2.2). Examples of applicable standards are listed for some layers to help relate the layers to known concepts, but the list is not intended to be exclusive. New standards were specifically developed for the OSI Transport Layer and the layers above. They are simply referred to as the Transport, Session or Application layer protocols. In some respects, the upper layers have no parallels in other architectures. The layers are described in detail in subsequent chapters.

Physical Layer Depicted at the bottom of the layered protocol stack, the Physical Layer provides the path for transmission of bits between systems. Physical Layer standards define the mechanical, electrical, functional and procedural interfaces to transmission services. Examples of physical interface standards include:

- V.24, V.28 (RS-232);

- X.21, X.21 bis;

- IEEE 802 series LANs;

- I.430, I.431 ISDNs.

Data Link Layer This layer sends blocks of data over a link between systems, and provides protection against transmission errors. Example of data link protocols include:

- High level Data Link Control (HDLC);

- Logical Link Control (LLC) for LANs;

- Link Access Procedure Balanced (LAPB) for X.25.

Network Layer Whereas the lower two layers operate point to point, the Network Layer joins together concatenated subnetworks and links to provide a path for the end to end transfer of data. It is responsible for controlling access to the subnetworks, and for routing and switching data across them. An important aspect is the provision of a global addressing scheme for all open systems. Examples of protocols include:

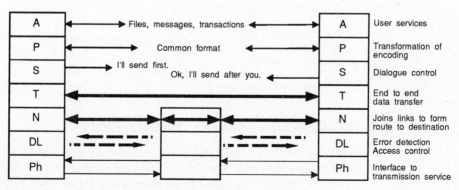

Figure 2.2   Purpose of the OSI layers

- packet level of X.25;

- connectionless network protocol (ISO 8473).

Transport Layer

A universal, reliable data transfer capability is provided by the Transport Layer. Conceptually, it adjusts its behavior to enhance the performance of the lower layers. It operates end to end only; i.e. intermediate systems do not implement the Transport Layer or the layers above.

Session Layer

The applications in the end systems need a mechanism to co-ordinate their activities. The Session Layer provides a standard set of signals, like electronic punctuation marks, that higher layers can insert in the data flow between end systems. The signals are interpreted by the higher layers to control and structure the data exchanged between them, e.g. to delimit the start and end of a processing activity, to pause transmission or to query progress.

Presentation Layer

It is common for computer applications to deal with complex data structures (e.g. a personnel record made up of various fields of different data types). To exchange such data, both ends need to know the structure and the way the data will be encoded for transmission. If necessary, the Presentation Layer transforms data from the Application Layer into a form suitable for common interpretation by both end systems. (This is distinct from the presentation of data on a screen for viewing by humans. Such matters are not covered by OSI.)

Application Layer

The Application Layer provides services to end users. A large number of standards are already in place for this layer and it is the subject of on-going development. Each standard builds on the common services provided by the lower layers to provide specific capabilities for user applications. Some standards are:

- Message Handling Systems (MHS, X.400);

- directory services (X.500);

- file handling (FTAM);

- Virtual Terminals (VT);

- Transaction Processing (TP).

2.1.4 Relationships between OSI Standards

Standards developed under the OSI umbrella fall into two families: services and protocols. The service standards define the functional capabilities provided by a layer to the immediately higher layer, and the "abstract" interface to the layer. The protocol standards detail the rules or etiquette for the behavior of the layer, i.e. the format and contents of the control information exchanged between the corresponding layers on opposite sides of a network. Examples of these two types of standards are seen in the ISO Transport Layer, where ISO 8072 is the Transport Service Definition and ISO 8073 is the Transport Protocol Specification. In some layers, multiple protocol standards are provided to support different network or application requirements. The task of systems designers then, is to choose the appropriate combination of the OSI standards for use in a particular environment.

Three levels of abstraction have been introduced in the foregoing discussion as illustrated in Figure 2.3, and summarized below:

Reference Model	Conceptual framework, definition of constraints and relationships between layers, broad statement of the seven layers.
Service definition	Abstract definition of "what" the layer provides.
Protocol specification	Detailed specification of "how" the layer provides the service.

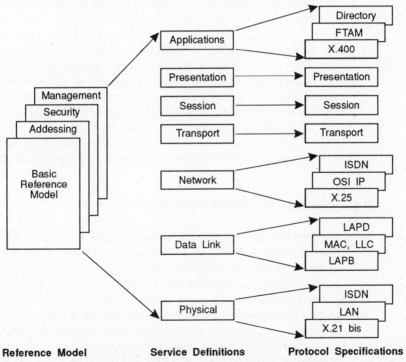

Reference Model   Service Definitions   Protocol Specifications

Figure 2.3   The Reference Model and service definitions are abstract specifications – only the protocol specifications have concrete requirements that can be implemented.

The relationship between a layer service and protocol is shown in Figure 2.4.

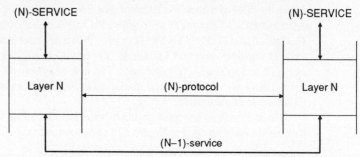

Figure 2.4   Each layer builds on the services of the layer below to provide additional services to the layer above.

Service definition

The concept of a service definition was devised by the standards community to facilitate the stepwise refinement of layer requirements. A service definition specifies "what" capabilities a layer provides without prejudice to "how" it is implemented. There is one service definition for each layer and it defines the services, functions, and facilities provided by that layer. Furthermore, the services are described in abstract terms in order to avoid unnecessary constraints on the internal design of real systems.

Protocol specification

It is the protocol standards that constitute the definitive interpretation of OSI. They specify, in concrete terms, how the defined service for a layer may be implemented by the exchange of protocol control information and data between peer systems. A protocol specification details the protocol headers, rules for control of communications and handling of data. There may be multiple protocols that can provide the service defined for the layer. The protocol standards are intended to be general enough to cater for the total range of user requirements, without restricting future extensions.

2.2 SERVICE DEFINITIONS

The term "service" refers to interactions between layers at each end of a communication, i.e the "vertical" interactions in Figure 2.5. A service is defined by listing the interactions and their associated parameters. In a sense, the service is defined in terms of the things that the two layers can ask each other to do. The interactions are defined as abstractions (called primitives); i.e. we specify what one layer can ask another to do, but we do not specify the physical mechanism by which the request is made. This is because in most cases, adjacent layers will be implemented by the same organization, so there is no need for the details to be subject to international standardization. In other words, a service definition covers the semantics of the service provided by a layer. Although a more precise syntactic specification would benefit both implementors and applications programmers, particularly in the case of user interfaces to Application Layer services, such interface specifications are outside the scope of the standards committees. (As a separate exercise, a number of industry groups have developed interface specifications for OSI layers or "APIs" as described in Section 24.1.1 on page 413.)

Service provider

In order to define the functions provided by a layer without prejudice to its implementation, the service definition is based on an imaginary "black box" called the *service provider* (see Figure 2.5). The layer is then described in terms of its interaction with the service users in the layer above. The service provider contains the layer being described, and all lower layers and intermediate systems.

(N)-service

The *(N)-service* is the set of capabilities made available by the (N)-service provider to the users in layer (N+1). Only those capabilities that involve both end systems are included, e.g. open a connection, transfer data. A service definition defines the semantics of the service only, not how it is realized. It specifies:

- the interactions or events that occur at the boundary between layers;

- the data associated with such interactions; and,

- the relationships between service interactions in the distributed system.

The conventions used in service definitions are defined in a technical report ISO/TR 8509. These descriptive conventions will be illustrated after a brief digression to discuss communication mode.

2.2.1 Connection Oriented and Connectionless Mode

In their initial formulation, the Reference Model and associated standards assumed a mode of operation in which a procedure to set up communications was observed before data transfer could take place. This is known as the connection oriented mode. The connectionless mode, which by-

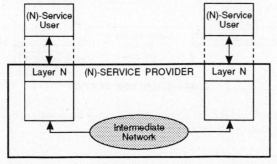

Figure 2.5   The (N)-service provider models layer N and the layers below.

passes the set-up procedures, was a later addition to OSI although it is equally as important. Figure 2.6 illustrates the concepts.

An implementation may offer either or both of these modes for a particular layer, although any instance of transmission between end systems must use the same mode in each layer. The differences between these modes have many ramifications, particularly in the lower layers (i.e. Transport and below). Although standards exist for both modes for all layers, at the time of writing, there is no practical implementation of OSI connectionless mode in the upper layers. The two modes are characterized below and the subject will recur in later chapters.

Connection oriented   A service that the original Reference model specified as being offered by all layers is that which associates two or more systems in a *connection*, for the purposes of transferring data and other information. A connection has a distinguishable lifetime which progresses through defined phases. The process of communication between peer end systems would be:

- Establish a connection.

- Transfer data ...

- (some time later) Release the connection.

This mode of operation is somewhat analogous to a telephone call where the address of the called party (i.e. telephone number) is supplied to the

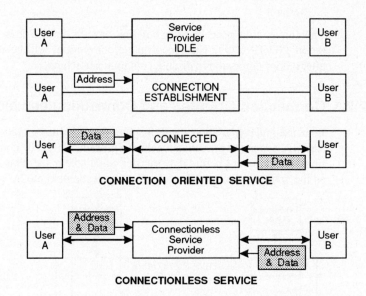

CONNECTION ORIENTED SERVICE

CONNECTIONLESS SERVICE

Figure 2.6   Each instance of communication may be in either connection oriented mode or connectionless mode.

network, and then the caller waits for the network and the called party to agree to communicate (i.e. answer the connection).

Three services are always provided in connection oriented mode:

Connection   A three party agreement is negotiated between the ser-
establishment   vice provider and the users concerning the addresses, communications parameters and service options that will apply for the duration of the connection. The connection must be successfully established before data transfer can proceed.

Data   The connection, in effect, provides a clear pathway for
transfer   data transfer. It provides a context within which succes-sive data transfers can be logically related and avoids the overheads of address resolution for each transfer. Some layers provide for several categories of data, e.g. normal data, expedited data, etc. These categories will be ex-plained in the layers where they occur.

Disconnection   Disconnection terminates data transfer and releases resources associated with the connection. Depending on the layer, disconnection may be initiated by either of the users or the provider. Disconnection may be caused by errors or it may be the normal end of communication.

A variety of other services may be provided during the data transfer phase.

Connectionless   A later extension to the Reference Model covered a *connectionless* mode of operation; i.e. data could be passed between peer systems without a connection being established first. For this to occur, each unit of data being transferred must be accompanied by enough address information to enable it to reach its destination. This mode of operation is analogous to sending letters or telegrams, and is often referred to as a datagram service. Each data transfer is regarded as a single unit and it has no relationship to other data units (at least as far as the service provider is concerned). There is only one service:

Unit data   All of the addresses and communications parameters
transfer   required to deliver the data unit are presented together with the user data in a single access to the service provider. Each unit of data may be routed and delivered independently of other data units by the service provider.

Much of the interest in connectionless operation has come from the development of LANs, many of which provide connectionless services. There are also applications, such as Electronic Funds Transfer at Point of Sale (EFTPOS), which can be inherently connectionless.

2.2.2 Primitives

**Service
primitive**
The flow of information between the layers, i.e. between service provider and service user, takes place in OSI in the form of a *service primitive*. The Reference Model defines a primitive as "an abstract, implementation independent interaction between a service-user and service-provider". Note that there is no prescription of how a primitive is to be implemented: it could be a subroutine call, a system call, a message in a queue, etc. A primitive is just a conceptual representation of an interaction and its associated data.

There are four types of primitives, as shown in Figure 2.7. These are described below using the telephone service as an illustration.

Request   A primitive issued by a service user to the service provider to invoke some procedure. For example, to request a telephone connection, the initiating party dials a number (a parameter).

Indication   A primitive issued by a service provider to indicate that a procedure has been requested by the peer service user. The phone at the destination rings.

Response   A primitive issued by a service user to complete a procedure previously invoked by an indication. The called party picks up the phone.

Confirm   A primitive issued by a service provider to complete some procedure previously invoked by a request. Ringing tone ceases at the initiating end.

In the telephone example, only the interactions with end to end significance are represented as primitives. Other interactions (e.g. pick up the handset and wait for dial tone) are regarded as local interface matters and are not represented as primitives.

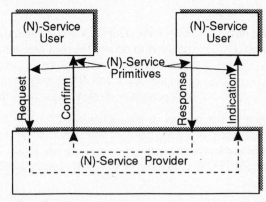

Figure 2.7   Service primitives are a conceptual representation of the interactions between adjacent layers.

A primitive may convey data parameters between layers. The parameters may be a simple data value or a complex data structure. The service conventions define tabular techniques for defining these data parameters and the relationships between parameters in different primitives (e.g. user data carrier by an indication primitive is the same as the user data of a preceding request). Such tables form a large part of service definitions, although the detail is beyond the scope of this book. The labeling convention for primitives is to use the initial letter of the layer concerned, followed by one or more words that identify the activities associated with the primitive. For example, the primitive for initiating a transport connection is: T-Connect request.

Sequence diagrams

Service definitions specify the allowed sequences of service primitives that may be exchanged between the peer users and the service provider. Two complementary descriptive techniques are used: state transition diagrams and tables; and, sequence diagrams. State transition techniques are the formal approach but they are beyond the scope of this book. The sequence diagrams, however, are a very useful intuitive descriptive tool. A slightly modified version of the sequence diagram technique is used throughout this book. An example appears in Figure 2.8. The two vertical bars represent the boundary between a service provider and the users. Horizontal arrows represent service primitives exchanged between the provider and the users. The lines between the bars represent the relationship between different primitives. These lines slope downwards to depict the passage of time while the service provider conveys the primitives between the distributed systems, and performs associated actions. Time increases down the page. In this book, only salient events are shown in the sequence diagrams for clarity and space reasons.

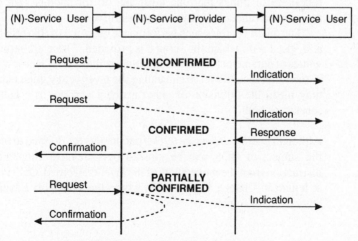

Figure 2.8   Sequence diagrams for service definitions

2.2.3 Dialogues

In providing a service to a higher layer, the service provider frequently is called upon to support a dialogue between the service users, i.e. a flow of information, either data or control information, or both. There are two broad types of dialogue: unconfirmed, and confirmed. Intermediate types of dialogues, known as partially confirmed dialogues, are also used in service definitions.

Unconfirmed   A service element in which a request at one service access point leads only to an indication at the other. Examples of unconfirmed dialogues include data transfer after a connection has been established; and connectionless data transfer.

Confirmed   A service element in which a request at one service access point leads to an indication at the other, which provokes the service user into issuing a response, leading to a confirm at the originating service access point. Examples are the connection establishment phase of most layers; and various forms of acknowledged services.

Partially   Various forms of partially confirmed dialogues are per-
Confirmed   mitted when the service provider confirms some previous request, but without waiting for destination response.

2.2.4 Quality of Service

OSI distinguishes between a service and the quality of that service. These are orthogonal aspects of a layer's behavior. The service defines the repertoire of things that one layer can do for another. The service is represented functionally by service primitives.

The quality defines such performance quantities as the reliability, cost and speed with which the service is provided. These are represented as values of parameters contained in certain primitives. If we view each layer in the Reference Model as enhancing the layer below, then enhancement may mean the provision of either a richer service, or a better quality service, or both.

QOS   Although *Quality of Service (QOS)* parameters are defined in most layers, the subject of QOS will be glossed over in most chapters to avoid distraction from the main theme of the layer concerned. QOS is discussed at length in Chapter 9 (page 158) where the Transport Layer provides convenient examples.

2.3 MODEL OF A LAYER

Entity

An open system is divided up into layers, each layer comprising one or more entities. An *entity* is defined as the active element of a layer — in other words, the thing that does the work of a layer in each open system. There must be at least one entity in each layer in each open system. Entities are conceptual modeling tools which do not necessarily relate to real implementations. Entities can be realized in hardware, software or both. Entities at layer N are known as (N)-entities.

Service access points

Each layer, except the highest, provides services to the layer above. The logical interface between an (N+1)-entity and an (N)-entity, over which the services are offered, is known as an *(N)-service access point*, or (N)-SAP for short. Each (N)-SAP is the logical interface between only one (N+1)-entity and only one (N)-entity. An (N)-entity, however, can service several (N)-SAPs, and an (N+1)-entity can use several (N)-SAPs. These aspects are illustrated in Figure 2.9. A SAP can support multiple instances of communication (i.e. several simultaneous connections and/or multiple connectionless data transfers). Each (N)-SAP has a unique address (known as an (N)-SAP address) that can be used for locating it at the layer boundary.

Addresses

Within the framework of the Reference Model, a particularly important role is played by *addresses*. In general, an (N)-address identifies a set of SAPs at the boundary between the (N) and (N+1) layers. An (N)-SAP address is an (N)-address which identifies only a single (N)-SAP. Some implementations have multiple addresses for each layer to distinguish between different entities in the layer above.

When an entity, say at layer (N+1), wishes to establish a connection with another (N+1)-entity, it invokes some form of a connection request

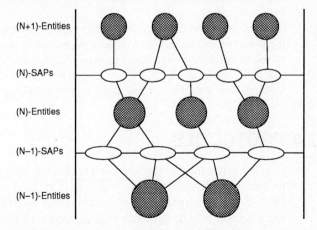

Figure 2.9   Service Access Points (SAPs) identify the entity in the layer above. The SAP address is used to locate entities in adjacent layers.

primitive containing as parameters both the called and calling (N)-SAP addresses. As appropriate, the (N)-entity maps these addresses onto (N–1)-SAP addresses.

The role of the addresses differs between the upper and lower layers of the model. The physical and data link addresses distinguish:

- between different physical pieces of equipment on a transmission circuit or LAN; and,

- between different uses of the circuit or LAN, e.g. between different upper layer protocols.

Addresses in these two layers are local to the end system and its associated intermediate system.

NSAP address

The Network SAP (NASP) addresses are particularly significant. They provide a globally unambiguous address for each OSI end system. Every end system that participates in OSI communications must be allocated one or more NSAP addresses — much like the international telephone numbering scheme. The details of this global NSAP numbering scheme are explained in Chapter 8 on internetworking.

Presentation address

In the Transport Layer and above, SAP addresses take the form of a selector that provides a way of distinguishing between different entities within a layer in one end system. By analogy, the NSAP address is like the telephone switchboard number for an organization, and the selectors are the extension numbers to reach individuals. Multiple simultaneous conversations between different endpoints can take place through the switchboard. The *presentation address* is the concatenation of an NSAP address and the upper layer selectors; i.e.:

Presentation address = P selector, S selector, T selector, NSAP address

To transfer information to another end system, the application entity in the initiating end system must supply the complete presentation address of the destination. This address may be obtained from locally available information, or, as the X.500 standards become more widely implemented, from an electronic Directory service database.

2.4 PROTOCOLS

In general, it is not possible for a single entity in one system to perform its services and functions unilaterally. Both entities, one at each end of the link, must co-operate to implement the functions of a layer. In order to co-ordinate their actions, they must exchange control information in an agreed way. This interface between peer entities is termed the layer protocol and it corresponds to the "horizontal" interactions between the entities. Since the two different entities in any particular communication may well be implemented by different organizations, it is necessary for the protocol to be specified, not just in abstract form, but also in physical implementation form, i.e as defined bit patterns.

Layered protocols mimic the encapsulation of a letter in an envelope:

- The starting point is the text of the letter that is to be transmitted through the postal network.

- The upper layer of the protocol adds addresses, a salutation and a signature to the text to form the body of the letter.

- The next layer encapsulates the body in an envelope for transfer through the postal system.

In common with other protocol architectures, each OSI layer encapsulates the information with a header that is used to co-ordinate communications with its peer (see Figure 2.10). (The Data Link Layer also includes a trailer.) The header, which is generated by the sending entity, conveys Protocol Control Information (PCI) to its peer entity. The information in the PCI header may include:

- requests for actions to be performed by the peer entity;

- acknowledgements for receipt of data or the completion of previously requested actions; and,

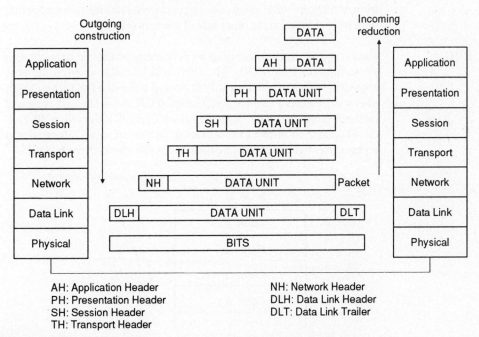

AH: Application Header   NH: Network Header
PH: Presentation Header   DLH: Data Link Header
SH: Session Header   DLT: Data Link Trailer
TH: Transport Header

Figure 2.10   Construction and reduction of protocol headers

- data from upper layers.

The protocol standards specify in detail the external behavior of an entity. The specification entails the mapping of an N-service request into some appropriate protocol exchanges between peer entities to achieve the desired service and to deliver appropriate N-service indications and confirmations. A protocol specification typically includes:

- a state transition table that defines the allowed sequences of events; and,

- a definition of the format and encoding of the header (and trailer).

For the purposes of this book, an extension of the sequence diagram technique will be used for intuitive description of the mapping between services and protocols. This technique will be introduced in Chapter 5 (page 70) because the Physical Layer provides a convenient example.

Null layers or null protocols are not permitted in OSI. However, protocol functionality may be minimal for a layer if the required service is already supplied by lower layers. In effect, some layers simply pass through services from the layer below.

A key part of the layered approach of OSI is the principle that, once data is passed to a lower layer, its content and format are transparent to, and untouched by, the lower layers. (The exception to this is the Presentation Layer that may transform users' data to a common format for transfer.) Each layer will usually add some additional information in the form of a header (or in some cases, trailer) to enable effective interaction with its peer layer on the other side of the network.

PDU   Data is passed from an entity to its peer entity across the network as a *Protocol Data Unit (PDU)*. The PDU will be made up from the next highest layer's PDU (temporarily known as a Service Data Unit (SDU)) plus some Protocol Control Information (PCI). As a data unit is passed between adjacent layers, some Interface Control Information (ICI) is called upon to co-ordinate the operation. Interface Control Information is an implementation dependent matter and is not standardized by OSI.

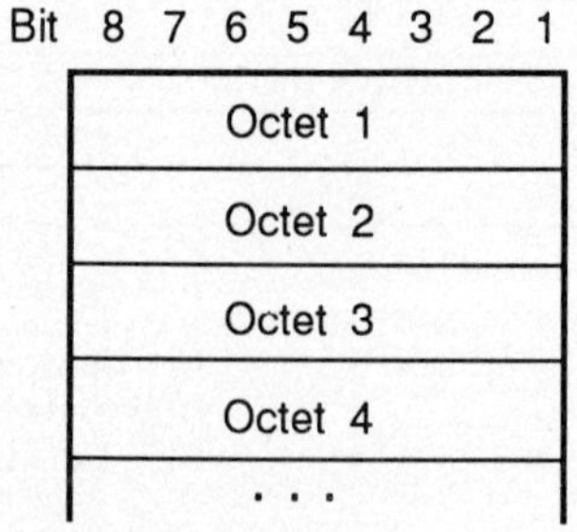

Bit 8 7 6 5 4 3 2 1

| Octet 1 |
| Octet 2 |
| Octet 3 |
| Octet 4 |
| . . . |

Figure 2.11   Layout of PDU format diagrams

PDU formats   Figure 2.11 illustrates the notation used to describe the PDU headers. The headers are described as a series of octets (i.e. eight bits), with the first octet to be transmitted depicted at the top, and subsequent octets below it. Bits of an octet are numbered from 8 to 1 where bit 1 is the low order bit and is transmitted first. Within an octet, bits are shown with bit 8 to the left and bit 1 to the right. This is aligned with the format diagrams in most of the standards (the exception being the IEEE 802 series for LANs which show bit 8 to the right).

2.4.1 Layer Functions

In addition to the externally visible services, layers perform a variety of internal functions to support their operation. The activities within a layer as it goes about its business are termed the functions of the layer. In general, services are also functions, but not all functions are services. If an activity within a layer is not visible in the form of a primitive, then that activity is a function and not a service. Some general functions are briefly defined below (see Figure 2.12). More concrete examples of these functions will be found in subsequent chapters.

A number of functions are related to the handling of data units, in particular the process of taking an SDU from a higher layer, adding PCI and creating a PDU. Among the main such operations are:

Segmenting/ reassembling   It is possible to divide the contents of an SDU between two or more PDUs (to meet, say, a limitation on message size).

Blocking/ deblocking   A PDU can be built up from several SDUs and their accompanying PCIs for efficiency reasons.

Concatena- tion/separat- ing   Two or more PDUs can be incorporated into a single SDU, once again for efficiency.

Other important functions are:

Multiplexing/ demultiplex- ing   This occurs when an (N)-layer uses one (N–1)-connection to send SDUs from two or more (N)-connections, like a single large pipe carrying the flow from a number of smaller inlets. The purpose of this function is resource sharing.

Splitting/ combining   This is the reverse of multiplexing, where several (N–1)-connections are used for one (N)-connection to perform load sharing. Splitting provides higher resilience or throughput than a single connection.

Relaying   The forwarding of data by an entity in an intermediate system from one entity to another peer entity. This is the main function of the lower three layers in intermediate systems. It operates in conjunction with routing and switching.

Protocol identifier   A layer may have one or more protocols to choose from when communicating to its peers. When an information transfer is initiated, the protocol used must be specified. This would be indicated in a *Protocol Identification (PID)* field in the header (PCI) for that layer.

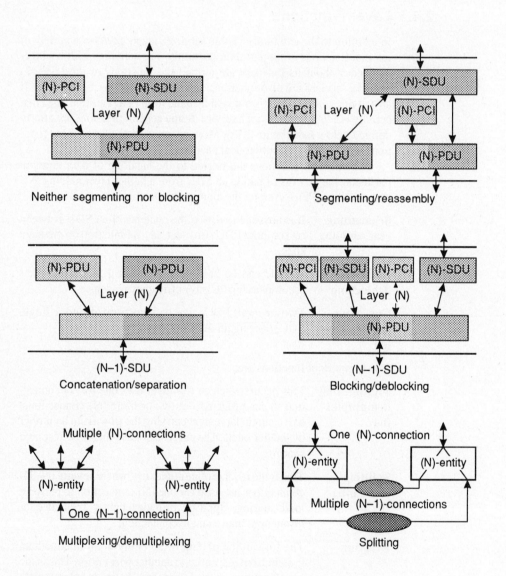

Figure 2.12   Layer functions

2.5 QUESTIONS

Question 2.1   Which OSI layer is responsible for global addressing for all end systems?

Question 2.2   All layers except one transfer user data unchanged. Which layer may transform the bits transmitted for a common interpretation at both ends?

Question 2.3   The service mode (i.e. connection oriented mode or connectionless) may restrict the dialogues. What types of dialogues can be supported by a connection oriented service? What dialogues can be supported by connectionless?

Question 2.4   Do the diagrams in Figure 2.13 correctly represent the allowed relationships between entities and Service Access Points?

Question 2.5   What do "PDU" and "SDU" stand for? Describe how they are related.

Question 2.6   Draw a sequence diagram for a successful telephone connection. Also show disconnection by the called party. Use the following service primitives:

- Dial request

- Ring indication

- Answer response

- Cease ring confirmation

- Hang-up request

- Busy tone indication

- Hang-up response.

Question 2.7   Draw a sequence diagram for the successful connectionless delivery of a letter using the postal service. Use the following primitives:

- Post letter request

- Deliver letter indication.

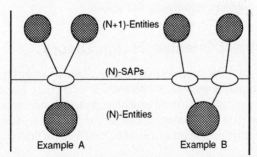

Figure 2.13   Question: Which example is correct and which is incorrect, and why?

3 Object Oriented Specifications

3.1 INTRODUCTION

The size and scale of the effort to implement Open Systems Interconnection (OSI) place great demands on application and systems programmers to interpret correctly the complex specifications of OSI services and functions. These demands can be met only if there are consistent and universally accepted specification guidelines and methods. In particular, there has been great benefit from the use of object oriented methods in the development of the OSI Application Layer standards. Object oriented methodology has also been used at the lower OSI layers for modeling objects such as circuits, route tables and interfaces, etc. for management purposes. It is therefore very important that object oriented design be reasonably well understood if OSI standards are to be used. Without an understanding of the object oriented principles described in this chapter, many of the aspects of the OSI standards for the upper layers will be difficult to follow.

Organization   This chapter is organized into the following sections:

- the theory of object oriented design;

- a comparison of non-object oriented design and object oriented design;

- the relationship between objects and protocol;

- the application of objects to OSI;

- implications of objects within the standards;

- object conformance and testing.

3.1.1 Object Oriented Design Theory

In the basic model of computing, data structures are manipulated by a processing module. As computing technology progressed, data became shared between a number of processes, to enable more complex operations and data distribution. If uncontrolled access to data was permitted, any specific data structure could be modified (or destroyed) by any one of its accessors in a random fashion without any recourse to the other parties who were also using it. This would obviously lead to very unreliable processing systems. To overcome this very fundamental problem, where data is accessed by a number of parties, a consistent interface for those parties is needed to eliminate uncontrolled use of the data; i.e. an interface protocol is needed for data access. The term "protocol" is used in the general sense (as the rules of the dialogue) and not as the realization of protocol data units transferred between the object and its accessor. In this model, the data structure in effect becomes "encapsulated" and access to it is via a protocol. The data becomes an "object" and the protocol is a set of operations on the data that perform a required functions and protect the data from becoming inconsistent. The protocol design dictates how the data is accessed and manipulated; i.e. the protocol becomes the access rule for the data (see Figure 3.1).

Objects themselves can therefore be defined to represent combinations of data structures, processes, functions or even complete systems. Control of an object is achieved by issuing operations on the object's defined interface (i.e. using its protocol).

Object properties

The object oriented paradigm provides properties which are very useful in the data modeling process. These properties are as follows:

Inheritance   Inheritance refers to a type of dependence between object classes. Objects when they are defined are classified (i.e. are given a class). Any further refinement of this class becomes the subclass of the original class. Thus, the subclass "inherits" the properties of the class as well as having its own additional properties. An example of this inheritance is a "House" object class that has the properties of a roof, walls, floors, doors, etc. A subclass of house is a "Furnished House" that inherits the above properties but, in addition, contains curtains, carpets and furniture, etc. There can also be a further refinement to an "Occupied House" that refines these above classes by the addition of people properties. Inheritance is an aspect derived from the structure definitions of an object and therefore provides the ability to reuse and refine the object's original definition.

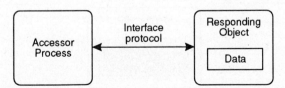

Figure 3.1   Basic object and protocol concept as used between two processes in one system

Data abstraction   Data abstraction means that the object's features and the operations that are performed on them are described at a high level without recourse to the object's real structure or its real interface.

Encapsula-tion   Encapsulation means that access to the object (and its internal functions and data) is permitted only by its specific interface via its defined protocol. It also means that operations on its interface are atomic at the object boundary. (There are no subdivisions of an object operation.)

Data hiding   Data hiding means that the real internal structures and processing algorithms of the object are hidden from the accessors of the object. Because of this, the object's interface need not reflect the actual mechanisms and data within used within the object.

3.1.2 Object Oriented Design

Figure 3.2 illustrates the object oriented design principle. In the upper diagram, traditional design principles are used. Each individual software

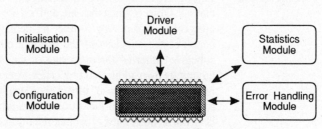

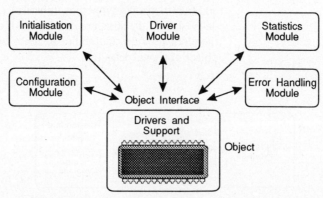

Figure 3.2   Object oriented design uses data encapsulation and defined interfaces.

module can independently access the software, data structures and hardware registers of the communications interface (the hardware device and its support software). In this situation, there is obviously no co-ordination of operations on the interface components or any control to inhibit inconsistent actions. The lower diagram represents the object oriented design approach to the problem. The hardware and the driver module are "encapsulated" and access to these internal components is via a defined interface or protocol. Thus, the internals of the object are hidden from the accessing modules and integrity of the operations is assured by the procedures permitted on the object's interface.

3.1.3 The Relationship between Objects and Protocol

When objects are defined, the attributes of the object and the operations applied to it are made available to the object's accessors via the interface protocol. Because of this, the interface reflects the object's definition. For example, if an object's definition has a status attribute that can be read and another attribute that can be written and read, then the object's protocol may define:

* Read and Write operations;

* which type of attribute is accessed; and,

* the ability to carry attribute values.

3.2 OBJECTS IN OSI

The object oriented paradigm is an important foundation for the OSI Application Layer standards. At a very basic level, an object has a protocol that is used to access it. If the object is a part of an OSI end system, then the protocol used to access the object is an OSI protocol. Consequently, the OSI Application Layer standards define appropriate objects and their properties, and the application protocols reflect the OSI objects defined by those standards. This is represented in Figure 3.3.

Typically, an Application Layer standard deals with multiple objects arranged in some structure or hierarchy. An inverted tree is the typical object organization for OSI end systems such as file stores, management

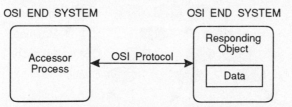

Figure 3.3   In OSI, the accessor process is in a separate end system and it communicates with objects via an OSI protocol.

systems or the Directory. As an example, a typical object tree identifying a world of network circuits is shown in Figure 3.4. At the "top" is a root object. Where subordinate objects exist within (or under) the root object, then a naming scheme is used to reference the subordinate objects.

3.2.1 Objects in OSI Standards

Because OSI standards use objects, both in the definition of the service they provide and in the protocols for accessing those services, there are many references to objects. Typically, an OSI object has the following properties:

Class An object's structure is defined by it's class, i.e. the attribute types it must contain and the attribute types it may contain.

Name A name (or an address) uniquely identifies an instance of a class.

Attributes An object's attributes are of specific types and contain values relevant to the syntax of the attribute type.

Operations Objects generally support a range of operations, e.g. Read and Write.

Notifications Objects generally have internal events which cause notifications on their interface.

Behavior The behavior of an object determines what the object does under its permitted conditions; e.g. a Delete operation on the object causes it to destroy itself.

To illustrate the use of the above notation, a simplified definition of a "House" object is shown in Figure 3.5. (For examples of object definitions, see ISO 10165/X.720 - X.723 for OSI management objects.) The object definition process gives a clear indication of what an object contains (i.e. its attributes) and what can be performed on those attributes

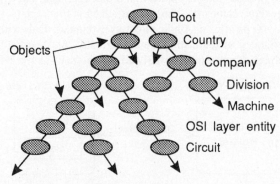

Figure 3.4   Example of an OSI object tree

by the defined operations (protocol). The above example definition is a simplification of the process used in a standard.

3.2.2 Object Identifiers

OID

Within the OSI standards, numerous aspects of an object need to be explicitly identified. It is necessary to label (and to be able to encode the label) of such things as an object's name, its class, the operations and notifications the object supports, and the object's attributes. Therefore, a common data item has been defined within OSI to enable the labeling of objects and their component parts. This label is called an *Object Identifier (OID)*. In essence, an OID is a structured number that is carried in a

```
OBJECT CLASS: House
ATTRIBUTES :    {
                MUST CONTAIN          {mandatory attributes}
                        State         { e.g. Occupied, Powered, etc.}
                        Doors         {quantity}
                        Floors
                        Windows
                        Walls
                        Roof
                MAY CONTAIN           {optional attributes}
                        Skylights
                        Stairs
                }
OPERATIONS:     {
                Read Attributes
                Power On
                Power Off
                }
NOTIFICATIONS: {
                Dry Rot Detected
                Roof Leaking
                }
BEHAVIOR:       {
                The attribute values are returned on a Read Attributes operation.
                The power is enabled with a Power On operation and the state attribute
                is changed to Powered.
                The power is disabled with a Power Off operation and the state attribute
                is changed by resetting Powered.
                If there is a Roof Leak event detected, a notification is given.
                If there is a Dry Rot event detected, a notification is given.
                If a People Present event is detected the state attribute is
                changed to Occupied.
                If a No People Present event is detected, the state attribute is
                changed by resetting Occupied.
                }
REGISTERED AS: House object class {an object identifier for the class}
```

Figure 3.5   Generalized illustration of the definition of an object class

specific format. The allocation of such numbers is generally the responsibility of the standards organizations, although the use of privately defined OIDs is permitted in cases where the products containing OSI components have specific extensions. The following list highlights the requirements of object oriented mechanisms within OSI:

- Objects have an object class definition; thus classes are identified with a specific OID.

- Objects, once created, represent an instance of the object; thus object instances must be identified. Objects therefore have an object instance name and/or address. Typically, object instances are identified by either an OID or a Distinguished Name. (Distinguished Names are used in the X.500 Directory and X.700 Systems Management standards).

- Objects have attributes of specific types. Therefore, attribute types require unique identification. OSI object identifiers identify OSI defined attribute types (and syntaxes) as well as the object's class.

- OIDs are carried in OSI protocols. The syntax of an OID is defined in Abstract Syntax Notation One (ASN.1). (ASN.1 is described in Chapter 13.)

To support the object oriented definition of OSI application layer protocols, the Remote Operations Service Element (ROSE) (an Application Layer service and protocol) has been defined (see Chapter 14). ROSE is used by many of the Application Layer standards.

Scope   Objects are used widely within the Application Layer standards, e.g.:

- messaging functions in Message Handling Systems;

- to define the object classes of the entries in the Directory;

- managed objects in the systems management standards;

- files and file directories in File Transfer, Access and Management (FTAM); and,

- data stores and terminal control mechanisms in the Virtual Terminal standards.

3.2.3 Object Conformance Testing

An important aspect of realizing implementations of OSI standards (which are abstract) is the issue of conformance testing. OSI conformance testing can be applied only to defined interfaces to OSI objects. Figure 3.6 represents the boundaries of conformance.

Real effects The real resource of a system is represented by an abstract object. To test an object, then generally, some real event must occur and be monitored, either when the object is controlled or when the resource itself causes an event. Conformance testing applies only to the object's defined interface. The actual real results as determined by an implementation of the object cannot in fact be the subject of the standard or a conformance test. In other words, conformance tests evaluate only the OSI defined protocol, not the mapping from the abstract object to the real implementation.

3.2.4 Summary

Object oriented design provides an approach to development where specifications and implementations can be modeled in a consistent manner. The object and protocol concept forms one of the foundation principles of OSI design.

Objects have classes, attributes, operations and notifications. Objects themselves are abstract and they are realized by mapping them onto real resources by the product implementation.

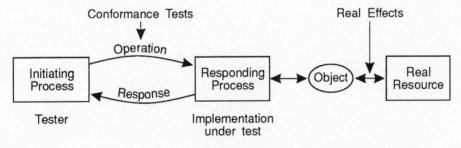

Figure 3.6 Object conformance testing does not test the "real effects".

Part 2 — Standards for Computer Networks

4 The Lower Four Layers

4.1 OPEN DATA COMMUNICATIONS

The lower four layers (Physical, Data Link, Network and Transport) can be grouped together from a technical viewpoint, because their common purpose is to provide a transparent data transfer mechanism between end systems. This grouping is also reflected in the structure of the various T profiles (i.e. Transport profiles). Transparency means that user's data is delivered unchanged and without error, from sender to receiver. Building on the basic "roadworks" of the Physical Layer, each layer increases the reliability of the path over which data is transferred. Often, the transfer path traverses multiple networks of different types, which like the public roads and highways, are transport resources shared among a large number of users. At a basic level, the functions of these lower layers include:

- Error control procedures to prevent corruption of data by noise and from other sources (a rough analog is the road rules to prevent collisions).

- Flow control and congestion control to ensure equitable sharing of the network resources, like a traffic policeman on intersection duty.

- Addressing schemes to identify the source and destination end systems. Addresses may be required in several layers, like a street address and a room number to locate an individual in a large building.

- Routing and relaying functions to transfer the data across a series of concatenated links and networks.

A complicating aspect of Open Systems Interconnection (OSI) is that the allocation of these functions to each of the layers is not fixed, but may vary depending on the network technology. The purpose of this chapter is to give an overview of the main combinations — i.e. connection oriented X.25 networks, connectionless Local Area Networks (LANs), and Integrated Services Digital Networks (ISDNs) — before each layer is covered in detail. This is a complex matter that is explained step by step in following chapters. To give an overview in this chapter, some generalizations and simplifications are used for clarity in the following discussion. For instance, the scope of the discussion is limited to the provision of the connection oriented transport service. (Although standards exist for the connectionless transport service, it is not yet widely implemented. Connectionless transport, however, has potential for application over LANs similar to the use of the User Datagram Protocol (UDP) from the TCP/IP suite, described on page 57.)

4.1.1 Network Alternatives

A perplexing array of network technologies is available today. For example, most networks would have a selection of a number of the following:

- Wide Area Networks (WANs) using point to point operation, or switched operation using X.25 packet switching, ISDNs, or circuit switched data networks; and,

- various types of LANs.

For each type of network technology, there is a further choice of protocol combinations that can be used. Why are there so many, and what is the purpose of the different types? Although there are many factors involved, the background for the answer to these questions is the decreasing cost, but increasing capacity of transmission services. Spectacular technical advances, firstly in digital technology and more recently in fibre optics, have dramatically altered potential network architectures. New protocols have developed to take advantage of the improved technology, but these operate side by side with earlier systems that still have a long and viable lifetime.

The following sections give an introduction to packet switching (over WANs and LANs), ISDN and addressing issues.

4.2 PACKET SWITCHING

Before explaining the details of network protocols, it is necessary to give some insight into the internal operation of packet switching networks. Both connection and connectionless modes are discussed.

Why packet switching? The basic concept of packet switching is the breaking of data into "packets" of 100–200 octets before sending them through a network. The data packets from many sources and to many destinations **share** the network's resources, i.e. the communications lines and the switching processors. This is a form of statistical multiplexing.

For brevity in this discussion, the switching processors are called nodes (see Figure 4.1). The nodes are OSI intermediate systems — they are commonly called Packet Switching Exchanges (PSEs) in an X.25 network, or routers in a connectionless environment. The standards generally govern the interface between an end system and its corresponding node for subnetwork access. Internode protocols may be proprietary or they may be based on the access standards. In effect, the nodes are queuing systems:

- A node receives and (temporarily) stores packets from end systems or other nodes.

- Packets are sorted according to their destination – this is the *routing* function. The node chooses one of a number of possible data links to forward the packet, either to the next node along the path to the destination, or for delivery to those destinations that are directly attached.

- The node then queues the packets for on-going transmission.

Together, the nodes form a homogeneous subnetwork that is administered by some organization. So in addition to routing, switching and relaying packets, nodes must also perform management and accounting functions.

Addressing and routing

Sharing of the network resources is achieved by interleaving packets from many different computer conversations on the transmission lines. In order to sort the packets, the header (i.e. Protocol Control Information, PCI) of each packet must identify the destination. Each end system in a network is allocated a unique numeric address (i.e. a string of digits like a telephone number). Each node has a routing algorithm or table to which it can refer, like a local road map, to choose an appropriate outward data link path for specific addresses.

Packet size

User data in packets is variable in length up to a predetermined maximum. Maximum packet length is kept quite small (often a maximum of 128 or

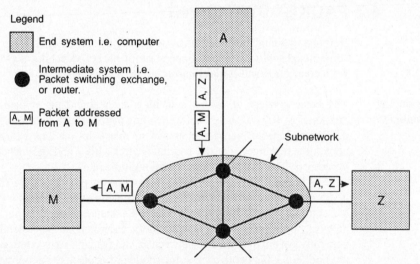

Figure 4.1   Network model – packets exchanged between different computer end systems are interleaved on the transmission lines.

256 octets). Although larger packets would be more efficient on network resources, shorter packets have the effect of reducing the transit delay of a message as it traverses a network. If a full display screen of 2,000 octets were sent as one packet, a complete transmission delay would be incurred for each link in the network. By breaking the 2,000 octets into, say, 8 packets the earlier packets can be moving on to other links while the later packets were arriving.

The use of small packets also facilitates the interleaving of data from several sources. But small packets have relatively higher overheads for protocol header information than large packets.

4.2.1 Connection Oriented Networks

Limited bandwidth
Early packet switching networks, which lead to the development of the X.25 standard for public data networks, were designed to optimize communications with the limited speed and error prone transmission services that were available at the time. They have the following characteristics:

- Each computer is connected to a PSE by a separate access line.

- Each PSE is interconnected to multiple other PSEs.

- The transit delay for data to travel from source to destination is in the order of hundreds of milliseconds.

The consequences for the protocol architecture are:

- For reliable operation, error detection and recovery procedures are implemented in the Data Link Layer on each transmission link. (End to end error recovery would incur unacceptable delays.)

- For equitable sharing of the limited network resources in a commercial, public environment, strict traffic control is required in the Network Layer. The traffic flow control regulates data entry to the network to avoid traffic jams, and ensures that data is delivered correctly in the sequence in which it was submitted. Because of the delays in the wide area network, the function of the traffic policeman is performed by the PSEs, which advise transmitting end systems when there is room for more traffic and whether parking space (i.e. data storage buffers) is available at the destination.

- Since each access line is dedicated to one computer, all addressing and routing are resolved in the Network Layer and no addressing is needed in the Data Link Layer.

- The destination address is supplied once in a connection establishment procedure that sets up a temporary route, called a virtual circuit, for subsequent data packets. Like a scout vehicle that sets up temporary route signs at each intersection, the nodes perform routing only at the start of a connection. The data packets need then carry only abbreviated channel numbers to distinguish between different virtual circuits. Each node maintains a list of channel numbers and their corresponding outward data link. This simplifies handling of data packets; i.e. by analogy, at each intersection, each driver follows the sign bearing the route number that has been previously allocated.

- Because of the robust nature of the lower layers, most typical applications can operate without further error controls in the Transport Layer.

X.25   X.25 is a good general purpose communications protocol and has many advantages for public and private network operation. X.25 interfaces are universally available from computer vendors and network suppliers. Public X.25 networks operate globally and will be viable for a long time to come. However, in comparison with the other network technologies, it has some disadvantages when there is bandwidth to burn. The main disadvantage is connection establishment delay. Inherent in the way that the X.25 traffic policeman operates, a three party agreement has to be reached between the network and the communicating end systems before data can be transferred. The connection management and data flow control are also an overhead on transmission capacity (although it is generally insignificant). The trade-off is that, once the connection is in place, data transfer can proceed with minimal transmission overhead; i.e. protocol data units are transferred with small headers and minimal processing. Furthermore, X.25 networks have many flow control options to fine-tune the performance of the network.

Complexity   Another disadvantage is that the establishment and maintenance of the connections require complex software and high processing power. This is compounded by the addition of a wide range of sophisticated facilities — more for marketing reasons than for technical necessity. The options now required for conformance to the standard mean that X.25 packet switching devices are increasing in complexity. The rich (heavyweight) connection oriented protocols in the Data Link and Network layers mean that the cost of the processing equipment for the switching nodes for such protocols is relatively higher than that of the simpler nodes that are possible using connectionless protocols.

4.2.2 Connectionless Networks

Bandwidth glut   To overcome some of the limitations of the above, high speed communications interfaces were developed. These interfaces were limited in distance (typically 1 km), but had a great speed advantage (e.g. 10 Mbit/s). Because of its initial physical distance limitation, this technology is referred to as a Local Area Network (LAN). LANs have been and still are under continual development to improve speed and distance. The new LAN technologies have now effectively started to erode the use of traditional wide area technology such as X.25. The distinguishing feature of a LAN is that multiple end systems are attached to a common high speed, low error rate transmission medium. The consequences for the protocol architecture are:

- So long as the bandwidth exceeds the peak demands of all of the attached systems, there is no need for a traffic policeman in the Network Layer.

- Since the error rates are very low, error recovery is not required in the Data Link or Network layers. Any corruption of data or congestion problems are simply resolved by discarding data. Data recovery is performed on an end to end basis by the Transport Layer. In other words, the highway is so empty that the LAN operates with few road rules. Any infrequent accidents that occur are cleaned away, and the damage is quickly repaired later in the Transport Layer on an end to end basis.

- The main remaining function of the Network Layer is addressing and internetworking, i.e. the linking of LANs and other networks by routers. (This is not required at all if communications are confined to the one LAN.)

- The Network Layer header of each packet contains full source and destination addresses, necessitating a separate routing action for each packet at each router node, like drivers having to look up the road map at every intersection.

- Although the Data Link Layer is simpler on account of not necessarily performing error recovery, it has picked up two other duties. Firstly, Medium Access Control (MAC) arbitrates permission to transmit on the LAN. This is a traffic policeman but is much simpler than that in the X.25 Network Layer because it operates in a local environment only. In effect, each station can "see" the traffic on the LAN. Additional addressing is also required in the Data Link Layer to distinguish between the different end systems.

Internet Protocol

A very convenient model was available for the OSI standards group to follow when devising a protocol stack for this environment. It was the Transmission Control Protocol/Internet Protocol (TCP/IP), widely used by the US Department of Defence and in UNIX systems. It evolved from the original ARPANET project, and uses connectionless protocols for Data Link and Network (IP) layers, and connection oriented for the Transport (TCP) Layer. Certain extensions were necessary to make the original IP suitable for global internetworking; so the standards committee started with a clean slate and developed the OSI connectionless protocol (also called OSI IP). TCP/IP is not OSI, but has a direct analog in the OSI connectionless protocol and transport protocol class 4.

The main reasons for using connectionless protocols are for inter-working across different types of networks, and for their simplicity that is appropriate in high bandwidth environments. The heavyweight X.25 protocols are replaced by data link MAC protocols that can be implemented cheaply in silicon, and a simple Network Layer protocol. All of this leads to cheaper network interface hardware for the computers, and cheaper routers for internetworking. Although OSI connectionless is just starting to be deployed, it is expected to proliferate during the 1990's. Connectionless is not without its trade-offs, however:

- Each data transfer has to carry full source and destination addresses and other communications parameters. This addressing information can be a considerable overhead in the header of short data units. Also, address resolution and routing take place for each individual data transfer in all intermediate systems. These matters are not troublesome on a LAN, but are a disadvantage when interworking between LANs over a lower speed wide area network via routers. In X.25, the address resolution is performed once only per connection for a potentially lengthy exchange of many data units.

- A robust and complex transport protocol is essential in end systems for end to end reliability over a connectionless network. In contrast, X.25 end systems can operate with a relatively simple Transport Layer.

- There is little scope to optimize the network as in the X.25 flow control options. The main way of managing performance limitations is to add more transmission capacity — but bandwidth is less of a problem these days.

4.3 INTEGRATED SERVICES DIGITAL NETWORKS

In the initial stages of network development, data and voice communications were considered separately. Since most organizations need both data and voice services, this required access via dual transmission plant to the subscriber's premises. Such duplication was due to the independent and quite distinct evolution of the services. The advent of digital telephone exchanges and advanced transmission technology, that allows the carriers to gain much more capacity out of the existing copper wire, has eliminated the need for such duplication. With economic pressure to remove the multiplicity of cabling and service (exchange) points associated with different networks, the *Integrated Services Digital Network (ISDN)* was formulated. Essentially, ISDN provides circuit switched Physical Layer bandwidth on demand. The bandwidth is allocated in 64 kbit/s time division multiplexed channels and it may be used for voice, data or other applications. Controlling the use of this bandwidth, say to establish a

64 kbit/s path to a specific destination, requires the use of a separate channel for signalling control information between the terminal equipment and the ISDN exchange.

4.3.1 ISDN Access

ISDN provides a mechanism by which a user can have a single managed access to the different services as previously provided by different networks. The essence of an ISDN interface is a set (two or more) of Bearer (B) channels and a D channel that is used to assign the connection and usage of the B channels. Each B channel may be used to provide an independent circuit switched connection for either end to end Pulse Code Modulated (PCM) voice conversation, or Physical Layer connection for data transfer or for image communications. The D channel is a statistically multiplexed signalling channel that is used for multiple purposes, i.e.:

- to control the B channels;

- for ISDN management; and,

- for access to a packet mode service.

Two types of access are offered by ISDN networks — *Basic Rate Access (BRA)* and *Primary Rate Access (PRA)*. Associated with each type of access is framing information that is used by the ISDN equipment for synchronization and control. The framing information is transparent to the user. Figure 4.2 illustrates potential interconnections via an ISDN.

BRA   Basic Rate Access provides two B channels at 64 kbit/s and one 16 kbit/s D channel. The total 2 B + D + framing is 192 kbit/s. The BRA service may be used by digital

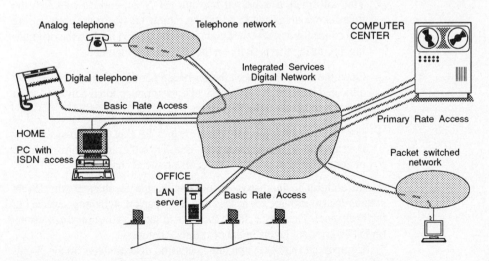

Figure 4.2   Example of integrated voice and data access on an ISDN

voice or data terminals or Group 4 facsimile terminals fitted with ISDN interfaces. Multiple terminals may concurrently share access to one BRA. Existing terminals using older interfaces are accommodated by Terminal Adapters (TAs). Basic rate is intended as a replacement for the traditional telephone service but with the inducement of providing multiple services and additional facilities. Basic rate can use the existing pair of copper wires that previously supported a single analog telephone, thereby maximizing the use of the carrier's investment in the existing customer access network.

PRA

Primary Rate Access is either 23 B + D + framing or 30 B + D + framing for a 1.544 Mbit/s or 2.048 Mbit/s stream respectively. (2.048 Mbit/s is used in Europe and Australia, 1.544 Mbit/s is used in North America and Japan.) For PRA, the D channel is 64 kbit/s. The PRA is typically used by PABXs (private telephone switchboards) and larger computer systems.

B channel assignment

To highlight the operation of ISDN technology a typical scenario is described below.

- The user's Terminal Equipment (TE) accesses the D channel in order to signal to the Network Equipment (NE).

- Once access has been achieved, the TE requests a B channel connection by signalling, on the D channel, information relating to the destination address (e.g. ISDN number) and the B channel use (e.g. whether a PCM coded channel for voice or a clear channel for data).

- This information is passed into the ISDN network to establish the internal resources and to signal the remote party. Progress signalling and connection acceptance signalling are passed back to the originating TE during this activity on the specified D channel.

- Once the call is accepted, the users are permitted data access to the allocated B channel; i.e. a Physical Layer connection is activated from end to end between the two users.

- For OSI data communications, the user's TA (i.e. OSI end systems or intermediate systems) must now establish either connection oriented or connectionless network protocols on the B channel.

As an additional alternative to the use of the B channel, the ISDN standards also provide for access to a X.25 packet switching service via the D channel. These aspects are further explained in the specific sections on ISDN protocol layers in the next three chapters.

Compared to a packet switching network, data transfers on the circuit switched ISDN B channel will encounter significantly lower transit delays. The trade-off is the need for heavyweight connection oriented signalling protocols on the D channel i.e. a traffic policeman is required in the Network Layer to arbitrate between competing requests for the bandwidth.

4.3.2 Impact on Network Planning

New high speed technologies are emerging for WANs, e.g. Metropolitan Area Networks (MANs), Fibre Distributed Data Interface (FDDI), frame relay, broadband ISDN using Asynchronous Transfer Mode (ATM), etc. These will continue the trend for simpler network protocols, i.e. OSI connectionless. However, whatever the future holds, LANs and other high speed services will need to co-exist and interwork with X.25 based systems and ISDN for a considerable time to come. Neither X.25 nor connectionless nor ISDN can be ignored in any organization's network plans.

The divergence between connection oriented and connectionless networking is a dichotomy that OSI could well do without. The debate about the two options has been divisive, and regional preferences have emerged (Europe generally prefers X.25, the USA connectionless). The technical differences complicate internetworking between LANs and WANs. To achieve such internetworking, implementations of the Network Layer must sometimes run dual protocols (i.e. both X.25 and connectionless). The Transport Layer is also necessarily more complicated — it must be able to convert from either X.25 or connectionless to provide a uniform service to the upper layers. Fortunately, however, once above the Transport Layer, applications are, in principle, isolated from these differences.

4.4 NETWORK ADDRESSING

As different communications technologies developed, so did their addressing requirements. Addressing may at first seem to be a minor issue, but a good rule to follow is: "The first action of any network design is to determine the naming and addressing scheme". This point can be brought home by considering the cost to a business of changing its telephone numbering scheme after some years of network service. Each type of public network has its own numbering forms:

E.163   Public Switched Telephone Network (PSTN).

E.164   ISDN.

X.121   X.25 Public Data Networks (PDNs).

Subnetwork addresses   These network dependent address forms are called *subnetwork addresses* in order to distinguish them from OSI Network Layer addresses defined later. Subnetwork addresses are numeric and are generally defined in

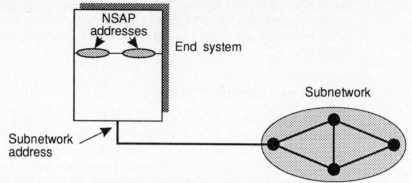

Figure 4.3   The subnetwork address identifies end systems to the subnetwork; the NSAP address is network independent.

terms of country, area, terminal number and subaddress. They are allocated by the carriers to identify the point of attachment of the customer's terminal equipment to the public network. The addresses are network dependent and are quite sufficient to define the end points on a single global network. However, these public schemes did not accommodate all of the requirements of private networks that needed their own numbering plan for subnetwork addresses. Furthermore, the allocation of numbers in private networks and LANs was not co-ordinated with other networks, leading to inconsistencies when interworking between them. For example, duplicated numbers may occur. Revision of all existing public and private network numbering plans for consistency was impractical, so a separate, global addressing scheme has been established for OSI Network Layer addresses (see Figure 4.3).

NSAP addresses

All end systems that wish to participate in the global open network must be allocated one (or more) *Network Service Access Point (NSAP) address(es)*. Such addresses are required to be:

- unambiguous, i.e. each identifies only one NSAP in one end system;

- global, i.e. able to be used anywhere and still identify the same end system;

- independent of routing, i.e. the route to be taken is not constrained; and,

- structured to facilitate allocation of numbers, and to simplify routing analysis.

A number of NSAP address formats have been standardized and are explained in Section 8.4.1 (page 143) on internetworking. In summary, an NSAP address may be up to 40 digits long, and it is allocated by addressing authorities in a hierarchical structure. For simple cases, a default format, based on a public network number (e.g. from the X.121

Format Identifier	Country Code	Organization Identifier	Network Identifier	Computer Number

Figure 4.4   Example of Network Service Access Point (NSAP) address format

number plan) may be used. For a network independent address, another alternative format consists of a series of prefixes as illustrated in Figure 4.4.

Routing   Since NSAPs are different from subnetwork addresses, Network Layer entities must be able to perform routing on NSAP addresses, and map from NSAPs to subnetwork addresses. Furthermore, NSAP addresses must be carried through the subnetworks as well as subnetwork addresses. X.25 can carry NSAPs in its facility fields and ISDN E.164 formats permit the use of NSAP fields. However, another solution to the problem is to use the OSI connectionless protocol over the subnetwork and let it carry the NSAP addresses independently of the underlying subnetwork technology. The use of the OSI connectionless protocol today is primarily directed at this use as it provides an end to end network protocol, and gateway and routing functions are performed at this level.

4.5 RELAYS

Relaying may occur in any of the lower three layers of intermediate systems. The implementation of relaying, and the allocation of relaying functions to the layers in a particular case depends on a balance between technology, performance and cost. Relaying is also intimately associated with addressing, routing, and switching. Some examples of relay functions are listed below:

Physical Layer   A Physical Layer relay copies bits from one physical medium to another as the bits arrive. In WANs, modems and network terminating units are relays. In a circuit switched network, such as an ISDN or X.21 public data network, the exchanges are relays that also perform switching. Repeaters are physical relays in a LAN environment. Repeaters are low level amplifying devices that join separate cable segments of the same type.

Data Link Layer   Data Link relays are store and forward devices which exchange entire frames between links. (A frame is the unit of data transfer in the Data Link Layer.) Frame relay is a new technique for transport of packetized data in WANs. Bridges store and forward frames between LANs at the Data Link Layer. Typically, bridges link two LAN segments of the same type.

Network   Packet switching exchanges and routers store and forward
Layer   packets in the Network Layer. Routers, in particular, may
                     provide routing and relaying between multiple dissimilar
                     types of networks and typically operate with multiple
                     protocol stacks.

Relays progressively become more sophisticated, going from the Physical
Layer to the Network Layer. When activated, repeaters merely forward
all bits. Bridges, on the other hand, filter frames by making a decision on
whether or not to forward each frame based on the location of the
destination. Routers choose from a number of alternative routes to find a
path on which to forward data to the destination.

4.6 WHAT'S NEXT?

The topics introduced in the preceding discussion will be explained in
detail in the following five chapters. Chapters 5 and 6 cover the standards
that apply in the Physical and Data Link layers. The coverage is at an
overview level because the technical details of the operation of these
standards are well covered elsewhere, and the aim is to consolidate the
existing Physical and Data Link layer standards with OSI. The Network
Layer has such an important role in OSI that two chapters are devoted to
it. Chapter 7 covers the protocols, and Chapter 8 covers internetworking
and addressing in detail. Chapter 9 deals with the Transport Layer.

5   Physical Layer

5.1 INTRODUCTION

The Physical Layer provides a bit pipe for transmission of data between open systems. It is affectionately called the "sewer" because it is concerned with the plumbing at the bottom of the seven layer stack.

At the time of the development of the Open Systems Interconnection (OSI) Reference Model, a variety of physical media were in use for communication, using a number of different control procedures and interfaces (RS-232, V.24, X.21, V.35). New standards for Local Area Networks (LANs) and Integrated Services Digital Networks (ISDNs) were also being formulated. In the Reference Model it was considered appropriate to isolate the tasks associated with these interfaces into the Physical Layer. The OSI committees aimed to develop a uniform way of modeling the large amount of pre-existing and developing standards in this area, rather than develop new interfaces for OSI. The Reference Model defines the task of the Physical Layer as providing the mechanical, electrical, functional and procedural means to activate, maintain and deactivate physical connections for bit transmission between Data Link entities. Note that other standards define the interface at the boundary between the Physical Layer and the real physical transmission media. The four main aspects of the interface are:

Mechanical   Plug/socket and pin sizes and shapes.

Electrical   Specification of the signalling voltages, etc. associated with the interface.

Functional   Meaning of the signals.

Procedural   Combinations and sequences of signals on the interfaces.

Many interface standards are applicable and on-going development adds new standards to the list. The purpose of this chapter is to recap the main standards and technology that apply in the Physical Layer and to give a simple example that relates the OSI sequence diagram technique to familiar concepts. Other standards have been omitted from this chapter for space considerations but are not excluded from application in OSI.

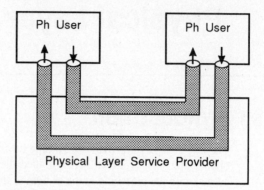

Figure 5.1   Model of Physical Layer

5.1.1 Physical Layer Services

The Reference Model specifies a number of broad services that may be provided by the Physical Layer. A model for the Physical Layer service provider is given in Figure 5.1; i.e. it is modeled as a pair of bit streams carrying data between open systems. The model basically reflects what is available from existing interface standards. Many of the services are self-evident and some could be implemented probably only with difficulty. In consequence, some services are defined as optional. The major services are:

Physical connections   Transparent connections are modeled by an (optional) connection activation/deactivation service between two or more physical entities. This allows for point to point operation between two open systems, or multi-endpoint operation as in a LAN. The model also allows for multiple circuits and relays, i.e. a series of more than one sequential circuits.

Data transfer   The physical Service Data Unit (SDU) is defined as 1 bit. Delivery, however, may be affected by transmission errors and transit delays.

Sequencing   The bits must be kept in order.

Management   Fault condition notification (optional) may be provided for layer management.

Quality Of Service (QOS) parameters are defined for aspects such as error rate, desired transit delay, etc.

Service definition   Because the Physical Layer is dependent on the transmission media, there is no requirement for the Physical Layer to conform to one service definition. The physical service definition ISO DIS 10022/CCITT X.211, in effect, models existing standards. The key requirement is for the

Physical Layer to support the Data Link and Network layers in the provision of the network service. The service definition for a full duplex point to point service may differ from the physical service of a LAN. Figure 5.2 illustrates the sequence diagram for full duplex point to point operation. Connection activation occurs independently in either direction.

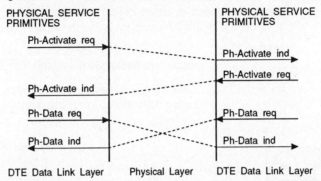

Figure 5.2   Sequence diagram for full duplex Physical Layer service showing physical connection activation and data transfer

5.1.2 Physical Layer Interface Standards

Much of the standards development activity affecting the Physical Layer has been concentrated either on the different interfaces to physical circuits (RS-232, V.35, etc.) or LANs where the emerging standards such as the IEEE 802 and ISO 8802 cover both the Physical and Data Link Layers. Furthermore, the growing adoption of ISDN now provides a flexible, high speed alternative for interconnection of computer systems using the CCITT I-series Recommendations.

There is no single interface standard for the Physical Layer. Instead OSI systems use established standards in a way that supports the Data Link and Network layers in the provision of the network service. Although the model generally permits the use of asynchronous transmission and half-duplex operation, most implementations use full duplex synchronous operation. Figure 5.3 summarizes the standards that are discussed in this chapter. Each standard will be covered in turn.

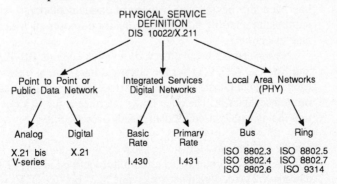

Figure 5.3   Some OSI Physical Layer standards

5.2 POINT TO POINT SERVICES

The most commonplace standards for physical interfaces are concerned with point to point transmission, or access to a Public Data Network (PDN) over leased lines. The transmission lines may be based on analog telephone bearers or newer digital services. Some of the terminology associated with this environment is illustrated in Figure 5.4.

DTE   *Data Terminal Equipment*, i.e. the user's terminal, computer or an intermediate systems such as a router.

DCE   *Data Circuit terminating Equipment*, i.e. a modem in analog networks or a network terminating unit in digital networks.

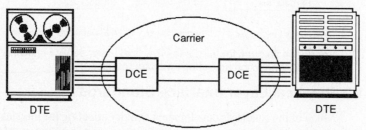

Figure 5.4   Model and terminology for point to point Physical Layer

RS-232   The Physical Layer interface is defined between the DTE and DCE. Despite a number of technical shortcomings and many predictions about its demise, the RS-232 interface standard, and its CCITT equivalents, V.24 and V.28, continue to be dominant in the Physical Layer. The first variant of RS-232 appeared in 1960 and the fifth revision, now called EIA/TIA-232-E, is currently being considered by the technical committees of the Electronic Industries Association (EIA) and the Telecommunications Industry Association (TIA).

RS-232 is usually associated with the 25 pin (ISO 2110) plug, although this was not part of the original standard. One of its many problems has been the bewildering variety of implementations, with different manufacturers using different circuits for purposes such as flow control and "paper out".

Newer standards have been developed, such as RS-423/X.26/V.10 and RS-422/X.27/V.11 for the electrical interface, and RS-449 or X.21 for the procedural and functional interface. However, these have met with limited acceptance. The other major interface is the V.35 Recommendation that is widely used for data speeds over 48 kbit/s.

X.21 and   For the OSI Physical Layer, the usual combinations of these standards for
X.21 bis   point to point or circuit switched circuits is defined in CCITT Recommendations X.21 (for digital networks) and X.21 bis (for DTEs with V-series

interfaces). X.21 and X.21 bis define the procedural characteristics for the OSI Physical Layer interface and refer to other X or V-series Recommendations to cover the full definition of mechanical, electrical and functional characteristics. The mechanical and electrical characteristics are summarized in Table 5.1.

X.21 bis is one of the essential compromises in communications standards that emerged as it became apparent that few manufacturers would provide full X.21 interfaces. X.21 bis is essentially a subset of V.24 to control the functioning of a synchronous circuit. It can use either V.28 or X.26 electrical signaling.

Functional characteristics standards assign meaning to the individual circuits making up the interface. X.21 bis refers to V.24 (RS-232) for the definition of circuits. V.24 uses one circuit per function and many functions are defined. X.21 bis uses only a subset of the V.24 circuits.

Table 5.1   Summary of point to point Physical Layer standards

X.21 AND X.21 bis STANDARDS			
Common Name	**X.21 (Digital)**	**RS-232 (Analog)** < 20 kbit/s	**V.35 (Analog)** > 20 kbit/s
Mechanical (plug)	ISO 4903	ISO 2110	ISO 2593
Electrical (voltages)	V.11 (or V.10)	V.28	V.35
Functional (signal meaning)	X.21	V.24	V.24
Procedural (signal sequences)	X.21	X.21 bis	X.21 bis

MECHANICAL CHARACTERISTICS	
ISO 2110	25 pin connector used with RS-232/V.24/V.28
ISO 2593	34 pin connector used with V.35 Recommendation
ISO 4902	37 and 9 pin connectors used with RS-449
ISO 4903	15 pin connector used with X.21 and X.22

ELECTRICAL CHARACTERISTICS			
Standard	**Voltages**	**Type**	**Distance**
V.28/RS-232	Logical 0: 5 V < V < 15 V Logical 1: –5 V > V > –15 V	Unbalanced signaling	Limited to < 20 kbit/s and distances < 10 m
V.10/X.26/RS-423	Logical 0: 4 V < V < 6 V Logical 1: –4 V > V > –6 V	Unbalanced signaling with wave shaping	1000 m at 3 kbit/s or 10 m at 300 kbits/s
V.11/X.27/RS-422	+/– 2 V to 6 V	Balanced differential signaling	1000 m at 100 kbit/s or 10 m at 10 Mbit/s

The *Send Data* and *Receive Data* circuits convey the serial data stream. When the control circuits are in the logical On state, their functional indication is:

DSR   Data Set Ready. The modem is powered on and ready for operation.

DTR   Data Terminal Ready. The terminal is on and ready for operation.

RTS   Request To Send. The terminal initiates a transmission.

CTS   Clear To Send. Modem acknowledgement to the Request to Send.

RLSD   Receive Line Signal Detector. Carrier has been detected and the modem is receiving incoming data.

The X.21 bis and associated standards specify the procedures for accessing public data networks by DTEs designed for modem interfaces. In other words, how to use RS-232 or V.35 for access to packet switched networks. These procedures can also apply for point to point connections between two DTEs.

Figure 5.5 illustrates the relationship between the sequence diagram used earlier to define the physical service, and the events at the X.21 bis (RS-232) interface. The various modems and transmission facilities that make up the physical medium are depicted by the vertical box in the center of the diagram. Basically, the Ph-Activate request from the Data Link Layer causes the physical entity to turn DTR On, thereby connecting the modem to the line. When carrier (RLSD On) is detected at the remote modem, the physical entity issues a Ph-Activate indication to the data link entity in the layer above. After the Physical Layer is activated, data

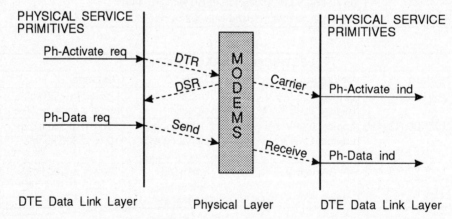

Figure 5.5   X.21 bis procedures

transfer may proceed. Although the relationship depicted in the diagram is trivial, the example serves to relate the descriptive notations used in this book to real life. This technique will be used in subsequent chapters to illustrate the mapping between services and protocols.

Note that the activate service is optional in the physical service definition. In typical implementations, the physical connection is activated automatically when the DTEs and modems are switched on.

5.2.1 The X.21 Recommendation

X.21, which was first approved in 1972, is intended as the standard for DCE/DTE interface to digital Public Data Networks (PDN). PDNs in this case include both circuit and packet switched networks. X.21 may be used in point to point, or multipoint leased line service, and circuit switched service. As X.21 preceded the ISO Reference Model, its structure is not clearly divided into layers. For example, its circuit switch mode includes some Data Link and Network layer aspects.

X.21 uses a 15 pin plug (ISO 4903) and uses X.27 (RS-422/V.11). For speeds of 9.6 kbit/s and below, the DTE may optionally use X.26 (RS-423/V.10) electrical characteristics.

Functional characteristics Compared with RS-232, and its 21 interchange circuits, X.21 has only six circuits plus a signal ground. X.21 codes multiple functions on a relatively small number of circuits. The various states associated with setting up and clearing connections are indicated by combinations of the circuits.

Despite its technical elegance, and its effectiveness in PDNs, the main applications of X.21 have been confined to high speed (48 kbit/s or higher) access to digital networks. Such networks include Telecom Australia's Digital Data Service (DDS) and a number of European circuit switched networks. It has not been well accepted in the USA. Use of X.21 is increasing in the role of a high speed interface for terminal adapters for ISDN access.

5.3 INTEGRATED SERVICES DIGITAL NETWORKS

The CCITT Recommendations for Integrated Services Digital Networks (ISDNs) were developed during the same period as the OSI standards. Consequently, ISDN from the outset conforms to the OSI requirements for the lower three layers. The objective of ISDN is to extend the benefits of digital transmission and switching, which is already pervasive within the telephone network, to the customers' premises. ISDN allows switched 64 kbit/s circuit switched channels to be established end to end between customers' terminals for voice, data or image communications.

ISDN uses time division multiplexing to support multiple switched 64 kbit/s channels (called B channels) over the physical link to the ISDN exchange. Two access modes are defined: Basic Rate Access (BRA, two B channels) and Primary Rate Access (PRA, 23 or 30 B channels). In addition, a separate signaling channel (called the D channel), is provided to control the use of the circuit switched channels. This calls for a sophisticated model for the ISDN Physical Layer as described in the next section.

5.3.1 ISDN Reference Points

The standards associated with ISDN are the CCITT I-series and the CCITT Q-series. There are many separate standards in the series and the major ones for the ISDN Physical Layer are:

I.430   Layer 1 for Basic Rate Access (BRA).

I.431   Layer 1 for Primary Rate Access (PRA).

The Recommendations define the mechanical characteristics of the plugs/sockets used, the electrical characteristics of the interchange circuits, and the framing and signaling used on those interchange circuits. These Physical Layer characteristics of ISDN are defined in the Recommendations in terms of the reference points depicted in Figure 5.6. The figure depicts two types of Terminal Equipment (TE1 and TE2), a Terminal adapter (TA), Network Terminations (NT1 and NT2) and Exchange Termination (ET). TE2 represents existing equipment using traditional interfaces (i.e. X-series or V-series) that accesses the ISDN network via a TA. TE1 represents terminals fitted with ISDN interfaces. Multiple TE1s, TE2s and TAs share the BRA. The NT1, NT2 and TA may exist as separate devices or they may be integrated into one unit with support of the various interfaces.

Reference point R is for non-ISDN equipment (i.e. TE2). Reference point S is a 4 wire interface (two send, two receive) and provides the interface for ISDN compatible terminal equipment (TE1).

Reference points T and S have the same physical characteristics. They are provided in order to allow splitting (distribution) of the T reference point; e.g. a PABX (private telephone switch) is represented by an NT2 multiplexing a number of TAs and ISDN BRA interfaces. Reference point T (like S) is a 4 wire interface and defines the user interface to NT1

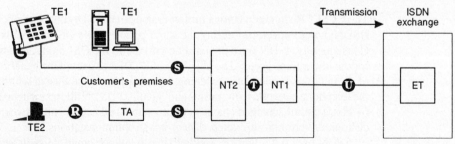

Figure 5.6   Physical Layer Model for ISDN

equipment. The NT1 terminates the transmission media supplied by the carrier. Reference point U is the actual transmission line between the user premises and the exchange. Its physical characteristics depend on the type of access and transmission technology.

The PRA and BRA interfaces are quite distinct. BRA uses multi-point operation (multiplexed attachment of multiple TE1s and TAs to the service), whereas PRA is only point to point (attachment is by a single PRA multiplexer or PABX). Salient aspects of the S and U interfaces for BRA and PRA are described in the following sections.

5.3.2 Basic Rate Access

Mechanical

The mechanical aspects of the ISDN interfaces depend on the type of equipment; e.g. a TA may use RS-232, X.21 or RJ type connectors. At the S/T reference point, an 8 pole RJ type connector is used for Basic Rate Access. The connector is defined in ISO 8877. A number of physical configurations are possible. In a typical configuration, the S/T interface is installed as a 4 wire bus with multiple outlets in a home or office. Multiple ISDN voice, data and image terminals may share the bus; i.e. up to eight TE1s or TAs may plug into the bus. The maximum bus length is 100 m and the maximum length of the drop to the TE or TA is 10 m.

Electrical

CCITT Recommendation I.430 details the electrical characteristics for the BRA S/T interface; i.e. it covers waveform timing diagrams, voltage and impedance specifications, and the encoding scheme (Pseudo Ternary). In addition to a 4 wire transmission interface, the S/T reference point also defines two pairs of wires for a power source between the TE and the NT equipment. The power source and sink can be either the TE or the NT or both in order to retain voice services in the event of a power failure. The applicability and use of the power source is subject to the capabilities of the equipment and the policies of individual carriers.

Framing

CCITT I.430 also defines the framing structure used to multiplex multiple channels on the physical circuit. Each direction of transmission at the S/T reference point is time division multiplexed into frames that have fixed timeslots for the B channels and D channels. Functions are also assigned to bits in the frame for Physical Layer signaling. The two B channels and the D channel require 144 kbit/s and there are an additional 48 kbit/s of framing and signaling information. The composite transmission speed on the S/T interface is 192 kbit/s. The frame transmitted from the TE to the NT is repeatedly encoded every 250 µs as shown in Figure 5.7. The frame transmitted from the NT to the TE is slightly different and is delayed by two bit times. This is done to enable D channel access collision management by the TEs.

Framing bits (F) are used to define where the frame is in a time sequence (timeslot identification); i.e. the framing bits determine which octet is the B1 channel and which octet is the B2 channel.

Access to the B channel is controlled by D channel signaling (i.e. for connection establishment). A contention control mechanism must be used to manage access to the shared D channel by multiple TEs. For contention control, the D channel transmissions by the TEs are echoed back to the TEs from the NT (in the E bits in Figure 5.7). As a TE transmits on the D channel, it monitors the echoed D channel (delayed by two bit times). If it is not as transmitted by the individual TE (i.e. other TEs are transmitting at the same time), then transmission is ceased and a retransmission is attempted after a predefined period. This mechanism is similar to CSMA/CD used on LANs (see page 77), but in this case separate transmit and receive cables are used.

Procedural   The Activation bit (A) is used in conjunction with the other bits (B, D, E, F) for the level 1 signaling procedures between the NT and TE. The level 1 procedures of BRA perform a Physical Layer activation/deactivation/resynchronization function for the equipment. The procedures use messages that are briefly described as follows:

Info 0   Defined as no signal on any bits. Indicates that the NT
(NT to TE)   wishes to deactivate the TE.

Info 2   Defined as B, D, E and A bits set to zero. Indicates that
(NT to TE)   the NT wishes to activate the TE (as the TE is sending
                    Info 0).

Info 4   Defined as B, D, E operational and A bits set to one
(NT to TE)   (active). Indicates that the NT is transmitting normally.

Info 0   Defined as no signal on any bits. Indicates loss of frame
(TE to NT)   alignment, power up, etc.

Info 1   Defined as a positive, a negative and six ones in a bit
(TE to NT)   sequence. Indicates that the TE wishes to activate the NT
                    and requests the NT to send Info 2 (activate to the TE).

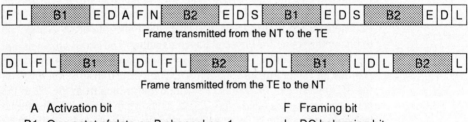

Frame transmitted from the NT to the TE

Frame transmitted from the TE to the NT

A   Activation bit   F   Framing bit
B1 One octet of data on B channel no. 1   L   DC balancing bit
B2 One octet of data on B channel no. 2   N   N framing bit
D   D channel bit   S   Spare bit
E   Echo bit (echo of TE D channel)

Figure 5.7   ISDN Basic Rate Access (BRA) frame structure.

INfo 3   Defined as B and D channels operational. Indicates that
(TE to NT)   the TE is operational.

There is also a level 1 arbitration and priority mechanism applied to the
D channel. Signaling traffic is given a higher priority than user data. This
arbitration mechanism relies on the state of a stream of E bits transmitted
by the NT.

Transmission   The NT1 terminates the S/T 4 wire bus and interfaces to the transmission
service at the U reference point. Transmission from the NT1 at the
customer premises to the ISDN exchange takes place on an ordinary 2
wire twisted pair circuit to achieve an effective full duplex data transfer
rate of 144 kbit/s.

5.3.3 Primary Rate Access

The Primary Rate Access (PRA) operates on a point to point circuit
between the NT and TE equipment. It provides the user–network interface
at the S/T reference point at 1,544 kbit/s (23 B + D) and 2,048 kbit/s
(30 B + D) for use by a single PABX or large computer system.
Transmission between the ISDN exchange and the NT takes place over
conditioned 4 wire circuits or fibre optic systems.

Mechanical   The standard 8 pole connector for the PRA S/T interface is ISO 10173.
Coaxial connectors are also used by some administrations on an interim
basis.

Electrical   The electrical characteristics for PRA are defined in CCITT G.703. This
recommendation provides waveform timing diagrams, impedance and
voltage specifications, and the encoding scheme.

Framing   The CCITT G.704 recommendation defines the frame format (timeslot
allocation), framing control, signaling and error detection schemes. The
multiplexing hierarchy is defined in G.732. For 1,544 kbit/s, the frame
structure consists of a framing bit followed by 24 consecutive timeslots.
The 2,048 kbit/s frame is divided into 32 timeslots — one of which is used
for framing. Each timeslot is 8 bits with a frame repetition rate of 125 µs
giving 64 kbit/s per timeslot.

Procedural   For PRA, one timeslot in the above-mentioned frame structures is
reserved for D channel access and the remainder are used for B channels.
Since the D channel operates in a fixed point to point mode, no contention
control is necessary.

5.3.4 Broadband ISDN

The mass introduction of ISDN will be justified mainly by the replacement and extension of the telephone service. As a side benefit, the lower costs and the integrated access of ISDN will attract many data users who were previously confined to costly dedicated low speed data circuits. However, many users require higher speed access than is provided by BRA and PRA, e.g. for LAN bridging. New standards are emerging for broadband ISDN to meet this need.

Broadband ISDN is based on new switching technology called fast packet switching — it is also referred to Asynchronous Transfer Mode (ATM). The technology has been evolved for wideband applications such as video and High Definition Television (HDTV). (ATM is described briefly in the next chapter on the Data Link Layer.) At the Physical Layer, broadband ISDN can use fibre optic transmission systems or can be carried over wideband multiplexing schemes such as Synchronous Digital Hierarchy (SDH) that defines multiplexed transmission for rates from 155 Mbit/s to 2.48 Gbit/s and beyond.

5.4 LAN PHYSICAL LAYER

LAN technology introduced a range of physical medium types, e.g. co-axial, twisted pair, fibre optic. The choice of LAN media type is generally determined on the nature of the bandwidth required, the availability of equipment with such interfaces, the operating environment and the protocol characteristics of the LAN itself.

The IEEE developed a number of standards for LANs, and these have also been republished by the ISO. The standards encompass both the Physical and Data Link layers. In fact the LAN standards are specified in three parts:

PHY   Physical Layer.

MAC   Medium Access Control sublayer.

LLC   Logical Link Control sublayer.

The LAN PHY standards correspond to the OSI Physical Layer, and the MAC and LLC standards correspond to the OSI Data Link Layer. For each LAN technology, one LAN standard (i.e. each of those listed in Figure 5.4) covers the PHY and MAC. The LLC is a generic standard for all LANs. The Physical Layer aspects of the standards are outlined here, and the data link aspects are covered in the next chapter. Since the technical details of the interface are not of concern to OSI, only the salient aspects of the LAN Physical Layer standards are summarized in this chapter.

LANs can be grouped into two categories, corresponding to bus and ring topology. The following discussion refers to the logical topology of the LAN. The physical wiring topology can assume a star, bus, ring or tree configuration, depending on the cabling strategy.

Bus   For the bus LANs, each computer system or (station) effectively taps into the high speed transmission medium.

Ring   Stations on ring LANs intercept the transmission medium and regenerate signals received in the incoming side for outgoing retransmission.

Each transmission reaches all stations on the LAN; i.e. the LANs operate in a multi-endpoint broadcast mode. The right to transmit (insert a frame) on the transmission medium by a station is governed by the MAC protocols operating in the Data Link Layer.

5.4.1 ISO 8802-3/IEEE 802.3 CSMA/CD

CSMA/CD stands for Carrier Sense, Multiple Access/Collision Detect. This is based on the original Ethernet technology but it is not compatible with it. CSMA/CD operates with a bus topology in a broadcast contention mode (Figure 5.8). Any station with data to send may transmit provided that the LAN cable is not being used by another station. It typically uses direct baseband modulation of omni-directional cable at 10 Mbit/s (broadband is also supported). The maximum cable path between any two stations may be up to 2.5 km depending on the configuration. A number of cable types may be used for the transmission medium:

10base5   "Thick Ethernet"; 50 ohm co-axial cable with tap connection.

10base2   "Thin Ethernet"; 50 ohm co-axial cable with BNC connectors.

10broad36   "Broadband"; permits operation over co-axial cable using radio frequency modulation.

10baseT   Unshielded twisted pair (UTP) in a star wired topology.

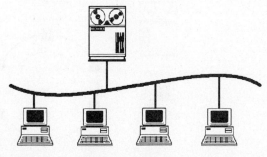

Figure 5.8   LAN bus topology for IEEE 802.3 and 802.4

5.4.2 ISO 8802-4/IEEE 802.4 Token Bus

A Token Bus LAN forms a broadcast bus at the Physical Layer (Figure 5.8), but a logical ring at Data Link Layer. The token is a special data link frame that circulates between LAN stations. The station which holds the token has momentary control, and may broadcast data. The LAN can operate with omni-directional or single direction of transmission, and it uses either Cable Television (TV) technology (broadband) or direct baseband modulation. The broadband (CATV) option uses transmit and receive channels allocated in the region from 59 MHz to 300 MHz. It is the preferred LAN for the Manufacturing Automation Protocol (MAP).

5.4.3 ISO 8802-5/IEEE 802.5 Token Ring

This is the same as the IBM Token Ring product. Stations are hard wired in a ring topology (Figure 5.9), and a special data link frame called a token circulates between stations. Ownership of the token determines whether the station may insert data onto the ring or acts as a repeater of incoming data. It operates with baseband uni-directional transmission at 4 Mbit/s or 16 Mbit/s, over shielded twisted pair cable.

5.4.4 ISO 8802-6/IEEE 802.6 Distributed Queue, Dual Bus (DQDB)

Known as a Metropolitan Area Network (MAN), because of its indefinite distance coverage, DQDB uses a dual uni-directional bus, one for each direction of transmission (Figure 5.10). It operates at 140 Mbit/s. The MAN bandwidth is divided into a number of fixed length timeslots by a control station. The control station generates a series of 125 µs time division multiplexed frames that propagate along the transmission medium. Each frame is divided into approximately 400 timeslots. Timeslots are 53 octets long, comprising 5 octets of header and 48 octets of user data (or payload).

Bandwidth is managed in two ways to enable both real time synchronous traffic and packet mode traffic to share the MAN. Real time

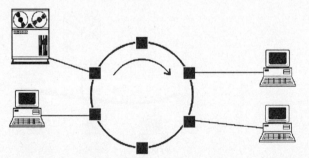

Figure 5.9   ISO 8802-5/IEEE 802.5 LAN ring topology

traffic is allocated certain reserved timeslots. Access to an unreserved timeslot for packet mode traffic is based on a distributed queue algorithm. DQDB can serve as a backbone network linking lower speed LANs and it is compatible with developing standards for broadband ISDN using Asynchronous Transfer Mode (ATM). DQDB is similar to the Switched Multi-megabit Data Service (SMDS).

5.4.5 ISO 8802-7/IEEE 802.7 Slotted Ring

Based on a fixed timeslots scheme, the slotted ring originated in the UK as the Cambridge ring but it is not popular elsewhere.

5.4.6 ISO 9314 Fibre Distributed Data Interface (FDDI)

A dual fibre optic token ring system developed by ANSI rather than IEEE, FDDI operates at 100 Mbit/s with up to 1,000 physical links and distances of up to several kilometres between systems. Operation of an FDDI LAN is similar to a token ring LAN. It can serve as a backbone, interconnecting a number of lower speed LANs.

5.4.7 Integrated Voice and Data LAN (IEEE 802.9)

An amalgam of ISDN, circuit switching and LAN transmission, this technology is still very much in its infancy. Essentially, at the transmission level time division multiplexing at 4.096 Mbit/s is used. This bandwidth is divided into 125 μs per frame slots giving 8,000 frames per second. The frame is partitioned to carry the framing overhead, one ISDN D channel, two ISDN B channels (at 64 kbit/s each), a C channel for circuit switching and a P channel for MAC (LAN) traffic. The ratio of bandwidth between the C and P channels is configurable.

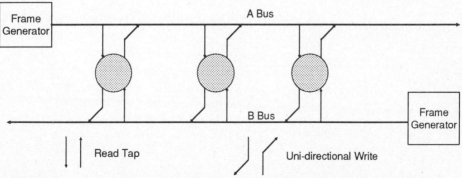

Figure 5.10   IEEE 802.6 Distributed Queue, Dual Bus Metropolitan Area Network

5.5 QUESTIONS

Question 5.1   What are the four main aspects of the Physical Layer?

Question 5.2   The Physical Layer provides four services. What are they?

Question 5.3   What are the main groups of Physical Layer interfaces and what are the main differences between these groups?

Question 5.4   Describe the functions of DSR and DTR.

Question 5.5   What physical interface do the R, I, T, C interchange signals belong to and what is their purpose?

Question 5.6   What transmission speeds are used for ISDN BRA and PRA?

Question 5.7   What services do the B and D channels perform?

Question 5.8   List the ISDN reference points and explain their purpose.

Question 5.9   What is the difference between the S and T reference points?

Question 5.10   Why are there two distinct Physical Layer standards for ISDN?

Question 5.11   What is ATM?

Question 5.12   What are the characteristics of 10base5, 10base2 and 10baseT?

Question 5.13   What OSI layer do the MAC protocols belong to and why?

6 Data Link Layer

6.1 LINK PROTOCOLS

The purpose of the Data Link Layer is to organize the data from the higher layers into blocks of bits, called frames, for orderly transmission and error control.

HDLC

The Data Link Layer is another example of a layer that was conceived around an existing area of standardization — in this case the so-called line or link protocols. Since the very earliest days of data communications, protocols had been developed for the formatting, delimiting, synchronization and error control of messages on data lines. Early protocols are generally termed "character oriented" as they used special ASCII (American Standard Code for Information Interchange) or EBCDIC (Extended BCD Interchange Code) characters for formatting and delimiting. The most common such protocol is known variously as Binary Synchronous Control (BSC) and ISO Basic Mode. Later protocols removed the need for special characters to delimit the fields of communication messages and are generally termed "bit oriented" protocols. The major such protocol is High level Data Link Control (HDLC). IBM's Synchronous Data Link Control (SDLC) is a subset of HDLC.

HDLC, in one form or another, appears in all OSI data link standards. These are known as:

LAPB Link Access Procedure Balanced — used in X.25.

LAPD Link Access Procedure for D channel — used in Integrated Services Digital Networks (ISDNs).

LLC Logical Link Control — used in conjunction with Medium Access Control (MAC) in Local Area Networks (LANs).

6.1.1 Purpose of the Data Link Layer

The Data Link Layer is primarily concerned with the passing of data (i.e. data link Service Data Units, SDUs) over communications lines, and the detection and, optional correction of any errors that may occur. Both connectionless and connection oriented modes are used in the Data Link Layer, with some implementations supporting both simultaneously. For

81

connection oriented mode (e.g. X.25 LAPB), the purpose of the layer is as follows:

- The Data Link Layer provides the functional and procedural means to establish, maintain and release data link connections among network entities. A data link connection is built upon one or several physical connections, and the Network Layer is able to control the interconnection of data circuits within the Physical Layer.

- Data link SDUs are correctly transferred, in sequence, between network entities. The Data Link Layer detects and attempts to correct errors that may occur in the Physical Layer e.g. due to corruption by electrical noise.

- Irrecoverable failures in the data link operation (residual errors) are signaled to the Network Layer by disconnection of the data link. The Network Layer can force the data link to reset to a known state (possibly causing the loss of data).

The connectionless service (e.g. LAN LLC type 1) simply transfers data units one at a time, without error recovery. Any corrupted transmissions are discarded and losses are not reported to the sender.

Multi-endpoint operation is also used in ISDN and LAN applications. Data link addresses are supported in order to distinguish between the multiple systems sharing the multi-endpoint physical service.

6.1.2 Service Definition

Along with the Physical Layer, the data link service definition (ISO 8886/CCITT X.212) is an outline of functional requirements rather than a single specific service that is globally supported. Thus, each data link protocol (e.g. LAPB for X.25, LAPD for ISDN, and LLC for LANs) may have a slightly different realization of the data link service. The key

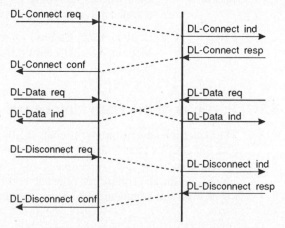

Figure 6.1   Sequence diagram for data link connection oriented service

requirement is that the Data Link Layer supports the Network Layer in the provision of the network service.

For example, the connection establishment service for LAPB is modeled by a confirmed dialogue as shown in Figure 6.1, whereas it is modeled by a partially confirmed dialogue for LLC on a LAN.

6.1.3 Data Link Standards

Figure 6.2 illustrates the relationships between the main standards. HDLC is not one document, but a series of standards that define a broad family of data link control protocols. The family of HDLC standards has seen a protracted period of development since the basic concept of the protocol was devised by Jack Houldsworth in the late 1960's. There are several quite different "modes" within HDLC, with the most recent not being finalized until 1981. IBM's SDLC, which was defined in 1972, was based on early ANSI drafts and appeared well before HDLC became a standard.

A subset of HDLC was adopted by the CCITT as the link protocol for X.25 in 1976, where it was originally known as the Link Access Protocol (LAP). This was later modified and improved to become the LAPB. A further variant of HDLC is used on the D channel of ISDN and is known as LAPD, while HDLC-like message structures are used in the Logical Link Control (LLC) standards for LANs. LAPD and LLC emerged in the mid-1980's while the OSI standards were being developed, and so they have been aligned with the OSI concepts.

The following sections give an overview of the HDLC standards and then cover its realization in the various OSI environments.

6.2 HIGH LEVEL DATA LINK CONTROL

In HDLC, each station on a link is classified as either a Primary or a Secondary, which bestows certain powers and responsibilities such as initiating connections, timeouts, etc.

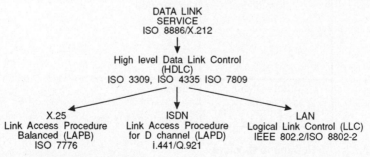

Figure 6.2   Data link standards

Each frame (i.e. data link Protocol Data Unit, PDU) sent in HDLC is classified as either a Command or a Response. A Command is sent by a Primary station, and a Secondary station will reply with a Response. The response of the secondary station may be one or more frames but the last frame must be indicated by a special bit (the F bit) being set.

Modes

HDLC has within it three subprotocols known as its modes of operation. They are:

Normal Response Mode (NRM)   In this mode a secondary station can transmit only in response to a command frame from a primary station. The primary station is responsible for timeouts, transmission, etc.

Asynchronous Response Mode (ARM)   A secondary station can initiate transmission of a frame or group of frames. The secondary is then responsible for timeout and retransmission. This mode is used in point to point links and is now considered obsolete.

Asynchronous Balanced Mode (ABM)   Each station is equivalent and communicates in a symmetrical fashion. With ABM each station is regarded as a combined primary/secondary. ABM mode is usually employed for OSI applications and is the mode used in the LAPB implementation of X.25.

6.2.1 Frame Structure

In HDLC, all transmission takes place in "frames" with a structure as illustrated in Figure 6.3. The fields of a frame are:

Flags   Each frame is delimited by 8 bit flags. The flag pattern is unique and consists of 01111110. To make sure that a

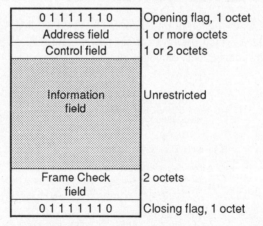

0 1 1 1 1 1 1 0	Opening flag, 1 octet
Address field	1 or more octets
Control field	1 or 2 octets
Information field	Unrestricted
Frame Check field	2 octets
0 1 1 1 1 1 1 0	Closing flag, 1 octet

Figure 6.3   HDLC frame structure

flag pattern cannot occur within a frame the bit stream is monitored and whenever a continuous pattern of five "1"s occurs a "0" is automatically inserted. This is known as zero bit insertion (or bit stuffing).

Address field This contains the address of a station for both command and response. It may also contain a global address. The field is 1 octet long in LAPB. In ISDN and LAN implementations, the field is 2 octets and it contains data link Service Access Point (SAP) addresses.

Control field Indicates the type of frame being sent. For connection oriented mode, it includes sequencing numbers for error recovery and flow control. It is typically 1 octet long, but 2 octets may be used to allow larger sequence numbers, e.g. for long delay satellite circuits.

Information field This contains any user data being transmitted. The format and content of user data are unrestricted and its length may be any number of bits (up to a network dependent maximum size).

Checksum A 16 bit CRC checksum (see below).

6.2.2 Error Detection

The most prevalent method used for error detection in data communications is to calculate and append a checksum field to a message during transmission, and recalculate and compare the checksum on reception. There are several techniques for checksum generation; the one used by HDLC is known as Cyclic Redundancy Code (CRC).

In a CRC, a special bit pattern is "divided" into the message using modulo 2 arithmetic. The remainder from the division is then used as a checksum. This technique is also known as a polynomial code, as both the message and the special check pattern can be regarded as polynomials with coefficients of either 0 or 1; e.g. 1101001 would be:

$$X^6 + X^5 + X^3 + 1$$

CRC codes can be generated very simply in hardware using shift registers and Exclusive-Or gates. They are very effective in detecting error bursts; e.g. the 16 bit checksum generated by the CRC CCITT polynomial will detect:

- all single and double bit errors
- all errors of an odd number of bits
- all burst errors of length less than or equal to 16 bits
- 99.997% of 17 bit burst errors

- 99.998% of 18 bit burst errors.

Both the HDLC transmitter and receiver perform the same division and if a discrepancy is found the received frame is ignored.

6.2.3 Frame Types

There are three types of frames determined by the contents of the control field:

- Numbered Information frames (I frames) convey data for the connection oriented service.

- Supervisory frames are used in the connection oriented service for error control and flow control.

- Unnumbered frames are used for connection establishment, or for connectionless data transfer.

The format of the control fields for these three types is illustrated in Figure 6.4. The components of the Control field are as follows:

S bits	Determine type of supervisory commands and responses.
U bits	Determine type of unnumbered commands and responses.
N(S)	Transmitted frame sequence number. $N(S)$ is incremented by the transmitting station for each successive frame being sent. Normally $N(S)$ ranges from 0 to 7 (modulo 8), requiring 3 bits as illustrated. The control field may be extended to allow for $0 - 127$ (modulo 128).
N(R)	Received frame sequence number. $N(R)$ identifies the number of the next expected I frame to be received by the station. If a frame is not correctly received $N(R)$ is not incremented. Thus $N(R)$ confirms the correct reception of all frames to $N(R) - 1$.

NUMBERED INFORMATION FRAME (I)

0	N(S)	P/F	N(R)

SUPERVISORY FRAME (RR, RNR, REJ)

1	0	S	S	P/F	N(R)

UNNUMBERED FRAME (SABM, UA, DISC, DM, UI, XID, etc.)

1	1	U	U	P/F	U	U	U

Figure 6.4   HDLC Control field coding

P/F   The Poll/Final bit is sent by a station either to request a response (i.e. poll) or to indicate that the final frame is being transmitted as the response to a poll.

6.2.4 Functions of the Frames

I frames   Numbered Information frames in HDLC are used for passing user data along the communications link. Each I frame carries a sequence number N(S) that is incremented by the transmitter. Many of the frames transmitted in HDLC are I frames.

Supervisory   There are four supervisory frames:

     RR   Receive Ready. Acknowledges receipt of error free frames up to N(R)–1 and solicits the transmission of further I frames.

     RNR   Receive Not Ready. Acknowledges receipt of error free frames up to N(R)–1 and inhibits the transmission of further I frames.

     REJ   Reject. Requests retransmission of I frames starting with N(R).

     SREJ   Selective Reject. Requests retransmission of I frame N(R).

Unnumbered   Unnumbered frames perform a variety of tasks:

     SABM   Set Asynchronous Balanced Mode. Used to establish the data link connection and reset the link if irrecoverable errors occur.

     SABME   Set Asynchronous Balanced Mode, Extended. Establishes link with modulo 128 sequence numbering.

     DISC   Disconnect. Signals disconnection of the link.

     UA   Unnumbered Acknowledgement. Positive acknowledgement to SABM.

     UI   Unnumbered Information frame. Used for connectionless data transfer.

     FRMR   Frame Reject. Signals the reception of an unrecognizable frame.

     DM   Disconnect Mode. Unable to transfer data.

     XID   Exchange Identification. Exchanges identification and communication parameters.

6.2.5 Error Recovery

Although error detection is used in both connectionless and connection oriented modes, error recovery is possible only in the context of a data link connection. (Connectionless data transfer simply uses the UI frame only.)

Retransmission A copy of each I frame sent by the transmitting station is held in a retransmit buffer (Figure 6.5). The copy is held until a positive acknowledgement is returned by the receiver, providing a feedback loop. Upon the receiver detecting an error (a frame out of sequence), the usual approach is to send back a special negative acknowledgement frame (REJ) on the link, requesting the retransmission of the frame in error, and all subsequent frames. This technique is sometimes called Automatic Repeat Request (ARQ). In the case of error free frames, some positive acknowledgement is sent instead.

Timers To further guard against the loss of acknowledgments or the loss of the last frame in a sequence, the transmitter starts a timer for each frame. The timer is canceled when a positive acknowledgement is received for the frame. If the timer expires, the transmitter invokes retransmission procedures. Retransmission may be repeated a number of times until a positive acknowledgement is returned. If nothing is heard after a reasonable time, the link may be declared out of order and disconnected.

Early data link protocols (e.g. BSC) tended to wait after each frame until some form of acknowledgement was returned before proceeding (stop and wait). Later protocols (i.e. HDLC) were able to overlap the data transmission and acknowledgement and achieve a greater utilization of the link. The permitted number of outstanding unacknowledged I frames is called the window size.

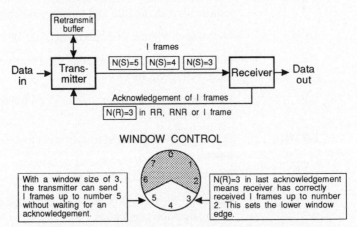

Figure 6.5   Model for flow of HDLC frames (only one direction shown)

**Acknow-
ledgements**
If an I frame has been received successfully, this must be advised to the transmitting end to enable it to continue with further transmission. Acknowledgement is achieved by sending a frame with the N(R) sequence number in the control field containing a value one greater than the correctly received frame. If I frames are flowing in the reverse direction, the N(R) of the next I frame will be used for this purpose. This is known as "piggybacked" acknowledgement as no specific acknowledgement frame is sent. If no I frames are being sent, an RR (or RNR) supervisory frame is sent.

Errors
If an I frame (or any frame) is received with a faulty CRC, it is ignored by the receiver. The loss of a frame is detected by either the receiver noticing the N(S) sequence to be incorrect in the next I frame and sending a REJ frame, or the transmitter having to wait too long for an acknowledgement and a timer expires.

6.3 X.25 LAPB

From its beginning, X.25 has used HDLC as its Link Access Protocol (LAP). In the first (1976) version of X.25 ARM was the HDLC mode specified. In the 1984 and later versions of X.25, LAP was replaced by a subset of ABM, termed LAPB (Balanced), for point to point links.

LAPB is a quite strict subset of HDLC/ABM. The only unnumbered frames permitted are SABM/SABME, DISC, UA, DM and FRMR. The SREJ supervisory frame is not supported. Figure 6.6 illustrates connection control and error recovery sequences for LAPB, and the mapping between

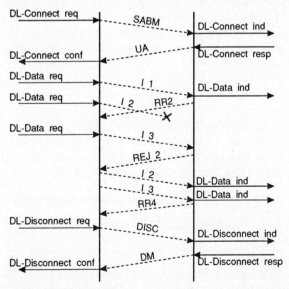

Figure 6.6   X.25 LAPB procedures

the data link service and the HDLC protocol. LAPB also supports splitting and recombining using optional Multiple Link Procedures (MLP) based on ISO 7478.

LAPB uses a single address octet because only two stations are communicating on the link (i.e. the DTE side and the DCE side of the interface). (LAPD and LLC use 2 octets for station addressing.) The value of the LAPB address field is either 01 or 03 (hexadecimal) depending on which station originated the frame and whether the frame is a command or a response. For sending commands, the DTE uses the 03 address and the DCE uses 01. For sending responses, the DTE uses 01 and the DCE uses 03.

Note that LAPB defines the link protocol between the user and Packet Switching Exchanges (PSEs) in a public packet network. It is not necessarily the protocol used within the network.

6.4 INTEGRATED SERVICES DIGITAL NETWORKS

6.4.1 Narrowband ISDN

D channel   A new variant of HDLC, known as LAPD, is used on the ISDN D channel. It is perhaps the most complicated implementation of HDLC as it is designed to support multiple Network Layer entities that share the physical link between Terminal Equipment (TE) and the ISDN exchange. The purpose of LAPD is to reliably convey connection control information between network entities across the ISDN user – network interface on the D channel. The B channels are "protocol independent" and are considered as 64 kbit/s streams of unspecified data with respect to the ISDN standards. Separate, independent data links operate on the B channels as required for user to user data communication. The LAPD is defined in CCITT I.440 (Q.920) and CCITT I.441 (Q.921). LAPD˙has a high similarity with LAPB. For the sake of brevity only the differences are defined below.

LAPD provides both a connectionless and a connection oriented Data Link service. The connectionless service is called "unacknowledged". These data services are mapped onto unnumbered and numbered information HDLC protocol units respectively. The data services provided are:

- DL-Unit-Data-request/indication — unacknowledged data service.

- DL-Establish-request/indication — connection services.

- DL-Data-request/indication — acknowledged data service.

There are also Management services to assign data link addresses and to co-ordinate the use of the D channel. These are called the MDL services.

Addressing   For Basic Rate Access (BRA), LAPD provides multi-point operation to support multiple terminals (similar to multi-dropped lines). Furthermore, LAPD provides for separate data links to be multiplexed onto the D channel:

- A signaling data link for call control of the B channels and user to user information transfer.

- A packet data link that can convey X.25 formatted data packets to provide a packet switching service. Implementation of this service is a national option.

- A link for allocation of link addresses and D channel management functions.

To permit this type of operation, independent link level LAPD addresses are used to differentiate between the actual signaling streams (to one or more TEs in the case of BRA). However, these user related link level addresses are not pre-assigned and therefore must be dynamically assigned before any connection establishment and use of the actual B channel(s). To distinguish between the multiple users of the D channel, LAPD uses 2 bytes for the HDLC address field.

SAPI and TEI   The address is divided into two fields: a pre-assigned *Service Access Point Identifier (SAPI)* and a dynamically allocated *Terminal Endpoint Identifier (TEI)*. The SAPI identifies the use of the data link. The fixed allocation of the SAPI is as follows:

SAPI = 0   Call control procedures (management of B channels).

SAPI = 16   X.25 packet mode procedures (use of D channel as an X.25 access path).

SAPI = 32–47   Reserved for national use.

SAPI = 63   Management procedures (allocation of TEI addresses for use with SAPI 0).

Others   Reserved for future use.

The TEI distinguishes between different terminals (e.g. on a BRA interface). TEIs are grouped as follows:

TEI = 0   Pre-assigned point to point/single SAP for Network Termination type 2 (NT2) equipment.

TEI = 1–63   Non-automatic assignment user equipment.

TEI = 64–126   Automatic assignment user equipment.

TEI = 127   The group TEI.

Address allocation   The total LAPD address (i.e. the DL-SAP address) is a concatenation of the SAPI and the TEI. To allocate the TEI, the TE transmits a UI frame to the NT with SAPI = 63 and the TEI set to 127. A Management Entity Identifier (MEI), a Reference Number, a Message Type and Action Indicator are also supplied as separate fields within the UI frame. The Reference Number is a random number used to identify this instance of the TEI allocation process; the Message Type is set to 1 indicating an Identity Request; and the Action Identifier is set to a TEI value as follows:

AI = 127   Any TEI value is acceptable.

AI = 0–126   Preferred TEI value.

The NT responds accordingly and once this TEI allocation has been achieved the SAPI/TEI address can then be used between the TE and NT to exchange B channel allocation and call information signals. The Message Type field is used to indicate responses and denials of this allocation process.

LAPD format   The format of the LAPD protocol is shown in Figure 6.7. The control field has three formats: numbered information, numbered supervisory and unnumbered. The control fields can be either extended mode (2 octet — frame numbering is modulo 128) or normal mode (single octet — frame numbering is modulo 8). For connection oriented services, the control field format and procedures are identical to those of LAPB, i.e. I, RR, RNR, REJ, SABM, UA, DISC and FRMR. However, there are three additional unnumbered commands used in LAPD. These are Unnumbered Information (UI), Sequenced Information 0 (SI0) and Sequenced Information 1 (SI1). The sequenced commands are used to send single sequenced acknowledged information frames between the data link entities over the link. The UI command is used for BRA TEI assignment procedures, and D channel management.

B channels   After the D channel has been used to establish a 64 kbit/s path (i.e. a Physical Layer connection) between two ISDN terminals, separate data link procedures must be invoked on the B channels. To support X.25

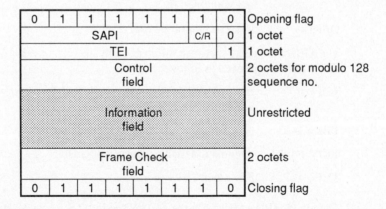

Figure 6.7   Format for ISDN LAPD frame

communication over the B channel (e.g. to access a packet switched network from an ISDN terminal), LAPB is used. LAPB requires an initial exchange of SABM and UA over the B channel before data transfer can start. Alternatively, for connectionless mode (e.g. for interworking between LAN routers), UI frames can be sent as soon as the B channel is established.

6.4.2 ISDN Evolution

Frame relay

Frame relay is a new development for data link bridging for Wide Area Networks (WANs). It stems from CCITT work on ISDN, but it is not confined to the ISDN environment. Frame relay is a data link protocol defined by CCITT I.122. It is an addition to the ISDN set of protocols. In the ISDN environment, frame relay allows the statistical multiplexing of user data from multiple B channels.

ATM

Standards for Asynchronous Transfer Mode (ATM) have been developed for broadband ISDN. Briefly described, it uses statistical multiplexing based on a cell of 53 octets (comprising 5 octets of header and 48 octets for the payload data) and simplified virtual circuit protocols. Because of the high transmission speed used on ATM (150 Mbit/s or higher), the short cell size and the use of simple protocols, ATM is an ideal mixed mode technology for the transmission of video, image, data and voice.

6.5 LOCAL AREA NETWORKS

Much of the development of standards in Local Area Networks (LANs) has been carried out by Technical Committee 802 of the IEEE. The work, in the early 1980's, resulted in a family of standards that encompasses several types of LANs. While the early standards (802.3 to 802.5) are limited to coverage in the order of 1 km or so, more recent effort has seen the emergence of high speed networks that do not have such restrictive distance limitations and are described as Metropolitan Area Networks (MANs).

MAC standards

The IEEE 802 structure provides for multiple Medium Access Control (MAC) standards operating under a single Logical Link Control (LLC) standard. The MAC standards covered in this chapter are:

- IEEE 802.3/ISO 8802-3, a bus using CSMA/CD access method;

- IEEE 802.4/ISO 8802-4, a bus using token passing as the access control method;

- IEEE 802.5/ISO 8802-5, a ring using the token passing access method; and,

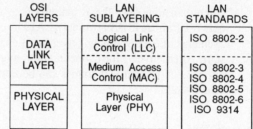

Figure 6.8   LAN standards

- IEEE 802.6/ISO 8802-6, a Distributed Queue, Dual Bus (DQDB) MAN.

Other LAN and MAN standards have been developed, notably Fibre Distributed Data Interface (FDDI) ISO 9314.

LLC standard   IEEE 802.2/ISO 8802-2 defines a HDLC subset, called Logical Link Control (LLC), that combines with the MAC sublayer to provide an OSI Data Link Layer between stations on a LAN or MAN. The relationships between the PHY, MAC and LLC standards and the OSI layers are illustrated in Figure 6.8. The following sections firstly cover the MAC standards and a description of LLC follows. Note that some other non-OSI protocols do not necessarily use LLC, e.g. the US Department of Defense Transmission Control Protocol/Internet Protocol (TCP/IP).

6.5.1 LAN Access Control

There are many techniques for controlling and resolving the competing demands of terminals for access to the physical medium. LAN operation depends on the co-operation of all stations to observe correctly the access control standards. The MAC standards define the access control procedures and the format of frames transmitted on the LAN. Common MAC standards are described below and the frame formats are shown in Figure 6.9.

CSMA/CD   Carrier Sense Multiple Access/Collision Detection (CSMA/CD) is used on bus networks, and it involves terminals only transmitting when the bus is idle. It has back-off procedures for resolving collisions, and it may have indeterministic delays as traffic load is increased. This is generally caused by stations internally queuing messages whilst the LAN is seen to be busy by that station. Once the LAN is perceived to be free, the station transmits the message and hopefully other stations will see that the LAN has now become busy and wait to avoid collisions. Thus the scheduling characteristics of a CSMA/CD LAN is "use it if you can" and no credence is given to any high priority, or "real time" or fixed bandwidth messages. It should be noted, however, that, because of the bandwidth available on a

CSMA/CD LAN (10 Mbit/s) when used in average personal computer LAN installations, this delay rarely causes difficulties in data throughput.

The preamble and start fields serve to synchronize the receiver and delimit frames. The address fields identify both the destination and source stations. Normally, they are 6 octets each. For collision detection to operate in all circumstances, there must be sufficient overlap of frames that are transmitted simultaneously from opposite ends of the LAN cable; i.e. the time taken to clock out the frame must exceed the maximum propagation delay. Each frame must have a minimum length of 64 octets. If the data field is less than 46 octets, padding is added in the PAD field. The length field specifies how many octets are present in the data. The MAC data field carries the LLC header and, finally, the user's data.

Token passing In token passing, a special control frame (token), is passed from station to station, carrying permission to transmit. Token passing is used on both bus (IEEE 802.4/ISO 8802-4) and ring (IEEE 802.5/ISO 8802-5) networks. These technologies are directed at process control, digitized voice and video bandwidth requirements, as well as computer communications, etc. Token passing resolves the issue of indeterministic delays by managing a token. The ownership of the token controls who can transmit onto the LAN. Stations are configured with maximum token holding times and may transmit any data they wish during that period once they have captured the token. Once data transmission is completed, the token is then relaunched to the next station. This round robin operation ensures that there is an upper bound on the LAN data link transit delay.

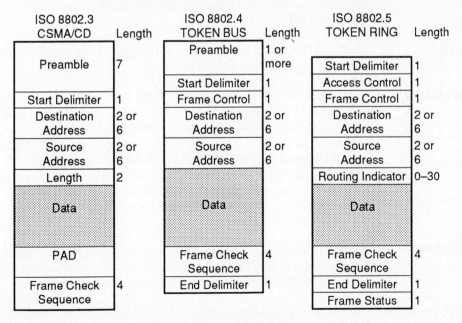

Figure 6.9   MAC frame formats (lengths in octets)

Token bus   The token bus (IEEE 802.4/ISO 8802-4) technology uses Cable
                     Television (CATV) broadband technology to support multiple channels.
                     Although it uses bus physical topology, it forms a logical ring at the MAC
                     layer. It has three priority levels within each channel and these are
                     maintained by the use of Target Rotation Timers. These timers ensure that
                     the token is fully circulated by the stations on that channel at determined
                     times for that priority. Thus a guarantee of throughput is maintained
                     according to the configuration parameters.

                     The MAC frame format is similar to CSMA/CD, with the addition of
                     a Frame Control field. Its main purpose is to distinguish between the token
                     and information frames when the LAN is operating normally. Other frame
                     types and procedures are specified to set up the logical ring initially, or to
                     recover from failures.

Token Ring   In a Token Ring (IEEE 802.5/ISO 8802-5), a special 3 octet frame, called
                     a token, circulates around the ring when all stations are idle. When a
                     station has data to transmit, it waits until it receives the token. Receipt of
                     the token gives the station the right to output its data. A station may hold
                     the token for the token holding time, which is typically 10 ms. After all
                     pending frames have been transmitted, the station regenerates the 3 octet
                     token frame and transmits it onto the ring.

                     A significant difference between IEEE 802.4 and 802.5 is that all
                     stations in an 802.4 LAN are equal. In IEEE 802.5, however, each token
                     ring LAN has a monitor station to oversee and manage the ring.

                     Additional frame types are defined to manage the ring and to bypass
                     failed stations. The ring protocols include priority mechanisms to further
                     control access to the ring.

FDDI   The Fibre Distributed Data Interface (FDDI, ISO 9314) protocols and
                     frame formats are similar to the Token Ring.

DQDB MAN   In the IEEE 802.6 Distributed Queue, Dual Bus (DQDB) scheme, the
                     traffic on each bus consists of a series of timeslots. Timeslots or "cells"
                     are 53 octets long, comprising 5 octets header and 48 octets user data (or
                     payload). This structure is designed to be compatible with future broad-
                     band ISDN services. The 5 octet header controls access of stations to the
                     slot. The 48 octet payload may be used for a variety of data, voice or image
                     services. For data applications, a segmentation scheme allows multiple
                     fixed length timeslots to be combined to convey longer variable length
                     connectionless MAC frames.

Cell types   Bandwidth is managed in two ways to give priority to real time traffic.
                     The protocol cells have a type bit indicating that the cell is "pre-arbitrated"
                     or "queue arbitrated". Both cell types have the same protocol format.

Pre-arbitrated   The real time bandwidth requirements are met by the pre-arbitrated cells.
                     The octets within these pre-arbitrated cells are referred to as Isochronous

Service Octets. Pre-Arbitrated cells are launched by the MAN control station at the rate that is compatible with the overall composite real time bandwidth required for all stations on the MAN. Each station that requires real time bandwidth is configured to recognize pre-arbitrated cells and fill the payload field with its real time data accordingly. On receive, the destination station retrieves the data from the respective cell.

Queue arbitrated

Queue arbitrated cells are also launched by the MAN control station but these are only launched during the non-pre-arbitrated periods. As the queue arbitrated cell is available to stations by demand, a priority field is used to request empty cells. Thus the DQDB system offers both fixed real time and "on demand" bandwidth characteristics.

Another point with this technology is that, because cell payloads are a fixed 48 bytes, MAC level segmentation must be used between DQDB stations. So a further data link sublayer is used. Above the DQDB cell protocol, an Initial MAC Protocol Data Unit (IMPDU) is used. This IMPDU contains the overall link level data (e.g. LLC type 1) and it contains fields indicating the MAC addresses, their length and type (i.e. normal IEEE 802.3,4,5 address forms can be carried) and fields relating to sequencing and bridging. This protocol unit is then segmented into a number of Derived MAC Protocol Data Units (DMPDUs) for insertion into the cell payload. These DMPDUs indicate the Beginning of Message, Continuation of Message and End of Message. Once reassembly is complete, the IMPDU is decoded and the higher level data passed to the MAN access device (user).

6.5.2 MAC Layer LAN Bridging

Bridge

A common occurrence with LANs is the interlinking of several LAN segments to achieve virtually a single LAN. A "bridge" performs such relaying at the Data Link Layer, i.e. the MAC level. A bridge may be attached directly to geographically co-located LAN segments as shown in Figure 6.10, or the bridge may be split into two components interconnected by a leased line to cover a wide area. (There is no international agreement on the protocols used between the two halves of a remote bridge.) Bridges allow the combined LANs to extend beyond the physical constraints of a single LAN. The reasons for taking this approach often relate to either a mixture of LAN media, e.g. an optic fibre backbone LAN

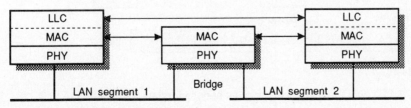

Figure 6.10   MAC level LAN bridge

and a co-axial LAN on each floor of a building, or the length and terminal number limitations placed on many LANs. Operating in a store and forward mode (not like a repeater that is just an amplifier), a bridge also acts as a filter. The bridge performs routing based on MAC header addresses. It only forwards MAC frames that need to pass from one LAN segment to another.

Bridged LANs effectively form one subnetwork from a number of LAN segments. Although very effective when interconnecting LANs of the same type, bridges become complicated when interconnecting different types of LAN or when a WAN is also required. These complications arise from the protocol differences illustrated in Figure 6.9; e.g. what does a bridge do if a long frame from an 802.4 LAN exceeds the maximum frame size for the 802.3 LAN it is addressed to?

Another inconsistency is in the addressing schemes and routing schemes. When two or more LAN segments are joined, there is the need for some method of identifying which terminals are on which segment, and passing frames between segments. Two techniques for achieving this have been standardised, one initially proposed by Digital Equipment Corporation (DEC) and one by IBM.

Transparent bridge

The LAN bridging technique originally proposed by DEC can operate with CSMA/CD and token based LAN protocols. In such LANs, the MAC addresses for each station may be assigned either locally by the network administrator or (usually) globally by the IEEE. This gives a flat address space that is randomly populated. Any station can uniquely address any other by giving the right 48 bit address.

The bridge units "listen" to messages on the two LAN segments. Each bridge observes the traffic, and builds up dynamic address forwarding tables for the MAC terminal addresses in each segment (see Figure 6.11). When active, the bridge will forward to the other LAN segment any frame

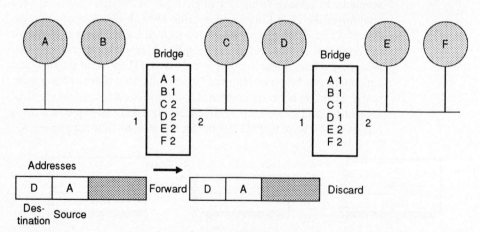

Figure 6.11   Operation of transparent bridges for data transfer from A to D

whose address it cannot positively identify as belonging to the originating segment. Procedures are also defined to update the tables to accommodate changes to the LAN configuration.

Spanning tree The spanning tree algorithm (specified in ISO 10038) ensures that no loops are formed in LANs with multiple interconnections. If multiple alternate paths are present between two active LAN stations, the spanning tree algorithm forwards frames on a single active path — the other paths are put on standby (idle). To do this, the bridges broadcast details of their topology. A distributed algorithm finds the shortest path between every LAN segment. The objective of these schemes is to simplify LAN installation — configuration of a bridge entails assignment of path priorities and weighting factor. Thereafter, the bridges broadcast to each other to determine the "least cost path". While very effective in a small to medium size LAN environment, the size of routing tables and the delay in propagating routing updates become unmanageable in large networks.

This procedure has been adopted as part of the IEEE 802.1/ISO 8802-1 standard for LAN MAC bridges.

Source routing Source routing was proposed by IBM and may be used in Token Ring LANs (see Figure 6.12). In this routing scheme, the sending station determines the route that the frame will follow and includes the routing information in the frame. Bridges read the routing information to determine whether they should forward the frame. An hierarchical address structure is used for rings and bridges. For 6 octet addresses, this comprises a unique 14 bit number for each ring and a 32 bit station address. If a station wishes to communicate with another on a remote LAN, it must specify the complete path in the MAC header, i.e. a series of route

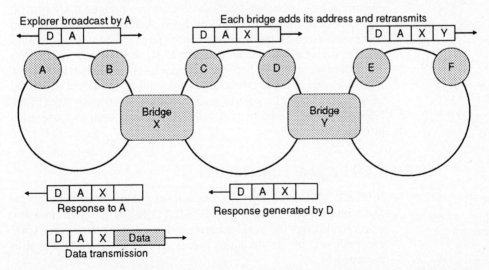

Figure 6.12   Operation of source routing LAN bridges (showing contents of RI field)

designators. Each designator corresponds to one hop and consists of a 12 bit ring number and a 4 bit bridge number. For source routing, MAC data frames contain an additional Routing Information (RI) field. The RI field contains a chain of such designators that are used by the bridges to determine whether they are responsible for forwarding the frame.

How, then, does a station first obtain the path? If a LAN station wants to establish communication with another station on a remote LAN, it must first broadcast a special Explorer frame. Each bridge adds its address to the Explorer frame and passes it on; i.e. it broadcasts to all other LAN segments to which it is attached a copy of the Explorer frame. The destination station sends the addressing information from the Explorer frame back as a Response frame, thus providing the source station with the full address.

Routing

By way of comparison:

- Source routing for Token Ring requires simpler bridges but more complicated end systems than transparent bridging. Its philosophy is akin to connection oriented operation — the source must first find a path to the destination before data transfer can commence. The end systems must also make adjustments if the topology changes due to failures or network reconfiguration.

- Transparent bridging using the spanning tree algorithm for CSMA/CD and token passing uses simpler end system procedures and relies on intelligence in the bridges to find a path. The bridges also automatically adapt to changing configurations, masking the details from end systems.

Both techniques have advantages and disadvantages that will not be elaborated here. Although both can co-exist in a bridged LAN system, they are unable to share routing information. Although new proposals are being considered by the standards committees to allow interoperability between the two LAN routing standards, MAC protocol incompatibilities will still hinder bridging between different LAN environments. For this reason, routers at the Network Layer are required for mixed networks. (Since some non-OSI protocol stacks do not have an equivalent of the Network Layer, bridging is a must for those LANs that use such protocols.)

6.5.3 LAN Logical Link Control

IEEE 802.2/ISO 8802-2 defines a logical link control sublayer for operation with the MAC sublayers. IEEE 802.2 is similar to HDLC in many respects, although the MAC sublayer handles such matters as the CRC checksum and the delimiting of frames. The LLC format is shown in Figure 6.13.

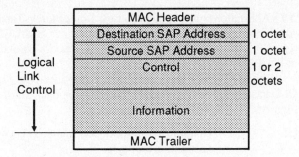

Figure 6.13   Logical Link Control (LLC) format

Addresses   Two 8 bit fields in the LLC format are used for addressing:

DSAP   Destination Service Access Point address field. One bit discriminates between either individual or group address. The remaining 7 bits are the actual address (either individual or group).

SSAP   Source Service Access Point address field. One bit is used as an HDLC command/response identifier and the remaining 7 bits are the actual address (always individual).

Draft Technical Report ISO DTR 10178 guides the allocation of individual addresses to distinguish between certain upper layer protocols. Examples of reserved data link SAP addresses are:

- Test address.

- Management address.

- A single address is reserved for all proprietary protocols. A separate mechanism (using 40 bits in the LLC information field) is used to distinguish between such proprietary protocols as Systems Network Architecture (SNA), XNS, Novell, Netbios etc.

- ARPANET IP.

- Standard network protocols. These are self-distinguishing according to ISO TR 9577.

LLC types   IEEE 802.2 originally had two main options within it:

LLC type 1   An unacknowledged connectionless service.

LLC type 2   A connection oriented service similar to LAPB.

A third type has now been added:

LLC type 3   Acknowledged connectionless mode service.

All LAN stations must implement type 1 procedures. The other types are additional options. LLC type 1 is common in CSMA/CD LANs. LLC type 2 is used in IBM token ring environments, in particular for support of SNA.

With LLC type 1, there are only two primitives: Dl-Data request and Dl-Data indication. A sequence diagram for data transfer is shown in Figure 6.14. The HDLC frames used are:

UI	Unnumbered Information frame. This conveys the connectionless user data.
XID	Exchange Identification frame. Used to convey the types of LLC services supported.
TEST	Test frame for maintenance purposes.

LLC type 2 has similar primitives, frames and procedures to LAPB previously described (see page 90). However, modulo 128 sequence numbering is used.

Commentary   It is unfortunate that the divergences between the various LAN committees created such unnecessary incompatibilities and complexities for LAN bridging. Nonetheless, LAN technology has proven to be a very cost effective solution to many network requirements, and the veneer of the LLC sublayer isolates the upper layers from the differences between LANs. The LLC sublayer also plays an important role in allowing multiple protocols to co-exist on the one LAN. Because future networking will inevitably expand to include various types of networks, a good rule of thumb is "Use routers where you can, use bridges only when you must!".

Figure 6.14   LLC type 1 sequence diagram

6.6 QUESTIONS

Question 6.1   What is the purpose of the Data Link Layer?

Question 6.2   What are the three modes of HDLC?

Question 6.3   What is bit stuffing used for?

Question 6.4   What is the Poll/Final bit used for?

Question 6.5   What is the significance of the LAPB address and how is it used?

Question 6.6   How is data link flow control achieved with HDLC?

Question 6.7   Are LAPB and LAPD point to point or multi-point protocols?

Question 6.8   What is a SAPI and a TEI and what purpose do they serve?

Question 6.9   What is the relationship between MAC and LLC protocols?

Question 6.10   What is the difference between LLC1, LLC2 and LLC3?

Question 6.11   What is spanning tree?

7 Network Layer

7.1 INTRODUCTION

The Network Layer co-ordinates routing, switching and relaying across one or more networks to provide a path for end to end transfer of data. Like the intersections that form the nodes of the road network, network entities join together concatenated data links which are the roads and highways of computer networks. The aim is to provide a uniform data transfer service between systems, independent of network and location; i.e. the Network Layer isolates the Transport Layer from routing or relay considerations.

Subnetworks   The Network Layer operates over multiple real networks of different technologies, e.g. X.25, Integrated Services Digital Networks (ISDN) and Local Area Networks (LANs). In OSI terminology, these are called *subnetworks*. To accommodate these different technologies, Network Layer standards govern both:

Subnetwork access   The attachment of end systems to intermediate systems.

Internetworking   Linking and communicating across different subnetworks.

In order to model both of these aspects, the Network Layer is divided into sublayers. To facilitate comprehension, this chapter deals with the network standards one at a time, operating over a single subnetwork. The next chapter explains how they can be combined in interrelated sublayers to operate over multiple subnets. The standards covered here are:

- X.25 packet level protocol;

- ISDN D channel Layer 3 protocol; and,

- ISO 8473 OSI connectionless protocol.

Background   The existence of the Network Layer in its initial form can be attributed to the early development of CCITT Recommendation X.25, and the ready acceptance of X.25's "packet level" interface as a viable standard for the generalized interface to public networks. This is quite in accordance with the principles of layer selection: "Select boundaries at a point that past experience has demonstrated to be successful". Some commentators are of the view that, had it not been for the prior existence of X.25, some alternative that included services now associated with the Transport Layer may have emerged.

X.25 in its turn has been influenced by the Reference Model, with many of the changes made to produce the 1984 version aimed at satisfying the services of the Network Layer, a process that has continued with later versions.

However, the rising popularity of the connectionless or datagram approach to networking, particularly in LANs and some private networks, has been reflected in amendments to the Reference Model and the development of new OSI standards for connectionless networking. Thus, there are two distinct modes for the Network Layer:

CONS   Connection Oriented Network Service, i.e. using X.25 in the upper sublayer.

CLNS   Connectionless Network Service, i.e. using the ISO 8473 protocol in the upper sublayer.

Figure 7.1 illustrates the Network Layer standards. The network service is defined in ISO 8348/CCITT X.213. In fact, it has three parts:

- ISO 8348 itself covers CONS.

- Addendum 1 covers connectionless service (CLNS).

- Addendum 2 covers addressing (described in the next chapter, page 144).

This chapter commences with the CONS followed by CLNS.

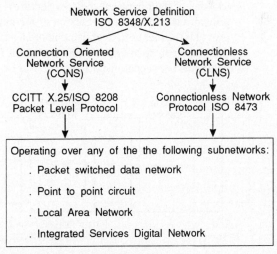

Figure 7.1   Family tree for Network Layer standards

7.1.1 Scope

The Network Layer caters for a wide range of configurations; e.g.:

- The Network Layer is required even in the simplest case of two end systems directly connected by a cable.

- More generally, it allows an end system to support multiple simultaneous communications with other end systems across a single subnetwork or a series of subnetworks.

- End systems may access a number of subnetworks. Such end systems may have to support multiple access protocols and be able to perform routing.

For clarity, the examples and illustrations used in this chapter will depict end systems that access a single subnetwork. Extension to the other cases is a straightforward matter.

The Network Layer operates on a hop by hop basis to provide an end to end service. The end to end service is achieved by stringing together the various links and subnetworks to provide a path for data transfer as shown in Figure 7.2. Intermediate systems use only the lower three layers for relaying and routing of messages. As an internal matter, intermediate systems typically use proprietary protocols between themselves, or they may use the standards.

7.2 CONNECTION ORIENTED NETWORK SERVICE

Purpose

The basic service of the Network Layer is to provide the transparent transfer of data between transport entities. In the case of CONS, such transfer takes place in the context of a connection. The Network Layer provides the means to establish, maintain and terminate network connections between open systems, and the means to exchange network service data units between transport entities over network connections. It makes

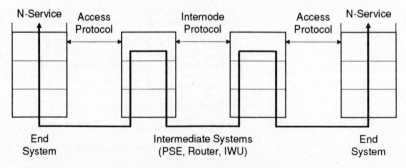

Figure 7.2   Hop by hop operation of Network Layer protocols

invisible to transport entities how underlying resources such as data link connections are used to provide network connections. The Network Layer contains functions necessary to provide the Transport Layer with a firm network/transport layer boundary that is independent of the underlying communications media in all things other than Quality of Service (QOS). Thus the network layer contains functions necessary to mask the differences in the characteristics of different transmission and subnetwork technologies into a consistent network service.

Service

The services provided are similar to those in lower layers: connections, data unit transfer, error notification, etc. These services are explained in conjunction with the protocol description in Section 7.3.3. Services that are unique to the Network Layer are:

- Expedited Data;
- Reset service; and,
- Receipt Confirmation.

Expedited

Expedited Data provides a means to transfer a small amount of data independently of normal data flow. For instance, normal data transfer may be temporarily suspended by flow control mechanisms because of network congestion, i.e. a traffic jam in the network queues. If it were necessary to perform some urgent action or perhaps to abandon processing of the data in transit, the Expedited Data service could be used to bypass the traffic jam of data in the normal flow to send a special interrupt signal to the other end.

Reset

Reset is used by the end systems or the network itself to signal some error condition. It purges data in transit, and resets the connection to a known state, but without losing the connection.

Receipt Confirmation

Receipt Confirmation provides acknowledgement by the network that data has been delivered to the destination (but not necessarily that the destination has processed the data).

Functions

In addition to providing the externally visible service, layers perform a variety of activities that go on within the layer. All of these functions are reflected in the particulars of the protocols that operate within the layer in order to provide the network services. Many of the functions, e.g. multiplexing and error recovery, are quite invisible to the higher layers.

7.2.1 Service Definition

Primitives

The Network Layer service is defined in terms of the primitives that operate at the Transport/Network Layer boundary. There are four types of primitives: request, indication, response, confirmation. The labeling convention within OSI for primitives is to use the initial letter of the layer concerned, followed by one or more words that identify the activities associated with the primitive. For example, the primitive for initiating a connection is:

- N-Connect request

and for signaling the arrival of data is:

- N-Data indication.

Table 7.1 summarizes the network service primitives. Each carries one or more parameters such as:

- Originating and Destination Network Service Access Point (NSAP) addresses;

- QOS parameters that indicate the error rate, availability, throughput, delay or cost for the connection;

- User Data that is transparently transferred between the end systems; and,

- a request to use certain options.

Note that these primitives and parameters are defined in an abstract sense only. If a real product supplies a network service interface, the primitives may be realized by system calls with different names and there may not be a one to one mapping to the primitives. Likewise, in some products, different parameters may be present. For instance, local parameters that control the real interface are necessary but are not defined by OSI. Sometimes, the QOS parameters may not appear at all, in which case the Network Layer operates with default values. To correspond to the OSI network service, a product requires the existence of some mapping between the real interface and the service definition.

Primitive sequences

In ISO 8348, the permitted sequences of primitives are defined in terms of a state transition machine that specifies the allowed ordering of inter- actions at the Network/Transport Layer boundary. This is coupled with a queue model for the network service provider to define formally the

Table 7.1   Network service primitives

PRIMITIVES	PARAMETERS
Connect	Addresses, Quality of Service, Options, User Data
Data	User Data, Confirm Request option
Expedited Data	User Data (limited length)
Receipt Confirmation	—
Reset	Reason
Disconnect	Reason, User Data

overall behavior of the distributed system. The main elements of the service are depicted in the sequence diagram shown in Figure 7.3. This is illustrative only — the complete service definition is much more complex. Examples of confirmed, partially confirmed and unconfirmed dialogues are shown.

Note that Expedited Data and Receipt Confirmation are provider options; i.e. they may not be available in some subnetworks.

Rather than just modeling existing protocols as did the service definitions for lower layers, the network service definition resolved some ambiguities in the original X.25 standard. The X.25 standard is cast as a definition of the interface between an end system (Data Terminal Equipment, DTE) and a Packet Switching Exchange (PSE), and it was first developed (in 1976) without the aid of a service definition. Hence, it was not initially clear to implementors whether certain X.25 features should be implemented with end to end significance or whether they had local significance only. As a result, products were built that conformed to the standard, but that used X.25 in different, incompatible ways. These problems are now resolved by the service definition which clearly defines the significance of interactions by the means of service primitive dialogues.

7.3 X.25 PROTOCOL

The 1984 (or later) version of X.25 inherently provides the Connection Oriented Network Service (CONS). It is used as an example in this chapter

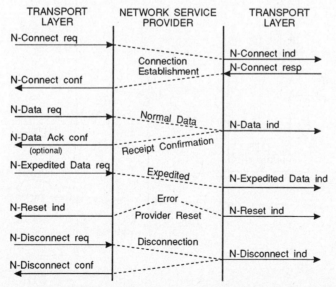

Figure 7.3　　　Sequence diagram for Connection Oriented Network Service

to illustrate salient OSI concepts. The treatment of X.25 here is not intended as a definitive description of the X.25 standard.

7.3.1 Virtual Circuits

In CONS, the connection corresponds to a virtual circuit in an X.25 network. (X.25 has two types of virtual circuits: switched virtual circuits (SVCs), which are established as required, and permanent virtual circuits (PVCs), which operate continuously). On request from the user in the end system, the network establishes a path through the network between two NSAPs that is used for the duration of the data transfer between the two end systems.

Multiplexing   One of the important functions in the Network Layer is that of multiplexing, i.e. sending Service Data Units (SDUs) from several N-connections over a single data link connection. This is implemented in an X.25 environment to allow a single access link to a packet switch network to support one or more virtual circuits. The multiplexing of virtual circuits onto a single link is achieved by allocating each circuit to a discrete "logical channel". The logical channel is indicated by a unique channel number in each packet. A packet can be associated with only one logical channel, although packets from several virtual circuits will be interleaved on the access link.

The logical channels are allocated during connection establishment. The logical channel numbers have local significance only. The network entities maintain a table that associates the logical channel numbers on different data links, pointing to the path that packets follow on each virtual

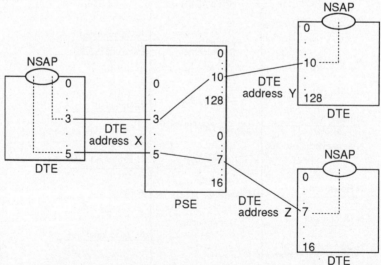

Figure 7.4   X.25 virtual circuits are set up on logical channels. Virtual circuits convey data between DTEs. N-connections operate between NSAPs.

circuit. The relationships between connections, virtual circuits and logical channels are illustrated in Figure 7.4.

7.3.2 Data Units

The embedding of an X.25 packet within the Information field of a numbered Information frame (I frame) illustrates the relationship between the various layers (see Figure 7.5). There is a one to one mapping between a packet (a network Protocol Data Unit, PDU), a data link SDU and a data link PDU (a frame).

Normally, systems are configured to set up the Physical and Data Link layers automatically after the equipment is switched on. The lower two layers normally remain ready to serve the Network Layer.

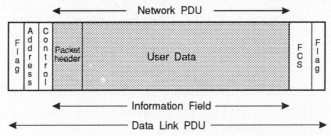

Figure 7.5   Relationship between Network and Data Link layer data units

Packet format   The role and purpose of the Protocol Control Information (PCI) can be seen by examining the various fields of the packet headers in X.25. Every X.25 packet includes a basic 3 octet header in the format shown in Figure 7.6. Some packet types have additional octets of header information as required.

The General Format Identifier is a 4 bit field in the form XX01 if sequence numbers in the packet are cycling modulo 8, or XX10 if they cycle modulo 128. The XX bits are set according to the requirements of the individual packet types. (In other Network Layer protocols such as

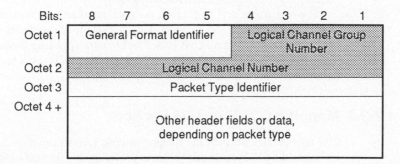

Figure 7.6   X.25 packet header, general format

Table 7.2   X.25 packet types

Network Service Supported	X.25 Packet Types		Packet type (octet 3). Bits: 8 7 6 5 4 3 2 1
	DTE to DCE	DCE to DTE	
Connection Establishment	Call Request Call Accepted	Incoming Call Call Connected	0 0 0 0 1 0 1 1 0 0 0 0 1 1 1 1
Disconnection	Clear Request DTE Clear Confirm	Clear Indication DCE Clear Confirm	0 0 0 1 0 0 1 1 0 0 0 1 0 1 1 1
Data Transfer	DTE Data	DCE Data	x x x x x x x 0
	DTE RR DTE RNR	DCE RR DCE RNR	x x x 0 0 0 0 1 x x x 0 0 1 0 1
Expedited Data	Interrupt Request	Interrupt Indication	0 0 1 0 0 0 1 1
	DTE Interrupt Confirm	DCE Interrupt Confirm	0 0 1 0 0 1 1 1
Reset	Reset Request DTE Reset Confirm	Reset Indication DCE Reset Confirm	0 0 0 1 1 0 1 1 0 0 0 1 1 1 1 1
Management	Restart Request DTE Restart Confirm	Restart Indication DCE Restart Confirm	1 1 1 1 1 0 1 1 1 1 1 1 1 1 1 1
	Diagnostic	Diagnostic	1 1 1 1 0 0 0 1
	Registration Request	Registration Confirm	1 1 1 1 0 0 1 1

ISDN and ISO 8473, bits 5 and 6 of the first header octet are set to 0 to distinguish them from X.25.)

Virtual circuits are identified by the combination of the 4 bit Logical Channel Group Number and the eight-bit Logical Channel Number. In most cases, these are combined to form a single 12 bit number, providing up to 4,095 logical channels. Channel 0 is reserved for special packets (i.e. Restart packets).

Packet types   The packet-type octet is unique to each of the packet types. The various packet types are shown in Table 7.2. (Some optional packet types have been omitted from the table for clarity, i.e. Reject, Diagnostic and Registration packets.) Note that in many cases the same packet type identifier code is used by the DTE and DCE (Data Circuit terminating Equipment representing the PSE) to represent different (but related) packets, e.g. Call Request and Incoming Call.

The originating and destination network interfaces are independent. The Call Request header submitted by a DTE to the network is not identical to the Incoming Call issued to the corresponding destination. They will probably refer to different logical channel numbers and other parameters will be different.

7.3.3 Mapping CONS to X.25 Packets

The relationship between the major Network Layer primitives and the corresponding X.25 packets is shown in the following diagrams. Note that there is not always a one to one relationship between primitives and network PDUs (packets). In some cases they are one to one; e.g. one N-Connect request generates one Call Request. On the other hand, a single primitive may result in several packets; e.g. one N-Data request generates multiple data packets and Receive Ready (RR) packets.

Some packets, such as those providing for flow control (RR and Receive not Ready, RNR), are not directly associated with primitives. They are used to control the X.25 protocol state machine.

Connection control

The connection establishment procedures, illustrated in Figure 7.7, perform the following functions:

- allocate a logical channel to the connection for the multiplexing function;

- convey address information to the subnetwork and destination for the routing function;

- negotiate the QOS and the use of options; and,

- prepare for data transfer by resetting sequence numbers to zero.

The logical channel number used to provide multiplexing has local significance only for a particular DTE/DCE interface, and is not carried across the network. Ranges of logical channel numbers are specified at the time a DTE is connected to a network. The convention is that a DTE will select the highest available channel number, and a DCE will choose the lowest when establishing a circuit.

If a connection cannot be established as requested, the network will issue an N-Disconnect indication to the calling user instead of an N-Connect confirm. The Disconnect primitive indicates the reason for connection refusal.

Fast Select

The Fast Select facility may be used for connection establishment if the user's data in the N-Connect request primitive is more than 16 octets. Fast Select is an option that can be requested in the Facilities field of the Call Request packet. Fast Select also enables the exchange of small amounts of data between DTEs without setting up a complete connection. In

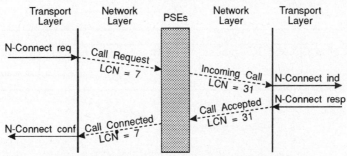

Figure 7.7   Sequence diagram for X.25 connection establishment

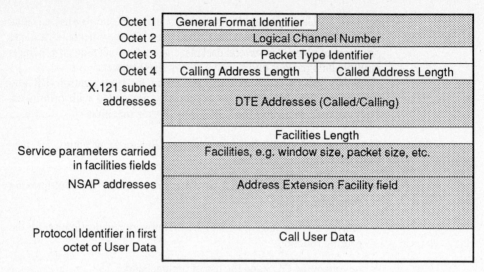

Figure 7.8   X.25 Call Request/Incoming Call packet format

ordinary Call Request packets, up to 16 octets of user data can be carried. With the Fast Select option this is increased to 128 octets in the Call Request, Call Accepted and Clear Request packets. A typical sequence would be for one DTE to send some data in a Call Request (Fast Select) packet and for the other DTE to reply with some data in a Clear Request packet. The actual level of use of Fast Select will be driven by tariff considerations.

Call packets   The structure of the Call Request and Incoming Call packets is shown in Figure 7.8 and the mapping from parameters in N-Service primitives to the various packet fields is shown Figure 7.9.

It will be recalled that two important parameters in the N-Connect primitive are the called and calling addresses, i.e. the NSAP addresses of the entities being interconnected. These parameters are mapped, by address translation functions in the end system network entity, into the DTE

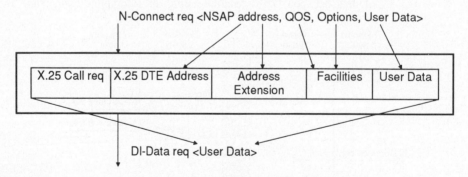

Figure 7.9   Relationship between network primitive and X.25 PDU

Address fields of the Call Request packet. The DTE Address fields are subnetwork addresses.

The X.25 DTE Address fields are encoded in 4 bit (semi-octet) numbers, with the length being zero if either the Called or Calling DTE Address is not present. The called DTE Address is mandatory in Call Request packets and the calling DTE Address is mandatory in Incoming Call packets. Different networks use different address formats. In public networks, DTE Addresses are typically a maximum of 14 digits. (This was extended in the 1988 version of X.25 to 17 digits for interworking with other networks as described in the X.300 series of Recommendations.) CCITT Recommendation X.121 defines the international numbering plan for DTE Addresses.

If it is necessary to also convey the full NSAP address, as distinct from the DTE Address, a separate optional field is provided. This is called the Address Extension Facility field and support of the field is mandatory for conformance to 1984 or later versions of X.25. The Address Extension Facility is used for internetworking with private X.25 data networks, that have numbering schemes that are not administered under X.121.

Protocol identification   X.25 can be used to support a number of OSI and non-OSI applications. For example, an X.25 interface could simultaneously support on different virtual circuits:

- the CONs for an OSI transport entity;

- the CLNS in conjunction with ISO 8473 connectionless protocol;

- the X.29 protocol for Packet Assembler/Disassembler (PAD) for terminal users;

- proprietary protocols such as Systems Network Architecture (SNA) using the IBM Qualified Logical Link Control (QLLC) protocol.

PID   A method is needed therefore, to distinguish between these different higher level protocols. ISO TR 9577 and CCITT X.244 define techniques for protocol identification in the Network Layer. Essentially, the first octet of the Call User Data field of the X.25 Call Request packet is reserved to act as a *Protocol Identifier (PID) field.* (Additional octets may also be reserved by some protocols.) The value of the PID field is set by the originator of the call to signal to the destination which high level protocol will apply for the duration of the connection.

Parameter mapping   Many of the parameter values in the X.25 calling packets can be derived from the parameters supplied in the corresponding N-Service primitive. In some cases this mapping is straightforward, and for other parameters it may require a complex transformation.

For example, there are a number of different numbering schemes for NSAP addresses. In one scheme, the DTE Address is a component of the NSAP address and only a simple mapping is required. In other schemes, the NSAP address is independent from the DTE Address and a more complicated address translation is required. If required, the full NSAP address is conveyed in the Address Extension Facility field.

Some of the network service parameters are mapped into parameters in the X.25 facilities fields. The fields enable details to be exchanged about a number of optional facilities. Some of the facility options are concerned with non-OSI issues; others may be determined from the QOS parameters in the OSI connection primitives:

Cost   Reverse charge acceptance.

Security   Closed User Group (CUG).

Delay   Optional packet sizes.

Throughput   Window size.

These facilities give X.25 network administrators a high level of flexibility to fine tune network performance.

Data transfer   Once a virtual circuit has successfully been established by the exchange of the Call Accepted and Call Connected packets, data transfer can commence. The structure of a data packet is shown in Figure 7.10. (An extended format using 2 octets for the packet type is also defined but not illustrated here.) Note, for later comparison with the connectionless protocol, that only 3 header octets are required for each data packet.

Within the data packet, there are fields and mechanisms which implement several important network services and functions, i.e.:

- sequencing;

- flow control;

- segmentation;

- receipt confirmation.

These are illustrated in subsequent sections.

Q bit   The Q (Qualifier) bit is carried transparently through the network. It may be used to differentiate between control information and pure data.

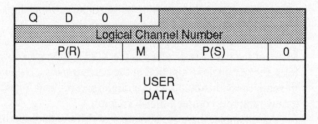

Figure 7.10   X.25 data packet format for modulo 8 sequence numbering

X.29 uses the Q bit for this purpose for terminal access via a PAD. Note that the Q bit is not related to any OSI network service.

Sequencing   The sequencing service is provided by use of the P(R) and P(S) fields. These sequence numbers function in a similar manner as the equivalent sequence numbers in HDLC (High level Data Link Control); i.e. they are used for acknowledgement and flow control. However, X.25 does not provide error recovery. Any out of sequence error is reported as a Reset. Normally, these sequence numbers only have significance over the local DTE/DCE link.

Flow control   Each X.25 virtual circuit has a flow control mechanism based on sequence number windows. Each direction of data flow on a connection is controlled by a separate window.

To illustrate flow control, the sequence diagram for data transfer in Figure 7.11 has been modified to represent the buffer occupancy in the network entities of two DTEs communicating via a packet switch. One direction of transfer is shown and the mechanism has been greatly simplified for clarity. The elongated rectangles represent the state of a buffer in the packet level of the sending DTE, the PSE and the receiving packet level. A buffer is a temporary data storage area where packets wait

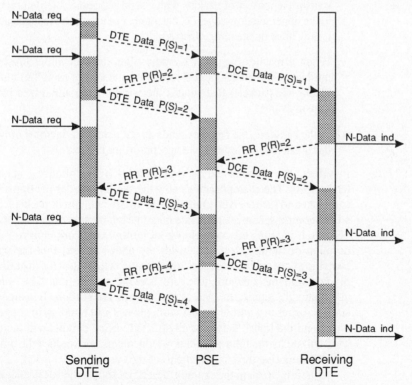

Figure 7.11   X.25 data transfer — flow control example

in a queue for an opportunity for transmission to the next node. A packet waiting for transmission is shown as a shaded area, and an empty buffer is unshaded.

For the illustration, the packet level window size is set at 1, and there is only one buffer in each of the nodes. (In a practical network, there would be a large, but finite, pool of buffers that are shared by a number of virtual circuits; and typically, the packet window size is 2 or 3.) At the network service boundary, the sending user can only issue N-Data requests if the buffer in the sending DTE is unoccupied, i.e. there is space in the queue. (How this is signaled to the user is not defined — it is assumed that "back pressure flow control" is somehow exerted across the network service interface.) For the purposes of illustration, assume that the receiving DTE is slow and that the received data remains in the buffer for some time before the N-Data indication is processed.

In general, the objective of flow control is to control the number of packets flowing into the network. Like a freeway, if the rate of packets entering the network exceeds the packet output, then traffic jams will occur, performance will degrade, and packets may be lost if all buffers are full. Flow control acts as a traffic policeman for the network. The procedure is as follows:

- The transmitter in the sending DTE (and the PSE) is allowed to transmit a number of packets with a send sequence (P(S)) number up to the upper window edge; i.e. the number of unacknowledged packets it may have outstanding is the window size.

- When it reaches the upper window edge, the transmitter must wait until an acknowledgement is returned (in this case as a P(R) number in the RR packets) that rotates the window and authorizes further transmissions.

- In the example, the receiver sends an RR acknowledgement only if it has sufficient buffer space to accept further packets.

In effect, the receiver exerts flow control by withholding acknow- ledgements. The example shows how the sending rate of the transmitter is matched to the receiver's output after the first couple of packets. Such a flow control scheme can operate only in a connection oriented network because it requires the co-operation of multiple network entities for the duration of the data transfer. It has the added benefit that the packet switching network can use the same mechanism to control the overall flow of data into the network to avoid network congestion. The scheme automatically adjusts to increasing network congestion. If congestion starts to occur in a part of the network, queues will build up in congested nodes and the transit delay for all affected virtual circuits will increase. This will delay the return of acknowledgements, and reduce the amount of traffic entering the congested part of the network.

As a refinement to the example described above, the RR packet is not the only one that carries P(R) acknowledgement numbers. If a Data packet happens to be traveling in the return direction, it can convey the P(R) number instead of an explicit RR. The RNR packet acts as an explicit request to stop sending, regardless of the window. After an RNR, data flow is resumed by an explicit RR packet.

In contrast, connectionless networks cannot perform flow control on an individual user basis (see page 133).

Segmentation

The segmenting and blocking service is provided by use of the M (More) bit as shown in Figure 7.12. A sequence of packets is defined as one or more full packets with M=1 followed by a packet with M=0. The network will deliver these packets as a correct sequence. The procedures allow for different packet sizes to be used on each data link. For example, the two end systems may have chosen different maximum packet sizes during call set-up at each end of the connection — the network entities will segment and reassemble data units as required to match the selected packet sizes.

Receipt Confirmation

The user of the network service can optionally request confirmation of delivery of the data. In X.25 this is implemented through the D (Delivery confirmation) bit in Data packets. If the D bit is set, the acknowledgement returned via the next P(R) field confirms end to end delivery to the receiving DTE. Not all networks support the D bit and its usage can result in delays. The D bit can also be set in the Call Request/Incoming Call and Call Accepted/Call Confirmation packets to enable DTEs to test the availability of the D bit service.

The D bit technique for obtaining an end to end acknowledgement is used to implement the Network Layer's acknowledged data service. There is no primitive to request an acknowledgement; instead a "confirmation request" parameter is set on the normal N-Data request. After the data is

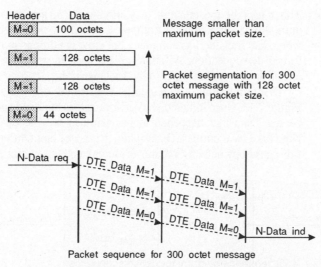

Figure 7.12   X.25 data transfer — segmentation using the M bit

delivered in an N-Data indication, an N-Data Acknowledge primitive is subsequently issued to the sender.

Interrupt

Up to 32 octets of data can be sent to another DTE using the Interrupt Request packet. This bypasses normal flow control procedures and would normally be used for urgent protocol management reasons. Only one unconfirmed interrupt can be outstanding for a virtual circuit, a restriction that aims to prevent the flooding of the network.

The interrupt packet is used to implement the Network Layer's expedited service via the N-Expedited Data request and indication primitives.

Reset

Whenever an irrecoverable error is encountered on a virtual circuit, a Reset packet can be used to reinitialize the circuit. This causes P(R) and P(S) to be reset to 0 and all data and interrupt packets in progress to be discarded. The network user would be informed via a N-Reset indication, as data may have been lost. Public data networks strive to minimize the risk of network generated resets, but there remains a finite probability that a reset will be used as a last resort if severe congestion or equipment failure occurs.

A user can also initiate a reset via a N-Reset request. This step might be taken, for example, if an end system detected some error condition. Note that although the network service specification defines the N-Reset confirmation as having end to end effect, most early X.25 implementations provided only a local significance. However, this has changed as implementation of 1984 X.25 has increased.

The outcome after a reset is indeterminate for data in transit at the time. Higher layer protocols are needed to resolve the situation and recover after a reset.

Disconnection

Either user or the network may disconnect at any time. This would normally be initiated by one of the users, and it would usually take place when data transfer was complete, but error conditions may also cause a forced disconnection. A failure or a refusal to complete a connection establishment is also signaled by disconnection.

Disconnection is a partially confirmed service, as shown in Figure 7.13. Once initiated, the network path is removed and data transfer ceases. Data that happened to be in transit will be discarded by the Network Layer entities. Once again, the risk of unintentional disconnection caused by network failures is minimized but remains a possibility.

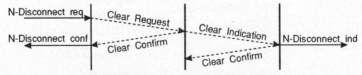

Figure 7.13   X.25 sequence diagram for user disconnection

7.3.4 X.25 Management Packets

Management packets are not directly related to connection establishment or explicit data transfer. These packets perform overall initialization, error management and subscriber related facilities as is described below.

Restart

To initialize equipment when a link to a network is first established, the restart service effectively clears all logical channels. It is also an important feature in times of major failures in the network. The restart results in all logical channels being reinitialized, with switched virtual circuits being disconnected and permanent virtual circuits being reset. Restart packets are sent on Logical Channel 0 as they affect all logical channels on the access link.

Diagnostic

The Diagnostic packet enhances the error management capabilities of the X.25 protocol. Typically, errors in X.25 are communicated by the clearing or reset cause and diagnostic code (1 byte each). In the case where additional information is useful or the error is considered outside the scope of the normal operation (e.g. invalid packets or protocol timer expiry is detected) the Diagnostic packet is used to convey the error related information between X.25 entities.

Registration

The Registration Request packet is used by the X.25 subscriber to issue network facility requests to the X.25 network on a dynamic basis. This facility enables the subscriber to optimize, e.g. on a daily or weekly basis, the level of service provided by the network. Typically, a subscriber may wish to change the packet size and throughput class for different service quality levels depending on the nature of the applications being used over these specific periods.

7.3.5 X.25 and Related Standards

Recommendation X.25, as standardized by CCITT, in fact describes the DTE/DCE interface protocol from the point of view of the DCE or network. ISO has developed a companion standard referred to as ISO 8208. The ISO standard describes the interface from the point of view of the DTE and also covers DTE to DTE connection.

The X.25 (1984/88) Recommendation and ISO 8208 are richer in functions than is strictly necessary to support the CONS. Because of this, a further standard ISO 8878 has been developed to specify the precise X.25 to CONS mapping. This is straightforward in the case of the full 1984 or later version of X.25. The relationships between these standards is illustrated in Figure 7.14.

X.75

The network service assumes that the basic service may be provided by several networks, and that relay functions and "hop-by-hop service en-

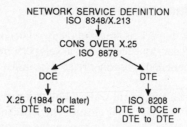

NETWORK SERVICE DEFINITION
ISO 8348/X.213

CONS OVER X.25
ISO 8878

DCE   DTE

X.25 (1984 or later)   ISO 8208
DTE to DCE   DTE to DCE or
DTE to DTE

Figure 7.14   OSI connection oriented standards

hancement protocols" will be involved to interconnect the networks. One such set of relay functions is provided by X.75.

X.75 is a variant of X.25 to enable packet networks to interwork. It differs from X.25 only at the packet level, at which level it has additional information to enable reconciliation of differences between networks. X.75 is not normally provided as an access protocol to interface to private users. Private X.25 data networks usually access the public network via an X.25 interface. The normal application of X.75 is to interconnect public data networks at the international level. As such, it creates one homogeneous X.25 subnetwork out of all the public data networks in different countries.

7.4 INTEGRATED SERVICES DIGITAL NETWORKS

An ISDN service can support the network service in a number of ways. D channel messages are exchanged between Terminal Equipment (TE) and the ISDN network to set up a B channel for communication. The B channel is a 64 kbit/s physical link between TEs that may be used for voice or image communications, or for a variety of switched data com-

Protocol Discriminator	0	0	0	0	1	0	0	0
	0	0	0	0	Call Reference Length			
	Flag	Call Reference Value						
	0	Message Type						
	Element 1							
Information Elements	Element 2							
	Element 4							
	Element 5							

Figure 7.15   ISDN network header format

munication applications. In addition, data communications may take place over the D channel independently of the B channel.

The ISDN level 3 recommendations cover only the D channel Network Layer protocol — the B channel protocols are user dependent. In this section, the D channel protocol is described first followed by an explanation of the alternatives for ISDN data communication.

Standards   The ISDN level 3 services and protocols for the D channel are defined in CCITT I.450 (Q.930) and CCITT I.451 (Q.931). Their purpose is to establish and maintain B channel connections. Since multiplexing of the bandwidth is performed by the Physical Layer in order to provide a signaling channel that is separate from the Bearer channels, the ISDN call signaling is performed "out of band" (on the D channel). In contrast, X.25, which performs both multiplexing and call control in the packet level is a form of "in band" signaling. Furthermore, because ISDN is used for a diverse range of voice, image and data services, ISDN signaling is more complicated than the X.25 call procedures previously described.

7.4.1 ISDN Messages

An example of the structure of the network header (called a message in ISDN) exchanged between a TE, e.g. computer or PABX (private

Table 7.3   Examples of ISDN message types

MESSAGE TYPE	TYPE VALUE	Direc-tion	MESSAGE TYPE	TYPE VALUE	Direc-tion
CALL ESTABLISHMENT					
Alerting	1	B	Call Proceeding	2	B
Connect	7	B	Connect Acknowledge	15	B
Setup	5	B	Setup Acknowledge	13	B
CALL INFORMATION					
Resume	38	UN	Resume Acknowledge	46	NU
Resume Reject	34	NU	Suspend	37	UN
Suspend Acknowledge	45	NU	Suspend Reject	33	NU
User Information	32	B			
CALL DISESTABLISHMENT					
Disconnect	69	B	Release	77	B
Release Complete	90	B			
MISCELLANEOUS					
Cancel	96	B	Cancel Acknowledge	104	B
Cancel Reject	112	B	Facility	98	B
Facility Acknowledge	106	B	Facility Reject	114	B
Register	100	B	Register Acknowledge	108	B
Register Reject	116	B	Status	125	B
Congestion Control	121	B	Information	123	B

Legend: NU   Message is applicable from network to user only.
         UN   Message is applicable from user to network only.
         B   Message is used in both directions.

telephone switchboard), and the Network Termination (NT) is shown in Figure 7.15 (page 122). Table 7.3 (page 123) lists the message types. The first 3 octets are in fixed order and are present in all messages. The Protocol Discriminator distinguishes between the D channel signaling protocol and other protocols. The Call Reference is assigned at the beginning of a call by the originating side. It is used to identify all subsequent messages associated with that call and it has local significance only.

Message types   The third octet distinguishes between the various message types. The main elements of the network level signaling are divided into a number of message groups as listed in Table 7.3 (page 123). The table also lists the Message Type field values.

Access procedures   D channel messages are exchanged, as illustrated in Figure 7.16, to set up a B channel for communication. There are many scenarios for call establishment (e.g. user initiated or network initiated, plus alternatives for the use of progress messages). The purpose of the diagram and the following description of the messages is to identify the general role of the message types in the overall scheme of ISDN signaling.

    The user initiates the call by sending a Setup message which contains the calling and called party address and facilities fields. The network replies with a Setup Ack message which confirms that the Setup parameters were acceptable and indicates that the call process has been initiated. An Alerting message indicates that the called party has received

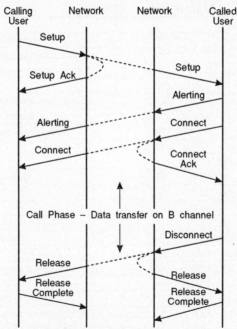

Figure 7.16   ISDN signaling procedures

Table 7.4   Selected ISDN message elements

BEARER CAPABILITY: This element indicates the type of channel required and its use, e.g. either clear 64 kbit/s for data or Pulse Code Modulated (PCM) encoded voice channel. It provides a broad spectrum of information relating to coding standards, transfer capability, mode (circuit or packet), transfer rate (bits per second), configuration (point to point/multiplexed), symmetry (call direction), and layer and protocol details (speed, A-law or μ-law PCM encoding, Adaptive Differential PCM) supported by the network.

CALL IDENTITY: This element is used to identify a suspended call so that it can be resumed.

CALL REFERENCE: This element is assigned by the call originator and provides a reference for the lifetime of the call. It has local significance only.

CALL STATE: This element describes the current state of the call (Call Delivered, Active, etc).

CAUSE: This element is complex and provides the reason for generating certain messages and related diagnostic information.

CCITT STANDARDIZED FACILITIES: This element indicates the facilities required on the call. For example, these facilities are reverse charging, throughput negotiation (X.25 packet mode), call charging and connected address required.

CHANNEL IDENTIFICATION: This element identifies the B channel within the interfaces controlled by these signaling procedures. The element comprises interface type (basic/primary), exclusivity control, channel map (subrates), channel number, timeslot map, etc.

CONNECTED ADDRESS: This element provides the actual address of the called party (as the call may have been redirected).

DESTINATION ADDRESS: This element is provided by the calling party and is the address of the preferred called party.

LAYER COMPATIBILITY: This element provides compatibility information for checking the bearer capability and the higher and lower layer capability. Its content is for further study.

MESSAGE TYPE: This element identifies the message (Alert, Connect, Information, etc).

NETWORK SPECIFIC FACILITIES: This element provides information of the attached network, e.g. network specific facilities.

ORIGINATING ADDRESS: This element is the address of the calling party. It can be encoded to indicate the type and format of the address used, e.g. national/local number, E.163, E.164, X.121 or maritime/land mobile.

PROTOCOL DISCRIMINATOR: This element identifies the message as user to network call control (other types are to be defined).

SIGNAL: This element conveys specific network (telephony) signals, e.g. busy tone, answer tone, dial tone, off hook tone, etc.

USER–USER INFORMATION: This element conveys user dependent data in the call set-up messages (Setup, Alerting, etc).

the Setup message (for a voice call this would cause ring tone to be simulated in the caller's telephone). A Call Proceeding message indicates that the called party has begun call establishment. A Connect message indicates that the called party has accepted the call. At this point the called and calling parties can transfer data on the specified B channel. An optional Info message could also be exchanged during the call establishment or call connected phase to convey additional call related information.

Information elements   For each message type, a set of information elements (parameters) is defined. The elements may be 1 or more octets long. The first octet indicates the format of the parameter (i.e. single or multiple octet format). They must appear in a defined order in a message, although an element may be missing if it is not required. CCITT Recommendation I.451 provides a complete list of message types and their applicable parameters. Selected message elements are described in Table 7.4 (page 125).

7.4.2 ISDN Data Communications

CCITT Recommendation X.31/I.462 and ISO 9574 describe the use of ISDN to support data communications. Alternatives include:

End to end B channel   A B channel can be set up between the end systems that wish to communicate. After the B channel is established, a separate data link and network protocol is then used end to end on the B channel (see Figure 7.17). Either X.25 Link Access Procedure Balanced (LAPB) and the packet level protocol would be used for CONS, or the HDLC Unnumbered Information (UI) frames with ISO 8473 for CLNS could be used on the B channel as required.

Access to packet network   The B channel terminates on a port on a public packet switched data network. X.25 protocols are then used on

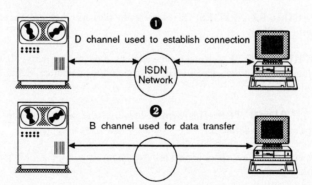

Figure 7.17   Provision of network service on ISDN B channel

the B channel to establish connections across the data network.

D channel user–user signaling
The D channel is used to set up a connection to an ISDN user. This may be either with an associated B channel or without a B channel. The user Info message can then be used to provide a data communications service between the two ISDN users. This is used for PABX to PABX control signaling rather than OSI data communications.

D channel packet access
A separate data link connection can be supported for X.25 protocols on the D channel to allow access to packet switched facilities. This is a multiplexing function in the Data Link Layer rather than the Network Layer.

The above alternatives are provided for in the CCITT Recommendations although some alternatives are not supported by all carriers.

7.5 CONNECTIONLESS NETWORK SERVICE

CLNS
The initial services specified for the Network Layer were based on connection mode. As a result of the development and use of LANs, and support from the US military, an alternative *Connectionless Network Service (CLNS)* was defined as Addendum 1 to ISO 8348. CONS and CLNS are two alternatives for networking — end systems may choose to implement one or the other or both modes. The standards do not express a preference for one or the other. Note that two end systems must both use the same mode for an instance of communication.

Service definition
CLNS provides transparent transmission of an N-SDU, of length up to 64,512 octets, between N-SAPs without prior establishment of an N-Connection as shown in Figure 7.18. The only primitive provided is N-UnitData (request and indication), which carries NSAP addresses and user data, and optionally some QOS parameters such as Transit Delay and Priority.

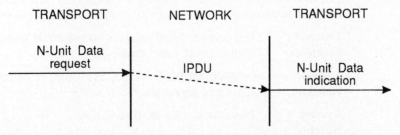

Figure 7.18   Sequence diagram for the Connectionless Network Service

7.5.1 Connectionless Network Protocol

CLNP

The *Connectionless mode Network Protocol (CLNP)* standard is ISO 8473 (there is no CCITT equivalent). CLNP was specifically developed for OSI to provide the CLNS over a variety of subnetworks. For this reason, it is also referred to as the ISO Internet Protocol (IP). It is functionally similar to, but not compatible with, the US Department of Defence Internet Protocol used in TCP/IP.

CLNP has two main functions. Firstly, it provides the CLNS over individual networks, with functions such as segmenting N-SDUs if the subnetwork's packets are too small. Secondly, CLNP supports internetworking by conveying N-SAP addresses, routing parameters, recording paths, providing priority mechanisms, etc.

IPDU

CLNP operates by exchanging *Internetwork Protocol Data Units (IPDUs)* in datagram fashion. It assumes minimal functionality from subnetworks; i.e. it requires an ability to deliver data only from one point to another within a subnetwork. It is assumed that the underlying subnetwork can support a service data unit size of at least 512 octets. Routing of connectionless data units (IPDUs) can either be left to the discretion of the switching nodes, or specified by the sender using a source routing option.

Implementation of CLNP over LANs involves the use of the Logical Link Control (LLC) type 1 "unacknowledged connectionless" service, with straightforward mapping of IPDUs to data link frames. Implementation over an X.25 subnetwork results in IPDUs being sent as M bit sequences of data packets. X.25 virtual circuits are established as required for this purpose. When ISO 8473 is used over an X.25 virtual circuit, the originator sets the first octet of the Call User data field in the X.25 Call Request packet to all zeros (i.e. 0000 0000). This acts as a protocol identifier (PID) to distinguish the CLNP from other uses of X.25.

7.5.2 IPDU Format

The format of IPDUs is shown in Figure 7.19 using the Data IPDU as an example. The various fields are explained below. (Note the length of the header in comparison with the relatively compact X.25 data packet.)

Protocol Identifier   This is set to a fixed value to distinguish this header from other Network Layer protocols.

Length Indicator   Length of the header. The header length is the same for all derived segments.

Version Number   This is set to 1 for the first version.

PDU Lifetime   The remaining lifetime of the PDU in units of 500 ms. This is set to an initial value by the end system that originates the IPDU. Each node that the IPDU passes through decrements the lifetime value by an amount corresponding to the time that it has taken to transit the node. When the lifetime value is decremented to zero, the IPDU is discarded. This mechanism guards against buffer overflow due to congestion and indefinite looping of IPDUs.

SP Segmentation Permitted flag. This should be set for OSI applications.

MS More Segments flag. Like the X.25 M bit, this indicates that the IPDU has been segmented. When it is set to 1, the IPDU has been segmented and further segments follow. When reset to 0, the segment contains the last octet of the data.

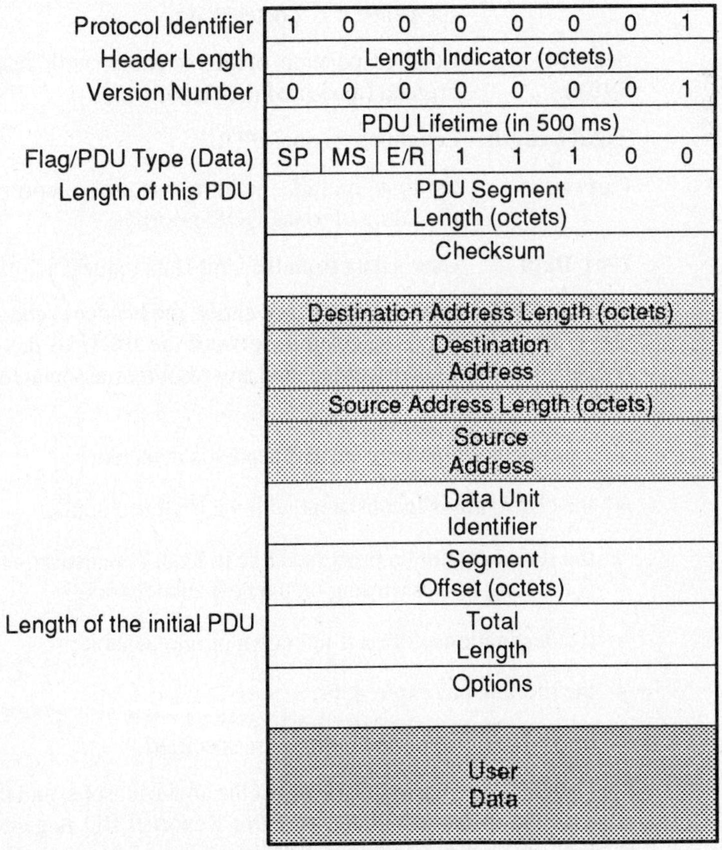

Protocol Identifier	1	0	0	0	0	0	0	1
Header Length	Length Indicator (octets)							
Version Number	0	0	0	0	0	0	0	1
	PDU Lifetime (in 500 ms)							
Flag/PDU Type (Data)	SP	MS	E/R	1	1	1	0	0
Length of this PDU	PDU Segment Length (octets)							
	Checksum							
	Destination Address Length (octets)							
	Destination Address							
	Source Address Length (octets)							
	Source Address							
	Data Unit Identifier							
	Segment Offset (octets)							
Length of the initial PDU	Total Length							
	Options							
	User Data							

Figure 7.19   Format of a Connectionless Network Protocol Data Unit

E/R	Error Report flag. If it is set by the sender, an Error Report IPDU is returned to the sender if the IPDU is discarded.
PDU Type code	Type of IPDU — either Data (DT) encoded as 11100, or Error Report (ER) encoded as 00001.
Segment Length	Length of this segment of the IPDU.
Checksum	Header error check bits. An IPDU received with an invalid checksum is discarded.
Addresses	Variable length fields are used to convey NSAP addresses according to ISO 8348 Addendum 2. Binary encoding of the NSAP addresses is used. Both Source and Destination addresses are included.
Data Unit Identifier	This field is given a unique value by the originating network entity to identify the initial PDU and all derived segments. It is 2 octets long.
Segment Offset	Relative position of this segment with respect to the original (measured in octets).
Total Length	Length of original IPDU.
Options	Options include padding, security, source routing, recording of route, QOS, priority.
User Data	User's data from the Unit Data request primitive.

When an IPDU arrives at a network entity, the header is checked; and if it is correct, a route is selected to forward the IPDU to the destination N-SAP. The IPDU is discarded, and any resources associated with it are released if:

- a protocol violation or invalid header is detected;

- the checksum is inconsistent with the IPDU contents;

- the IPDU cannot be processed due to local congestion, or because it is too long for forwarding on the next subnetwork;

- the destination address is unknown or unreachable;

- the lifetime has expired; or,

- invalid or unsupported options are specified.

If a Data IPDU is discarded for any of the above reasons, and the E/R flag is set in the discarded IPDU, an Error Report IPDU is generated. The network entity that discards an IPDU attempts to return the Error Report to the source network entity. The Error Report identifies the discarded PDU and type of error. Note that the error is not reported to the user in the Transport Layer, so this is a local problem resolution facility. Furthermore, an Error Report is subject to discard or suppression in the same way that Data IPDUs are. Discarding an Error Report does not generate another error report.

Segmentation Since the sending end system does not necessarily know the maximum data unit size that can be conveyed through subsequent subnetworks, one of the main CLNP functions is segmentation (see Figure 7.20).

The sending end system forms its IPDUs up to the maximum size of the originating network. Subsequent intermediate systems may need to divide the original up into a number of smaller segments. The Data Unit Identifier, Segment Offset and Total Length fields are then used to associate the derived segments so that they can be reassembled by the destination. The length of headers is not changed by intermediate systems although they may alter the header contents. Intermediate systems do not perform reassembly.

Reassembly by the receiving end system involves the use of timers and the header lifetime parameter to avoid waiting indefinitely for lost packets.

7.5.3 Routing Protocols

ES–IS ISO 9542 is a standard for the exchange of routing information between End Systems and Intermediate Systems (ES–IS) in a connectionless network. Its typical use is for LANs that support multiple end systems, and one or more intermediate systems as routers for off LAN traffic. For instance, in such a LAN, how does each system know which NSAPs are reachable on the LAN and which can only be reached via the router? Furthermore, what is the corresponding data link MAC address for each

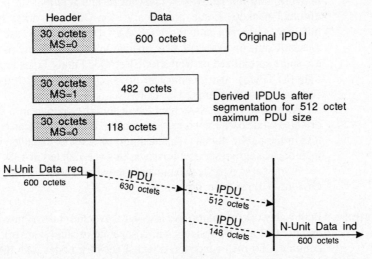

Figure 7.20 CLNP — segmentation example

NSAP? The ES–IS protocol is a distributed algorithm to resolve these routing questions. The protocol has three PDUs:

ESH   End System Hello PDU.

ISH   Intermediate System Hello PDU.

RD   Redirect PDU.

These are broadcast to all stations on the LAN at intervals by each of the end systems or intermediate systems. Each PDU contains a list of the NSAPs or a range of NSAPs which can be reached by the system that broadcasts it. The RD PDU notifies of any changes to previously advised routing information. By listening to the broadcasts, all systems can build up the necessary routing tables.

IS–IS

Nearing final approval is DIS 10589 that is for the exchange of routing and configuration information between Intermediate Systems and Intermediate Systems (IS–IS). It is designed to operate in large, heterogeneous connectionless networks, consisting of different types of subnetwork technologies. In the standard, large networks are organized hierarchically into a number of areas. Each area corresponds to one router, and the routing is performed at two levels. The first level deals with routing to destination end systems in an area, and routing paths into and out of the area. Routing between areas is treated as a second level.

7.5.4 Comparison of CONS and CLNS

Connectionless operation is sometimes termed a "datagram" service. Packets with full addressing information are handled singly by the network. There is no association between the end systems established by the network, and the network is unaware of any relationship between individual packets. Some proprietary, non-OSI networks, specialized military networks and most CSMA/CD (Carrier Sense Multiple Access/Collision Detect) LANs operate in connectionless mode. There are some specialized networks for Electronic Funds Transfer at Point of Sale (EFTPOS), and a number of private networks which use the OSI connectionless standards.

All public packet switching data networks operate in a connection oriented mode because it is easier to manage and operate than connectionless in the public domain. (Interestingly, X.25 was extended in 1980 to include a datagram service; however, this was deleted in 1984.)

A comparison of the two modes is shown in Table 7.5. One of the less obvious distinctions is flow control.

Flow control

Public network operators have no control over the end systems and cannot assume that all end systems will co-operate to share network resources equitably. So the connection oriented network nodes take the role of a

Table 7.5 Comparison of Connection Oriented and Connectionless Network Service

DESIGN ISSUES	CONNECTION ORIENTED	CONNECTIONLESS
Addresses	Only needed in circuit set-up	In every data unit
Error Control	Done in subnetwork	Left to end user
Flow Control	Provided by subnetwork	Not provided by subnetwork
Packet Sequencing	Delivered in transmitted order	Delivered in arrival order
Initial Set-up	Notifies availability of destination	Not possible

traffic policeman that can control the flow of data entering a network on an individual virtual circuit.

Flow control in a connectionless network is not as refined. Instead of the network performing the role of traffic policeman, CLNS relies on a trustworthy Transport Layer to regulate traffic entering the network. If congestion problems occur, and buffers start to fill up, a connectionless network cannot identify individual users to control and all users may be forced to throttle back. If congestion becomes severe, the network's only recourse is to discard packets.

Management Another distinction is in the amount of information supplied in error situations. For instance, the connection establishment procedure supplies immediate feedback if the network is unable to complete the connection. Disconnect reason codes identify whether network congestion is to blame, or whether other problems such as wrong number, destination busy, destination out of order are the cause of non-performance. In connectionless, nothing may be returned after a Data Unit request in error situations. Other management procedures are required to identify the problem.

Header size The connectionless protocol requires a much larger header (approximately 30 octets) to carry the full NSAP addressing information. By comparison, X.25 data packets have a meager 3 octets, which is much more efficient than connectionless for small data units over wide area networks.

7.6 QUESTIONS

Question 7.1 What is a subnetwork?

Question 7.2 What are CONS and CLNS?

Question 7.3 What is the difference between a network service and a network protocol?

Question 7.4 What is the mechanism for multiplexing network connections across a single link in the X.25 protocol?

Question 7.5   Why is ISO 8473 referred to as IP?

Question 7.6   How do connectionless networks perform congestion control?

Question 7.7   What are ES–IS and IS–IS?

8 Internetworking

8.1 INTRODUCTION

The purpose of OSI is to achieve interworking between various open systems connected together by a network, or a concatenation of networks. From the very beginning, it was envisaged that the network would in fact be constructed from an aggregation of many different types of subnetworks (see Figure 8.1). Early thinking in OSI was that connection oriented mode, through network protocols like the X.25 packet level protocol, would come to dominate networking. Since the initial drafting of the Reference Model, an immense development has taken place in Local Area Networks (LANs), with effectively connectionless operation at the Data Link and Network layers. The existence of two broad families of networks, operating under connection and connectionless modes, and their formalization as standards, have provided a particular focus on the design of the Network Layer to encompass multiple access protocols.

To facilitate standardization, a model for the Internal Operation of the Network Layer (IONL) was devised. The model is defined in ISO 8648. It isolates the components of the problems involved in network interconnection, and provides a framework for developing solutions. The IONL standard develops about twenty examples of interconnection scenarios to explore general solutions to the interconnection problem. A simplified treatment of the subject is given in this chapter. The general principles of

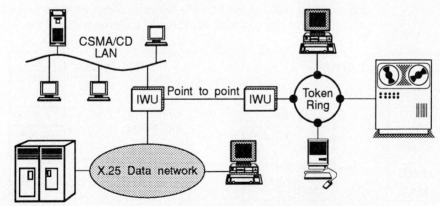

Figure 8.1   Example — internetworking between different subnetworks

internetworking based on the IONL standard are covered first and then the practical use of the internetworking standards is outlined.

8.2 INTERNAL ORGANIZATION OF THE NETWORK LAYER

IWU

The IONL standard classifies network components into real end systems, real subnetworks and *Interworking Units (IWUs)*. A simple internetworking example, shown in Figure 8.2, will serve to illustrate the concepts. An IWU is an OSI intermediate system that intervenes between networks, typically supporting multiple subnetworks and their different access protocols. The IWU is a logical concept. Physically, it may be a separate piece of equipment or it may be integrated with a subnetwork node. In the LAN environment, an IWU is usually called a "router". The distinction between an IWU and a bridge is that the IWU links subnetworks at the Network Layer, not the Data Link Layer as a bridge does.

In order to allow communication between end systems attached to different subnetworks, IONL identifies three approaches to internetworking:

- interconnection of subnetworks which support all the elements of the network service;

- hop by hop harmonization over individual subnetworks; and,

- use of an internetworking protocol over two or more subnetworks.

In the first approach, each subnetwork involved has a single Network Layer protocol that fully supports the N-service. The interconnection of such subnetworks is relatively straightforward, involving relay and routing functions and mapping between N-service components by the IWU. An example of this approach would be the interconnection of two X.25

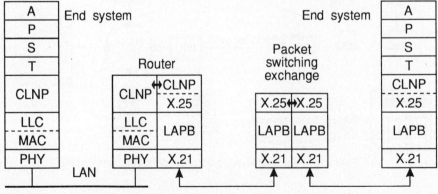

Figure 8.2   Protocol stacks for Interworking Unit

networks using X.75. The IWU may even be physically omitted in this case, existing only as a logical component in the interconnected Packet Switching Exchanges (PSEs).

In the hop by hop approach, one or more of the subnetworks would not fully support the desired N-service. Such subnetworks would need to be enhanced or modified by the addition of protocol functions, provided by an appropriate "convergence" protocol operating in conjunction with the subnetwork access protocol. An example of this mode is the provision of the connection oriented service over a circuit switched data network or an ISDN.

The internetworking protocol approach involves a special convergence protocol operating across all subnetworks, supported by different sets of protocol capabilities in different subnetworks. An example is the OSI connectionless protocol operating over an X.25 subnetwork. The key point recognized in these approaches is that multiple protocols may need to operate in the Network Layer; i.e. it has sublayers corresponding to:

Subnetwork access   Concerned with the access to, and operation over, a single subnetwork using subnetwork addressing.

Internet-working   Concerned with convergence protocols to implement the desired network service, and interworking between different subnetworks. The internetworking sublayer interprets Network Service Access Point (NSAP) addresses and performs the necessary routing and translation to subnetwork addresses.

(The IONL standard actually defines three sublayers. The description here is a simplification.)

Network service   The purpose of this sublayering is to provide a uniform network service interface to the network user, but permit the underlying use of different network technologies. Depending on the internetworking scenario, each sublayer may operate with a separate protocol, or one of the sublayers may not have a protocol associated with it, or a given protocol may perform both access and internetworking roles. In practical terms, the protocols for the internetworking sublayer are: X.25 for connection oriented; and ISO 8473 for connectionless. The most likely protocols for subnetwork access are: X.25 for packet networks or the Layer 3 D channel protocol for ISDN. No separate network access protocol is necessary for LANs because access control effectively takes place in the Data Link Layer.

8.2.1 Protocol Combinations

The different combinations of protocols to be used in providing the network service has led to yet another standard that defines how the various protocols are interrelated and how they operate. The standard is ISO 8880, and it has three parts:

ISO 8880-1   Protocols to provide and support the OSI network service — general principles and conformance.

ISO 8880-2   Protocols to provide and support the OSI network service — provision and support of the Connection Oriented Network Service (CONS).

ISO 8880-3   Protocols to provide and support the OSI network service — provision and support of the Connectionless Network Service (CLNS).

CONS   ISO 8880-2 defines how the CONS can be provided in three environments: LANs, X.25 packet switched networks and point to point connections. The corresponding protocol stacks for end systems and IWUs are listed in Table 8.1. Basically, the X.25 packet level protocol must be used in an internetworking role.

In the packet switched environment, ISO 8208 (i.e. X.25) is specified, in its full DTE to DCE mode, with LAPB for link access. In other words, X.25 fulfils both the access protocol and internetworking role. The 1984 or later versions of the X.25 standard incorporate facilities such as the Address Extension Facility field for the full CONS across single or multiple packet networks. (Earlier versions of X.25 can also be used in conjunction with an additional convergence protocol, but this is no longer necessary since implementations of the 1984 standards are readily available.)

For point to point, ISO 8208 is also used, in its DTE to DTE mode, for both access and internetworking.

For LANs, no access protocol is used in the Network Layer. The X.25 packet level acts as an internetworking convergence protocol according to ISO 8881 "Use of X.25 Packet Level Protocol in LANs". The ISO 8802-2 LAN environment (i.e. Logical Link Control, LLC) is required and both LLC type 1 and 2 are handled. Some of the issues addressed in ISO 8881 are:

- timers and retransmission counts;

- special packet start-up procedures for LLC type 1 where there is no link management; and,

Table 8.1   Protocol combinations for the Connection Oriented Network Service

LAYER	SUBLAYER	LOCAL AREA NETWORK	X.25 NETWORK	POINT TO POINT WAN
Network Layer	Internet	ISO 8208/8881	X.25/ISO 8208 DTE/DCE	X.25/ISO 8208 DTE/DTE
	Access	–		
Data Link Layer	LLC	LLC 1 or 2	LAPB/ISO 7776	LAPB/ISO 7776
	MAC	MAC		
Physical Layer		PHY	X.21/X.21 bis	X.21/X.21 bis

Table 8.2   Protocol combinations for Connectionless Network Service

LAYER	SUBLAYER	LOCAL AREA NETWORK	X.25 NETWORK	POINT TO POINT WAN
Network Layer	Internet	ISO 8473	ISO 8473	ISO 8473
	Access	–	X.25/ISO 8208	–
Data Link Layer	LLC	LLC 1	LAPB/ISO 7776	LAPB or HDLC UI
	MAC	MAC		
Physical Layer		PHY	X.21/X.21 bis	X.21/X.21 bis

- mapping of LAN DTE addresses and logical channels.

CLNS   ISO 8880-3 defines how the CLNS is to be provided, again in three environments: LANs, X.25 packet switched networks, and point to point and Circuit Switched Data Networks (CSDN) (see Table 8.2). Basically, ISO 8473 must be used as the internetworking protocol.

In the LAN environment, i.e. ISO 8802-2, LLC type 1 is specified to provide a basic underlying connectionless service, with service mapping for ISO 8473. No network access protocol is used.

In the X.25 packet network environment, the DTE to DCE procedures of ISO 8208 are specified as the network access protocol. ISO 8473 is used as the internetworking protocol and the ISO 8473 standard covers operation over X.25.

For point to point operation, no network access protocol is required and ISO 8473 operates directly over the Data Link Layer. Data link protocol choices include:

- use of LAPB in full, with flow control and error recovery;

- using Unnumbered Information (UI) frames to send the Internetwork Protocol Data Unit (IPDU), thus providing an equivalent combination to the LAN LLC type 1 approach.

ISDN   Integrated Service Digital Networks (ISDNs) can also be used as a bearer for OSI data communications. A dual protocol stack is required to support both the D channel and B channel as shown in Table 8.3. CCITT Recommendation X.31, in conjunction with ISO 9574, defines the use of ISDN

Table 8.3   Protocol combinations for OSI use of ISDN

LAYER	SUBLAYER	CONNECTION ORIENTED		CONNECTIONLESS	
Network Layer	Internet	X.25	–	ISO 8473	–
	Access	–	ISDN level 3	–	ISDN level 3
Data Link		LAPB	LAPD	LAPB or HDLC UI	LAPD
Physical Layer		B channel	D channel	B channel	D channel

for data communications. These standards define provision of the CONS over an ISDN B channel. The ISDN D channel is used as the access protocol to establish a switched B channel which acts as the physical medium for an OSI Data Link and Network Layer. For CONS, the X.25 packet level is used as an internetworking protocol over LAPB over the B channel. CLNS over ISDN is not defined as a separate standard, but such a service is achieved by using ISO 8473 over either LAPB or HDLC UI frames as for CLNS point to point operation.

8.3 INTERNETWORKING SCENARIOS

Terminology   The terms "bridges", "routers", "IWUs" and "gateways" have all been used at various times to describe alternatives for the interconnection of networks. There has been little consistency in the use of these terms by the industry, so it is necessary to define them for the purposes of this chapter.

Bridge   Within the standards community, the term "bridge" has been formalized as an interconnection in the Data Link Layer. This topic was covered in Section 6.5.2, and Figure 8.3 puts bridging into context with the Network Layer. In effect, the bridge routes within the local subnetwork Medium Access Control (MAC) address domain and its operation is transparent to the network entities.

Router   A router performs interconnection at the Network Layer, often involving different network access protocols. It is an intermediate system in the Network Layer. The router operates with NSAP addresses and performs the necessary translation to subnetwork addresses. Other terms for this function include:

- Network Layer relay

- Interworking Unit (IWU).

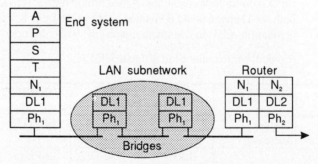

Figure 8.3   Internetworking and LAN bridging – bridges make a LAN conglomerate appear as a single subnetwork.

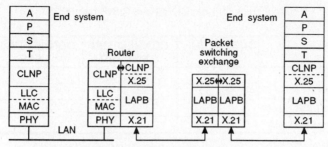

Figure 8.4   Routers interconnect subnetworks.

Protocol stacks for some common internetworking examples are shown in Figure 8.4.

Gateway   "Gateway" is a less specific term that implies interconnection and protocol conversion above the Network Layer, typically at the Application Layer. A gateway performs a mapping of applications between two incompatible architectures (e.g. Figure 8.5). The gateway itself must implement dual protocol stacks. It is one way for the adaptation of existing proprietary systems, but suffers from limitations and bottlenecks.

8.3.1 Interworking CONS and CLNS

Although both CONS and CLNS can co-exist in one network, the standards provide no mechanism for interworking between them. (A Transport Layer IWU which facilitates such interworking has been proposed but it has not been accepted as a standard.) For interworking between two end systems, both end systems and all intervening routers must support a common mode.

Commentary   If different communication modes are chosen by system implementors and purchasers, there is a danger of forming two isolated OSI communities i.e. those using CLNS only and those using CONS only. This incompatibility is precisely what OSI set out to avoid! Yet the current purchasing policies of governments, as expressed in Government OSI Profiles

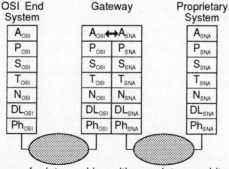

Figure 8.5   Gateways for interworking with proprietary architectures

Table 8.4   Protocol stack for both CONS and CLNS over X.25

LAYER	SUBLAYER	CONNECTION ORIENTED	CONNECTION-LESS
Network Layer	Internet	X.25/ISO 8208	ISO 8473
	Access		X.25
Data Link Layer		LAPB/ISO 7776	
Physical Layer		X.21/X.21 bis	

(GOSIPs), are entrenching this dichotomy. The USA favors CLNS and Europe CONS.

The practical solution to this dilemma is to recognize that CONS is already widely implemented on an international basis in X.25 packet switching WANs. Many X.25 CONS end systems will not need to implement CLNS if they interwork only with other X.25 hosts. The main reason for the rising application of CLNS in LANs is the simplicity of the Connectionless Network Protocol (CLNP). For this reason, LAN systems cannot be expected to welcome the extra complexity of CONS (this observation is made despite the preference for CONS LANs by the UK GOSIP). The problem boils down to interworking between an end system on a LAN and an end system attached to an X.25 network. The conclusion to be drawn is that end systems that are attached to an X.25 network will need to implement both CONS and CLNS to achieve any to any internetworking. A dual protocol stack, illustrated in Table 8.4 can achieve such operation.

8.3.2 Issues for Internetworking

Internetworking protocols are just one aspect of the design of IWUs and routers. Many of the major issues associated with internetworking are summarized in the list below. Some of these issues are the subject of standardization (i.e. addressing), while others are issues to be taken into account for the design and selection of routers.

Addressing   Providing the ability to identify a destination and source LAN/WAN station uniquely by a NSAP.

Buffering   Particularly when stations on dissimilar LANs are communicating directly (or via a WAN) with each other and throughput rates vary significantly.

Error handling   Related to the Data Link and Transport layers and the separation of functions between LAN stations and IWUs. It includes the ability to control the retransmission of data not correctly received at the designated LAN station. A connection oriented Transport Layer is assumed.

Flow control   Related to the Data Link, Network, and Transport layers and the separation of functions between LAN stations and IWUs. It is the ability to prevent overrunning a receiver's buffering capabilities.

Routing   Translating NSAP addresses to DTE addresses or MAC header addresses, and the selection of an appropriate path or set of paths to transmit data so that a destination station may be reached.

Protocol conversion   The mapping of elements of one protocol onto another when the two offer similar services, but are dissimilar in protocol composition.

Segmenta-tion and reassembly   Specifically, the ability to resolve a data unit (such as a packet) size disparity between subnetworks. The method includes dividing, at a transmitter LAN station or an IWU, the larger data unit into smaller units that can be managed by the subnetwork, then recombining the smaller data units into the original larger data unit at the receiver.

Congestion control   The ability to respond to an overloaded condition within a network. It is usually accommodated by detecting a potential overload and routing around it (or using flow control in a connection oriented network). If that is insufficient, some data (usually of a low priority) is discarded to free resources for other (higher priority) data. Discarding data is done only as a last resort and should be an exception condition in a properly designed network.

8.4 NETWORK LAYER ADDRESSES

In recent years, considerable attention has been paid to the question of addressing in open systems. The addressing question assumes particular importance in the case of several subnetworks being connected together. There are in fact two types of addresses that must be considered:

- OSI network addresses which uniquely identify OSI end systems. These are in fact NSAP addresses encountered earlier in Section 4.4 (page 62).

- Subnetwork addresses that are used within subnetworks for identifica-tion and routing. Examples include DTE addresses in X.25 networks and MAC addresses on LANs.

8.4.1 OSI Network SAP Addresses

ISO 8348 Addendum 2 specifies that NSAP addresses belong to hierarchically organized "domains" each of which has an associated

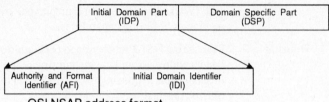

Figure 8.6   OSI NSAP address format

"authority". NSAP addresses are structured in two parts as shown in Figure 8.6:

IDP   Initial Domain Part, effectively prefix numbers for an organization that are allocated by higher level addressing authorities.

DSP   Domain Specific Part that identifies networks and individual computers within an organization.

The IDP is divided into two parts: the Authority and Format Identifier (AFI) and the Initial Domain Identifier (IDI). The AFI, which is 2 decimal digits, specifies the format of the IDI, the authority for allocating values to the IDI and also the syntax for the DSP. AFI values are listed in Table 8.5. The DSP can be up to 40 decimal digits or 20 binary octets. For example, an AFI of 37 defines an X.121 IDI and a binary DSP, whereas an AFI of 36 defines an X.121 IDI and decimal DSP.

Formats   At present there are seven IDI formats. Four are under the authority of the CCITT (X.121 for packet switched networks, E.163 for the public switched telephone network (PSTN), E.164 for ISDN and F.69 for Telex), two use pre-existing ISO numbering standards (i.e. ISO 3666 for 3 digit Data Country Codes (DCC) and ISO 6523 International Code Designator (ICD) for registered organisations). The seventh has no IDI and is intended for non-OSI operation.

The DSP is allocated by the network administrator. Typically, the DSP itself would have hierarchical structure, with prefixes that designate:

Table 8.5   Authority and Format Identifier (AFI)

IDI FORMAT	DECIMAL SYNTAX	BINARY SYNTAX	ASCII SYNTAX	NATIONAL CHARACTER
X.121 public X.25 address	36, 52	37, 53		
ISO Data Country Code (DCC)	38	39		
F.69 public telex number	40, 54	41,55		
E.163 public telephone number	42, 56	43, 57		
E.164 ISDN number	44, 58	45, 59		
ISO International Code Designator (ICD)	46	47		
Local IDI format	48	49	50	51

- Departmental divisions within an organization;

- different subnetworks; and,

- different NSAPs on the end systems attached to the subnetworks.

Network administrators should choose an IDI format appropriate to their organizational hierarchy. Examples of addresses for selected formats are shown in Table 8.6 and described below.

X.121 IDI The first example is a simple case where an organization's networking is based on end systems that are directly attached to X.25 public networks. With minimum fuss, the organization can adopt the X.121 numbers already allocated to its computers by the X.25 carrier for its IDI. The DSP is allocated as needed by the administrator of the end system. Other end systems on remote subnetworks would use an NSAP address similar to the example shown in Table 8.6 to communicate with such an end system. Use of an X.121 IDI does not constrain the routing algorithms to use the public network and does not prevent the end systems being connected to other networks. The X.121 address is simply being used as a unique and unambiguous number.

ISO DCC A larger organization, with a private network, and possibly multiple connections to a public network, would probably prefer an address which was independent of any subnetwork address. In the ISO DCC scheme, the IDI consists of a 3 digit code for countries allocated according to ISO 3166. Within each country, organizations will then need to approach the ISO member, or its delegate, for an allocation of an organization identifier code. The allocation of the organization identifier will need to take into account the size of the organization and its likely future addressing needs. This is the format chosen in the UK GOSIP.

Table 8.6 Examples of NSAP addresses

AFI	IDI	DSP	
36 X.121	505231234567 Up to 14 digits allocated by carrier	89 DSP allocated by system administrator	
38 DCC	826 3 digit DCC for UK government	1234 Organization code allocated by British Standards Institute	56789 Network number allocated by system administrator
47 ICD	0005 4 digit ICD code for US government	12 2 octet organization code allocated by NIST	3456789 7–11 octet number allocated by organization

ISO ICD   Certain larger international organizations registered with ISO, are allocated a 4 digit ICD to serve as the IDI. This is the format chosen in the US GOSIP.

Lest the NSAP addressing seem unwieldy, it is worth comparing it with the international telephone number plan. If we all thought up our own telephone numbers arbitrarily, the telephone network would be unworkable. Instead, numbers are allocated in a hierarchy as a series of prefixes. The country codes are allocated internationally by CCITT. Within a country, there are area codes, exchange zones and finally a number for each telephone. Within the number plan there are alternate formats for toll free dialing etc.

The hierarchical NSAP address structure serves a number of purposes:

- It guarantees the uniqueness of each address provided that each addressing authority never allocates the same number to different organizations.

- Responsibility for management of the scheme is devolved among a number of authorities to make it manageable. The higher levels in the hierarchy are concerned only with the broad sharing of the number space between competing interests; responsibility for day to day allocation of numbers in subnetworks is delegated to the network administrator.

- The hierarchy facilitates routing by providing a predefined structure, but it does not constrain the path chosen by routing algorithms.

8.4.2 Addressing and Routing

The issues encountered when considering the addressing used in internetworking can be seen in Figure 8.7. If end system A wishes to communicate with end system B, not only are the called and calling NSAPs required, and carried in the NPDU (Network Protocol Data Unit), but also the subnetwork address of the router is needed by end user A, and the subnetwork (MAC/LLC) address of end user B is needed by the router.

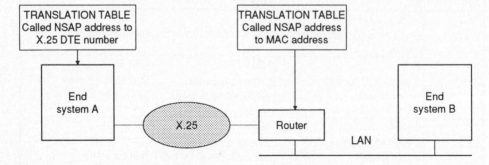

Figure 8.7   Address translation for internetworking

These subnetwork addresses must be derived from the NSAP addresses supplied by the originating party in a N-Connect or Unit Data request. There are several strategies available for dealing with these issues, which are of course bound up with the practical problem of routing the NPDU through the networks.

Address translation

Translation from NSAP to subnetwork addresses is done hop by hop in the network entities in the originating end systems and any IWUs or routers in the path. The network entities would then choose an appropriate data link to forward the PDU. The address translation and routing are typically performed by the use of look-up tables or a routing algorithm in each network entity. In the future, reference may also be made to an X.500 Directory to assist with address translation — although local tables will still be needed to minimize delays for frequently used addresses. Updating these address translation tables to reflect changing network configurations is a management task that should not be overlooked. The hop by hop approach outlined above will minimize the disruption caused by local changes to address structures.

Address transfer

In the CLNS and its associated protocol, the task of carrying NSAP and subnetwork addresses is partly devolved to the subnetworks and the access protocols that may be used. It is up to each network entity and relay to select the required subnetwork addresses on the basis of the NSAPs provided and to convey the subnetwork address in the access protocol. The CLNP (ISO 8473) is responsible for carriage of the NSAP address independently of the subnetwork, and this is the primary role for CLNP in networks today. (ISO 8473 also has an option in which a string of addresses of relays can be provided in the data packets to perform source routing.)

In the CONS, where a connection must be established, identification of subnetwork addresses from the NSAP address is also required by network entities. X.25 has the ability to carry both the subnetwork address (DTE Address field) and it has a Called Address Extension facility that can cater for the carriage of the full NSAP address. ISDN E.164 formats also permit the use of NSAP addresses.

8.5 QUESTIONS

Question 8.1
Bearing in mind that the first step in network design should be to determine the naming and addressing scheme, devise an addressing scheme for your organization. Show the hierarchical address structure that suits your organization now, and allow scope for expansion as your organization's use of computers grows to one computer per person.

Question 8.2
What is the distinction between an NSAP and a subnetwork address?

Question 8.3
What are E.163, E.164 and X.121 and how are they used?

Question 8.4   Complete the sequence diagram in Figure 8.8 showing the exchange of Protocol Data Units (PDUs) to provide the Connectionless Network Service (CLNS) interworking over an X.25 subnetwork and a LAN.

Notes: Assume that the link levels are established but no virtual calls are connected at the start of the sequence. The Connectionless Network Protocol (CLNP, ISO 8473) is used between the OSI end system on the LAN and the network relay. ISO 8473 over X.25 is used between the relay and the OSI end system on the packet network. The X.25 Call Request and Incoming Call packets contain a Protocol Identifier (PID) in the Call User Data field that signifies that ISO 8473 is the user of the call. This allows the X.25 end system automatically to accept the call and prepare to receive connectionless data units. Show the Network Layer service primitives and PDUs for connectionless mode internetworking between the end systems. (Do not show RRs etc.) Use the following abbreviations:

SERVICE PRIMITIVES:

N-UD req   N-Unit Data request

N-UD ind   N-Unit Data indication

CONNECTIONLESS PDUs:

IPDU   Connectionless Internetwork PDU

X.25 PACKETS:

Call-Req   X.25 DTE Call Request packet

Inc-Call   X.25 DCE Incoming Call packet

Call-Acc   X.25 DTE Call Accepted packet

Call-Con   X.25 DCE Call Connected packet

Data   X.25 DTE or DCE Data packet

Assume that it is required to transfer two Unit Data primitives between the end systems. The first has 50 octets of user data — the second has 128 octets. Assume that the maximum size of the data field in X.25 data packets is 128 octets and that the IPDU header is 30 octets.

Question 8.5   Continuation of the previous question: For how long should the X.25 virtual call be held open?

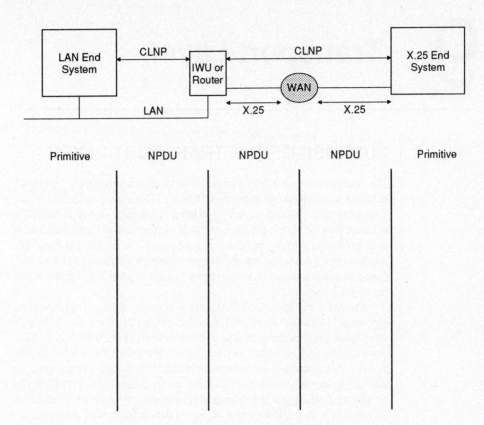

Figure 8.8   Question 8.4 – interworking between LAN and WAN. (Photocopy this diagram to serve as a worksheet for the question.)

9 Transport Layer

9.1 PURPOSE OF THE TRANSPORT LAYER

The transport service in effect provides an idealized, full duplex "bit pipe" between two communicating end systems. The interface between the Transport and Session layers is relatively simple. In its connection oriented form, it allows the session entities to open a transport connection and exchange binary patterns, regardless of how the patterns are transported or what the patterns mean. Although standards exist for the connectionless transport service, they are rarely implemented and will not be covered here.

Above the transport service, there may be many different applications, e.g. virtual terminal, file transfer, specific user applications, etc. Although all of these involve the exchange of binary information, they may require connections with different characteristics. For example, a file transfer system may require a connection with very high data throughput; an interactive application may tolerate a lower throughput, provided the propagation delay is not too long; a financial application may require a connection with the lowest probability of data being lost or corrupted.

Below the transport service there may be several alternative network mechanisms, e.g. a packet switched network, a dedicated line and a satellite link.

QOS   When a application needs a connection, it makes a request, via the Presentation and Session layers, for a connection with a specified Quality of Service (QOS). The transport service attempts to provide a connection of the required quality in the most cost effective way. First, the transport service must chose the most suitable network mechanism (if more than one is available), i.e. choose between the Connection Oriented Network Service (CONS) and the Connectionless Network Service (CLNS). Second, the transport service may have to enhance the basic network service, e.g. by recovering from certain types of error not handled by lower layers, and by multiplexing to reduce costs.

Thus, the amount of work done by the Transport Layer in a particular case may be almost nothing, if the quality of the network service is already good enough for the requested connection, or may be considerable, if a high quality connection is requested over an unreliable network service. In other words, Transport adjusts its behavior according to the QOS required.

9.1.1 Differences between Transport and Network

There is often confusion over the differences between the Transport and the Network layers, since both are involved with providing a reliable mechanism for transporting binary information over a possibly complex network. Perhaps it is best to think of them not as fundamentally different, but as two sides of a single coin.

Network Layer The Network Layer is dominated by the sheer mechanics of networking; it is concerned with issues such as identifying the intended destination of a message (i.e. addressing), finding a suitable path through the network (i.e. routing), recovering from the failures of links or intermediate nodes, and avoiding congestion in links and internal nodes. The Network Layer may also have to deal with the situation where a connection crosses several subnetworks of widely differing characteristics.

Transport Layer The Transport Layer is dominated by user related issues, such as QOS and cost. Any data communications mechanism must have some limitations in maximum throughput, propagation delay, uncorrected error rate, probability of link failure, etc. In principle, some of these parameters may be improved, but at a price. Different applications require connections with different QOS, and it is the job of the Transport Layer to provide connections with suitable QOS in the most cost effective way.

Subnetworks Consider the case of communications through a concatenation of different subnetworks as shown in Figure 9.1. In the Network Layer, although the purpose is to transmit data end to end, the mechanisms to do this must operate hop by hop. Thus the integrity of the network service depends on the correct operation of the end systems and all the intermediate nodes. The network service must often be implemented using major subnetworks which are outside the administrative control of the end users, e.g. public packet switching networks; such subnetworks have to be used "as is". The exact format of a network Protocol Data Unit (PDU) may change as it moves from one subnetwork to another; e.g. in an X.25 network, different packet sizes may used in different parts of the network, and so packets

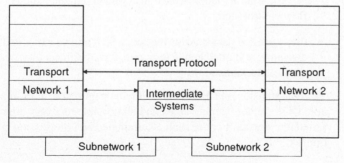

Figure 9.1 The Transport Layer operates end to end.

may be fragmented or reassembled as they progress. Different subnetworks may even use different network protocols.

The Transport Layer operates end to end; i.e. it is implemented entirely within the two end systems of the connection. Provided a network service of some sort is operating, the integrity of the transport service does not depend on the correct operation of any intermediate nodes. Thus the transport service is always under the administrative control of the end users. The transport PDUs exchanged are not altered as they progress through the network.

9.2 THE CONNECTION ORIENTED TRANSPORT SERVICE

The following sections provide an overview of the transport service, functions and service primitives. The transport services are:

- connection establishment and release; and,

- normal and expedited data transfer.

Connection   Connection establishment provides the means by which a session entity can request a transport connection with a specified QOS. The QOS of the connection actually established is negotiated between the session entities and the transport service. The Transport Layer uniquely identifies each session entity by its Transport Service Access Point (TSAP) address. More than one transport connection may be established between the same pair of transport addresses. The operation of one transport connection is independent of the operation of all others, except for the limitations imposed by the finite resources available to the Transport Layer, and the constraints imposed by the overall demands of concurrent session entities.

Data transfer   The transport connection allows the full duplex exchange of data. Two types of data transfer are allowed on any connection:

- the normal data transfer service, which allows transport service data units of arbitrary length to be transferred in sequence subject to normal flow control; and,

- the expedited data transfer service, which allows expedited transport data units of limited length to be transferred, subject to a separate flow control mechanism.

The data transfer is in accordance with the negotiated QOS. If an acceptable QOS cannot be maintained and all possible recovery attempts have failed, the transport connection is terminated and the session entities are notified.

Disconnect The disconnection service provides the means by which either session entity can release a transport connection and have the correspondent session entity informed of the release. Disconnection by the service provider is used to signal failure of the connection.

9.2.1 Transport Layer Functions

Transport connection During connection establishment, the following internal functions may be performed by a transport entity:

- Map transport addresses onto network addresses (NSAP addresses). When a session entity requests a transport connection it identifies the intended peer session entity by means of its transport address, i.e. a TSAP address that is a concatenation of a T-selector and an NSAP address. Since the transport service operates end to end, it can map the target transport address directly onto a target network address for requesting a suitable network connection. Many transport addresses may be associated with a single network address.

- Obtain a network connection (if using CONS) which best matches the requirements of the session entity taking into account cost and quality of services.

- Decide whether multiplexing or splitting is needed to optimize the use of network connections.

- Establish the optimum transport protocol data unit size; i.e. the Session Layer may request transfer of data units whose size is not appropriate for the network service used and so segmentation may be required.

- Select the functions that will be operational upon entering the data phase.

- Provide identification of different transport connections between the same pair of transport service access points; i.e. this identification will be used in subsequent service requests by the Session Layer. It is comparable to the Logical Channel Number used in X.25 to identify virtual circuits.

- Transfer data; i.e. during connection establishment, a limited amount of data may be transferred on behalf of the Session Layer.

Data transfer During data transfer, the following functions may be used, if selected during the establishment phase: sequencing, blocking, concatenation, segmenting, multiplexing or splitting, flow control, error detection, error recovery, expedited data transfer, transport Service Data Unit (SDU) delimiting, transport connection identification.

Disconnection   During connection release, the following functions may be used: notification of the reason for release, identification of the connection released, transfer of a limited amount of data.

9.2.2 Transport Service Definition

The transport service definition is contained in ISO 8072/CCITT X.214. The connection oriented transport service is straightforward as can be surmised from the transport primitives listed in Table 9.1. No other interactions are possible. Note the absence of the resets and data acknowledgements which appeared in the network service.

Establishing a connection is a confirmed service. The required sequence of primitives is:

- The initiating Transport Service (TS) user issues a T-Connect request.

- The TS-provider at the target issues a T-Connect indication.

- The target TS-user accepts by issuing a T-Connect response.

- The TS-provider at the initiating end issues a T-Connect confirm.

Thus the connection is not established until the TS-provider and both TS-users have agreed that the connection is acceptable and they have been informed on the level of options and QOS that can be sustained (see below on negotiation).

Both normal and expedited data transfer are unconfirmed services. Once the connection is established, either TS-user may issue T-Data request or T-Expedited Data request at any time. Since the service is reliable (to the extent of the agreed QOS), it can be assumed that the data will be delivered to the corresponding TS-user with a T-Data indication or T-Expedited Data indication. There are no explicit confirmations.

As is the case in other layers, there are no explicit flow control operations in the transport service. In practice, any implementation of the primitives will allow the recipient of a T-Data indication to delay acceptance of incoming data — so some mechanism internal to the TS-provider may subsequently inhibit the acceptance of further T-Data requests at the other end of the connection as a result of "back pressure" within the

Table 9.1   Transport service primitives and their parameters

PRIMITIVES	PARAMETERS
T-Connect	Called Address, Calling Address, Expedited Data Option, Quality of Service, TS-User Data
T-Data	TS-User Data
T-Expedited Data	TS-User Data
T-Disconnect	Reason, TS-User Data

TS-provider. This implicit flow control mechanism operates independently for the two different directions.

Expedited data A similar, but independent, implicit flow control mechanism operates for T-Expedited Data requests and indications. The primary use of the expedited data service is to allow higher level entities to exchange control messages (i.e. protocol units), even if the normal data service is blocked due to implicit flow control.

Releasing a connection is also an unconfirmed service. It may be invoked at any time by either TS-user, or by the TS-provider itself, if, for example, the network connection fails.

9.2.3 Sequence of Primitives

The transport service definition specifies the allowed sequences of primitives observed by the service provider by a combination of state transition tables and a queue model. A simplified sequence diagram is used for an intuitive explanation in this section. Figure 9.2 shows the use of the following primitives:

* a connection being established using T-Connect;

* data being exchanged using T-Data and T-Expedited Data;

* and the connection being released using T-Disconnect.

The initiating end cannot send data until it has received the T-Connect confirm. The receiving end cannot send data until it has issued the T-Connect response. Any data so sent will not overtake the T-Connect confirm.

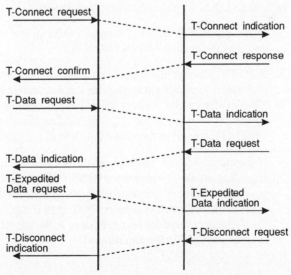

Figure 9.2   Typical sequences of connection oriented transport primitives

Once the connection is open, either end can send data or expedited data at any time (subject in practice to implicit flow control) until the connection is released; i.e. a transport connection is always full duplex.

In each direction, the sequencing of data is maintained; i.e. data from one T-Data request cannot overtake data from an earlier T-Data request. Similarly, the sequencing of expedited data is maintained. However, the relative sequencing of data and expedited data is not necessarily maintained. In practice, expedited data may overtake normal data, although this is not an essential characteristic of the expedited data service. The important thing about the expedited data service is that it is not affected by flow control in the normal data service.

The data unit delivered in a T-Data indication is exactly the same as the data unit that was sent in the corresponding T-Data request; i.e. the data unit may be segmented within the transport service if it is too large for the underlying network service, but it will be exactly re-assembled before delivery at the receiving end.

Either end may release an open connection by issuing a T-Disconnect request. Having done so, it may not issue further T-Data or T-Expedited Data requests and will not receive further T-Data or T-Expedited Data indications. Similarly, once the other end has received a T-Disconnect indication, it may not send and will not receive further data or expedited data. Data still in transit when the connection is released may be lost. It is a function of the Session Layer to provide orderly connection release by end user request with no data loss.

9.2.4 Negotiation during Connection Establishment

In the normal case in which a transport connection is successfully established, the two TS-users and the TS-provider may negotiate over the options and QOS for the connection, as follows:

- In the parameters of the T-Connect request, the initiating TS-user specifies the desired options and QOS.

- If the TS-provider can support the requested options and QOS, then it supplies identical parameters in the T-Connect indication. If the TS-provider cannot support the requested options or QOS, then it supplies parameters in the T-Connect indication corresponding to the subset of the requested options and QOS that it can support.

- If the called TS-user can support the options and quality of service requested in the T-Connect indication then it supplies identical parameters in the T-Connect response. If the called TS-user cannot support the requested options or QOS, then it supplies parameters in the T-Connect response corresponding to the subset of the requested options and QOS that it can support.

- The options and QOS parameters in the T-Connect confirm will be identical to those in the T-Connect response. This is because, if the TS-provider could not support the options or quality of service in the original T-Connect request, then it would have already subsetted them in the T-Connect indication and so there is no need for a second subsetting.

- After the originating TS-user receives the T-Connect confirm, then it should check if the options and QOS on the connection obtained are acceptable, in view of the options and quality of service originally requested. If not, then the originating TS-user should immediately release the connection using T-Disconnect request.

All of the T-Connect primitives carry a TS-User Data parameter that is of no significance to the TS-provider. It allows the TS-users to "piggyback" a limited amount of data in each direction during connection establishment.

Parameters The parameters of the T-Connect primitives, listed in Table 9.1 (page 154), form the basis of the negotiations over facilities and QOS for the connection.

Addressing The Called Address conveys the address of the Transport Service Access Point (TSAP) to which the connection is requested. Note that it must appear in the request and the indication, but is not needed in the response and the confirm since the information is then known.

The Calling Address similarly conveys the address of the originating TSAP.

The Responding Address conveys the address of the TSAP to which the connection is eventually established. Currently, it must be the same as the Called Address, but may in future be a specific address in response to a call to a generic called address.

Expedited Data Option The Expedited Data Option indicates whether this option is requested for this connection. The negotiation process is as follows: If this option is not selected in the request, then the option will not be available on the connection. If this option is selected in the request, then it must appear as selected in the corresponding indication; i.e. the TS-provider cannot deny this option. However, the called TS-user may then accept or reject this option in the corresponding parameter in the response, and the same value must then appear in the corresponding parameter in the confirm; i.e. this option can only be selected if both TS-users agree.

QOS The Quality of Service parameter is a composite item, with fields corresponding to those given in Table 9.2. In principle, numerical values may be given to each of these fields, although any particular implementation may allow default values or may enforce fixed values. The negotiation process is as follows: In the request, any defined value is allowed. In the

Table 9.2   Quality of Service parameters of T-Connect primitives

PHASE	PERFORMANCE CRITERION	
	SPEED	ACCURACY/RELIABILITY
Connection Establishment	Establishment delay	Establishment failure probability (mis-connection, refusal)
Data Transfer	Throughput, Transit delay	Residual error rate, (corruption, duplication, loss), Resilience of the connection, Transfer failure probability
Connection Release	Release delay	Release failure probability

indication, the values may be equal to those in the request, or may be worse if the TS-provider cannot provide the requested QOS. In the response, the values may be equal to those in the indication, or may be worse if the target TS-user cannot support the requested QOS. In the confirm, the values must be equal to those in the response.

User Data   The User Data parameter has no significance to the TS-provider, but it allows the TS-user to piggyback some data in each direction during connection establishment.

9.2.5 Use of T-Disconnect

The T-Disconnect primitives may be used in several different ways. The T-Disconnect primitives have a parameter, User Data, that is of no significance to the TS-provider, but allows a TS-user initiating release to piggyback a limited amount of data across the connection during release.

The T-Disconnect indication primitive also has a disconnect reason parameter which allows the TS-provider to specify why disconnection has occurred, i.e. whether disconnection was initiated by the remote TS-user or by the TS-provider, and, in the latter case, what the specific reason for release was.

The following are examples of the use of T-Disconnect:

Normal disconnect   This is the most usual case in which a TS-user requests connection release.

Disconnection by provider   A connection is released by the TS-provider, e.g. because of a failure of the network connection.

Refusal by provider   The rejection can be initiated by the transport entity at either end. The initiating transport entity may have rejected the request, e.g. because it is not possible to establish a network connection. Alternatively, the receiving transport entity could have rejected the request, e.g. because the called transport address is invalid or not currently active. In the latter case, higher level entities at the receiving end were not consulted about the connection attempt.

Refusal by   A connection request can be rejected by a higher level
peer user   entity at the receiving end, for example, because insufficient resources were available for the connection, or communication with the calling end system is prohibited.

In summary, the transport service is very simple. The TS-user can open a connection, exchange data, optionally exchange expedited data, and close the connection — that is all. The network service is apparently almost identical, except that the network service has additional primitives for non-catastrophic failures termed resets and for optional explicit acknowledgements for data sent. What then is the purpose of the Transport Layer, apart from hiding acknowledgements and resets?

To understand this it is necessary to distinguish between a service and the quality of that service. If each layer in the Reference Model is seen as enhancing the service of the layer below, then the Transport Layer does not provide a richer service than the Network Layer, but a better quality one. Most of the value adding, QOS improving, activities within the Transport Layer are internal to the layer and, therefore, are functions and not externally visible services.

9.3 THE TRANSPORT PROTOCOL

TPDU   The Transport Protocol Specification is ISO 8073/CCITT X.224. The transport protocol is relatively conventional and its features closely resemble those of X.25 levels 2 and 3. The transport entities co-operate by exchanging binary patterns called *Transport Protocol Data Units*, henceforth called *TPDUs*. These are conveyed between the transport entities by the network service. Eleven different types of TPDU are defined. Each TPDU has two parts:

- A header containing information private to the transport entities. One field within the header is the TPDU code that specifies what type of TPDU this is.

- A data field containing information being carried on behalf of the TS-user. This information will have been supplied in the User Data parameter of a request or response primitive and will be delivered in the corresponding parameter of an indication or confirm primitive. This field is not carried in some types of TPDU not directly associated with a primitive.

The transport protocol is therefore defined by specifying:

- The format of TPDUs;

- the meaning of TPDUs, i.e. the circumstances under which a transport entity may send each type of TPDU and what effect that TPDU should have on the receiving entity; and,

- the permitted order in which TPDUs may be sent.

Transport classes
The protocol has five variants, called *classes*. These are necessary because different circumstances require different combinations of functions in the transport service. The key factor is the difference between the QOS requested by the TS-user and the quality of service available from the network service. If the QOS available from the network service is already good enough, then few Transport Layer functions need to be invoked and a simple, low overhead class of transport protocol can be used. However if the required QOS is much better than the network service can deliver, then many Transport Layer functions must be invoked and a complex, higher overhead class of transport protocol must be used.

The class of protocol used on a transport connection is negotiated when the connection is established. Both ends use the same class for the duration of the connection.

9.3.1 Errors and Types of Network Connection

A data communications network is a very complex system and there are many different types of error or failure that can occur. The most frequent types of error can be detected and corrected within the lower layers of the OSI model. For example, line transmission errors will normally be detected, and corrected by retransmission, entirely within the Data Link Layer. The discussion here is not concerned with any errors or failures that can be fully corrected at the Network Layer or below. The concern is about residual errors and signaled errors within the network service.

Residual error
A *residual error* is one that has not been detected by lower layers and that therefore could not be corrected by them. For example, there is a small but finite probability that a transmission error will not be detected by the usual Cyclic Redundancy Code (CRC) check in most data link protocols — there is also a possibility that the CRC checking circuitry will fail. There are also circumstances when it is appropriate to use a connectionless network service; e.g. when operating over a Local Area Network (LAN) or where complex internetworking is required. A connectionless network service is liable to lose, duplicate or change the order of data units sent.

Signaled error
A *signaled error* is one which the Network Layer can detect, but from which it cannot recover. The Network Layer reports such events to the Transport Layer through the N-Reset indication primitive. The most common cause of such an event would be a Reset occurring in a packet switching network, e.g. as a result of a temporary switching node failure. When such an N-Reset occurs, it can be assumed that data already

Table 9.3   Classification of network types

Type A	Acceptable rate of residual errors Acceptable rate of signaled errors	Reliable leased line or packet network
Type B	Acceptable rate of residual errors Unacceptable rate of signaled errors	Unreliable packet network
Type C	Unacceptable rate of residual errors Unacceptable rate of signaled errors	Connectionless network

delivered was correct, but an arbitrary amount of data in transit will be lost.

What matters for a given transport connection is not the absolute rates of residual and signaled errors, but how they compare to acceptable rates for the particular application. For example, an acceptable rate for online program development may be quite unacceptable for a financial system involving very high value transactions.

For a given application, a particular network connection can be classified as shown in Table 9.3.

9.3.2 Classes of Protocol

According to circumstances, it may or may not be appropriate to provide mechanisms in the Transport Layer to recover from residual errors and signaled errors. Also, it may or may not be appropriate to provide mechanisms to implement multiplexing, splitting or the use of the CLNS.

It is not feasible to devise a single transport protocol suitable for all circumstances. Instead, the standards define five classes of transport protocol as depicted in Table 9.4. The part of the transport protocol which deals with establishing a transport connection is identical for all classes, and therefore the class to be used for a given connection is negotiated at connection establishment time. Not all implementations of the Transport Layer will support all classes, but all conforming implementations must support Class 0.

The existence of these classes is not visible in the transport service, i.e. there may be five classes of protocol, but there is only one class of service. When a TS-user issues T-Connect request, the transport entity compares the requested QOS with its own internal knowledge of the quality of the available network services and it makes an appropriate choice of protocol class. It then negotiates with its peer transport entity that may agree to the proposed class or suggest a lower class. Neither TS-user will know which protocol class is being used, but they will be informed what QOS has been agreed.

Transport classes

Class 0 is the simplest, providing minimal functionality (and overhead). If a network signaled reset or disconnect occurs, Class 0 simply disconnects and attempts no recovery. Hence it is suitable for type A networks only. Class 1 retains a copy of data for retransmission to recover from

Table 9.4   Classes of Transport protocol

CLASS	NAME	NETWORK TYPE	FEATURES
0	Simple Class	A	No multiplexing. No recovery from signaled errors. No detection of or recovery from residual errors.
1	Basic Error Recovery Class	B	No multiplexing. Recovery from signaled errors. No detection of or recovery from residual errors.
2	Multiplexing Class	A	Multiplexing. No recovery from signaled errors. No detection of or recovery from residual errors.
3	Error Recovery and Multiplexing Class	B	Multiplexing. Recovery from signaled errors. No detection or recovery from residual errors.
4	Error Detection and Recovery Class	C	Multiplexing. Splitting and connectionless networks. Recovery from signaled errors. Detection and recovery from residual errors.

network resets and disconnects and is suitable for type B network environments. Class 2 allows multiple transport connections to share one network connection; however, it has no recovery functions. Class 3 effectively combines the features of classes 1 and 2. Classes 0 to 3 require the CONS.

Class 4 is a very robust (and complex) transport protocol. It is the only class that can operate over either CONS or CLNS. It converts a connectionless network into a connection oriented transport service. Class 4 has its own checksum to detect residual errors. It can accept TPDUs in any order, and uses timers to initiate retransmissions of lost TPDUs.

9.3.3 Use of the Network Service

Notionally, the transport entities co-ordinate their activities by exchanging TPDUs directly. In practice, they must use the services of the Network Layer to convey the TPDUs as NSDUs (Network Service Data Units). If the CONS is used, then the TPDUs are sent using the NS-User Data field in N-Data primitives, except for the TPDUs encoding T-Expedited Data, which are sent using the N-Expedited Data primitives.

CONS   When using the CONS, it is simplest to map each transport connection onto its own network connection, as in classes 0 and 1. Thus when a transport entity receives a TPDU through an N-Data or N-Expedited Data indication for a specific network connection, there is no confusion over which transport connection the TPDU belongs to. Also there is no need to provide a separate flow control mechanism at the Transport Layer, since the Network Layer flow control mechanism can be used. Such a one for one mapping of transport connections onto network connections is acceptable where only a small number of transport connections is needed between the same pair of end systems, or where network connections are freely available.

Multiplexing   In many cases, a large number of transport connections is needed between two particular NSAPs and either there is an implementation limit on the number of network connections or there are per network connection cost factors (e.g. most public packet networks levy a connect time charge for each virtual circuit). In these cases, it is appropriate to multiplex many transport connections onto a single network connection (as in classes 2 to 4). However, this makes the transport protocol more complex, as TPDUs must carry transport connection identifiers, and independent flow control mechanisms must be provided for each transport connection.

Splitting   Where a very high throughput or high resistance to link failure is required, it may be appropriate to split a transport connection across several network connections. This places even more demands on the transport protocol, because TPDUs sent over different network connections may not arrive in the order in which they were sent.

CLNS   Finally, in some circumstances, it may be appropriate to support a transport connection over a CLNS, e.g. when the Connectionless Network Protocol (CLNP) is used over a LAN, or complex internetworking is required. All TPDUs are sent in the NS-User Data field in N-Unit Data primitives. Since there is no network connection, the concepts of multiplexing and splitting do not apply. However, the transport protocol must now be powerful enough (i.e. class 4) not only to identify the transport connection of incoming TPDUs and implement flow control, but also to recover from lost, duplicated or out of order TPDUs.

NCMS   In the basic transport protocol standard, assignment or reassignment of transport connections on an existing network connection is restricted to the transport entity which initiated the network connection. Addendum 1 to the transport protocol standard specifies optional extensions for an *Network Connection Management Subprotocol (NCMS)*. NCMS allows the acceptor of a network connection to assign transport connections also.

9.4 TYPES OF TPDU

The TPDU types are summarized in Table 9.5. Most of these TPDUs are similar in use to corresponding packet types in X.25. There is one major difference — in X.25 packets are conveyed through an active network and so all packet types come in pairs, from Data Terminal Equipment (DTE) to Data Circuit terminating Equipment (DCE) and vice versa, whereas the TPDUs operate end to end. For example, to establish a switched virtual circuit in X.25, a DTE inserts a Call Request packet into the network and

Table 9.5   Types of transport PDUs and their use

TPDU TYPE	NAME	Validity in class				
		0	1	2	3	4
CR	Connection Request	x	x	x	x	x
CC	Connection Confirm	x	x	x	x	x
DR	Disconnect Request	x	x	x	x	x
DC	Disconnect Confirm	—	x	x	x	x
DT	Data	x	x	x	x	x
ED	Expedited Data	—	x	O	x	x
AK	Data Acknowledgement	—	O	O	x	x
EA	Expedited Data Acknowledgement	—	x	O	x	x
RJ	Reject	—	x	—	x	—
ER	TPDU Error	x	x	x	x	x
PI	Transport Protocol Identifier					

LEGEND

  x   means used in this class.

  —   means not used in this class.

  O   means used in this class if appropriate option selected when connection was established

an Incoming Call packet is then delivered to the DTE at the other end. Although the Call Request and Incoming Call packet formats are similar, the packets are not identical and the packet switching network transforms the one into the other. By contrast, to establish a transport connection, one transport entity sends a Connection Request TPDU and that is exactly what is received by the other transport entity.

Acknow-ledgements

Acknowledgements are not used in Class 0 because it is assumed that the network service is reliable. Other classes use acknowledgements, but they are not piggybacked inside Data TPDUs the way they are in X.25 data packets. A separate Data Acknowledgment TPDU is used, but this may be concatenated with a Data TPDU in one NSDU. Flow control in the non-multiplexing classes (0 and 1) relies on the network flow control mechanism, whereas in the multiplexing classes (2 to 4) a credit mechanism is used (see below).

In Classes 0 and 2, it is assumed that the network service never loses Data TPDUs and so the Reject TPDU is not used. In Classes 1 and 3, Reject is only used after the network service has signalled an N-Reset. In Class 4, lost Data TPDUs are recovered by retransmission after timeout (other classes do not have timeout mechanisms).

The TPDU Error TPDU is sent by a transport entity when it detects a protocol error by the other transport entity, e.g. an invalid TPDU or a TPDU not used in the selected class.

PID

To allow coexistence with other transport protocols or proprietary protocols, the Transport Protocol Identifier TPDU can be used. The PID is sent just before a transport connection is established, to indicate which protocol is to be used.

9.4.1 TPDU Sequences

Connection   The relationships between T-Connect primitives and the Connection TPDUs is straightforward as shown in Figure 9.3.

- On receipt of a T-Connect request, a transport entity will send a Connection Request TPDU to its peer transport entity, which in turn will issue a T-Connect indication (assuming that no errors have occurred).

- On receipt of a T-Connect response, the remote transport entity will return a Connection Response TPDU and the originating transport entity will issue a T-Connect confirm.

The above exchange is sufficient for Classes 0 to 3, since it can be assumed that the underlying network service will not lose any TPDUs without issuing an N-Reset indication. However in Class 4, TPDUs may be lost without notification. If the calling transport entity does not receive a Connection Confirm TPDU, it can timeout and retry. The problem is that the called TPDU has no way of knowing if its Connection Confirm TPDU has been received, and so whether it is safe to start sending data on the new connection. In Class 4, the calling transport entity must therefore perform a "three way handshake", i.e. send a reply to the called transport entity after the Connection Confirm TPDU. The reply may be a Data or Expedited Data TPDU if there is one ready to be sent; otherwise a Data Acknowledgement TPDU is used.

Multiplexing   In those transport protocol classes which support multiplexing (i.e. 2, 3 and 4), it is necessary for each TPDU to carry some sort of "connection identifier" so that the receiving transport entity can determine which transport connection each TPDU belongs to. This is similar in concept to the Logical Channel Number in an X.25 packet. (The connection identifier

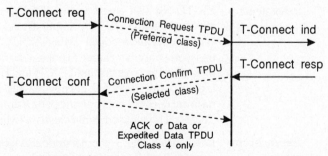

Figure 9.3   Establishing a transport connection

is distinct from TSAP addresses because it is possible to have more than one separate transport connection between the same pair of TSAPs.)

Connection references

As with X.25, the solution is to use the full address while establishing the connection and allocate a unique identifier to each particular connection. In order to allocate an identifier that is not already in use by either transport entity, each end allocates its own independent number — a 16 bit "reference". Each transport entity must know its own and its partner's reference for a particular connection. The references are exchanged during the connection establishment.

The connection TPDUs all carry a Source Reference (SRC-REF) and a Destination Reference (DST-REF). The SRC-REF is the number by which the sender knows this connection and the DST-REF is the number by which the destination knows this connection. In the Connect Request TPDU, the DST-REF must be all zeros. All other TPDUs carry only the DST-REF field, except for the Data TPDU for Classes 0 and 1, which carry neither reference because multiplexing is not implemented.

Data transfer

After the connection is established data may be exchanged in either direction. Figure 9.4 contains example sequences. Some important TPDU parameters used during data transfer are explained in the following paragraphs.

Sequence numbers

Depending on the class, Data TPDUs may have sequence number parameters. For normal data TPDUs, this number is called the TPDU send sequence number (TPDU-NR). The first Data TPDU sent in each direction after connection establishment has a TPDU-NR of 0 and subsequent Data TPDUs in that direction are numbered consecutively. The numbering is independent for the two different directions. The normal size of the TPDU-NR field is 7 bits and so the counting is modulo 128. However, an extended format can be negotiated at connection establishment time, in which case the TPDU-NR field is 31 bits.

Data TPDU numbering is not used in Class 0 and is subject to negotiation on Class 2. It is mandatory in Classes 1, 3 and 4 for the following purposes:

Acknow-ledgements

A Data Acknowledgement TPDU contains a field called YR-TU-NR that specifies the TPDU-NR of the next expected Data TPDU. This implicitly acknowledges all earlier unacknowledged Data TPDUs. The sending transport entity is then free to release the buffers holding those TPDUs. Note that unlike X.25 and High level Data Link Control (HDLC), acknowledging Data TPDUs received does not imply giving permission to send more. There is a separate credit mechanism to handle that.

Resynchroni-zation

In Classes 1 and 3, the network service may signal a network Reset, in which case NSDUs in transit may have been lost. After receiving an N-Reset indication, the transport entities exchange Reject TPDUs, which contain a field YR-TU-NR specifying the TPDU-NR of the next expected Data TPDU, from which retransmission should occur.

Resequencing Class 4 has the ability to detect and recover from lost, duplicated or out of sequence TPDUs. Lost Data TPDUs are retransmitted after the sending transport entity times out waiting for an acknowledgement. The receiving transport entity checks the TPDU-NR field of incoming Data TPDUs. Duplicate TPDUs are discarded. Data TPDUs which are expected, but arrive out of order, are held until the missing TPDUs arrive and they can be delivered to the TS-user in order.

Expedited Data TPDUs carry a field, Expedited TPDU identification number (ED-TPDU-NR) which is used in a similar way to the TPDU-NR field in Data TPDUs. Similarly, Expedited Data Acknowledgement TPDUs carry a field for identification of the Expedited Data TPDU being acknowledged (YR-EDTU-NR).

Credit In multiplexing classes (i.e. 2, 3 and 4), it is necessary to be able to flow control individual transport connections when the appropriate TS-user is unable to accept data fast enough. It is not satisfactory to let "back pressure" build up in the underlying network connection as that will limit

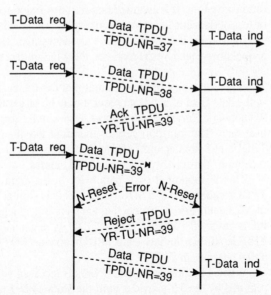

Figure 9.4 Data TPDU sequence numbering and acknowledgements

the flow of all transport connections simultaneously. The mechanism used in the Transport Layer is the use of "credit".

This is slightly different from the mechanism used in data link and packet layers of X.25. In these a "window size" is predefined for each connection. When a frame or packet is acknowledged, the lower edge of the window is set to the frame or packet number in the acknowledgement. Since the window is of fixed size, this also advances the upper edge of the window, thus authorizing the sender to send further frames, provided that they fall within the new position of the window. In other words, acknowledging frames or packets already received automatically grants permission to the sender to transmit more.

In the credit system used by the Transport Layer, acknowledging a Data TPDU does not of itself grant the right to the sender to transmit more Data TPDUs; i.e. it updates the lower edge of the window, but not the upper edge. There is a separate field in the Data Acknowledgement TPDU, Credit (CDT), which specifies the new window size, and hence the new position of the upper edge. The flow of data can be stopped altogether by sending an acknowledgement with a credit of zero. In Class 2, it is not permitted to withdraw credit previously given, but this is allowed in Classes 3 and 4.

The Connection Request and Connection Confirm TPDUs also carry a CDT field, so that an initial credit can be given for each direction of a newly opened connection. The Reject TPDU also carries a CDT field so that a suitable credit can be established after a network reset.

Congestion control
To avoid congestion, particularly when using Class 4 on connectionless networks, the window size is adjusted depending on the level of retransmissions. It is assumed that retransmissions occur mainly because of loss of data due to network congestion. The window size is reduced by the transmitter if retransmissions are necessary. As subsequent TPDUs are acknowledged by the receiver, the window size is gradually restored.

Segmenting
The maximum size of the data unit that the transport service can accept in the data field of a T-Data request may be larger than it can forward to the network service. The transport service must also add its header to the user data. The transport service therefore has the facility to segment a TSDU into smaller units for transmission and to reassemble them on reception. This facility is present in all classes.

This is supported by a parameter in the Data and Expedited Data TPDUs called End of TSDU (EOT). This is similar to the More Data bit in X.25 data packets, except that the meaning attached to the value of the bit is inverted. When a large TSDU is segmented into several Data TPDUs, all but the last Data TPDU carry an EOT bit of 0 and the last TPDU carries an EOT bit of 1.

When a sequence of Data TPDUs is received with EOT = 0, they are retained by the TS-provider until the Data TPDU with EOT = 1 arrives and they are then reassembled before being delivered by the T-Data indication. Thus the data field in the T-Data indication is always identical to the corresponding field of the originating T-Data request.

A similar bit in Expedited Data TPDUs provides a corresponding facility for the expedited data service.

Checksums   Class 4 is the class that must provide a reliable transport service over an unreliable network service. The standard mechanisms of Class 4 provide facilities to recover from lost, duplicated or out of order NSDUs. However, an extremely unreliable network service may even deliver NSDUs that have been corrupted in transit (rather than discarding or recovering them).

Class 4 therefore contains an optional mechanism, which can be negotiated at connect time, to detect corrupted TPDUs by means of a checksum. If selected, then every TPDU includes an additional parameter in the variable part of the header. This contains a 16 bit checksum covering all of the fields in the TPDU, i.e. both the header and the User Data fields. If any TPDU is received with an incorrect checksum, then the TS-provider discards it. Recovery is then by timeout, as if the network service had lost the TPDU. The algorithm specified for computing the checksum has been chosen so that it can be implemented efficiently in software.

Disconnection   Figure 9.5 illustrates release of a transport connection by a user. On receipt of a T-Disconnect request, a transport entity sends a Disconnect Request TPDU. On receipt of this, the other transport entity issues a T-Disconnect indication. In all classes except 0, the receiving entity returns a Disconnect Confirm TPDU. This is so that both transport entities can be sure that the connection has been released. Note that the transport service is not a confirmed service, since the Disconnect Confirm TPDU is generated internally to the transport entity, not as a result of a response primitive from the TS-user.

9.5 FORMAT OF TPDUs

A TPDU has two parts:

- A header containing information relevant to the transport entities.

- A data field carrying information on behalf of the TS-user. This field is not present in all types of TPDU.

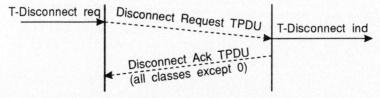

Figure 9.5   Releasing a Transport connection

The header varies in format according to the type of the TPDU and the class of the protocol, as shown in Table 9.6. (The table shows the format for 7 bit sequence numbers.) All headers have the following general format:

Length   This field specifies the length, in octets, of the header
Indicator   minus the Length Indicator field itself. (Field length 1 octet)

Fixed part   This contains frequently occurring parameters, the first of which is always the TPDU Type Code (1 octet). Its format is determined by the TPDU type and, in certain cases, by the protocol class and options negotiated at connection establishment time.

Variable part   This contains less frequently used parameters and its format is self-describing (see below). It consists of zero or more occurrences of a parameter.

A parameter in the variable part has the following format:

Parameter   This identifies the type of this parameter. (Length 1 octet)
Code

Parameter   This specifies the length, in octets, of the Parameter
Length   Value field. (Length 1 octet)
Indication

Parameter   The particular value of this parameter. (Variable length)
Value

Note that the TPDU contains no explicit specification of the length of the data field (if present). It is assumed that any implementation of the network service will inform the transport entity of the length of the NSDU that conveyed the TPDU. This NSDU will have been delivered as the User Data field of an N-Data, N-Expedited Data or N-Unit Data primitive. Since the length of the transport header is explicit, the transport entity can deduce the length of the data field.

In Classes 1 to 4, the transport entity may concatenate more than one TPDU into one NSDU for efficiency reasons, provided that either all, or all but the last, of the TPDUs are types having no data field.

Table 9.6   Formats of transport PDUs

Length 1 octet	Type 1 octet	Reference 2 octets	1 octet	1 octet	1 octet	Variable length	
LI	1110cccc **CR**	0 ... 0	Source Reference		Preferred Class & Options	Variable part	User data
LI	1101cccc **CC**	Destination Reference	Source Reference		Selected Class & Options	Variable part	User Data
LI	10000000 **DR**	Destination Reference	Source Reference		Reason	Variable part	User Data
LI	11000000 **DC**	Destination Reference	Source Reference		Variable part*		
LI	11110000 **DT**	Destination Reference (except in classes 0 & 1)	EOT TPDU-NR (except class 0)	Variable part*	User Data		
LI	00010000 **ED**	Destination Reference (except in classes 0 & 1)	EOT TPDU-NR (except class 0)	Variable part*	User Data		
LI	0110cccc **AK**	Destination Reference	Next TPDU	Variable part*			
LI	00100000 **EA**	Destination Reference	Next TPDU	Variable part*			
LI	0101cccc **RJ**	Destination Reference	Next TPDU				
LI	01110000 **ER**	Destination Reference	Reject Cause	Variable part*			

LEGEND

LI   Length Indicator

cccc   This field carries the CREDIT parameter in classes 2, 3 and 4.

EOT   End of TPDU (bit 8 of octet)

*   Variable part is optional and present in class 4 only.

▨▨▨ Variable length fields

9.6 QUESTIONS

Question 9.1   How many classes of transport protocol are there and what are the two major groups?

Question 9.2   What is the credit mechanism used for?

Question 9.3   What is the T-Expedited Data service used for?

Question 9.4   Draw the sequence diagram for the establishment of a transport connection and its associated network connection. Show the transport primitives and their mapping onto TPDUs. Assume that no User Data is required in the T-Connect primitives. Also show the network primitives used to create the underlying network connection and to carry the TPDUs.

Part 3 — Standards for Information Exchange

10 The Upper Layers

10.1 INTRODUCTION TO THE UPPER LAYERS

The lower four layers of Open Systems Interconnection (OSI) are concerned with how binary information can be transported reliably and economically through a communications network. Each layer improves on the one below, and connects together more links to make an end to end path. The service presented by the Transport Layer (the uppermost layer in the lower group of four) resembles that of an idealized "bit pipe". Using this service, the upper layers can open a connection between two points, exchange full duplex streams of binary information and then close the connection.

This low level telecommunications service, although vital, is not sufficient to enable worldwide open systems distributed computing to become a reality. It is no use a computer accurately receiving a binary pattern if it has no way of knowing what the pattern means, why it was sent and what is supposed to be done about it. Those who have ever been faced with trying to interpret a hexadecimal memory dump from a computer, or a hexadecimal printout of an unknown magnetic tape, will know that it is almost impossible to make sense of the data unless you have some idea of what it is supposed to mean. Raw strings of binary digits can represent anything!

Ultimately, the meaning of raw binary must be tied to a particular application, and so applications must also be standardized as appropriate to make true open systems working a reality. In most previous networking architectures, there have been attempts to standardize some applications above the binary Transport level, but each application has been standardized independently, with little attempt to identify any common aspects. In the standards for OSI, it has proved possible to isolate and standardize two aspects of the interpretation of binary data streams independently from the actual applications themselves, i.e:

- the structure and co-ordination of computer dialogues (the purpose of the Session Layer); and,

- the representation and encoding of data (the purpose of the Presentation Layer).

The subject of this chapter is the relationship between the upper layers (illustrated in Figure 10.1).

Session Layer   Application programs do not, in practice, bombard one another with continuous, unstructured, full duplex streams of data, any more than two people holding a conversation bombard one another with continuous, unstructured streams of words. Both people and programs interact in a much more structured way. This structuring forms the basis of the Session Layer.

Presentation Layer   What applications wish to exchange is information. What the Transport Layer allows them to exchange is strings of binary digits. There are many ways of encoding information into binary digits, e.g. different character codes, number representations, etc. When two computers need to communicate, then mutually agreed binary representations of the information must be selected and used for the data transfer. The Presentation Layer provides standardized ways of transferring Application Layer data as bit strings so as to preserve the meaning of the data.

Application Layer   To be worthwhile, open systems must deliver useful services to the end user, i.e. be able to exchange messages, files, transactions, etc. Yet the services provided by the Presentation Layer are rather generic and abstract. So Application Layer standards have two roles:

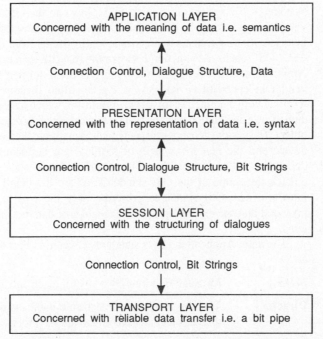

Figure 10.1   Relationships between upper layers in OSI, showing the nature of the parameters of service primitives passed between adjacent layers

- to standardize certain application services, e.g. to define the meaning of the information exchanged and the services provided to users of open systems; and,

- to define how the structuring and data representation services of the Session and Presentation layers are used for each application standard.

The following sections give an outline of each layer in turn, working from the Application Layer down.

10.2 APPLICATION LAYER

The Application Layer provides a range of system independent services to real "users" or user programs. It builds on the functions of the six lower layers to provide new services of particular use in the construction of distributed systems. In so doing, it also hides much of the complexity of the lower layers by taking responsibility for the co-ordination of the joint operation of distributed applications in peer systems.

Virtual devices At the outset, it was recognized that OSI would have to work within the framework of existing computer technology — it would not be reasonable for manufacturers to have to make major alterations to their operating systems or file systems to support OSI. How can the OSI objective for vendor independence be reconciled with the inconsistencies between, for instance, the file systems or electronic mail systems from different vendors? OSI makes a distinction between the real file system, and the OSI Application entity. An application entity is often defined in terms of a vendor independent *virtual device*, e.g. a virtual filestore or a virtual terminal with a defined set of service primitives which act on it. A virtual device is an abstraction of some real system resource represented as a data object. The system dependent aspects such as mapping between the virtual device and the real file system or terminal are performed by vendor dependent software elements. The specification of such mappings is outside the scope of the OSI standards, as are the details of the user interface. The OSI standards prescribe only the end to end service provided and the externally visible exchange of data between peer systems.

The main Application Layer standards covered in Part 4 of this book are:

MHS   Message Handling Systems for electronic mail.

Directory   The Directory — an electronic database of names, addresses and other communications information.

FTAM   File Transfer, Access and Management for file handling.

VT   Virtual Terminal for vendor independent communication between character mode terminals and applications.

Systems For control and management of network equipment and **Management** components.

DTP   Distributed Transaction Processing for linking online transaction processing systems.

A number of other Application Layer standards are available but are not covered in this book (e.g. Job Transfer and Manipulation, JTM, and Manufacturing Message Specification, MMS). New application standards will continue to emerge to fulfil user needs for distributed systems.

In addition to defining the mechanisms for exchanging messages and files over OSI, in some circumstances standards are also needed for the contents of the messages or files. In particular, content format standards are necessary to facilitate automatic processing of trade documents such as orders and invoices, or to edit word processing documents after they have been exchanged between systems. Two such content format standards are included in Part 5 because they will frequently be the *raison d'être* for OSI communications. The content standards are:

ODA   Open Document Architecture for the exchange of formatted documents.

EDI   Electronic Data Interchange for trade documents.

The Application Layer standards for Document Filing and Retrieval (DFR) for office automation are also covered in Part 5 of the book.

10.2.1 Distributed Systems

Usually, the applications involved in distributed communications using OSI will not be identical. They may be situated in different places, and implemented on different equipment by different people in different organizations. To exchange meaningful information, however, they should have something in common about which they need to communicate, e.g. a travel reservation system communicating with a banking system in order to obtain payment for travel booked. This "something in common about which the systems communicate" is sometimes called the *universe of discourse* for the two applications.

If two humans strike up a conversation, they usually have sufficient intelligence and flexibility in the use of language to negotiate a universe of discourse on the spot (think of people meeting at a party). Computers are not (yet) sufficiently powerful to do this. First, it is necessary for the people responsible for the communicating computers to identify the appropriate universe of discourse and formally define it. Next, the applications which will run in the computers can be implemented. Only then can the two computers establish communication between one another.

The development of distributed applications has always involved this three step process and OSI standardization does not change the situation. OSI simplifies the implementation process when the communicating systems are from different vendors.

Before a distributed application can be implemented, the appropriate universe of discourse must be precisely defined. Two aspects of this definition are semantics and syntax.

Semantics   Semantics refers to the meaning of the information exchanged. For example, in a financial system, the semantics of a data item might be that the data is a set of rates of exchange to be used in converting one currency to another. Semantics are entirely the concern of the Application Layer in OSI.

Syntax   Syntax refers to the representation of the information exchanged. For the above example, the syntax of the data item might be that it is an array of five real numbers. Syntax is the concern of both the Presentation and the Application layers.

A syntax definition specifies a set of data values and its structure.

10.2.2 Application Layer Modeling

Application Layer standards are defined in terms of a number of co-operating elements. (The general term "elements" is used here as a simplification of the Application Layer structuring concepts that include Application Service Elements (ASE), control functions and objects.) As a rough analogy, consider a conference telephone call between two teams of people working on a joint project. The call is initially established by secretaries who communicate with each other to ensure that the correct people are available. Project managers at each end discuss the progress of the project but defer to technical specialists and financial advisers for detailed conversations. Each speaker uses specific terms and jargon to convey information relevant to their specialization. Likewise, each of the elements of an application entity uses specific semantics and syntax to communicate with its peer element over a presentation connection.

Each Application Layer standard specifies one or more syntaxes specific to its requirements (e.g. the X.400 standard for message handling specifies a syntax for envelopes). In the OSI standards, all syntaxes are precisely defined and are given unique, registered names.

To enable a consistent modeling of applications, ISO 9545 defines the Application Layer structure. This standard defines the major components and terminology used in the formulation of OSI application standards. Details of the Application Layer structure are covered in Chapter 14.

10.3 PRESENTATION LAYER

Syntax negotiation

If a Japanese person and a French person need to converse on a common topic, one of the first steps is to select a language for discourse. Likewise, two open systems need to select common syntaxes for the transfer of information between them. In OSI, the Presentation Layer acts on behalf of the Application entities to determine the syntaxes to be used on a connection and selects encoding schemes to represent the information exchanged as a string of bits transmitted over the Session service. From the viewpoint of the Application Layer, data values from multiple syntaxes can be transferred unambiguously over the Presentation connection. The syntaxes can also be changed during the course of a connection.

Transforming bits

Once a common language is agreed between two foreigners, then one or both speakers will need to transform internally between their native tongue and the language of the conversation. Likewise, communicating computer systems may naturally use different internal encodings. It may therefore be necessary to transform the strings of bits one or more times during transmission, in order to preserve the overall meaning of the information.

In the past, if the two different systems used different internal data representations, then the transformation of data representations had to be implemented as part of the applications. If more than two computers regularly communicate using the same universe of discourse and each uses different internal data representations, then the number of data transformations that have to be embedded in each application starts to become prohibitive.

The aim of the Presentation Layer is to separate the data representations from the applications. The benefits of this approach include:

- application development is simplified;

- applications become more portable, especially if written in a high level language;

- bit transformations, if required, are internal to the Presentation Layer;

- operational flexibility can be improved, since appropriate transformations can be selected by the Presentation Layer at connect time; and,

- transformations can, in principle, be generated automatically.

These transformations of encoding are internal functions of the Presentation Layer and the transformations as such are not standardized.

10.3.1 Abstract Syntax Notation One

In order to define the syntax of the information making up a particular universe of discourse, some kind of precise notation must be used.

The Presentation Layer standards do not dictate that any particular notation must be used. However, one particular notation has been developed and is universally used for specifying the various standards within the Application and Presentation layers. This notation is also suitable for a wide range of user applications that exchange data consisting of common data types, e.g. boolean, integers, strings of characters, etc.

ASN.1

The notation is called *Abstract Syntax Notation One (ASN.1)*. ASN.1 provides a range of "built-in" basic data types corresponding to the data types found in most high level programming languages. ASN.1 also provides a way of composing a comprehensive range of structured data items whose value is derived from a number of basic data items. Furthermore, encoding rules are defined for the efficient representation of any ASN.1 data value as a bit string.

ASN.1 is the major contribution of OSI to vendor independent representation of data objects. It is used in all of the Application Layer standards and is a central unifying concept in the OSI upper layers. A tutorial style introduction to ASN.1 is given in Chapter 13.

10.4 SESSION LAYER

10.4.1 The Structure of Human Conversations

The purpose of the Session Layer can be understood by considering the way people structure human conversations. When talking, people do not usually spout continuous streams of words simultaneously at one another, although the communications media (i.e. air or the telephone) would allow us to do so. Instead, we communicate in a very structured way. We start by "striking up a conversation" with someone. If necessary, this may first involve making sure they know who we are. Next, we establish a "topic of conversation". Many of the words we use are ambiguous unless we know the context in which they are being used. During a complete conversation, we may change the topic of conversation several times, provided that this is mutually agreed. We may also interrupt a topic of conversation and introduce a more urgent one, later returning to finish off the original topic.

During a conversation, speakers take "turns to talk" since the conscious part of the human brain can normally deal with only one thing at a time. Usually the speaker will voluntarily give the other person a chance to talk every now and then, but from time to time one person may interrupt the other. For formal meetings and debates, there are usually agreed rules to control who has the right to speak. At other times, etiquette governs the right to speak and the use of the cues. Even when one person has the right to speak, he or she will pause from time to time to make sure that the other has understood what has been said. This is not a "transport level" acknowledgement (i.e. has the other person heard what I said?) but an "application level" acknowledgement (i.e. has the other person understood and accepted what I said?).

Finally, at the end of a conversation, people do not abruptly stop talking and walk away. We use polite ways of "taking our leave" from people, i.e. making sure that they know we have nothing more to say, and that there is nothing more they want to say to us.

Cues

In order to co-ordinate such structuring, people have to exchange special signals, which we can call "cues", to make their intentions clear. Examples of such cues include:

- "This is ... from the Computing Department here" (striking up a conversation);

- rise in pitch of voice (asking a question); and,

- nod of head (acknowledging what has been said).

This system of cues is fairly universal. We all use something like it for structuring conversations, regardless of what we are actually talking about or whom we are talking to. Therefore it is quite valid to regard our system of cues as being a form of communication distinct from the words that make up the body of our conversations. To illustrate how distinct, but universal, this system is, most of us have had the experience of going through the motions of a polite conversation with someone who is speaking a foreign language. It is quite easy to smile, nod and grunt in all the right places, using non-verbal cues, even though we do not understand what is being said.

10.4.2 Structure of Computer Conversations

The Session Layer provides a set of standard cues for applications to use in structuring their dialogues. Applications insert the cues into the data stream as appropriate. They act as universal control signals for the applications to:

- control which end has the right to transmit (interaction management);

- delimit the start and end of some processing task (activity management);

- confirm progress on the processing of data that has been transferred (synchronization); and,

- advise of exception conditions.

The Session Layer attaches no meaning to the cues, it simply encodes them as required and ensures that the correct etiquette is observed by the applications.

10.5 OVERALL OPERATION OF THE UPPER LAYERS

The operation of the upper layers is quite distinct from that of the lower four layers. Whereas the lower layers provided a transparent bit pipe, the Session Layer is used by applications to insert special cues or punctuation marks into the data stream. The Presentation Layer determines the encoding of the bit string that represents application information. Together, the upper layers focus on end user services and the problems of distributed systems.

The upper three layers work very closely together. All of the session services are passed directly through the Presentation Layer for use by applications. The main focus of the Presentation Layer is on data objects, rather than functions, and so its service is used directly by applications. The services provided by the upper layers are more complex than those provided by the lower layers and the service primitives are more numerous (see Figure 10.2).

This close relationship is also reflected in the packaging of products. Software for the upper layers is often packaged so that the three layers are implemented in one product without exposed interfaces to the Session or Presentation layers.

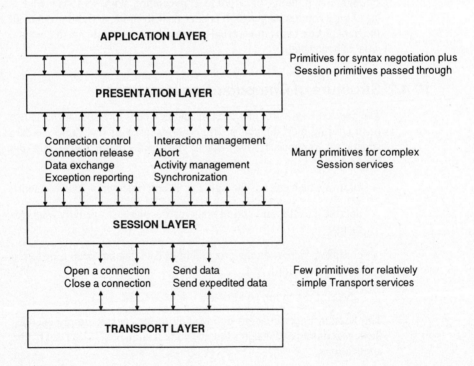

Figure 10.2   Upper layer primitives

Functional units

Another common aspect of the upper layers is that the standards are very comprehensive, covering most conceivable application requirements. In practice, a particular implementation does not need to implement the complete standard. So uniform subsets, called *functional units*, are defined within the standards themselves. Because the upper layers are so closely interrelated, this means that consistent subsets must be chosen across all three layers. The subsets to be used for a connection are negotiated for all three layers together during connection establishment. Negotiation allows systems with different capabilities to interwork — the more capable system operates with lower functionality when communicating with a less capable system.

10.5.1 Connection Establishment

It is often stated in informal descriptions of the Reference Model that the main function of the Session Layer is to establish and release sessions (or connections) between end users. Such a statement is wrong. In the OSI standards, all layers play a role in establishing and releasing connections. The confusion has probably arisen because, in IBM's Systems Network Architecture (SNA), there is a function called Session Control whose purpose is to activate and deactivate sessions (which are roughly equivalent in concept to connections in OSI). In OSI, connection establishment involves all layers. A simplified description follows (see Figure 10.3).

P-Connect

The initiative for opening a connection always comes from an application entity, which starts by issuing a P-Connect request primitive to the Presentation Layer. The connect primitive specifies the presentation and session functional units and other options required for the connection. At this point, the initiating presentation entity would like to send a Connect Presentation PDU (Protocol Data Unit) to its peer presentation entity, but cannot do so because there is no session connection open. So it issues a S-Connect request primitive to the Session Layer. The process repeats itself. The session entity would like to send a Connect PDU to its peer session entity, but probably cannot do so because there is no transport connection open. So it issues a T-Connect request primitive.

The Connect request primitives ripple down through the layers of the initiating side until a layer is found with a suitable connection already open. This will usually be no lower than the Data Link Layer, because most data links are opened at system initialization time. A connection may already be open at a higher level, e.g. if the Transport Layer is implementing multiplexing (as is the situation shown in the example).

Suppose the first open connection is at the Network Layer. The initiating Transport entity can now send a Connect Request Transport PDU (i.e. CR-TPDU) to its peer transport entity. That entity will then issue a T-Connect indication primitive to its session entity. If that entity accepts the connection, it will issue a T-Connect response primitive to its transport

entity that will return a Connect Confirm PDU (CC-TPDU) back to the
initiating transport entity. That entity will now issue a T-Connect confirm
to the initiating session entity.

At this stage, we now have an open connection at the Transport Layer,
i.e. one level higher than before.

Now, however, the Session Connect PDU, and the Presentation Connect PDU and the Application Connect PDU (i.e. A-Associate Request
PDU) are transferred together as transport user data. They are conveyed
in the first Data Transport PDU (i.e. DT-TPDU). This is necessary
because the upper layers act in concert and need to ensure consistent
selection of session and presentation services to support the application.
When the connections are confirmed (again in a combined PDU), the
application connection is open. Thus, in this overall mechanism, the

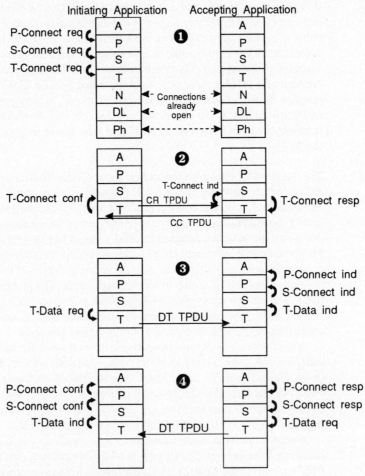

Figure 10.3   Connection establishment in OSI layers

Session Layer does play a part, but no bigger part than any of the other layers.

10.6 WHAT'S NEXT?

The remaining chapters of Part 3 work through the Session and Presentation layers, and then ASN.1 is covered in tutorial style before proceeding with the Application Layer. While some aspects of the Session and Presentation layers may seem abstract in isolation, the concepts will be drawn together in examples given when discussing the Application Layer standards. An appreciation of ASN.1 is vital to understand the operation of the upper layers or to delve into the Application Layer standards themselves.

11 Session Layer

11.1 THE STRUCTURE OF COMPUTER CONVERSATIONS

There are many similarities between the structure of a human conversation, described in the previous chapter, and the structure of a typical "conversation" between computers. Just as humans need a system of cues for co-ordinating the structure of their conversations, so also do computers. It is the function of the Session Layer to provide such a system of cues in a standard way. A typical conversation between two computers will be illustrated using the terminology of the Session Layer.

Two applications wishing to interact for a while create a session connection (i.e. strike up a conversation).

Activities
Within one session connection, there may be a number of phases corresponding to different but related "activities" (i.e. topics of conversation), and the meaning of the data exchanged may vary from one activity to another. For example, when word processing one might edit one file, run a spelling checker, print the file, edit another file, etc. Very often, the meaning of particular keystrokes varies depending on whether one is editing or running the spelling checker; so it is vital to establish unambiguously when one activity ends and another starts.

Interactions
Some applications do exchange data in full duplex mode, but many do not, for much the same reason as people do not; i.e. normally, programs are written to do one thing at a time. Mechanisms are needed for co-ordinating whether or not half duplex communication is to be used, and if so which application starts off with the right to transmit, and how the applications subsequently exchange that right.

Synchroniza-tion
Within one activity, one application must pause from time to time to make sure that the other has "synchronized" its processing (i.e. an application level acknowledgement). This is particularly true when the data transferred is being used to update a file or database on disk storage, and it is necessary to provide automatic recovery from system failures. Here it is not good enough just to confirm that the data has been received correctly (i.e. a Transport level acknowledgement); the applications also need to confirm that the data has been processed correctly and that the file or

database has been correctly updated (i.e. an application level acknowledgement), before the sender of the data can relinquish its responsibility for that data.

Finally, applications need to be able to "negotiate for the release of the connection" so that the two communicating applications can end their interactions in a controlled way. For example, after one application has signaled that it wishes to release the connection, it may still be necessary to exchange a limited amount of accounting data; so the connection cannot be broken immediately.

11.2 THE PURPOSE OF THE SESSION LAYER

In the past, the exchange of control information or "cues" has been implemented as part of the internal mechanism of the applications. The problem with this approach is that there is no standardization of the way cues are encoded. In OSI, the function of communicating standardized cues between applications has been removed from the applications themselves to form the Session Layer (see Figure 11.1). The Presentation Layer is totally transparent to these cues; so the Application and Session layers can be regarded as interacting directly.

It is still the function of an application entity to decide that a cue of a particular type should be sent, but instead of formatting up an application protocol unit, the Application Layer issues a Session Layer primitive request (via the Presentation Layer) asking that a cue be sent. When the peer session entity receives and decodes the session protocol unit, the session entity issues the appropriate primitive indication (again via the Presentation Layer) to inform its application entity of the arrival of the cue.

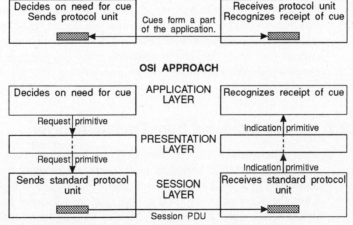

Figure 11.1   Transmission of cues by Session Layer

Standard cues   The Session Layer provides primitives corresponding to several different types of cue (roughly corresponding to the ones just described informally). Each primitive comes in request/indication pairs and some also have response/confirm forms (i.e. confirmed dialogues) as well. Each type of primitive is associated with rules (etiquette) about the order in which the primitives can be issued; e.g. data cannot be sent without first starting an activity, or, once the "turn to send" has been passed to the other entity, data cannot be sent until you get the turn back, etc.

The Session Layer attaches no ultimate meaning to the primitives; that is the job of the Application Layer. However, the Session Layer does enforce the rules about the ordering of primitives.

11.2.1 Service Provided to Presentation Layer

The Session Layer provides services to establish a session connection between two presentation entities, and supports orderly data exchange.

Connection   A session connection is created when requested by a presentation entity at a Session Service Access Point (SSAP). During the lifetime of the session connection, session services are used by the presentation entities to regulate their dialogue, and to ensure an orderly message exchange on the session connection. The session connection exists until it is released by either the presentation entities or the session entities.

A presentation entity can access another presentation entity only by initiating or accepting a session connection. Each presentation connection is mapped to one session connection. Both concurrent and consecutive session connections are possible between two presentation entities.

Addresses   The initiating presentation entity designates the destination presentation entity by a session address. In many systems, a transport address may be used as the session address; i.e. there is a one to one correspondence between the session address and the transport address. In general, however, there is a many to one correspondence between the session address and transport address. This does not imply multiplexing of session connections onto transport connections, but does imply that at session connection time more than one presentation entity is a potential target of a session connection establishment request arriving on a given transport connection.

11.2.2 Service Expected from Transport Layer

Most of the machinery in the Transport Layer faces downwards. It is there to deal with problems arising in lower layers (e.g. network resets, lost or duplicated data, etc.) and to present a simple interface to higher layers. Thus the services of the Transport Layer are relatively few, but the functions are many and complex. Most of the machinery is invisible to the layers above.

Many of the different types of Transport Protocol Data Unit (TPDU) and the fields within them are not directly related to the transport primitives; e.g. the Acknowledgement and Reject TPDUs and the connection reference, credit and sequence number fields. They are just part of "the machinery in the basement", working away unseen.

The Session Layer sits back to back with the Transport Layer. The only things that the two layers can say to one another are:

- Open a connection.

- Close a connection.

- Here is data.

- Here is expedited data.

11.2.3 The Connection Oriented Session Layer

Most of the machinery in the Session Layer faces upwards. This layer takes the simple interface provided by the Transport Layer and provides a richer set of facilities to the higher levels. The facilities consist almost entirely of communicating the "cues", or control signals, between session service users and policing the associated rules on the use of session primitives. Thus, the functions of the Session Layer are simple, but the services are many and apparently complex.

By contrast, nearly all of the Session Protocol Data Units (SPDUs) are directly related to particular session primitives, and the fields in the SPDUs are related to the parameters of those primitives. In fact, the SPDUs really are just primitives, suitably wrapped up and labeled for transmission through the network.

The session service has a total of 58 primitives, in 21 groups. Most of these groups represent a particular type of cue, or control message exchanged between Session Service (SS) users. Of these groups:

- ten involve request/indication pairs (i.e. unconfirmed dialogues);

- nine involve request/indication and response/confirm pairs (i.e. confirmed dialogues, two of which have both accept and reject forms of response/confirm); and,

- two involve indications only (for error reporting by the service provider).

The session protocol defines 36 different SPDUs.

11.3 THE SESSION LAYER SERVICES

11.3.1 Overview

The following services broadly correspond to the similar services in the Transport Layer:

- session connection establishment;

- orderly connection release and abort; and,

- data exchange: normal, expedited, typed and capability data.

Note that the release service allows presentation entities to negotiate orderly connection release without loss of data, and there are four forms of data. The specialized services provided by the Session Layer are:

- interaction management;

- session connection synchronization;

- activity management; and,

- exception reporting.

Turn control   Interaction management allows presentation entities to control explicitly whose turn it is to exercise certain control functions. It provides for voluntary exchange of the turn. The following types of interaction are permitted:

- two way simultaneous (i.e. full duplex);

- two way alternate (i.e. half duplex); and,

- one way (i.e. simplex).

Synchroniza-   The synchronization service allows presentation entities to:
tion

- define and identify synchronization points that are serially numbered markers inserted in the data flow; and,

- reset the connection to a defined state and agree on a resynchronization point.

Activities   A means is provided for presentation entities to start, end, interrupt, resume or discard a defined piece of work called an *activity*. This provides a way to:

- identify a new activity and commence synchronization; and,

- identify a previously interrupted activity and resume it.

Exceptions   This permits the presentation entities to be notified of exception situations not covered by other services.

11.3.2 Functions

Connections   At any one time, there is a one to one mapping of a session connection onto a transport connection; i.e. there is no multiplexing of session connections onto transport connections. The Session Layer will normally create a new transport connection for each new session connection attempt, but it may reuse an existing transport connection if a suitable one is currently idle.

Data transfer   Data transfer may involve segmentation of user data if the session entities agree to the use of a maximum Transport Service Data Unit (TSDU) size. There is no specific flow control mechanism in the Session Layer. Since session connections are not multiplexed onto transport connections, the transport back pressure flow control mechanism is used.

Expedited data   The transfer of expedited data units is accomplished using the expedited transport service.

Disconnection   The Session Layer contains the functions necessary to release the session connection in an orderly way, without loss of data, upon request by the presentation entities. The Session Layer also contains the necessary functions to abort the session connection with possible loss of data in error situations. The Session Layer may immediately disconnect unused transport connections or save them for reuse by subsequent session connection requests.

11.4 THE CONNECTION ORIENTED SESSION SERVICE

The session service definition is ISO 8326/CCITT X.215. Version 1 was published in 1988. Version 2 was developed during 1990 to incorporate unlimited user data and symmetric synchronization. The following description is based on Version 2. The session service primitives are listed in Table 11.1, and are described below and on subsequent pages. Not all applications require all of these services; so related services are grouped together into *functional units* to facilitate the selection of services during session connection establishment. The functional units defined for Version 2 are listed in Table 11.2.

A number of subsets were defined in Version 1 of the standard although this has not been retained in Version 2. For the record, the Version 1 subsets are:

Table 11.1   Session service primitives

SERVICE	PRIMITIVE	DIALOGUE
Connection establishment	S-Connect	Confirmed +/–
Normal data transfer	S-Data	Unconfirmed
Expedited data transfer	S-Expedited Data	Unconfirmed
Typed data transfer	S-Typed Data	Unconfirmed
Capability data exchange	S-Capability Data	Confirmed
Give tokens	S-Token Give	Unconfirmed
Please tokens	S-Token Please	Unconfirmed
Give control	S-Control Give	Unconfirmed
Minor synchronization point	S-Sync Minor	Confirmed
Major synchronization point	S-Sync Major	Confirmed
Resynchronize	S-Resynchronize	Confirmed
Provider exception report	S-P-Exception Report	Indication only
User exception report	S-U-Exception Report	Unconfirmed
Activity start	S-Activity Start	Unconfirmed
Activity resume	S-Activity Resume	Confirmed
Activity interrupt	S-Activity Interrupt	Confirmed
Activity discard	S-Activity Discard	Confirmed
Activity end	S-Activity End	Confirmed
Orderly release	S-Release	Confirmed +/–
User abort	S-U-Abort	Unconfirmed
Provider abort	S-P-Abort	Indication only

Indication only: indication primitive only
Unconfirmed: request and indication primitives
Confirmed: request, indication, response and confirm primitives
Confirmed+/–: request, indication, response and confirm primitives with accept and reject forms
of response and confirm.

Kernel   This is a minimal subset and it must be provided in all implementations.

Basic Combined   This adds support of half-duplex data exchange to the Kernel subset.

Basic Synchronized   This adds facilities for major and minor synchronization and typed data exchange to the Basic Combined subset.

Basic Activity   This adds the activity management facilities to the Basic Synchronized subset, but it removes the facilities for full duplex data exchange and synchronization.

11.4.1 General Services

Connection   S-Connect establishes a session connection. The S-Connect parameters include calling and called session addresses (from which transport addresses can be derived), a session connection identifier and the Quality of

Table 11.2   Functional units are defined logical groupings of the session services and primitives. Session entities negotiate on their use during connection establishment.

KERNEL: The kernel functional unit supports the basic services to establish a Session connection, transfer normal data, and release the connection.

NEGOTIATED RELEASE: The Session users may negotiate the orderly release of the connection. If this functional unit is selected, an attempt to release the Session connection may be refused by the accepting user.

HALF DUPLEX: The Session users may choose either the half duplex or duplex functional unit. Half duplex controls the right to send data (using the data token).

DUPLEX: This is used when the right to send data is not controlled.

EXPEDITED DATA: A limited amount of Session user data may be transferred if this functional unit is selected and if the Transport expedited flow is available.

TYPED DATA: This functional unit allows Session users to transfer (typed) data out of turn, i.e. not subject to the data token.

CAPABILITY DATA: When selected, this functional unit allows the sending of data when the activity management functional unit has been selected, but when no activity is in progress.

MINOR SYNCHRONIZE: This supports the minor synchronization service using a single serial number. Minor and symmetric synchronization cannot both be selected for the one connection.

SYMMETRIC SYNCHRONIZE: This functional unit allows the use of two independent serial numbers.

MAJOR SYNCHRONIZE: This supports the major synchronization points.

RESYNCHRONIZE: If selected, this functional unit allows the session users to modify the synchronization point number(s) and reassign tokens.

EXCEPTIONS: This allows the reporting of errors rather than aborting the session connection.

ACTIVITY MANAGEMENT: This supports the management and synchronization of logical pieces of work.

Service (QOS) parameters that will be passed down to the transport service. An important parameter is session requirements that are used to negotiate and select the functional units that will be used for the duration of the connection. Further parameters identify session service options for this connection, e.g. whether segmentation will be used or not, and, if so, the maximum TSDU size. An unlimited amount of user data may also be conveyed as a parameter of the S-Connect request primitive.

Data transfer   S-Data maps closely onto T-Data. However, T-Data may be issued at any time while a transport connection is open, whereas S-Data is subject to control by other session primitives (e.g. turn control). The length of user data is unlimited.

S-Expedited Data maps closely onto T-Expedited Data and is available only if the latter service is available. It is not subject to any S-Data flow control or to any of the other constraints on the use of S-Data (e.g. turn control). The User Data parameter of an S-Expedited Data may be 1 to 14 octets long.

Two other types of data transfer services are available, i.e. S-Typed Data and S-Capability Data. They are associated with other services and are described later.

Disconnection   S-Release provides for the orderly release of a session connection, avoiding the possible loss of data that can occur when a transport connection is released. The two session entities exchange SPDUs to ensure that the transport connection is empty before it is released. The session entity that did not initiate the release can veto the release and continue sending data with no loss.

S-U-Abort allows either session user to release instantaneously the connection without the agreement of the other. Data in transit will be lost.

S-P-Abort enables the session provider to inform the session users that the connection has been released for reasons internal to the provider, e.g. loss of transport connection. Data in transit will be lost.

Exceptions   Exception reports are provided to signal error conditions which are less severe than an abort. The S-P-Exception Report indicates an unanticipated error detected by the session service provider. An S-U-Exception Report is generated by one user to signal that it is unable to proceed unless some error condition is cleared. An exception report discards any data in transit and prevents delivery of synchronization points. Exception reports are cleared by:

- resynchronization;

- abort;

- activity interrupt or discard; and,

- give the data token.

The other session services are specialized facilities enabling the session users to structure the dialogue on the connection.

11.4.2 Tokens

The transport service is completely symmetric. Once a connection has been opened, either Transport entity may send data, send expedited data or release the connection. The entities may request these services simultaneously.

It is appropriate for the transport service to be structured symmetrically, since it is used by all applications. However, individual applications may not structure their dialogues so symmetrically. The session service therefore provides facilities for applications to introduce asymmetry into their dialogues deliberately. This is done means of tokens.

Tokens

A *token* is an abstract object. At any particular time, it is held by one of the SS-users, giving that user the right to use specific groups of session services. The other SS-user cannot use those services until the SS-user holding the token gives it the token. The SS-user without the token can ask for it, but may not seize it unilaterally. At session connection time, the SS-users negotiate on whether token control is to be used for specific groups of services, and if so, who is to be the initial holder. There are four tokens:

Data This is the formal mechanism for the facility previously described for controlling which SS-user has the turn to send data when the application uses the connection in a half-duplex (two way alternate) mode. It is only available if the half duplex functional unit was successfully negotiated at S-Connect time. Otherwise the connection operates in full duplex (two way simultaneous) mode and the token is not available. Possession of this token mainly affects the use of the S-Data request primitive, but not the use of the S-Expedited Data request, or S-Typed Data request.

Release This token controls which SS-user currently has the right to issue an S-Release request. It is only available if the negotiated release functional unit was successfully negotiated at S-Connect time. Otherwise both SS-users have the right to issue S-Release and the token is not available. This token does not affect the use of S-U-Abort request.

Synchronize Minor This token controls which SS-user currently has the right to issue an S-Sync Minor request (see below). It is only available if the minor synchronize functional unit was successfully negotiated at S-Connect time. If neither the minor synchronize nor symmetric synchronize functional units was selected, then neither SS-user can use S-Sync Minor and the token is not available. If the symmetric synchronize functional unit is being used, then both SS-users can use S-Sync Minor requests and the token is not available.

Major/ Activity This token controls which SS-user currently has the right to issue either an S-Sync Major or any of the S-Activity requests (see below). It is only available if either the major synchronize or the activity management functional unit, or both, were successfully negotiated at S-Connect time. If neither was negotiated then the token is not available.

There are three primitives associated with the use of the tokens. Figure 11.2 illustrates their use as described below.

Surrender tokens

S-Token Give request/indication allows the SS-user currently holding a token or tokens to surrender any combination of those tokens to the other SS-user. These primitives have two parameters: Tokens, specifying the particular combination of tokens to be given; and SS-User Data, an unlimited amount of user data.

Request tokens

S-Token Please request/indication allows the SS-user currently not holding a token or tokens to request a particular combination of tokens from the other SS-user. If the other SS-user is prepared to surrender the tokens, it must use S-Token Give to do so. S-Token Please has two parameters: Tokens, specifying the combination of tokens requested; and SS-User Data, which may be used to convey some sort of reason for the request.

Out of turn data

S-Typed Data request/indication operates almost identically to S-Data in that it allows an SS-user to send a data unit of unlimited size subject to normal flow control. However, it is not subject to token restrictions. S-Typed Data has one parameter: SS-User Data. The major use of this service is to carry protocol information for higher layers, rather than to carry application user data. It is therefore likely to have a predefined format or type, hence the name of this service. Note, however, that the format of the data is irrelevant to the session service.

One further primitive that affects tokens is S-Control Give which allows an SS-user to surrender the entire set of available tokens. This primitive is classed as part of the activity management function (see below).

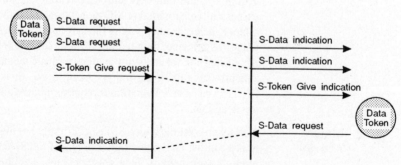

Figure 11.2   Use of session tokens to control the turn

11.4.3 Minor and Major Synchronization

In the transport service, the streams of data transmitted have no structure beyond being divided into TSDUs. Many applications need to be able to insert *markers* into the data stream to indicate significant points; e.g. a remote job entry system might need to mark the end of one job description and the start of the next. In some cases, it is enough for the sender to be able to place a marker in the data stream and then carry on sending data without waiting for confirmation, e.g. a remote job entry system. In other cases, the sender must pause and wait for an Application Layer acknowledgement before doing anything else. For example, the sender may be transmitting requests for updates to a remote database. Since a wide range of things can go wrong, the sender must retain responsibility for a given group of updates until the remote database confirms that the updates have been successfully committed.

Synchronization points   The general process of marking a data stream is termed *synchronization*. Since applications vary in just how rigidly they need to synchronize, two forms of service are provided by the Session Layer: minor and major synchronization. Any combination of minor and major synchronization services may be used on a given connection. Furthermore, there are two methods to identify a synchronization point:

- a single serial number (if the minor synchronization functional unit was selected at connection establishment); and,

- two serial numbers — one for each direction of data flow (if the symmetric synchronization functional unit was selected).

The primitives associated with synchronization are illustrated in Figure 11.3 and are described below.

S-Sync Minor normally has three parameters; Type: specifying whether or not explicit confirmation (by response/confirm primitives) is requested by the sending SS-user; Serial Number: a number in the range 0 to 999998 identifying this synchronization point; SS-User Data: unlimited length. In the case of symmetric synchronization, two Serial Number parameters are conveyed — one for each direction.

S-Sync Major is similar in form to S-Sync Minor, except that it does not carry a type parameter, since confirmation is mandatory.

The synchronization point serial numbers are maintained by the SS-provider and are allocated consecutively to successive synchronization points of either type.

Dialogue units   An S-Sync Major request must be acknowledged and most other requests, including S-Data, are forbidden until the confirmation is received. An S-Sync Minor request is optionally acknowledged and further requests, including S-Data and S-Sync Minor, are not inhibited, even though confirmation has not yet been received. One S-Sync Minor confirmation may acknowledge several outstanding requests. Major synchronization

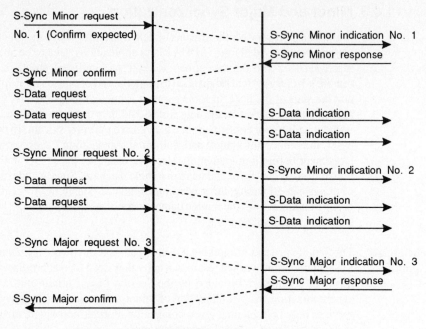

Figure 11.3   Minor and major synchronization

points divide the data stream into *dialogue units*, each of which is completely isolated from the others. Dialogue units may be further sub-divided by minor synchronization points.

The use of the S-Sync Minor request is controlled by the synchronize minor token and the use of S-Sync Major request is controlled by the major/activity token. In Version 1 of the session standards, both forms synchronize the data stream in one direction only. Version 2 adds a symmetric synchronization option that synchronizes the data streams in both directions.

11.4.4 Resynchronization

The resynchronization service permits SS-users to negotiate recovery and return to an agreed state after an error or lack of response by either the SS-user or the SS-provider, or after disagreements between the SS-users. S-Resynchronize is a confirmed service. It has the following parameters:

Type	Resynchronize type (not present in the response/confirm) indicates the type of resynchronization. Its value may be one of: abandon, restart or set (see below).
Serial Number	The synchronization point serial number(s) identifies a particular resynchronization point. The exact meaning depends on the previous parameter (see below).

Tokens   This parameter specifies the proposed placement for all available tokens following successful resynchronization.

Data   An unlimited amount of SS-user data may be carried in the primitive.

Either SS-user may issue S-Resynchronization. It is not subject to token control. Furthermore, if symmetric synchronization is being used, then resynchronization can be requested for either one or both directions. If symmetric synchronization is not being used, both directions are resynchronized simultaneously. Data in transit at the time of resynchronization is purged. The Type parameter has the following meanings:

Abandon   Abandon requests the SS-provider to resynchronize the connection to a new synchronization point whose serial number is greater than any previously used. It is used when one SS-user wants to cancel a data exchange currently in progress. For example, in a travel reservation system, the customer may be in the middle of booking a whole series of flights and then decide to cancel everything.

Restart   This is used to return to an agreed previous synchronization point, which cannot be any earlier than the last confirmed major synchronization point. It is implied that data sent since that synchronization point must be retransmitted, but that is the responsibility of the SS-users. For example, in database systems, it is usual to lock records which are being updated to prevent inconsistencies due to concurrent updates. It is possible for two concurrent sets of updates to deadlock. This can be recovered by killing one of the sets of updates, so allowing the other set to complete. The killed set of updates can then be repeated (i.e. restarted).

Reset   Reset is used to set the synchronization point serial number(s) to a new, negotiated value(s).

Note that recovery from failures must be organized by the Application Layer. S-Resynchronize is only used to enable the application entities to signal their intentions to one another.

11.4.5 Activities

Activity management is an optional service that allows SS-users to divide a data stream into activities, which are coarse grained units consisting of one or more logically related dialogue units. For example, a file transfer system might use a separate activity for each file transferred. The actual meaning of an activity is entirely the concern of the SS-users.

A key concept of activities is that they may be interrupted and then resumed later, possibly after several other activities have been completed, or even on a different session connection. The activity service is asymmetric. The right to issue activity primitives is controlled by the major/activity token. The service is illustrated in Figure 11.4 and the primitives are described below.

Activity Start   The SS-user indicates that a new activity is entered. A SS-user specified activity identifier of up to 6 octets must be supplied. The values for the synchronization point serial numbers are set to 1.

Activity End   The SS-user indicates that the current activity has ended. It also acts as a major synchronization point.

Activity Interrupt   The SS-user indicates that the current activity is interrupted. Work achieved before the interruption is not canceled and may be resumed later. A reason code may be given. Data in transit may be lost.

Activity Resume   The SS-user indicates that a previously interrupted activity is to be resumed. The activity identifier of the session to be resumed must be given and so must the session connection identifier if the session was on a different connection. The serial numbers are also set to values supplied by the SS-user.

Activity Discard   The SS-user indicates that the current activity is to be abnormally terminated. A reason code may be given. Data in transit may be lost.

Capability Data   The SS-users may exchange an unlimited amount of SS-user data, while no activity is in progress. It would

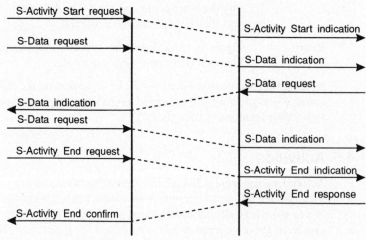

Figure 11.4   A session activity

normally be used to enable SS-users to exchange protocol information concerning their own capabilities before starting up a specific activity. It is subject to control by the data, synchronize minor and major/activity tokens.

Control Give   The SS-user surrenders the entire set of available tokens. It may only be used when no activity is in progress. It is subject to control by the data, synchronize minor and major/activity tokens.

During an activity, minor and major synchronization, and resynchronization services may also be used to co-ordinate the dialogues.

11.5 THE SESSION PROTOCOL

The Session Protocol Specification is ISO 8327/CCITT X.225. The following description is based on Version 2.

SPDU

The most striking thing about the *Session Protocol Data Units (SPDUs)* is their large number compared to protocols in other layers. However, this merely reflects the relatively large number of session service primitives. In most cases, the purpose of an SPDU is to convey the meaning of a session primitive across the connection. The SPDUs are listed in Table 11.3.

There is one SPDU type for each of the primitive request/indication pairs in the session service. Where services are confirmed, there is another SPDU type for the primitive response/confirm pairs. For two primitives, S-Connect and S-Release, there are two SPDUs associated with the response/confirm pairs, one signifying acceptance and the other rejection.

In the connection phase, two additional SPDUs are used to support unlimited data in S-Connect request primitives.

The primitives S-U-Abort and S-P-Abort share the same Abort SPDU, but there is also an Abort Accept SPDU used for internal acknowledgement within the session provider, even though the session service is an unconfirmed one. Similarly, for the S-Control Give service, there is a Give Tokens Ack SPDU for internal confirmation, even though the service is an unconfirmed one.

Prepare SPDU

One further SPDU, Prepare SPDU, is used only when the transport expedited data service is available. It is sent as a warning when the sending session entity is about to send one of the following SPDUs on the normal data service: Resynchronize SPDU, Resynchronize Ack SPDU, Major Ack SPDU, Activity Interrupt SPDU, Activity Interrupt Ack SPDU, Activity Discard SPDU, Activity Discard Ack SPDU, Activity End Ack SPDU. It is particularly useful if the normal data service is blocked by transport level flow control, since in some cases the receiving session entity can then discard Data Transfer SPDUs until the associated control SPDU emerges from the transport connection.

The following SPDUs can only be sent on the transport expedited data service: Expedited Data SPDU, Prepare SPDU.

The following SPDUs are sent on the transport expedited data service if it is available; otherwise they are sent on the transport normal data service: Abort SPDU, Abort Accept SPDU.

All other SPDUs are sent on the transport normal data service.

Table 11.3   Session Protocol Data Units (SPDUs)

SERVICE	SPDU	SI CODE (Decimal)	CATEGORY
Connection establishment	Connect	13	1
	Overflow Accept	16	1
	Connect Data Overflow	15	1
	Accept	14	1
	Refuse	12	1
Data transfer	Normal Data	1	2
	Expedited Data	5	1
	Typed Data	33	1
	Capability Data	61	2
	Capability Data Ack	62	2
Tokens	Give Tokens	1	0
	Please Tokens	2	0
	Give Tokens Confirm	21	1
	Give Tokens Ack	22	1
Synchronization	Minor Sync Point	49	2
	Minor Sync Ack	50	2
	Major Sync Point	41	2
	Major Sync Ack	42	2
	Resynchronize	53	2
	Resynchronize Ack	34	2
	Prepare	7	1
Provider exception report	Exception Report	0	2
User exception report	Exception Data	48	2
Activity management	Activity Start	45	2
	Activity Resume	29	2
	Activity Interrupt	25	2
	Activity Interrupt Ack	26	2
	Activity Discard	57	2
	Activity Discard Ack	58	2
	Activity End	41	2
	Activity End Ack	42	2
Orderly release	Finish	9	1
	Disconnect	10	1
	Not Finished	8	1
User and provider aborts	Abort	25	1
	Abort Accept	26	1

Concatenation   The session protocol makes extensive use of concatenation. In fact, certain SPDUs (e.g. Data) are always accompanied by token control SPDUs (e.g. Give Tokens or Please Tokens) for transfer over a transport connection. The concatenation rules are complex and they allow considerable flexibility in the implementation of the protocol. In brief, each SPDU belongs to one of the following categories:

Category 0   Give Tokens and Please Tokens SPDUs may be either transferred singly in one TSDU or they may be concatenated with one or more category 2 SPDUs.

Category 1   The category 1 SPDUs listed in Table 11.3 are always transferred singly in one TSDU.

Category 2   The remaining SPDUs are never mapped one to one onto a TSDU and are always concatenated with a category 0 SPDU.

11.5.1 Formats of Session Protocol Data Units

There are 36 types of SPDU, each of which may have several different parameters. SPDUs are mostly generated as a result of a primitive request or response and the parameters of the SPDU correspond to the parameters of the primitive.

The general format of an SPDU is illustrated in Figure 11.5. The SPDU fields are:

SI   SPDU Identifier: a 1 octet field indicating the type of this SPDU. Values are listed in Table 11.3. Some SPDUs have the same identifier code — the ambiguity is resolved by the concatenation rules.

LI   Length Indicator. Specifies the total length of the following parameters. This length does not include the SI, LI itself, or the user information field. A value of 0 means that there are no parameters. For lengths in the range 0 to 254, LI is encoded in 1 octet. For lengths in the range

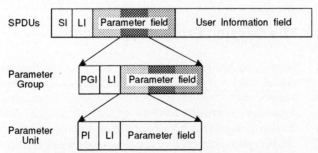

Figure 11.5   Illustration of the nested structure and formats of SPDUs, parameter groups and parameter units

	255 to 65,535, LI is encoded in 3 octets, the first of which has the binary value 1111 1111 and the other two being the length in binary.
Parameters	The Parameter field contains zero or more parameters (PI units) concatenated. For each SPDU type, some parameters are mandatory and others are non-mandatory. Each parameter carries a Parameter Identifier (PI) to identify it, since parameters cannot be identified by their position in the SPDU. In some cases, a group of parameters may be nested within a parameter group (PGI unit), whose overall format is the same as that of a parameter. A parameter group is identified by a Parameter Group Identifier (PGI).
User Information	The User Information field is present if permitted for this SPDU type, and SS-user data was supplied in the associated session primitive. It consists of 1 or more octets of data. There is no length specifier for this field, since the total length of the SPDU can be deduced from the length of the TSDU that conveyed it and the lengths of all other fields in the SPDU are known.

In some cases, SPDUs are mapped one to one onto TSDUs. In other cases, several SPDUs may be concatenated onto a single TSDU. There are complex rules concerning permissible concatenations of SPDUs and the order in which they must be processed by the receiving session entity. Each parameter (PI unit or PGI unit) has the following format:

PI	Parameter Identifier: a 1 octet field identifying this parameter type.
LI	Length Indicator: the length of this parameter, encoded the same way as the LI field for the SPDU as a whole (see above).
Value	Parameter field: 1 or more octets of parameter data. In the case of a PGI unit, this field contains nested parameters.

11.5.2 The Session Protocol Machine

Connection mapping	Session connection establishment allows some flexibility that is not available in lower layers as shown in Figure 11.6. Session connections are mapped one to one onto transport connections. Normally, a new transport connection is created for each session connection. However, when a session connection is released, the session entity may optionally retain the old transport connection in anticipation of future traffic. A later session connection can then reuse the old transport connection to avoid the transport establishment delay. Another feature allows an activity to span

multiple connections. If an activity is interrupted, and the session and transport connections are released, the activity may be resumed some time later on new connections. Transport connection reuse is an option in the standard which is not yet widely implemented.

Primitives and SPDUs

Once the connection is established, most of the actions of the Session Layer are as follows. When an SS-user issues a request primitive, the session entity formats up the associated SPDU and sends it using a T-Data request. When the peer session entity receives the SPDU via a T-Data indication, it decodes the SPDU and issues the associated indication primitive. If the primitive was for a confirmed service, then the above process is repeated in the reverse direction for the response/confirm primitives.

The session service enforces certain rules about the sequence in which primitives may be issued. Purely from the point of view of the session layer, these rules appear almost arbitrary. However, they are designed to

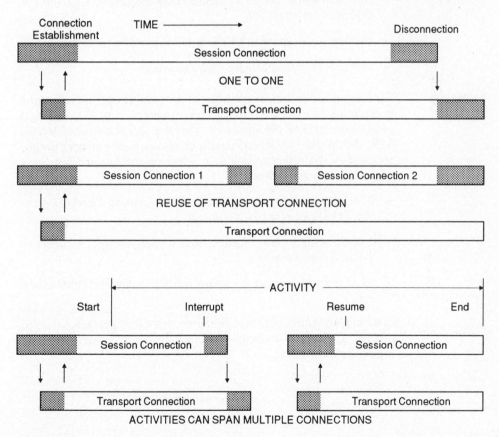

Figure 11.6 Session connection mapping

provide exactly the sort of services that applications need in practice. Because of the important, generalized role of Session Layer dialogue control to the Application Layer, and some requirements inherited from an earlier CCITT session protocol (Recommendation T.62), the session protocol is quite complicated. To highlight this sophistication (and complexity) the following data is provided.

Session protocol machine

Each session entity can be regarded as a Session Protocol Machine (SPM) (a specific sort of finite state machine). At any particular time, the SPM is in one of 32 different states, the actual state being dependent on the past sequence of primitives. Eighty different sorts of incoming event are defined:

- 32 of them correspond to the SS-user invoking different session service request or response primitives.

- 3 of them correspond to the transport service issuing T-Connect or T-Disconnect primitives.

- 44 of them correspond to SPDUs arriving from the peer session entity.

- 1 of them corresponds to the expiry of a timer.

State table

For each of the 32 states, a state table defines whether each of the 80 input events is legal for that state or illegal (i.e. a protocol error). For each legal combination of state and input event, the table specifies what action the SPM should take. An action consists of zero or more outgoing events, followed by a transition to a new state (which may be the same as before). There are 80 outgoing events:

- 32 of them correspond to the session service invoking different session service indication or confirm primitives.

- 3 of them correspond to the session service issuing T-Connect or T-Disconnect primitives.

- 43 of them correspond to sending SPDUs to the peer SPM/session entity.

The complete behaviour of session entities, hence the rules on the allowed order of primitives, is defined by state tables in the service definition and protocol specification.

11.6 QUESTIONS

Question 11.1   What is the purpose of the Session Layer?

Question 11.2   What impact does the Session Layer have on the application that uses it?

Question 11.3   What are the session functional units and how are they organized?

Question 11.4   What session services define the bounds of an application dialogue unit?

Question 11.5   What is the difference between the typed data and capability data services?

Question 11.6   What are tokens and how are they used?

Question 11.7   What session services are related to activities?

Question 11.8   What session services convey synchronization point references?

Question 11.9   What SPDUs map onto the T-Data and the T-Expedited Data services?

12 Presentation Layer

12.1 PURPOSE OF THE PRESENTATION LAYER

The session service allows end systems to exchange structured strings of binary digits (bits), particularly through the SS-User Data parameter of the S-Data request and indication primitives. However, there are an infinite number of different ways of encoding information onto strings of bits, and the communicating end systems may naturally use different, machine dependent encoding schemes for their internal representation of information. While not all applications will share a common method of representing information, in order to communicate they must agree about the subject matter of their communication, the meaning (semantics) of the information, and the data values of the information exchanged.

The purpose of the Presentation Layer is to negotiate and support a common representation of the information transferred in order to preserve its meaning. Making the Presentation Layer responsible for data representation has the following consequences:

- The data and Protocol Control Information (PCI) of application entities can be specified independently of their concrete representation (encoding).

- For each presentation connection, the presentation entities select compatible data representations to support information transfer. Different representations may be chosen in different circumstances.

- The common representation may or may not be the same as the internal encoding scheme used in either end system. Hence, the Presentation Layer may need to transform data representations in end systems.

There are two common reasons why the data representations may differ:

- natural syntax differences within end systems; and,

- the need to improve transmission or security.

Syntax differences
The natural data representations of the computers implementing the end systems may be different:

- Different word sizes; e.g. 16, 32, 36 or 60 bits.

- different character codes, e.g. ASCII and EBCDIC;

- different number representations, e.g. binary or binary coded decimal, sign and modulus or ones-complement or twos-complement;

- different ordering of bytes within words;

- different alignment rules for word sized data units on byte addressed machines; or,

- different formats or syntaxes for representing complex data objects.

Transmission It may also be appropriate to use a different encoding of data during transmission, irrespective of whether or not the two end systems use the same data representations. For example:

- Data compression may be used to reduce the volume of bits transmitted.

- The bit stream may be encrypted for improved security.

To illustrate the variability between different systems, alternative machine dependent encoding schemes for the number 345 are shown in Table 12.1. Any of the octet strings shown in the table could be used to transmit the value and they all have the same meaning provided that the sender and receiver are using the same scheme.

12.1.1 Syntax

The data exchanged between OSI applications may be quite complex. For example, the X.400 standards for message handling define separate data structures for:

- the envelope;

- alternate message headings depending on the message type;

Table 12.1 How the number 345 could be transmitted as a sequence of octets

ENCODING SCHEME	Low Address ⟶ High Address				
16 bit binary, most significant octet first, e.g. Motorola 68000	0000	0001	0101	1001	
16 bit binary, least significant octet first, e.g. Intel 8086	0101	1001	0000	0001	
Packed binary coded decimal, e.g. IBM System 370	0000	0011	0100	0101	
ASCII character set, mini- and micro-computers	0011	0011	0011	0100	0011	0101
EBCDIC character set, mainframe computers	1111	0011	1111	0100	1111	0101

- different content types, e.g. text, image, EDI (Electronic Data Interchange) etc; and,

- X.400 protocol control information which is a data structure representing the action to be performed on a message, or to ensure its reliable delivery.

Instances of these data structures will be present together in various combinations in the User Data parameters of presentation primitives. To provide a general solution for the representation of such arbitrary data structures, the Presentation Layer introduces the concepts of:

Abstract syntax	A high level description of data types and structures.
Transfer syntax	The bit-wise representation used in the transfer of data between systems.
Context management	The orderly identification and control of multiple syntaxes on a connection.

Syntax refers to the representation of the information exchanged. Three aspects to syntax are:

- The structure of the data. Very few universes of discourse consist of a single elementary data item. Most applications will exchange composite data, either arrays (in which the constituent items all have the same type), or records (in which the constituent items have different types).

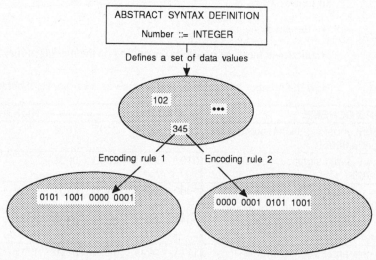

Figure 12.1   An example of an abstract syntax and two alternative encoding rules

- The types of the constituent data items, i.e. whether the data items are integers, strings of characters, booleans, etc, or whether they are themselves composite data.

- Encoding rules, i.e. how the structures and the elementary items are represented as strings of bits.

A syntax definition specifies a set of data values and their structure (see Figure 12.1).

12.1.2 Operation of the Presentation Layer

The operation of the Presentation Layer can be viewed at two levels:

- At a high level of abstraction, the standards for the Application entities deal only with abstract syntaxes and the Presentation Layer deals with data representation. Figure 12.2 illustrates this point of view which corresponds to that of the authors of the OSI standards.

- At a more detailed level, the software that realizes the application and presentation entities must also deal with the local data representations used on each end system. Figure 12.3 illustrates the view of the interaction between the Presentation and Application Layer software as seen by a software developer.

The terms used in the figures are elaborated below:

Abstract syntax   An abstract syntax is a specification of Application Layer data and PCI by a notation that is independent of the encoding used to represent them. It refers to the generic structure of the data and the types of the constituent data items, but without regard to the bit level encoding. An example of an abstract syntax is the data description in a program written in Pascal or a similar high level lan-

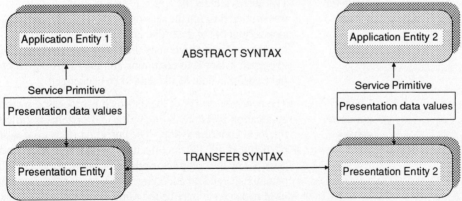

Figure 12.2   Syntaxes in Presentation and Application layer standards. The abstract syntaxes of data exchanged are the same to all entities.

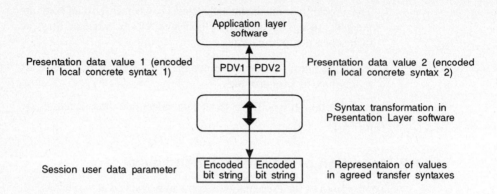

Figure 12.3   Syntax transformation is an internal function of the Presentation Layer.

guage. Abstract Syntax Notation One (ASN.1) is used to specify abstract syntaxes used by the OSI standards. The abstract syntax of data must be preserved as the data is transported from application to application.

Presentation data value   A value from an abstract syntax is called a Presentation Data Value (PDV). This is the unit of information which is transferred by the Presentation Layer. The value is serialised by the Presentation Layer according to agreed encoding rules for transmission. The User Data parameters of presentation primitives contain one or more PDVs, and their order is preserved after transfer.

Concrete syntax   A concrete syntax is a specific representation of data from an abstract syntax by the application of a set of encoding rules. The concrete syntax of a data item specifies the actual bit format of the data.

Transfer syntax   Transfer syntax is the concrete syntax of the data as it is transmitted through the session service; i.e. the transmission format of the data. The task of the transfer syntax is to represent unambiguously the PDVs as bit strings. For two open systems to communicate, they must agree on the transfer syntax of the data to be exchanged.

Local concrete syntax   The concrete syntax of the data as it is processed by the application software in one of the end systems is called the local concrete syntax. The encoding rules used will be dictated by the architecture of the computer and possibly by the compiler used for the application, i.e. the machine dependent encoding. The local concrete syntax used in a system may be the same as the transfer syntax or it may be different.

Syntax is the concern of both the Presentation and Application layers. The abstract syntax is preserved across the peer application and presentation entities. The Presentation Layer provides for a common representation (i.e. transfer syntax) to be used over a connection between application entities. This relieves application entities of any concern with the problem of the common representation of information; i.e. it provides them with transfer syntax independence.

Internally, the software which realizes the application entities can use any local concrete syntax and the presentation entities provide the transformation between these syntaxes and the common transfer syntax needed for communication between application entities. This transformation is performed inside the open systems. It is not seen by other open systems and therefore has no impact on the standardization of presentation protocols.

12.2 PRESENTATION LAYER SERVICES AND FUNCTIONS

To fulfil the above-mentioned purpose, the Presentation Layer builds on the services of the Session Layer in order to provide additional services concerned with the negotiation and selection of syntaxes. In fact, although the presentation service definition is quite complex, the incremental difference from the session service definition is small.

12.2.1 Services

Session services   All the services of the Session Layer for structuring dialogues are passed through the Presentation Layer unchanged. There are P-primitives for these services, since layer jumping is not permitted in the reference model, but their function is identical to the corresponding S-primitives.

Syntax selection   The externally visible services added by the Presentation Layer are summarized below.

Syntax selection   In order for the Presentation Layer to select an appropriate transfer syntax, it must know the abstract syntax of the data to be transferred. The Application Layer must therefore inform the Presentation Layer beforehand by selecting the appropriate syntaxes using parameters of presentation primitives provided for that purpose. Negotiation of syntax occurs at two levels:

- Before an application can transfer PDVs, it proposes to the Presentation Layer the name of the **abstract syntaxes** of the data to be transferred. Syntax selection is a confirmed service and the target application must also accept the use of the proposed syntaxes.

- During the above negotiation, the two presentation entities will also negotiate on behalf of the application entities to choose suitable **transfer syntaxes**. For each abstract syntax, a transfer syntax is selected to be used as a common encoding for data values associated with that abstract syntax.

Presentation context
The combination of an abstract syntax and the associated transfer syntax is called a *presentation context*. A presentation context represents a specific use of an abstract syntax. Several presentation contexts may be in use on one presentation connection. Presentation contexts can be re-negotiated during the course of connection (if the context management functional unit is selected).

DCS
A presentation connection can have more than one presentation context. Multiple contexts arise when a single application entity comprises several components (called *Application Service Elements, ASEs*) — each using different abstract syntaxes. The list of currently selected presentation contexts is called a *Defined Context Set (DCS)*.

Default context
One context which is always available to the presentation entities is the *default context*. If the DCS is null, then the Presentation and Application layers use the default context. The default context is also used for expedited data units. It is either fixed by some prior arrangement between the end systems or is selected at connection establishment. An example of the use of the default context is access to a remote database where the abstract syntaxes are unknown at connection establishment time and will depend on subsequent activity on the database. The peer presentation entities will assume a mutually understood default context, say IA5/ISO 646 (i.e. ASCII), until the DCS is defined. The default context is also used after errors to signal failures (e.g. in Abort primitives).

12.2.2 Establishing a Presentation Context

To illustrate context negotiation, suppose two end systems have available a range of presentation context types; i.e. they are aware of a number of abstract syntaxes, and they have transformations that can support specific transfer syntaxes for each abstract syntax. Figure 12.4 shows the sequence of steps involved in the establishment of a presentation connection as follows:

- One application entity initiates the process by requesting a presentation connection (using a called and calling presentation address, see page 36), specifying by name, one or more presentation contexts.

- The presentation entity checks that it knows of (i.e. it can support) the named contexts and that it has associated with each (i.e. it can support) the requested transfer syntaxes. Each association of a particular abstract syntax with a particular transfer syntax represents a proposed context. The connection request will be rejected if the supported proposed context list is empty, i.e. if none of the named abstract syntaxes are known or no associated transfer syntaxes are available.

- The initiating presentation entity then establishes a session connection and, using the presentation protocol, offers the proposed context list.

- The responding presentation entity checks each item in the proposed context list and rejects the item if it cannot support either the named abstract syntax or the associated transfer syntax. If none of the proposed contexts are supported, then the connection is rejected; otherwise the presentation entity invokes its application entity, informing it of the proposed connection and the list of acceptable presentation contexts.

- The responding application entity checks the proposed context list and rejects any items for which it cannot support the proposed abstract syntax. The updated list of acceptable contexts is returned to the presentation entity.

- Using the presentation protocol, the responding presentation entity returns the updated proposed context list to the initiating presentation entity. For each abstract syntax, the first acceptable transfer syntax will be the one used for the connection.

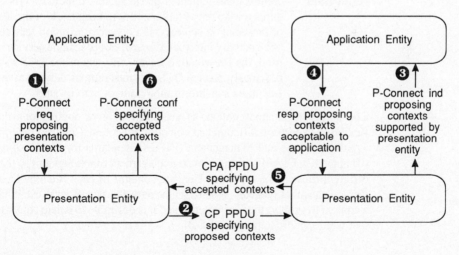

Figure 12.4   Establishing a presentation context

- The initiating application entity is informed that the presentation connection is established and which contexts are in operation. The presentation connection is now open.

Note how the application entities are concerned only with abstract syntaxes. It is the presentation entities that negotiate on transfer syntaxes. In addition to the selection of presentation contexts at connection establishment, similar procedures can be optionally used during the data transfer phase to alter the presentation contexts.

12.2.3 Functional Units

All of the session functional units are used in the Presentation Layer standards to identify the presentation user requirements during presentation and session connection establishment. Three additional functional units identify the user requirements for syntax selection and negotiation at different stages of a presentation connection:

Kernel
The kernel functional unit must be included in all implementations of the presentation standards. It provides the necessary procedures for syntax negotiation by application entities to select the DCS during connection establishment.

Context management
Context management is an optional functional unit. It provides for the alteration of contexts by the application entities during the data transfer phase. Contexts may be added to and deleted from the DCS.

Context restoration
Context restoration is optional and is available only if context management is also available. It includes procedures for the presentation entity to keep track of the use of presentation contexts. If a resynchronization service, or an activity interrupt, discard, end or resume service is used, the Presentation Layer will restore the DCS to a previously defined DCS, i.e. the contexts defined at the last major synchronization point or activity start.

The ability to change contexts is necessary to give applications the flexibility to perform different tasks on one connection. Consider the File Transfer, Access and Management (FTAM) standards for file handling (Chapter 17). FTAM uses the context management functional unit so that different files can be accessed. The data contents of each file may have different abstract syntaxes. When opening a file it is necessary to establish a context to support the file contents, and it is desirable to delete contexts that were specific to previous files.

12.2.4 Functions

The internal functions of the Presentation Layer include transformation of syntax and connection mapping:

- In each end system, the Presentation Layer performs any necessary transformations between the local concrete syntax and the transfer syntax. Transformation is an internal, system dependent function of the Presentation Layer and is not subject to standardization. An application entity simply requests an information transfer to its peer entity. As a part of the serialization that takes place in the Presentation Layer, each data value that is transferred is tagged with the identity of its associated presentation context. The tag is necessary for the receiving system to identify the context of each bit string in order to decode the value, and pass it to the destination application.

- Presentation connections are mapped one for one onto session connections. There is no multiplexing nor splitting. Therefore, the Presentation Layer must establish a suitable session connection to support a presentation connection. It must also release the session connection when the presentation connection is released.

Transforming syntax

An important issue in the Presentation Layer is the transformation of the concrete syntax of data whilst preserving its abstract syntax. This involves transforming one string of bits into another according to suitable rules. It is not appropriate in international standards to refer to any specific implementation of this process, but in the immediate future the most likely mechanism will be software, with possible hardware assistance in specific areas such as encryption.

The critical issue is: How will it be possible to define suitable rules for transforming bit strings and to implement these transformations, when the number of possible encoding rules is large and the number of abstract syntaxes is potentially infinite? Also, computers will need to exchange not just numeric and alphanumeric information, but also many other things, e.g. graphics information, digitized information (fingerprints, voice, etc), information in Chinese or Japanese writing systems, etc. There are two approaches to this:

- Define a certain number of data types and encoding rules as "international standard", implement these in the Presentation Layer and force all applications to operate in terms of these available elements. This approach is unacceptable, because it would be far too restrictive and because it would force constant revision of the standards to keep pace with new application areas.

- Regard the actual transformations and their implementations as being external to the Presentation Layer and so not subject to standardization. Then provide a standard mechanism in the Presentation Layer for allowing suitable transformations to be invoked and negotiated by name. Thus the range of transformations potentially available in an end system becomes unlimited.

The second approach is the one used in the Presentation Layer. Lest this seems like it avoids the problem, rather than solving it, consider that it is exactly the approach used in the command interpreters of interactive operating systems such as UNIX or MS-DOS. In earlier operating systems, the command interpreters had a fixed vocabulary of commands, programmed into the interpreter. It was therefore difficult to modify or enhance the available vocabulary.

In systems such as UNIX or MS-DOS, the command interpreter has very few commands built-in. When the user enters a string of characters representing a command, the interpreter checks that the command is in a legal format and is not a built-in command. It then looks in "well-known places" for an executable file with the name of the command, loads the program and runs it. Thus the vocabulary of such a system is completely open ended.

Likewise, presentation entities will have a repertoire of syntax transformations. For each abstract syntax supported in the system, a set of transformations between the local concrete syntax and one or more transfer syntaxes will be necessary. These will be invoked as required on a connection.

Presentation contexts

Conceptually, each presentation entity has available a "set of supported presentation context types". A common naming scheme is used to identify each abstract syntax and each transfer syntax uniquely by the use of Object Identifiers (OIDs). International standards have been developed to provide globally unique naming to enable end systems to identify and communicate widely about a variety of information.

For a presentation entity to support a particular presentation context, it must have available a mechanism for transforming a given data item (with known abstract syntax) between its local concrete syntax and its associated transfer syntax. One possible scenario for implementation is described below.

Define syntax

Suppose a group of organizations wishes to implement distributed processing using the OSI standards. A working party would identify the universe of discourse, specify its semantics and generate a precise description of the abstract syntax, e.g. using a notation such as ASN.1 (described in Chapter 13). The text of this formal description would then be distributed to each installation.

At each installation, there would be a manufacturer supplied utility program that would:

- understand the way in which data items would be encoded in the local concrete syntax for that system, e.g. as implemented in "native format" by the available high level language compilers;

- understand suitable standard encoding rules, such as the Basic Encoding Rules (BER) for ASN.1; and,

- when given an abstract syntax specification (e.g. in ASN.1), be able to generate a code module to transform the appropriate data items between the two different representations.

Compile code This utility would be similar to the "subschema compilers" supplied with many database management systems. The code module produced would be the physical representation of a presentation context, since it could be used by a presentation entity to support a given transfer syntax for a particular abstract syntax. Other versions of the utility would produce code to support other encoding rules, e.g. a null transformation for data transfer in the native format for that system, or a combination of the BER with encryption or data compression.

An example of the operation of a compiler for ASN.1 is illustrated in Figure 12.5. In the example:

- The abstract syntax of the Protocol Data Units (PDUs) for an application is defined in ASN.1.

- The Application Layer implementation requires data structures appropriate to the programming language and the function used; e.g. the local concrete syntax uses C language data structures for the main computational processing.

- The data transferred between the two end systems at the Presentation Layer must be in a common format. In the example, the transfer syntax is the BER of ASN.1 (see Chapter 13 for an explanation of BER).

The ASN.1 definitions of the protocol or application data structures are given as input to the compiler. The compiler then produces:

- C data structure definitions for use in the application software;

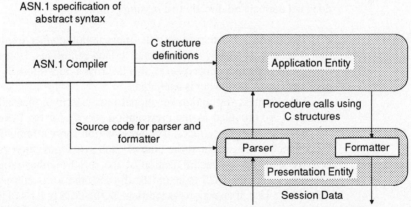

Figure 12.5   Implementation of presentation contexts by ASN.1 compiler

- C source code for formatting the C data structures submitted by the application into PDUs containing BER; and,

- C source code for parsing received PDUs containing BER into C data structures for the application.

The formatting and parsing code is then built into the Presentation Layer and the data structure definitions (as used by these formatting and parsing processes) are also used by the application. These data structures are used with the function calls representing the presentation service interface between the Presentation Layer and the Application Layer. Thus the whole process of constructing machine code with respect to its ASN.1 definitions, to perform conversion from internal data structures to Presentation Layer PDUs, is fairly automatic.

12.3 PRESENTATION SERVICE DEFINITION

The Presentation Service Definition is ISO 8822/CCITT X.216. Recent Addenda cover the connectionless service, symmetric synchronization and registration of abstract syntaxes. The primitives of the Presentation Layer (Table 12.2) map very closely onto the corresponding primitives of the Session Layer.

Connect   P-Connect is used to establish a presentation connection. It uses S-Connect to establish an underlying session connection, but in addition, a defined presentation context set, the default context and the available presentation functional units are negotiated between the two PS-users and the PS-provider.

Alter context   P-Alter Context is used after connection establishment if necessary to add or delete contexts from the DCS. The service is available if the context management functional unit is active. This primitive is the only one that does not correspond directly to a session primitive.

Abort   P-U-Abort and P-P-Abort release the presentation connection in a way that corresponds closely to the similar session primitives. However, the defined presentation context set is also destroyed, and a locally defined provider reason parameter is available.

If the context restoration functional unit is active, then additional functions are provided by the presentation service for the P-Resynchronize and P-Activity services. The presentation service remembers the DCS which was selected at the time of each synchronization point and activity start. For resynchronization, if the serial number returns to a previous value, the DCS is automatically restored to its corresponding value. Likewise, if an activity is terminated, the DCS reverts to the value at the start of the activity.

Table 12.2   Presentation Service Primitives

SERVICE	PRESENTATION PRIMITIVE	SESSION PRIMITIVE
Connection establishment	P-Connect	~ S-Connect
Alter context	P-Alter Context	—
Normal data	P-Data	= S-Data
Expedited data	P-Expedited Data	= S-Expedited Data
Typed data	P-Typed Data	= S-Typed Data
Capability data	P-Capability Data	= S-Capability Data
Give tokens	P-Token Give	= S-Token Give
Please tokens	P-Token Please	= S-Token Please
Give control	P-Control Give	= S-Control Give
Minor synchronization point	P-Sync Minor	= S-Sync Minor
Major synchronization point	P-Sync Major	= S-Sync Major
Resynchronize	P-Resynchronize	= S-Resynchronize
Provider exception	P-P-Exception Report	= S-P-Exception Report
User exception	P-U-Exception Report	= S-U-Exception Report
Activity start	P-Activity Start	= S-Activity Start
Activity resume	P-Activity Resume	= S-Activity Resume
Activity interrupt	P-Activity Interrupt	= S-Activity Interrupt
Activity discard	P-Activity Discard	= S-Activity Discard
Activity end	P-Activity End	= S-Activity End
Orderly release	P-Release	~ S-Release
User abort	P-U-Abort	~ S-U-Abort
Provider abort	P-P-Abort	~ S-P-Abort

LEGEND

= means that the presentation service is the same as the session service, apart from any transformations implied by the DCS.

~ means that the presentation service is approximately equivalent to the corresponding session service.

All other presentation primitives map exactly onto the corresponding session service primitives, with one important difference — PS-User Data parameters for these primitives refer to data transported across the presentation connection. Such data is subject to transformation according to the current DCS. This description does not imply that PS-User Data is always transformed in format at both ends of the presentation connection. During negotiations over presentation contexts, the presentation entities may determine that a null transformation is appropriate at either or both ends of the presentation connection. The latter would be the case if the communicating end systems used compatible native data representations.

12.3.1 Mode

The presentation service has two modes. This facility accommodates the original 1984 version of the X.400 messaging standard. Because the 1984 version of X.400 was prepared before the Presentation and Application layers were standardized, it assumes a "null" presentation service. The modes provided by the Presentation Layer are therefore "normal mode" and "X.410 mode". The mode is selected at connection time (by using a parameter of the P-Connect primitives). In the normal mode, the Presentation Layer performs the syntax transformation of the PDVs. In the X.410 mode, which is used only by 1984 X.400, all data contained within the PDVs is transferred untransformed between the application entities as an octet string. Thus, data in this mode is passed transparently through the Presentation Layer.

12.4 THE PRESENTATION PROTOCOL

The Connection Oriented Presentation Protocol Specification is ISO 8823/CCITT X.226. Addenda covering symmetric synchronization, registration of transfer syntaxes and protocol conformance have also been published. The connectionless presentation protocol is DIS 9576 but it is not discussed further.

PPDU

The Presentation protocol (Table 12.3) is similar in spirit to the session protocol in that each of the *Presentation Protocol Data Units (PPDUs)* is closely associated with a presentation primitive, and the fields of each PPDU are closely associated with the parameters of the corresponding primitive.

The Connect Presentation, Connect Presentation Accept and Connect Presentation Reject PPDUs are associated with the P-Connect primitives, and are concerned with negotiating the presentation DCS. They are conveyed through the session service in the SS-User Data parameter of the S-Connect primitives.

The Abnormal Release User and Abnormal Release Provider PPDUs are associated with the P-U-Abort and P-P-Abort primitives. They are conveyed through the session service in the SS-User Data parameter of the S-S-U-Abort and S-P-Abort primitives respectively.

The Alter Context and Alter Context Acknowledge PPDUs are associated with the P-Alter Context primitive and are concerned with renegotiating the DCS. They are conveyed through the session service in the SS-User Data parameter of the S-Typed Data primitives.

The Resynchronize and Resynchronize Acknowledge PPDUs are associated with the P-Resynchronize primitive. They are necessary because the synchronization procedure can influence the DCS. They are conveyed through the session service in the SS-User Data field of the S-Resychronize primitive.

The presentation Typed Data PPDU carries presentation protocol control information (PCI), as it shares the S-Typed Data primitive with the Alter Context PDUs, and the receiving presentation entity must be able to distinguish between them. The other Data PPDUs carry only

Table 12.3   Presentation Protocol Data Units (PPDUs)

PPDU	NAME OF PPDU	PURPOSE
CP	Connect Presentation	Context negotiation. Carried in session connection primitives
CPA	Connect Presentation accept	
CPR	Connect Presentation reject	
ARU	Abnormal release user	To specify context of user data in session abort primitives
ARP	Abnormal release provider	
AC	Alter context	Context management. Carried in S-Typed Data
ACA	Alter context acknowledge	
TTD	Transfer Presentation typed data	To tag context of user data in session data transfer primitives
TD	Transfer Presentation data	
TE	Transfer expedited data	
TC	Transfer capability data	
TCC	Transfer capability data acknowledge	
RS	Resynchronize	To reset context after resynchronization
RSA	Resynchronize acknowledge	

presentation protocol information concerned with the encoding of data, as they do not share their respective session primitives with any other types of PDU. They are conveyed through the session service in the SS-User Data fields of the corresponding session primitives.

12.4.1 Protocol Procedures

Basic aspects of the presentation protocol are illustrated in the sequence diagram in Figure 12.6. In order to establish a presentation connection with multiple syntaxes, the initiating presentation entity forms a Connect Presentation PPDU (CP PPDU). The Presentation Context Definition List parameter of the CP PPDU is a list of the abstract syntaxes and associated transfer syntaxes proposed for the connection. Each element of the list has three components:

- a presentation **Context Identifier** — an odd valued integer;

- an abstract syntax name (not encoded as a character string but actually encoded as a special ASN.1 data type known as an Object Identifier, OID); and,

- a list of the available transfer syntaxes for each abstract syntax (again encoded as OIDs).

The presentation entity does not wait for the establishment of a session connection before creating the CP PPDU. It passes the CP PPDU down in the user data field of the S-Connect request primitive.

    If the connection is accepted after negotiation with the remote application entity, the Connect Presentation Accept PPDU conveyed in the S-Connect confirm primitive contains a list of the selected contexts. The

Presentation Context Definition Result List parameter is a list in the same order as the proposed list containing:

- a result parameter — accepted or rejected; and,

- one of the proposed transfer syntaxes selected for encoding data values from the abstract syntax.

This completes the negotiation of a DCS for the kernel functional unit. If the context management functional unit is active, the DCS may be renegotiated, and similar negotiation procedures are used for the Alter Context PPDUs. The responding presentation entity uses even integers in the Alter Context PPDUs.

Once the DCS is selected, data transfers are "tagged" with the Presentation Context Identifier in order to allow the receiving entity to determine which syntax to use to decode the data. This applies to all user data fields — whether they are data transfer or control PPDUs.

For example, suppose an application entity issues a P-Data request with two PDVs. The presentation entity takes the information in the PS-User Data parameter and encodes it according to the current defined context set, so as to preserve its meaning, (but possibly change its representation). Each data value is effectively encapsulated with a header which includes the Presentation Context Identifier integer and a length parameter. The encoded data is then concatenated and passed as the SS-User Data parameter to an S-Data request.

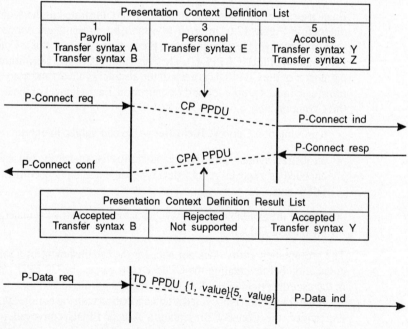

Figure 12.6   Example of presentation protocol sequence

At the receiving presentation entity, the received SS-User Data parameter from the S-Data indication primitive is decoded in order to interpret its value. The decoding scheme used depends on the Presentation Context Identifier associated with the encoded data. Finally the data is passed to the application entity as the PS-User Data parameter on a P-Data indication.

The explicit identification of the presentation context by the use of PDV lists as described above is known as fully encoded data. For flexibility, the presentation protocol also defines an alternative known as simply encoded data. Simply encoded data is interpreted as an octet string and it is passed to the presentation users as such (in the current context).

If the DCS contains only one context, or if the default context is used, then the encoding of user data can be simplified by omitting the tags.

In the presentation protocol specification, PPDUs are defined using ASN.1. So examples of the format of PPDUs are deferred until the next chapter which gives an introduction to ASN.1 (see Figure 13.2, page 233).

12.5 QUESTIONS

Question 12.1   What is the purpose of the Presentation Layer?

Question 12.2   What is the relationship between a transfer syntax and a presentation context?

Question 12.3   What parameters are passed from the Application Layer when requesting a connection of the Presentation Layer?

Question 12.4   What is a presentation address?

Question 12.5   What are the Presentation Layer's functional units?

Question 12.6   How does the resynchronization service affect the presentation context?

Question 12.7   What is a Presentation Context Definition List and how is it used during a presentation connection?

Question 12.8   What is the relationship between session services and presentation services?

Question 12.9   If new attributes and services are added to an application, how does it affect the Presentation Layer?

13 Abstract Syntax Notation One

13.1 NOTATION AND ENCODING RULES

13.1.1 Introduction

ASN.1
The techniques used to define the Protocol Data Units (PDUs) in lower layers (i.e. diagrams of the headers) are inadequate for the complex and variable data structures used in the Application Layer standards. Furthermore, it is desirable to share definitions of certain data structures between various Application Layer standards to promote reusable and modular design. So, before work could commence on the development of the application standards, a new technique had to be devised for machine independent and unambiguous definition of data types and structures. *Abstract Syntax Notation One (ASN.1)* is a formal notation for the definition of abstract syntaxes. It is a generic standard used throughout the Presentation and Application layers for the definition of PDUs and the information objects that applications use or refer to. It has an associated encoding scheme for the bit-wise representation of data transferred between systems.

ASN.1 is defined in ISO 8824/CCITT X.208. It is derived from an earlier CCITT Recommendation X.409. A new version of ASN.1 was jointly developed by ISO and CCITT to meet the CCITT deadline for publication of X.208 in 1988. The current ISO version (1990) incorporates recent extensions.

Built-in types
ASN.1 provides a way of composing a comprehensive range of structured data items whose value is derived from a number of basic data items. A range of "built-in" basic data types corresponding to most programming languages is defined in the standard, and a range of "constructor types" is used to define new types by reference to one or more other types. By implication, data items in ASN.1 carry not only a value but also a tag that identifies the type of the data item. It is also possible to give a data item a new tag that is different from other types. Thus, for example, one data item could be given a tag "destination reference number" and another the tag "source reference number". They would be of different types even though they might both be mapped onto integers.

226

BER

ASN.1 is an abstract syntax notation. It describes data but not the representation of the data. However, there is a further standard, *Basic Encoding Rules (BER)* for ASN.1, that specifies how data types in ASN.1 can be mapped onto specific sequences of bits. This standard is ISO 8825/X.209 and it has a similar history to ISO 8824/X.208. Data items encoded with these rules are represented by three components: an identifier (i.e. a tag) specifying the type of this item, a length field and a value field. Thus, the type and length of data items are explicit in the representation; i.e. the BER generate self-delimiting encodings. The transferred data can always be decoded without external rules.

One obvious option for the designers of distributed applications is to use ASN.1 for describing the abstract syntax of the data to be exchanged, and then combine this with the BER to define the transfer syntax of the data. It must be stressed that this is an option — current Presentation Layer standards do not mandate the use of ASN.1 for specifying applications or the use of the BER.

13.1.2 Chapter Contents

The purpose of this text is to impart sufficient understanding of the topic so that the reader can follow the use of ASN.1 in subsequent chapters. The reader is referred to Doug Steedman's book (listed in Appendix D) for a full tutorial or to the standards for a comprehensive definition of ASN.1.

The chapter provides an introduction to the notation and then describes the BER. The concluding section of the chapter gives a series of examples to illustrate how a value from an abstract syntax defined in ASN.1 notation is encoded according to the BER.

13.2 ABSTRACT SYNTAX NOTATION

A simplified description of ASN.1 notation is given to illustrate the main concepts. It is not intended to be definitive and some short-cuts are taken to facilitate comprehension and remove detail.

Module

When using ASN.1, a collection of data type definitions in a standard is termed a *module*. A module definition has the following form:

```
ModuleIdentifier          DEFINITIONS ::=
                          BEGIN
                                      Linkages
                                      Assignments
                          END
```

where:

Module-   Includes a textual name and, optionally, an Object Iden-
Identifier   tifier (OID), which provides an authoritative identity for

Table 13.1   Built-in ASN.1 data types

SIMPLE TYPES	
BOOLEAN	Takes a value of True or False
INTEGER	Positive and negative whole numbers including zero
ENNUMERATED	A set of values given distinct identifiers
REAL	A real value specified by three integers: a mantissa, base and exponent
BIT STRING	Ordered sequence of 0 or more bits
OCTET STRING	Ordered sequence of 0 or more octets
NULL	(indicates the absence of information)
OBJECT IDENTIFIER	An ordered list of numbers that uniquely identifies a registered information object
CHARACTER STRING AND USEFUL TYPES (11 types are defined)	
NumericString	Digits (0–9) and spaces
PrintableString	Upper case and lower case letters, digits, punctuation marks and spaces
IA5String	CCITT International Alphabet No. 5 (effectively ASCII)
GeneralizedTime and UTCTime	Represent date and time values
External	This is used within the data stream to switch to another Presentation context, e.g. switch to a data type defined by some other document or authority or syntax and possibly not defined using ASN.1.
ObjectDescriptor	Human readable text that describes an information object
CONSTRUCTOR TYPES	
SEQUENCE	Ordered sequence of items possibly of different ASN.1 types
SEQUENCE OF	Ordered sequence of items of same types
SET	A collection of tagged items in arbitrary order
SET OF	A collection of items of same type in arbitrary order
TAGGED	Item of another type
CHOICE	Item whose type is selected from several possibilities
ANY	Item whose type is any valid ASN.1 type

the module. A declaration as to whether implicit or explicit tags are used in the module may also be included (see Section 13.2.2, page 232).

Linkages   Allow this module to refer to and to use other modules by name, and, in turn, to be used by other modules. This facilitates the sharing and reuse of data type definitions between standards. The keywords EXPORT and IMPORT are associated with this part of the notation.

Assignments   Declare three aspects of the module: **types**, **values** (an instance of a type) and **macros** (a mechanism to extend ASN.1).

ASN.1 observes alphabetic case conventions to distinguish between different elements of a module. These conventions are introduced progressively. In particular, certain ASN.1 keywords are reserved and appear entirely in upper case. Some of the reserved keywords are listed Table 13.1 that shows the built-in data types. The format for rendition of ASN.1 on a printed page depends on personal style and preferences. The policy used here is a compromise between readability and space saving.

13.2.1 Types

Only the type declarations, which are the heart of ASN.1, are discussed further. The type notation can be likened to renaming. Its basic form is straightforward:

NameOfType ::=   Type

Type may be as simple as a single word (e.g. INTEGER) or a complex data definition spanning many lines with nested levels of constructed data types. By convention, the name of a defined type starts with an upper case letter. Although permitted by the standard, the definition of types whose names are all upper case is discouraged in order to distinguish them from the built-in types that are keywords in the ASN.1 standard.

Simple types   Suppose an application required access to a counter that indicated the number of items remaining to be dispensed by a vending machine. The count will be used for stock control and accounting purposes. (This is a contrived example, but it is based on a report about American researchers hooking up a vending machine to a network to avoid a wasted walk down the corridor for a can of cola!) The completed example appears in Figure 13.1 and it is progressively explained in the following sections. The status of the machine, i.e. whether it was working or non-operational, could be represented by:

Working ::=   BOOLEAN --True is OK, false is out of order

The number of items remaining could be represented by:

ItemCount ::=   INTEGER

(Text beginning with the character sequence "--" is commentary and is not part of the definition.)

13.2.2 Structured Types

Rather than define these as two separate types, ASN.1 allows the creation of composite types. For example:

```
VendingMachine ::=
          SET {
          status          BOOLEAN,
          count           INTEGER }
```

The order of items in a set is arbitrary; i.e. either the status or count values may be encoded for transmission first. Therefore, it is a requirement that the types of each component of a set are distinct. The example is satisfactory in this case because the encoding rules inherently distinguish between BOOLEAN, INTEGER and the other built-in types.

Note that the words "status" and "count" are human readable labels that are included for descriptive purposes — they do not contribute to bits on the line. Labels are always entirely lower case.

Further refinements for constructor types are the keywords OPTION-AL and DEFAULT. These allow components to be omitted if the resultant encoding is unambiguous. DEFAULT also permits the assignment of a value to an element if it is not present.

Tagged types   If the vending machine dispensed two types of products, a third component could be added. However, the following construction would be ambiguous:

```
SimpleExample    DEFINITIONS ::=                              -- Start of module

BEGIN

EXPORTS          VendingMachine
                           -- This data type may be reused in other modules
                                                          -- Imports nothing

VendingMachine ::=                              -- Start of data type assignment

          SET {                              -- An unordered collection of items

          status          BOOLEAN,                         -- False is out of order

          cola            [0] IMPLICIT INTEGER      OPTIONAL,
                                             -- This component may be omitted

          beer            [1] IMPLICIT INTEGER      OPTIONAL }
                                             -- This component may be omitted

OtherType        ::=          ...                       -- More type definitions

END
```

Figure 13.1   Example of the use of ASN.1 — data structure for vending machine

```
VendingMachine ::=
            SET {
            status          BOOLEAN,
            cola            INTEGER,
            beer            INTEGER }
```

The problem with the example is that cola and beer are not distinct types. Additional tags must be added, viz:

```
VendingMachine ::=
            SET {
            status          BOOLEAN,
            cola            [0] INTEGER,
            beer            [1] INTEGER }
```

This will cause additional octets representing the tags to be transferred in order to distinguish between the cola and beer values. In other words, the tag supplies additional information necessary to represent a multi-level data structure on a one dimensional bit string. The tag is a vital link between the abstract syntax and the transfer syntax. Effectively, the general notation for a type declaration is:

```
NameOfType ::=             [Tag] Type
```

The tag is a unique identifier that is specified by giving its class and a non-negative integer. The tag is either assigned by the ASN.1 standard or by the user of the notation. Table 13.2 lists the four classes of tags:

Universal   Universal tags are globally unique and are defined only in the ASN.1 standard. They correspond to the built-in

Table 13.2   ASN.1 notation for tagged types

CLASS	DESCRIPTION AND EXAMPLE OF NOTATION
UNIVERSAL	Generally useful, application independent, built-in types: EncryptionKey ::= **[UNIVERSAL 30]** OCTET STRING

APPLICATION	Defined within an application standard (e.g. from 1984 X.400):
	
	 CountryName ::= **[APPLICATION 1]** CHOICE {
	              NumericString,
	              PrintableString }

CONTEXT SPECIFIC	Used for distinguishing between types in a group: VendingMachine ::= SET { status BOOLEAN, cola **[0]** INTEGER, beer **[1]** INTEGER }
PRIVATE USE	For applications not covered by the standards: ProductNumber ::= **[PRIVATE 2]** INTEGER

types listed in Table 13.1. (Because each universal tag is associated with one of the reserved keywords, the tag is generally omitted from type declarations.)

Application   Application wide tags provide unique identification of a data type within an ASN.1 module. They are defined in Application Layer standards and their interpretation is specialized for a particular standard.

Context   Context specific tags are used to distinguish between
specific   different data elements in a group. Context specific tagging is typically used in SET or CHOICE types to distinguish between elements of the same type. (This was illustrated in the vending machine example.) It is used in SEQUENCE types when elements of the same type may be OPTIONAL. Different constructions in a module may use the same context specific tag to represent different types. The interpretation of such a tag is context sensitive, i.e. peculiar to a specific construction.

Private use   Private use tags are used by bilateral agreement within a given enterprise. They are reserved for applications not governed by the standards.

While tagging is necessary to make types distinct, in some cases the information contained in a tag about the underlying type is redundant. Provided that the outcome is unambiguous, the designer of an ASN.1 module may use the keyword IMPLICIT to suppress the encoding of tags. For example:

```
VendingMachine ::=
          SET {
          status      BOOLEAN,
          cola        [0] IMPLICIT INTEGER,
          beer        [1] IMPLICIT INTEGER }
```

When a data value is encoded for this example, only the tags [0] and [1] will be transmitted for the cola and beer components — the tag for INTEGER [UNIVERSAL 2] will be suppressed. An example of the effect of this construct is included in Figure 13.6 on page 239.

It is common for many of the types in a module to be implicitly tagged. In such cases, the keyword IMPLICIT (a declaration that implicit tags are used throughout the module) can be included in the heading of an ASN.1 module, and the keyword EXPLICIT can be used, if required, to force the encoding of the base type.

13.2.3 Other Features

Subtypes Subtypes are used to limit the values of an existing (parent) type. For example, a character string may be refined to reflect a particular alphabet. The general notation is:

SubType ::= ParentType   (-- subtype specification --)

Figure 13.2   ASN.1 definition of Presentation Layer PDUs

CP-PPDU ::=	SET {
	[0] IMPLICIT Mode-selector,
	[1] IMPLICIT SET {Components of RTS} OPTIONAL,
	[2] IMPLICIT SEQUENCE {
	[0] IMPLICIT Protocol-version DEFAULT {1},
	[1] IMPLICIT Calling-presentation-selector OPTIONAL,
	[2] IMPLICIT Called-presentation-selector OPTIONAL,
	[4] IMPLICIT Presentation-context-definition-list OPTIONAL,
	[6] IMPLICIT Default-context-name OPTIONAL,
	[8] IMPLICIT Presentation-requirements OPTIONAL,
	[9] IMPLICIT User-session-requirements OPTIONAL,
	User-data OPTIONAL, }
	OPTIONAL }

Presentation-context-definition-list ::= SEQUENCE OF SEQUENCE {
                  Presentation-context-identifier,
                  Abstract-syntax-name,
                  SEQUENCE OF Transfer-syntax-name }

Presentation-context-identifier ::= INTEGER

Abstract-syntax-name ::= OBJECT IDENTIFIER

Transfer-syntax-name ::= OBJECT IDENTIFIER

User-data ::=	CHOICE {
	[APPLICATION 0] IMPLICIT Simply-encoded-data,
	[APPLICATION 1] IMPLICIT Fully-encoded-data }

Simply-encoded-data ::= OCTET STRING

Fully-encoded-data ::= SEQUENCE OF PDV-list

PDV-list ::=	SEQUENCE {	
	Transfer-syntax-name	OPTIONAL,
	Presentation-context-identifier,	
	presentation-data-values CHOICE {	
	single-ASN1-type	[0] ANY,
	octet-aligned	[1] IMPLICIT OCTET STRING,
	arbitary	[2] IMPLICIT BIT STRING } }

Depending on the parent type, the subtype specification can include notation to define:

- single values or a range of values; or,

- all the values of the parent or values meeting certain constraints.

Macros

A macro is a powerful facility that allows the ASN.1 language itself to be extended. Note that this feature is more elaborate than the macro concept in some programming languages — the ASN.1 macro effectively allows an abstract syntax designer to write new rules for the ASN.1 language!

The macro notation is used extensively in certain Application Layer standards (particularly those that use the Remote Operations Service Element, ROSE) to provide a very concise specification of complex information objects and their semantics. However, the details of the notation are beyond the scope of the present discussion.

13.3 EXAMPLE — PRESENTATION PPDUs

Returning to the topic of the presentation protocol briefly, Figure 13.2 is an example of an abstract syntax defined in ASN.1 In fact, it is part of the definition of a Connect Presentation PPDU (CP PPDU) previously described in Figure 12.6 on page 224. Also shown is the encoding for user data. This encoding is used for the user data fields of all PPDUs.

The CP PPDU is a set of fields, most of which are optional. For comparison with the earlier example of the CP PPDU in Figure 12.6, note that the header contains a Presentation Context Definition List which is further defined to be a list of transfer syntaxes which support a particular abstract syntax. Each context in the list is identified by an integer — the Presentation Context Identifier. The Presentation Context Identifier also appears in the user data definition, effectively tagging the presentation context for each data value for all data transfers.

ASN.1 is used in this way throughout the upper layers to define protocols and services.

13.4 BASIC ENCODING RULES

BER

ASN.1 defines a formal syntax for the abstract description of the structure of data. The Basic Encoding Rules (BER), as described in the following pages, may be used to represent ASN.1 data values as a series of octets transferred between OSI end systems, i.e. a transfer syntax.

For the purposes of this book, the encoding rules are described first and then examples are given of the mapping between abstract syntax and the transfer syntax. It is easier to appreciate the nature of ASN.1 using an example than by study of the formal definition of the syntax.

In general, structured data are composed of one or more nested data elements as shown in Figure 13.3. The encoded data are of the form:

Identifier, Length, Contents

where:

Identifier Is the first part of each data element and it determines how the contents are to be interpreted. The identifier encodes the ASN.1 **tag**, and indicates whether constructed or primitive encoding is used.

Length Indicates the size of the contents field.

Contents Encodes the value of the data being transferred.

In the following diagrams, these fields are denoted as Tag, Length, Value for brevity. The encoding always generates an integral number of octets and the fields are octet aligned. There are two forms:

Primitive encoding The contents octets directly represent the value, e.g. for universal types.

Constructed encoding The contents octets are the complete encoding of one or more nested data values. The component values may themselves be constructed encoding or primitive encoding.

13.4.1 Type Identifier

The identifier encodes the tag (i.e. the class and number of the type of the data value to distinguish one type from another) and it governs the interpretation of the value field. It is generally 1 octet long although it may be extended as shown in Figure 13.4 (page 236). The four classes of types are encoded by bits 7 and 8 of the identifier:

Universal Built-in types.

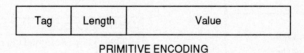

Figure 13.3 ASN.1 transfer syntax — tag (identifier), length , value (contents) format

Application wide   Types defined in application standards, e.g. by the notation: [APPLICATION 0].

Context specific   A specific type from a group, e.g. defined by the notation [1].

Private use   Types that are reserved for applications not covered by the standards.

The sixth bit distinguishes between two forms of data elements:

Primitive elements   These have no further internal structure of data elements; i.e. the contents are a single value.

Constructor elements   These have contents that are made up of one or more data elements; i.e. constructor elements may be nested. If the form bit is set to 1, then the first octet of the contents field is interpreted as the identifier (tag) of the first encoded component data element.

The remaining 5 bits of the identifier octet encode a numeric identifier code that distinguishes one data type from another of the same class. Each of the universal types is assigned a number by the ASN.1 encoding rules. Each application standard assigns a number to each data type defined by the application — this number completes the tag.

To facilitate the comprehension of the following examples, the type identifiers for selected types are reproduced in a condensed form in Table 13.3.

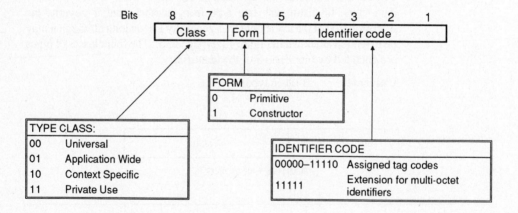

MULTI-OCTET IDENTIFIERS

| ccf11111 | 1xxxxxxx | ... | 0xxxxxxx |

Figure 13.4   ASN.1 encoding of identifier

13.4.2 Length Field

The length field specifies the length (in octets) of the contents of the data element. It may take three forms as illustrated in Figure 13.5 (page 238):

Short form   1 octet for contents less than 128 octets, i.e. a single octet of the form:

0LLLLLLL

Long form   From 2 to 127 octets for contents greater than 127 octets, i.e. multiple octets of the form:

1nnnnnnn LLLLLLLL ... LLLLLLLL

Table 13.3   Summary of type identifiers for selected ASN.1 types

TYPE	TYPE IDENTIFIER (HEX.)	
	Primitive	Constructor
UNIVERSAL CLASS:		
BOOLEAN	01	
INTEGER	02	
BIT STRING	03	23
OCTET STRING	04	24
NULL	05	
OBJECT IDENTIFIER	06	
ObjectDescriptor	07	
REAL	09	
ENUMERATED	0A	
NumericString	12	
PrintableString	13	
IA5String	16	
GeneralizedTime	18	
EXTERNAL		28
SEQUENCE and SEQUENCE OF		30
SET and SET OF		31
APPLICATION WIDE CLASS:		
[APPLICATION 0]	40	60
[APPLICATION 1]	41	61
[APPLICATION 2]	42	62
[APPLICATION 3]	43	63
etc.		
CONTEXT SPECIFIC CLASS:		
[0]	80	A0
[1]	81	A1
[2]	82	A2
[3]	83	A3
etc.		

Indefinite form	1 octet long plus an "end of contents" element that follows the last octet in the contents. The end of contents element is 2 octets both of value 00. The indefinite form can be used only for constructor elements. It has the form:

10000000 contents 00000000 00000000

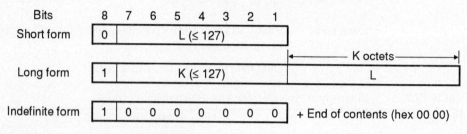

Figure 13.5   ASN.1 length encoding

13.4.3 Contents Fields

Universal types The contents for universal types are encoded as follows (note: this is not the complete list of ASN.1 types):

BOOLEAN	False is encoded as all bits 0. True is any other value.
INTEGER	Two's complement binary number.
REAL	Either a binary or decimal encoding of the sign, base, mantissa and exponent.
BIT STRING	Ordered set of zero or more bits. The first octet encodes the number of unused bits in the last octet of the Contents.
OCTET STRING	Ordered set of zero or more octets.
NULL	Valueless place holder with no contents.
SEQUENCE	Ordered set of zero or more values. Sequences of multiple types may have elements that are optional (i.e. may be omitted).
SET	Unordered set of values. Sets of multiple values may have optional elements.
IA5String	Ordered set of characters from International Alphabet No. 5 (i.e. American Standard Code for Information Interchange, ASCII).
Printable-String	Ordered set of characters from a subset of IA5.

Tagged types　　Tagging provides a means for creating new types from ones that already exist. The tag is simply the class and number that distinguishes the new type from others.

In the examples in Figure 13.6, type **Surname** is globally defined as an application wide type and it is encoded with a code of 0 in the type identifier. It is distinguished from **FirstName** with a code of 1 but the same base type of PrintableString.

A context specific type can be interpreted only within the group in which it was defined. Typically, this is a structured type, i.e. a

---

Surname ::=	[APPLICATION 0] PrintableString	Value:	DICKSON
Encoding	**Description**		
(Hexadecimal)			
60	Surname tag (APPLICATION 0, constructor)		
09	Length		
13	PrintableString tag		
07	Length of PrintableString		
44, 49, 43, 4B, 53, 4F, 4E	Value (DICKSON)		

FirstName::=	[APPLICATION 1] PrintableString	Value:	GARY
Encoding:	**Description:**		
61	FirstName tag (APPLICATION 1, constructor)		
06	Length		
13	PrintableString tag		
04	Length		
47, 41, 52, 59	Value (GARY)		

Surname ::=	[APPLICATION 0] IMPLICIT PrintableString Value:	DICKSON
Encoding:	**Description:**	
40	Surname tag (APPLICATION 0, Primitive)	
07	Length	
44, 49, 43, 4B, 53, 4F, 4E	Value (DICKSON)	

VendingMachine ::=		SET {	
		status	BOOLEAN,
		cola	[0] IMPLICIT INTEGER,
		beer	[1] IMPLICIT INTEGER }
Value:	true, 4 beer, 8 cola		
Encoding:	**Description:**		
31	SET		
09	Length		
01	BOOLEAN (status)		
01	Length		
FF	Value (true)		
81	Context specific 1, (beer)		
01	Length		
04	Value (4)		
80	Context specific 0, (cola)		
01	Length		
08	Value (8)		

Figure 13.6　　ASN.1 examples of encoding for simple data types

SEQUENCE, SET or CHOICE. In the example shown, cola and beer are distinguished by the identifier codes 0 and 1 that appear in the encoded bit string. However, the interpretation of these codes is not valid outside the SET construction.

The encoding of tagged values is derived from the complete encoding of the base type. The use of the keyword IMPLICIT has side effects when encoding tagged types.

- If the IMPLICIT keyword was *not* used in the definition of the type, the encoding form is constructed and the contents field is the complete encoding of the base type, i.e. including its identifier, length and contents fields.

- If the IMPLICIT keyword was used, the encoding form is the same as the base type, and the contents field is the same as the contents field of the base encoding, i.e. the identifier and length fields of the base encoding are omitted.

13.5 ASN.1 EXAMPLES

The purpose of the following examples is to highlight alternative ways in which a simple ASN.1 definition can be expressed and still effectively mean the same thing, but which result in different encodings. These examples also illustrate the options that can be taken by some implementations in encoding, e.g. the use or non-use of indefinite length indicators. Three related examples are given in the following sections.

13.5.1 Example 1

The following example demonstrates a simple definition of a personnel record. The personnel record is defined as an application wide data type consisting of three components: name, age and title.

```
PersonnelRecord ::=        [APPLICATION 0] IMPLICIT SET {
            Name,
            age        [1]        IMPLICIT INTEGER,
            title      [2]        VisibleString }

Name ::=                   [APPLICATION 1] IMPLICIT SEQUENCE {
            familyName [1]        VisibleString,
            middleName [2]        VisibleString      OPTIONAL,
            givenName  [3]        VisibleString }
```

For the definition of name, context tags are used because one field is optional. If this was not the case, then all the name components could be declared as:

```
                familyName    VisibleString,
                middleName    VisibleString,
                givenName     VisibleString
```

Context tags are needed only to distinguish fields that would be otherwise ambiguous when encoding and decoding the protocol, e.g. if some fields are declared as optional in a SEQUENCE or SET or they are a part of a CHOICE. The resultant encoding requires that explicit context tags are transferred between the two communicating entities to indicate which fields are in fact transferred. Figure 13.7 contains the encoded bit string that represents a personnel record with the following values:

Name   JOHN DAVID SMITH

Age   31

Title   Author

60	APPLICATION 0, PersonnelRecord tag (IMPLICIT SET constructed)
29	Length of PersonelRecord fields (41 decimal)
61	APPLICATION 1 Name tag (IMPLICIT SEQUENCE constructed)
1A	Length of Name fields, (26 decimal)
A1	familyName tag, (constructed)
07	Length
1A	VisibleString
05	Length
SMITH	familyName Value
A2	middleName tag, (constructed)
07	Length
1A	VisibleString
05	Length
DAVID	middleName Value
A3	givenName tag, (constructed)
06	Length
1A	VisibleString
04	Length
JOHN	givenName Value
81	Age tag (IMPLICIT INTEGER)
01	Length
1F	Value (decimal 31)
A2	Title
08	Length
1A	VisibleString
06	Length
Author	Value

Figure 13.7   ASN.1 BER encoding of example 1 showing the octet level representation of a personnel record. The type identifier and length octets are shown in hexadecimal form. The contents are in text for readability.

13.5.2 Example 2

If the definition of name is changed to make the components of the name IMPLICIT, then the visible string identifiers do not need to be transferred because both parties now "implicitly" know what the field type is (i.e. VisibleString).

```
Name ::=    [APPLICATION 1] IMPLICIT SEQUENCE {
            familyName    [1] VisibleString IMPLICIT,
            middleName    [2] VisibleString IMPLICIT         OPTIONAL,
            givenName     [3] VisibleString IMPLICIT}
```

The encoding for this definition is shown in Figure 13.8.

13.5.3 Example 3

Indefinite length encoding is illustrated in this example. Indefinite length encoding is usually done if the implementation is reading data from a disk to encode, but it does not know how long the data actually is. In this case, it formats the data, and inserts either an extended length field or an indefinite length indicator with an End of Contents (EOC) indicator. Figure 13.9 shows the result using the abstract syntax of the first example but with indefinite length encoding.

The use of indefinite length and EOC is optional and at the discretion of the sender. Thus all implementations receiving ASN.1 encoded protocols must cater for decoding protocol fields in either form.

60	APPLICATION 0, PersonnelRecord tag (IMPLICIT SET)
23	Length of PersonelRecord fields (35 decimal)
61	APPLICATION 1, Name tag (IMPLICIT SEQUENCE constructed)
14	Length of Name fields (20 decimal)
81	familyName tag
05	Length
SMITH	Value
82	middleName tag
05	Length
DAVID	Value
83	givenName tag
04	Length
JOHN	Value
81	Age tag {IMPLICIT INTEGER}
01	Length
1F	Value (decimal 31)
A2	Title
08	Length
1A	VisibleString
06	Length
Author	Value

Figure 13.8   Encoding for example 2

60	APPLICATION 0, PersonnelRecord tag (IMPLICIT SET constructed)
80	Length of PersonelRecord fields, Indefinite form
61	APPLICATION 1, Name tag (IMPLICIT SEQUENCE constructed)
80	Length of Name fields, Indefinite form
A1	familyName tag (constructed)
80	Length, Indefinite form
1A	VisibleString
05	Length
SMITH	Value
0000	EOC
A2	middleName tag (constructed)
80	Length, Indefinite form
1A	VisibleString
05	Length
DAVID	Value
0000	EOC
A3	givenName tag (constructed)
80	Length, Indefinite form
1A	VisibleString
04	Length
JOHN	Value
0000	EOC
0000	EOC to APPLICATION 1
81	Age tag (IMPLICIT INTEGER)
01	Length
1F	Value (decimal 31)
A2	Title
08	Length
1A	VisibleString
06	Length
Author	Value
0000	EOC to APPLICATION 0

Figure 13.9   Encoding of example 3 using abstract syntax of example 1 and showing indefinite length form

13.6 QUESTIONS

Question 13.1   What is ASN.1 used for?

Question 13.2   How many Application Layer standards use ASN.1?

Question 13.3   How does ASN.1 relate to the Presentation Layer?

Question 13.4   What is the relationship between ASN.1 notation and ASN.1 Basic Encoding Rules (BER)?

Question 13.5   What is a context specific tag?

Question 13.6   What is the constructor bit in the tag field used for?

Question 13.7   What are the options that can be used in encoding the length of a value field?

Question 13.8   What is the difference between ANY and EXTERNAL types?

Question 13.9   What is the purpose of an ASN.1 compiler?

14 Application Layer

14.1 INTRODUCTION

The OSI Application Layer standards define a range of system independent application services to support real "users" or user programs. It builds on the functions of the lower layers to support distributed systems. In so doing, it also hides much of the complexity of the lower layers by taking responsibility for the co-ordination of the dialogue between distributed applications in peer systems.

The complete realization of an application within a single end system is called an application process. The application process contains the application itself as well as OSI entities. Conceptually, an application process consists of two parts as shown in Figure 14.1:

- the user application — a local system dependent part that interfaces to the user, the operating system and to local resources such as a filestore and peripherals, and that uses the application services provided by an application entity for its OSI communications.

- the application entity (AE) — a system independent part that provides the standardized functionality of the Application Layer to the user application.

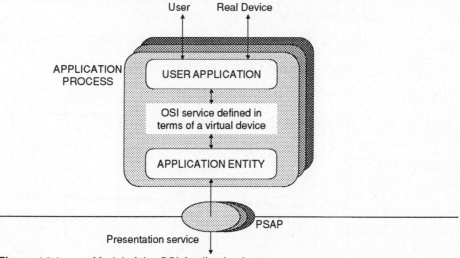

Figure 14.1   Model of the OSI Application Layer

245

This distinction is an important aspect that is used in OSI to achieve vendor independence. An application entity is often defined in terms of a vendor independent *virtual device*. The virtual device is represented as an information object with a defined set of service primitives that act on it. The system dependent aspects such as mapping between the virtual device and the real device are performed by the vendor dependent user element. The specification of such mappings is outside the scope of the OSI standards.

14.1.1 Application Layer Structure

There are many Application Layer standards. Standards such as File Transfer, Access and Management (FTAM) for file handling, X.400 Message Handling Systems, X.500 Directory services and X.700 System Management define their own individual set of functions, services and protocols within a unified Application Layer structure. There is no single service definition for the Application Layer — each Application Layer standard defines for itself the services provided to the applications.

ISO 9545 (Application Layer Structure) and its amendment (Extended Application Layer Structure) define the concepts, models and terminology used by all OSI Application Layer standards. The following paragraphs explain some of the definitions used in the Application Layer structure. It is important that these terms are reasonably well understood as they are used quite frequently in Part 4.

Within the application process, the application entity deals with the OSI services and communications. An application entity is defined in terms of Application Service Elements (ASEs), Association Service Objects (ASOs) and Control Functions (CFs). The ASO concept is a packaging tool for Application Layer components e.g. for control functions and ASEs. Internally, an ASO may consist of:

- one or more ASEs together with a control function;

- one or more ASOs together with a control function; or,

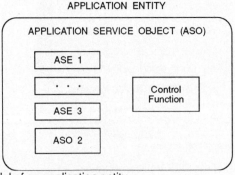

Figure 14.2   Model of an application entity

- one or more ASEs and one or more ASOs together with a control function.

An ASO may constitute all of the application entity or may be contained within successive ASOs iteratively until the ASO constituting the entire application entity is reached (i.e. an application entity is an ASO that may contain other ASOs). Figure 14.2 illustrates a simple configuration of these components and associated terms are defined in the following paragraphs.

Application process
: This is all those things needed to provide service to the end user. An *application process* represents a set of resources including processing resources, within a real open system that may be used to perform a particular information processing activity. Only those parts of the application process dealing with communications (i.e. the application entity) are subject to OSI standardization.

Application entity
: That standardized part of an application process which is uniquely identifiable as the source or destination of OSI communications. An *Application Entity (AE)* represents a set of OSI communication capabilities of a particular application process, e.g. the ability to exchange files or messages. An application process contains one or more application entities. (For simplicity, the discussion considers only one application entity per application process.) An application entity is made up of a collection of ASEs as shown in Figure 14.3.

Application process title
: An *application process title* is the globally unambiguous name of an application process.

Application entity title
: Multiple application entities (if they exist) are distinguished from each other by an application entity qualifier that is concatenated with the application process title to form the *application entity title*.

Application association
: Since a connection is defined in the Reference Model as a service to users in the layer above, the Application

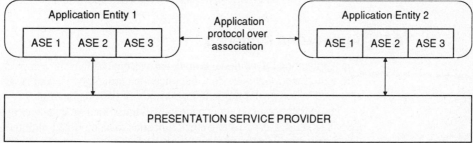

Figure 14.3   Model for Application Service Elements (ASEs)

Layer does not have connections. Instead, application entities establish *associations* for the exchange of information between application processes. An association is a co-operative relationship between two application entities formed by the exchange of Application Protocol Data Units (APDUs) over the presentation service.

Application service element

An *Application Service Element (ASE)* is a basic component of an application entity. It provides OSI communications capabilities for the interworking of application entities for a specific purpose. Each ASE is defined by a service and protocol standard. These ASEs are combined in various ways to form different types of application entities.

Application context

Each of the peer application entities communicating over an association must be composed of precisely the same ASEs, and must follow defined rules for their use. The set of ASEs comprising an application entity, their related options and the rules which define the combined behavior of the ASEs is called an *application context* i.e. the communications "template". In effect, the application context is a shared conceptual schema for the universe of discourse for communication. When an application context is defined by an Application Layer standard, it is assigned an Object Identifier (OID).

Application service object

An *Application Service Object (ASO)* is a composite component of an application entity that contains one or more ASEs and/or ASOs together with a control function. The ASO is a "packaging" concept for encapsulating ASEs, control functions and other ASOs.

Control function

The overall control of the application dialog exchanges and the peer to peer application association management is provided by a *Control Function (CF)*. A control function co-ordinates the component ASOs and ASEs within the ASO in which it resides. The control function provides sequencing control, APDU concatenation, mapping between services, association management, etc.

14.1.2 Application Modeling

The Application Layer model is modeled by a type and instance approach. The static functional behavior of application entities, ASOs and ASEs is specified by a type definition independently of their realization.

The invocation of an application entity requires active instances of the associated ASEs, ASOs and control functions to be modeled so that their dynamic behavior with respect to time can be considered.

Table 14.1   Application Layer standards

	NAME	ISO	CCITT
APPLICATION SERVICE ELEMENTS			
ACSE	Association Control Service Element	ISO 8649, ISO 8650	X.217, X.227
RTSE	Reliable Transfer Service Element	ISO 9066 parts 1 & 2	X.218, X.228
ROSE	Remote Operations Service Element	ISO 9072 parts 1 & 2	X.219, X.229
CCR	Commitment, Concurrency and Recovery	ISO 9804, ISO 9805	—
MHS	Message Handling Systems	ISO 10021 parts 1–7	X.400–X.420
EDS	Electronic Directory Services	ISO 9594 parts 1–8	X.500–X.521
FTAM	File Transfer, Access and Management	ISO 8571 parts 1–4	—
VT	Virtual Terminal	ISO 9040, ISO 9041	—
JTM	Job Transfer and Manipulation	ISO 8831, ISO 8832	—
DTP	Distributed Transaction Processing	ISO 10026 parts 1–3	—
MMS	Manufacturing Message Specification	ISO 9506 parts 1 & 2	—
CMIP	Common Management Information Protocol	ISO 9595, ISO 9596	X.710, X.711
RDA	Remote Database Access	DIS 9579 parts 1 & 2	—
APPLICATION SYNTAXES			
ODA	Open Document Architecture	ISO 8613 parts 1–8	T.411–T.418
EDI	Electronic Data Interchange	ISO 9735	—

For example, in the next section on the Association Control Service Element (ACSE), some of the parameters exchanged between applications in the association establishment process are the application entity titles (which contains the application process title) and the application process and application entity invocation identifiers. The "title" parameter is used to indicate the "type" of the application process and application entity. The invocation identifier parameters are used when the applications desire some co-ordination with their "instances".

14.1.3 Standards for Application Services

Table 14.1 lists the main Application Layer standards. For descriptive purposes, the standards for application services can be grouped into two categories as shown in Figure 14.4:

- The common services which are a collection of functions for general use by a variety of application entities. The four ASEs in this category provide generic services for distributed systems, and they are the subjects of this chapter.

- A number of standards have been defined for specific Application Layer functions, e.g. X.400 for electronic mail, FTAM for file handling, etc. Several such standards are listed in Figure 14.4, and some of them are covered in detail in Part 4.

Such categorization does not imply sublayering in the Application Layer, but merely that different tools are used at different times. An application

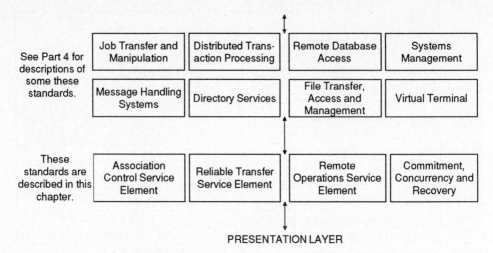

Figure 14.4   Some important application service elements

entity is not defined in terms of a single Application Layer standard. Typically, a standard such as FTAM defines a number of ASEs and refers to one or more other standard ASEs. The ASE specifications jointly define an application entity. The way the ASEs combine and interact with each other and the underlying layers defines the application protocol.

14.2 ASSOCIATION CONTROL SERVICE ELEMENT

ACSE   Although applications need to establish associations for a wide variety of purposes, a common set of functions dealing with the control of the association itself can be identified. The *Association Control Service Element (ACSE)* standardizes these basic facilities for the control of an association between two application entities. It provides these services independently of the reasons for such communication. Every application entity includes ACSE, with the exception of the 1984 version of X.400.

14.2.1 ACSE Service

The ACSE service is defined in ISO 8649/CCITT X.217, and the primitives and PDUs are shown in Table 14.2.

Association   The A-Associate service creates an association, and if successful, allows the other ASEs to use the association. The underlying presentation and session connections are established simultaneously. In order to establish the lower layer connections, ACSE must be supplied with the presentation address of the destination.

Because of the great variety of ASEs and their different lower layer requirements, application entities use ACSE to declare:

- the application context (i.e. the explicitly defined set of rules for use of the association);

- the application entity titles (i.e. names);

- the abstract syntaxes required to support the ASEs and any user data; and,

- presentation and session service requirements (e.g. required functional units).

The A-Associate primitives have over twenty parameters! However, half of these are passed directly to the presentation service which in turn passes many to the Session Layer below. This cascading effect makes the ACSE appear complex, although in reality most of the parameters introduced by ACSE are to do with naming.

Release
If successful, the A-Release service causes the graceful release of the association. Data in transit is delivered prior to release, and then the association and the lower layer connections are released simultaneously. However, the peer entity may refuse to release and the association would continue without loss of data.

Abort
The A-Abort and A-P-Abort primitives cause the abnormal release of the association due to irrecoverable errors with the possible loss of data in transit.

ACSE PRIMITIVE	ACSE APDU	PRESENTATION PRIMITIVE
A-Associate req/ind	A-Associate Request — AARQ [APPLICATION 0]	P-Connect req/ind
A-Associate resp/conf	A-Associate Response — AARE [APPLICATION 1]	P-Connect resp/conf
A-Release req/ind	A-Release Request — RLRQ [APPLICATION 2]	P-Release req/ind
A-Release resp/conf	A-Release Response — RLRE [APPLICATION 3]	P-Release resp/conf
A-Abort req/ind	A-Abort — ABRT [APPLICATION 4]	P-U-Abort req/ind
A-P-Abort ind	—	P-P-Abort ind

Table 14.2   ACSE Application Protocol Data Units (APDUs) and mapping between application and presentation primitives

Authentication   An addendum to the ACSE service definition on Peer Entity Authentication defines an additional functional unit for corroboration of the identity
of objects such as the application processes and human users of applications. The addendum provides additional parameters in the A-Associate
primitives to carry authentication information.

14.2.2 ACSE Protocol

The ACSE protocol is ISO 8650/CCITT X.227. ACSE provides fields in
APDUs to convey application information such as application process
titles, application entity qualifiers, version numbers, application context
name, etc. and specifies uniform procedures for controlling the establishment and termination of the presentation connection.

Each ACSE primitive maps one to one onto an ACSE APDU that in
turn maps directly onto a presentation service primitive. The very close
relationship between ACSE and the connection establishment PDUs of
the Presentation and Session layers is illustrated in Figure 14.5 (to fit on
the page, only a selection of the parameters are shown). Once the association is established, ACSE does not feature in the application entity
protocol until the release or abort services are used.

PDUs   The ACSE protocol defines five APDUs and allocates application wide
class ASN.1 tags to each. The APDUs are listed in Table 14.2.

14.2.3 Application Layer Naming

To establish an association, the application user element must supply the
destination presentation address and may optionally supply the application process title and entity qualifier, i.e. a name. To enable applications
to refer to each other by user friendly names, some kind of directory
service is desirable to translate from names to addresses.

ACSE is capable of conveying any ASN.1 defined data type for
application process title and application entity qualifier. However, with
the availability of the OSI Directory (X.500), these will generally take the
form of a Distinguished Name (i.e. an ASN.1 data type defined in X.500).
Typically, the mapping between names and presentation addresses will
use a combination of local tables for efficient look-up for commonly
accessed destinations, and enquiry of an X.500 Directory database for
infrequent destinations.

14.3 RELIABLE TRANSFER SERVICE ELEMENT

RTSE   The objective of the *Reliable Transfer Service Element (RTSE)* is to ensure
that bulk data requests (APDUs) from other ASEs are completely transferred exactly once or that an exception report is issued to applications.

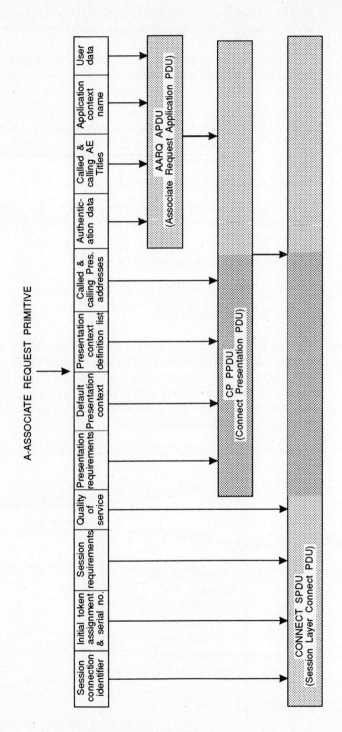

Figure 14.5 ACSE connection establishment

RTSE attempts to recover from communications and end systems failures and it hides the complexity of the underlying presentation and session services from the user.

RTSE uses the basic activity subset of the Presentation and Session layers. Each bulk data transfer forms one activity and the synchronization service is used for recovery after errors. There are two modes:

X.410 1984   This mode is a restricted version (called Reliable Transfer Service, RTS) compatible with the 1984 implementation of X.400. It is used with the X.410 mode for the Presentation Layer.

Normal mode   Normal mode is the full version.

If RTSE is included in an application context, then it is sole user of ACSE services. RTSE uses ACSE to establish an association and negotiate the following:

- two way alternate or monologue mode;

- checkpoint size in multiples of 1024 octets; and,

- window size (defaults to 3).

Activity   Each APDU is one activity and the sequence diagram for a successful transfer is shown in Figure 14.6. RTSE segments the APDU into Transfer PDUs of maximum checkpoint size. Each Transfer PDU is followed by a minor synchronization point with explicit confirmation expected, and each transfer is guarded by a timeout. There are three levels of error recovery depending on severity:

- Interrupt activity and restart from the last unacknowledged transfer.

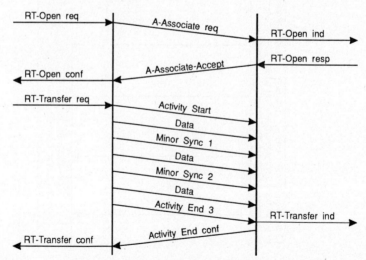

Figure 14.6   Sequence diagram for Reliable Transfer Service Element (RTSE)

- Discard activity, abandon data already transferred and restart a new activity.

- Abort the association and leave the application to recover.

The recovery procedures include the re-establishment of the association if necessary, (e.g. if it was lost due to communications failure) and resumption of a transfer.

14.4 REMOTE OPERATIONS SERVICE ELEMENT

Some Application Layer protocols are inherently interactive; i.e. they proceed from an application request to perform some function in a remote system, and then wait for that action to be completed. Examples of such protocols are: X.400 - P3 protocol, the Directory, Common Management Information Protocol (CMIP), Document Filing and Retrieval (DFR) and Remote Database Access (RDA). These all require particular operations to be performed remotely.

Furthermore, the majority of Application Layer standards are formulated using the object oriented paradigm. The standards define, for example, the major functional components (e.g. the X.400 Message Transfer Agents and the X.500 Directory System Agents) and data (X.400 messages and Directory entries) as objects. To perform actions on these objects, specific operations are defined.

ROSE

The *Remote Operations Service Element (ROSE)* is a vehicle for uniformly implementing interactive protocols. It provides a basic request/reply interaction (similar to an elementary procedure call mechanism) that is a tool for the construction of distributed applications operating on data objects. Other application service elements use ROSE together with ACSE and, optionally, RTSE to define the application protocol.

The ROSE standard has been developed from an earlier protocol that was incorporated in the 1984 version of X.400. ROSE, finalized in 1989 as ISO 9072/X.219 and X.229, has been extended to serve as a generic ASE.

14.4.1 Remote Operations Notation

In addition to the definition of the remote operations ASE, the ROSE standard defines a new notation to facilitate the definition of other application standards that use ROSE. Effectively, ASEs defined using the *Remote Operations Notation* (RO-notation) provide a uniform "operations interface" to the user element as shown in Figure 14.7. The notation specifies the external behavior of distributed systems at the interface and hides the details of the OSI communications from the application. This is an important characteristic for modern object oriented software design.

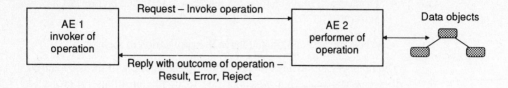

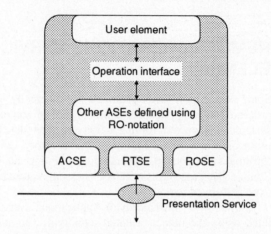

Figure 14.7   Model for Remote Operations Service Element (ROSE)

Together with ASN.1, ROSE and the associated notation are used by many other application standards.

The following types of remote operations form an operation interface:

- a **BIND** operation to establish an application association;

- a set of **OPERATIONS** and, for each operation, a list of **ERROR** (negative reply) reports; and,

- an **UNBIND** operation to release an association.

The RO-notation is a number of ASN.1 macros that are used by other applications to define the above remote operations. The ROSE protocol defines how the APDUs are transferred by means of the RTSE services, or directly by ACSE and the presentation service if RTSE is not used. Macros are also defined to facilitate the specification of an ASE and an application context. The details of the notation are beyond the scope of this discussion.

14.4.2 ROSE Protocol

There are only four basic ROSE APDU types as shown in Figure 14.8 (the ASN.1 definitions are simplified). These PDUs are conveyed in P-Data service primitives if RTSE is not included in the application context, or in the RT-Transfer service if RTSE is being used.

Using ROSE   Applications wishing to use ROSE define the following aspects using the RO-notation. For each operation define:

- an operation code (either an integer or an object identifier, OID)

- an argument

- a result

- possible errors.

For each error define:

- an error code (either an integer or an OID)

- a parameter.

Operations   ROSE operations may be classified according to whether the performer of an operation is expected to report its outcome:

```
ROSEapdus ::=   CHOICE {
                        [1] IMPLICIT  INVOKE,
                        [2] IMPLICIT  RESULT,
                        [3] IMPLICIT  ERR,
                        [4] IMPLICIT  REJECT}

INVOKE ::=      SEQUENCE {
                invokeID    INTEGER,
                linkedID    [0] IMPLICIT INTEGER              OPTIONAL,
                            OPERATION,
                argument    ANY                               OPTIONAL}

RESULT ::=      SEQUENCE {
                invokeID    INTEGER,
                            SEQUENCE {
                            OPERATION,
                result      ANY}                              OPTIONAL }

ERR ::=         SEQUENCE {
                invokeID    INTEGER,
                            ERROR,
                parameter   ANY                               OPTIONAL}

REJECT ::=      SEQUENCE {
                invokeID    CHOICE {INTEGER, NULL},
                problem     ProblemDescription}
```

Figure 14.8   ASN.1 definition of ROSE protocol data units

- in case of either success or failure (a result reply is returned if the operation is successful, an error reply is returned if the operation is unsuccessful);

- in case of failure only (no reply is returned if the operation is successful, an error reply is returned if the operation is unsuccessful);

- in case of success only (a result reply is returned if the operation is successful, no reply is returned if the operation is unsuccessful); or,

- not at all (no outcome is reported).

Two operation modes are possible:

- synchronous, in which the invoker requires a reply from the performer before invoking another operation; and,

- asynchronous, in which the invoker may continue to invoke further operations without awaiting a reply.

The class and mode are determined by the ASE that is using ROSE.

14.5 COMMITMENT, CONCURRENCY AND RECOVERY

CCR

If a master/slave relationship is required between two application entities, the *Commitment, Concurrency and Recovery (CCR)* ASE ensures that actions between them are atomic; i.e. either both parties jointly perform the actions or not at all. Typically, data is bound to the atomic action in order to ensure that both parties change over from an initial value to the final value in a consistent fashion. If errors occur during the action, the action may be rolled back to the initial state. No matter when errors occur, the subordinate is never left with an incomplete action that the master believes to be complete.

CCR is defined as a service and protocol between two applications over a single association. If more than two end systems are involved in a distributed application, it is up to the user of CCR to co-ordinate them (as defined in the Distributed Transaction Processing standard). The CCR procedures enable distributed applications to act in lock-step synchronization as illustrated in Figure 14.9. The master institutes application specific actions, then uses CCR to perform a two phase hand-shake:

- It requests agreement from subordinates to proceed.

- Then it demands commitment (or rollback, if agreement is not reached).

If any problems occur during the commitment phase, a recovery process must be initiated. The recovery procedures are not a part of the CCR standard, but are application specific.

The CCR standards were finalized by ISO in 1990. There are no CCITT equivalents. The standards are:

- ISO 9804 service definition; and,

- ISO 9805 protocol specification.

Table 14.3 explains the CCR service primitives and their mapping onto presentation service primitives.

14.6 QUESTIONS

Question 14.1   What is an application context?

Question 14.2   Describe the services provided by the ACSE, RTSE, ROSE and CCR standards.

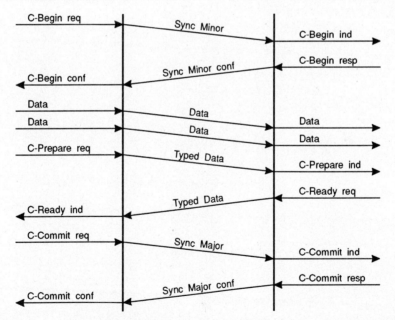

Figure 14.9   Sequence diagram for Commitment, Concurrency and Recovery (CCR) service element

Table 14.3   CCR service primitives

PRIMITIVE	TYPE	EXPLANATION	MAPPING
C-Begin	Optionally confirmed	Issued by superior to start atomic action	P-Sync Minor
C-Prepare	Non-confirmed	Used by superior to ask the subordinate for commitment	P-Typed Data
C-Ready	Non-confirmed	Issued by the subordinate only if it can offer commitment i.e. the bound data can be released in either the initial state (on commitment) or final state (if rollback)	P-Typed Data
C-Commit	Confirmed	Invoked by the superior to order commitment. Bound data is released in the final state	P-Sync Major
C-Rollback	Confirmed	May be invoked by either the superior or subordinate if unable to commit. Bound data is released in the initial state	P-Resync
C-Recover	Optionally confirmed	May be issued by either the superior (a confirmed service), or the subordinate (optionally confirmed) after a failure to indicate how to resume the action	P-Typed Data

Part 4 — Standards for Distributed Applications

15 Message Handling Systems

15.1 CONCEPTS OF ELECTRONIC MESSAGING

In the past, a variety of proprietary electronic mail systems were developed by computer vendors and service providers. Incompatibilities between these systems, however, limited the ability to transfer mail between users on different systems. The CCITT X.400 Recommendations for Message Handling Systems (MHS) (ISO 10021) provide a standardized way to interconnect electronic mail systems in order to provide a global service and overcome the technical limitations of existing systems.

Message

In X.400, as in other computer based mail systems, the information exchanged between two parties can be referred to as a message. This message is transmitted by the originator to a receiver (referred to as the recipient). The message itself may be stored for a period during its transmission, depending on the transmission medium or the availability of the recipient to receive it. The system may then acknowledge the originator of the message delivery or receipt. MHS is designed to support

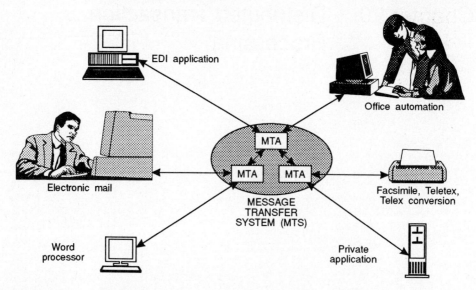

Figure 15.1   X.400 Message Handling Systems can be used for a variety of applications in addition to electronic mail.

a variety of different message types and to interwork with other services as illustrated in Figure 15.1. It may be used for interpersonal electronic mail or for more formal communication for the exchange of business documents.

This store and forward operation has advantages over other forms of electronic communication that require both the originator and recipient to be simultaneously available for information transfer. The originator can submit messages at any time and need not wait for the recipient to be willing to accept delivery. Equally, the recipient can read delivered messages at a convenient time and message transfer does not disrupt other activities.

15.1.1 Standards

The International Telegraph and Telephone Consultative Committee (CCITT) initiated work on message handling with the development of the landmark X.400 Recommendations in 1984. These early standards paved the way for many of the concepts in the Open Systems Interconnection (OSI) Application Layer. Since 1984, CCITT and the International Organization for Standardization (ISO) have been collaborating to extend and refine the standards and their texts are identical except for a few minor areas which reflect the different responsibilities of the two organizations:

- CCITT X.400 Message Handling Systems (MHS)

- ISO 10021 Message Oriented Text Interchange Systems (MOTIS).

The description of X.400 in this chapter is based on the 1988 version, although the focus is on those features that are common to both 1984 and 1988. Specific differences are mentioned where appropriate. The 1984 version is widely available from many vendors and as a public service in most countries. Implementations of the 1988 version started to appear in 1990. Possible extensions to the X.400 standards are summarized at the end of this chapter.

15.1.2 Basic Concepts

UA
The X.400 standards are defined in terms of a number of functional components, described below and depicted in Figure 15.2, that may be combined in various physical configurations to realize the MHS service. The MHS consists of a *Message Transfer System (MTS)* and a (potentially large) number of *User Agents (UAs)*. A UA acts as a user's mail-box and assists the user in the creation and receipt of messages. The user may be an individual or a computer application. There is one UA per user.

IPM
Different types of UAs can be supported. The UA defined initially by the standards is for *Interpersonal Messaging (IPM)*, i.e. electronic mail. An

additional standard was created specifically for Electronic Data Interchange (EDI) in 1990.

Originator,
Recipient

The message is created by the *originator*, and is *submitted* to the MTS via the UA. The MTS provides an application independent store and forward message transfer service. The MTS determines whether message delivery is possible and *delivers* the message to the *recipient* via the recipient's UA.

MTA

The MTS is a collection of co-operating *Message Transfer Agents (MTAs)*. An MTA is like a mail sorting and clearing house. Each UA is connected to only one MTA. The MTA exchanges messages between UAs attached to it, and connects to other MTAs for messages addressed to remote UAs. Where there is MTA to MTA exchange, the message is *transferred*. Messages are transferred through one or more MTAs in a store and forward fashion; i.e. messages are stored temporarily awaiting transmission toward the destination. If a path is temporarily unavailable, or if transmission errors disrupt message transfer, the MTAs may make several attempts to deliver (e.g. over a 24 hour period). However, MTAs do not normally store messages indefinitely — undeliverable messages are discarded and a non-delivery report is sent to the originator.

O/R Address

Central to the operation of the MHS and the routing of messages by MTAs is a hierarchical address for users. X.400 defines a global naming and address scheme whereby every user is unambiguously identified by an *Originator/Recipient Address (O/R Address)*. The structure of the address is defined later, but conceptually it is similar to a postal address.

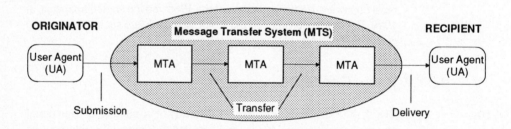

Figure 15.2   MHS functional models

Message store   To operate as described above, both the MTAs and UAs need to be highly reliable and available systems. This makes it difficult for personal computers, which are a desirable user interface to MHS, to act as UAs. Because personal computers may be switched off or engaged in other activities for long periods, MTAs may be unable to deliver messages to personal computer based UAs. To overcome this shortcoming, the 1988 version introduced the *Message Store (MS)*. The MS is an optional function interposed between the UA and its MTA. The MS complements a UA implemented, for example, on a personal computer by providing a more secure, continuously available storage mechanism to take delivery of messages on the UA's behalf. The MS is like an in-tray that supplements or replaces the message storage on a UA. Users can get counts and lists of messages, and fetch and delete messages held in the MS.

Other types of message services may participate in MHS via *Access Units (AU)*. The standards provide for the interworking with other Telematic services such as Telex and Teletex, and for the printed output of a message for delivery by postal services. A *Physical Delivery Access Unit (PDAU)* (defined in 1988) converts an MHS message to physical form (i.e. hard copy) for delivery to a postal address. Although not covered by the standards, some systems also interwork with Videotext services and can convert messages to facsimile images for transmission to a remote facsimile machine over the telephone network.

In total, the complete system is referred to as the Message Handling Environment.

15.2 MHS PHYSICAL CONFIGURATIONS

The main logical components of the MHS are the UA, MS and MTA. Various physical configurations of these components have been defined and incorporated into the overall design of MHS. The configurations range from a singlestand alone UA to a comprehensive system with multiple UAs, MSs, AUs and an MTA all co-resident in one computer system. Some typical examples are illustrated Figure 15.3 (page 266).

Co-located   In the first case, the UA(s) are combined with an MTA, thus providing a
MTA/UA   contained message system between its users' interfaces and communicating with other users via other MTAs. For example, this configuration might be implemented on a mini- or mainframe computer system.

Server   The second configuration is a number of detached UAs, and a combined MS/MTA. This might be used in a Local Area Network (LAN) environment where the MS/MTA is a server and the UAs are personal computers.

A combination of all components (not illustrated) would typically be offered by a public service provider.

The MTAs can be linked together by a variety of networks. X.25 public data networks are used by the public X.400 service providers for the backbone. Private X.400 systems could use LANs, leased lines or public and private X.25 networks.

The standards do not define the user interface to an X.400 UA. This is a matter for the system designer to determine and is an area for innovation and competition between vendors to come up with a user friendly interface. Some UAs are implemented as a gateway to an existing proprietary electronic mail product; some products have been developed from scratch and provide a native X.400 interface.

15.2.1 Message Storage and Transfer through the MHS

Within the MHS, there are many facilities such as delivery notification or non-delivery notification, multiple recipient delivery and copy list support. Should multiple recipients be specified by the originator on the original message submitted to the first MTA, then respective MTAs will create a copy of the original message and direct it to the required recipients.

Multiple copies Figure 15.4 illustrates a *multi-destination* message that is sent from user X through the MHS to users Y and Z. User Z is connected via a message store. The respective MTAs use the O/R Addresses of the recipients to process the message, i.e. to:

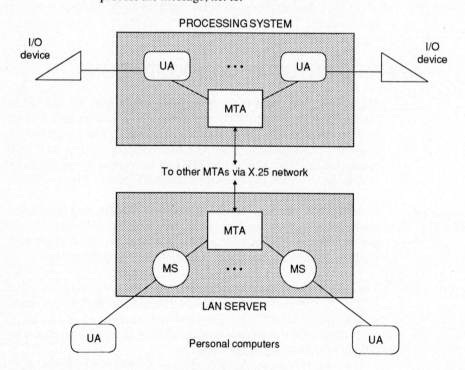

Figure 15.3   Possible MHS physical configurations

- deliver it if the recipient is on this MTA/UA;

- copy and forward it if a recipient is on this MTA and another recipient is on another MTA connected to this MTA; or,

- forward it to the next MTA if the recipient is on an adjacent MTA.

In the cases where an MTA actually delivers the message to one (or more) of the recipients or makes a copy for subsequent delivery, the MTA resets a flag in a special field for that recipient in the envelope. This indicates to other MTAs that previous MTAs have taken responsibility for delivery to this particular recipient and subsequent MTAs should ignore the recipient's entry. Thus, the last MTA receiving a message for multiple recipients should find all the recipients that are on prior MTAs have had their flag reset to zero.

Reports

Where the originator requests delivery advice, the recipient's MTA will send a *delivery report* back to the originator which specifies delivery or non-delivery. Delivery reports are generated by the destination MTA when delivery takes place either to the recipient's UA or to the recipient's MS. The originator can also specify *receipt notification* at the UA level. When the recipient's UA processes the message, a notification is generated by the recipient's UA and sent to the originator.

When subscribing to an MS (i.e. user Z), the messages are delivered to the MS only. Messages delivered to an MS are considered delivered from the MTS perspective. When a UA submits a message through the MS, the MS is in general transparent.

The delivery report and receipt notification are not exclusive. If both are requested by the originator of a message, then a report is generated when the message is "delivered" and a separate notification is generated when the message is "read". These are carried back to the originator as separate messages as illustrated in Figure 15.5 (page 268).

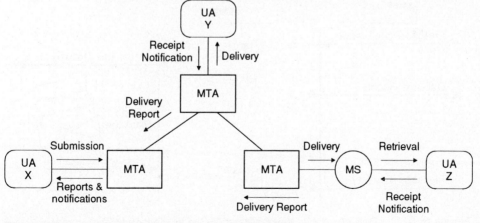

Figure 15.4   Message storage and transfer in MHS

Probe   UAs can also submit *probe* messages to the MTS. A probe is a test message without a message content but with a description of a potential message. It is used to test whether the described message length and content types could be delivered to a potential recipient. The probe is not actually delivered to the recipient, but the MTS sends back a delivery or non-delivery report depending on the success of the probe.

15.2.2 Elements of Service

The various capabilities of an MHS to transfer messages and the facilities offered to users are defined in the standards under the term *elements of service*. Some 93 elements of service are defined — some are mandatory and must be supported by all MHS implementations; some are optional. An indicative summary of selected elements of service is listed Table 15.1, together with an indication of the new elements introduced in 1988.

Conversion   The MTS provides conversion functions to allow users to input messages in one encoded format, called *Encoded Information Type (EIT)*, and have them delivered in another format to cater for users with various UA capabilities and terminal types. This increases the possibility of delivery by tailoring the message to the recipient's capabilities. CCITT Recommendation X.408 deals with conversion for the following:

- Telex

- IA5 text

- Teletex

- Groups 3 and 4 facsimile

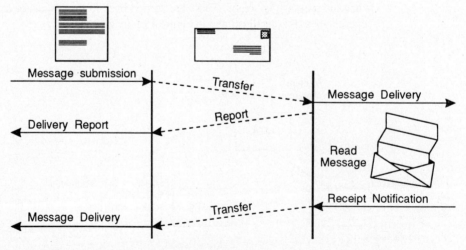

Figure 15.5   Delivery reports are generated by the destination MTA, and receipt notification messages are generated by the recipient's UA.

Table 15.1 MHS elements of service

MESSAGE TRANSFER SERVICE	
Multi-destination delivery	Distribution list expansion *
Delivery and non-delivery reports	Use of directory name *
Access management	Redirection *
Time stamps and trace information	Origin authentication *
Content conversion	Secure access management *
Alternate recipient control	Data confidentiality *
Deferred delivery	Message security labeling *
Hold for delivery	Message integrity *
Probe	Non-repudiation *
	Proof of submission and delivery *

INTERPERSONAL MESSAGING	
Multi-part, typed body	Expiry date; Obsoleting indication
Primary, copy and blind copy recipients	Authorizing user
Receipt and non-receipt notification	Sensitivity
Auto-forwarded and forwarded messages	Importance
Subject indication	Incomplete copy *
Cross referencing; In reply to indication	Language identification *

MESSAGE STORE	
Message deletion *	Message summary *
Message fetching *	Alert *
Message listing *	Auto-forwarding *

Legend : * means new service added in 1988 version.

- Videotex
- voice
- mixed mode.

15.3 MESSAGE STRUCTURE

Having looked at the path of a message through the MHS, the message structure will now be examined.

A message within the MHS has a defined structure consisting of an *envelope* and a *content* (very similar to a paper message, see Figure 15.6). The content consists of a *heading* and a *body*. The body may have multiple parts of different data types, e.g. text, image, binary data.

The originator creates the body and, with the assistance of the UA, creates the heading. The heading contains multiple fields with such details as To, From, cc, Confirmation criteria and Subject. The body contains the text of the message and attachments etc. This is encoded by the UA and submitted to the MTA in a submission envelope. For exchange within the MTS, the MTA then formulates and encodes a transfer envelope derived from the submission envelope, and transfers it to other MTAs for distribution. The envelope is the sole responsibility of the MTAs.

Message processing

The reason for the presence of a separate envelope and heading is that MTAs need to modify the envelope (e.g. postmark it) as a message progresses through the MTS. For multi-destination messages, each MTA that takes responsibility for delivery to a recipient resets a Responsibility flag in the appropriate recipient's reference (the Per Recipient field) on the envelope. This "stamping" mechanism informs subsequent MTAs of which recipients they should attempt delivery to. MTAs also append trace information to the envelope which acts as a time stamp and can be used to detect faulty routing of messages such as looping. The separate envelope allows the MTAs to modify delivery information without actually touching the original message. During message submission, much of the information in the heading is copied to the envelope, so that it can be processed independently by the MTAs.

Use of ASN.1

The MHS messages and protocols are defined using Abstract Syntax Notation One (ASN.1), and encoded according to the Basic Encoding Rules (BER). ASN.1 was specified originally by the 1984 CCITT standard X.409, but migrated to the generic OSI standards of ISO 8824/X.208 and ISO 8825/X.209 in 1988. ASN.1 was covered in Chapter 13.

The application wide identifier types that may be used within all parts of the MHS standards are listed in Table 15.2

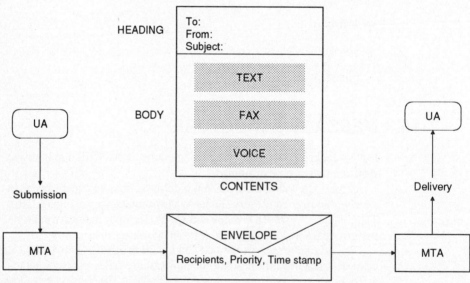

Figure 15.6   MHS message structure

Table 15.2 Application wide identifiers (tags) for MHS data types

ATTRIBUTE	MEANING	ASN.1 ID. (Hex)
O/R Name	Originator/recipient name	60
Country Name	Abbreviated name for country	61
ADMD Name	Administrative domain name	62
Global Domain ID	Message source identifier	63
MTS Identifier	Message identifier	64
Encoded Information Types	IA5, facsimile, Teletex, voice, etc.	65
Content Type	IPM 1984, IPM 1988, undefined, external	66
Priority	Normal, urgent, non-urgent	67
Per Message Indicators	Disclose recipients, conversion allowed, alternate recipient allowed, return content in delivery report	68
Trace Information	Inserted by the MTAs	69
Content Identifier	User's content identifier	6A
IPM Identifier	User's message identifier	6B

15.3.1 Transfer Envelope and IPM Message Construction

An ASN.1 definition of the message transfer envelope (i.e. as exchanged between MTAs) is shown in Figure 15.7, and the interpersonal message header (as exchanged between two UAs) is shown in Figure 15.8 (page 273). The illustrations are simplified, and details of the 1988 extensions are omitted. Throughout the X.400 standards and in the illustrations used here, implicit tagging is used unless otherwise specified (see page 232).

Envelope   The envelope contains a number of fields necessary to locate and deliver the message to the recipient(s). Each envelope has a unique identifier that is generated by the originating MTA (MTSIdentifier), and the originator's name. This allows delivery reports to be associated with the original message. The envelope carries a list of recipients that includes various flags per recipient for optional services.

IPM Message   The IPM user message consists of a heading and body. The heading consists of various fields that specify the originator, the primary recipients, the copy recipients and the blind copy recipients. Blind copy recipients are those who receive a copy of the message but are not indicated to other recipients in their messages.

Other fields in the heading provide such things as subject, time, importance and reply-by fields. These fields are typical of any paper message or memo currently used in an office.

```
MessageTransferEnvelope ::=    SET {
                               PerMessageTransferFields,
                               [2] SEQUENCE OF PerRecipientFields }

PerMessageTransferFields ::=   SET {
                               MTSIdentifier,
originator                     ORName,                          -- defined in Fig. 15.11
originalEIT                    EncodedInformationTypes                    OPTIONAL,
                               ContentType,
uaContentId                    ContentIdentifier,
                               Priority                          DEFAULT normal,
                               PerMessageIndicators                 DEFAULT {},
deferredDelivery               [0] Time                              OPTIONAL,
                               [1] SEQUENCE OF
                               PerDomainBilateralInformation             OPTIONAL,
                               TraceInformation,
                               [3] -- 1988 Extensions }

PerRecipientFields ::=         SET {
recipientName                  ORName,
                               [0] RecipientNumber,
                               [1] PerRecipientIndicators,
                                       -- Responsibility flag, delivery reports
                               [2] ExplicitConversion            OPTIONAL,
                               [3] -- 1988 Extensions }
```

Figure 15.7   MHS message transfer envelope — P1 protocol

15.3.2 X.400 Protocols

The previously defined functional components and configurations provide the model on which the MHS protocols have been designed. The MHS protocols are named P1, P2, P3 and P7. (PEDI is also used for Electronic Data Interchange, see Chapter 23.) The relationship of these protocols within the OSI Application Layer is shown in Figure 15.9 (page 274).

P1   The P1 protocol is used between MTAs to transfer messages.

P2   P2 procedures are used between IPM UAs across the MTS. The 1988 version of P2 is referred to as P22. For EDI exchanges, PEDI is used between UAs.

P3   The P3 protocol is used between an MTA and UA, and between an MTA and MS.

P7   The P7 protocol applies between an UA and its associated MS.

The X.400 system in total resides in the Application Layer. The MHS protocols are associated with distinct Application Service Elements (ASEs) in the Application Layer (the ASEs are not shown in the illustra-

IPM ::=	SEQUENCE { Heading, Body}	
Heading ::=	SET { IPMIdentifier,	
originator	[0] ORDescriptor	OPTIONAL,
authorizing-users	[1] { SEQUENCE OF ORDescriptor }	OPTIONAL,
primary-recipients	[2] { SEQUENCE OF Recipient }	DEFAULT {},
copy-recipients	[3] { SEQUENCE OF Recipient }	DEFAULT {},
blind-copy	[4] { SEQUENCE OF Recipient }	OPTIONAL,
replied-to-IPM	[5] IPMIdentifier	OPTIONAL,
obsoleted-IPMs	[6] { SEQUENCE OF IPMIdentifer }	DEFAULT {},
related-IPMs	[7] { SEQUENCE OF IPMIdentifer }	DEFAULT {},
subject	[8] EXPLICIT TeletexString	OPTIONAL,
expiry-time	[9] Time	OPTIONAL,
reply-time	[10] Time	OPTIONAL,
reply-to	[11] { SEQUENCE OF ORDescriptor }	OPTIONAL,
importance	[12] ENUMERATED	DEFAULT normal,
sensitivity	[13] ENUMERATED	OPTIONAL,
auto-forwarded	[14] BOOLEAN [15] -- 1988 Extensions }	DEFAULT false,
Body ::=	SEQUENCE OF BodyPart	
ORDescriptor ::=	SET {	
formal-name	ORName	OPTIONAL,
free-form-name	[0] TeletexString	OPTIONAL,
telephone-number	[1] PrintableString	OPTIONAL }
Recipient ::=	SET { [0] ORDescriptor,	
notification-request	[1] BIT STRING	DEFAULT {},
reply-requested	[2] BOOLEAN	DEFAULT false }

Figure 15.8   MHS Interpersonal Message (IPM) — P2 protocol

tion). X.400 MHS uses common service elements such as Association Control Service Element (ACSE), Remote Operations Service Element (ROSE) for the P3 and P7 protocol and Reliable Transfer Service Element (RTSE). RTSE uses the underlying services provided by a Basic Activity subset Session Layer.

The 1984 version of X.400 makes some exceptions to the OSI structure for the Application Layer. In fact, the 1984 version of X.400 made only minimal use of the Presentation Layer, and did not use ACSE since these were not standardized at the time. The 1988 version makes full use of the ACSE and revised ROSE, RTSE and Presentation Layer standards.

Protocols used by MHS below the network level are dependent on the network topology used, e.g. X.25 or LAN. However, for interworking with public X.400 services, Transport Class 0 and X.25 are mandatory.

In a complete MHS implementation, X.400 MHS will also use the Directory to resolve O/R addresses and MTA names to actual Presentation Service Access Point (PSAP) addresses. (Only the 1988 version has the capacity to use the Directory.)

15.3.3 Protocol Types and Standards

Within each MHS protocol there are a number of defined elements. These have been specified to suit the nature of the interactions across the functional units of the MHS.

P1

At the P1 level (MTA to MTA) there are only three protocol elements *Message*, *Probe* and *Report*. These are conveyed as Application Protocol Data Units (APDUs) by the RTSE RT-Transfer service. The Message conveys user protocol, i.e. messages. The Report contains MTA delivery reports (or non-delivery reports), and Probe is used to test the ability of the MTS to process and deliver a specific message. A simplified ASN.1 definition of the P1 follows:

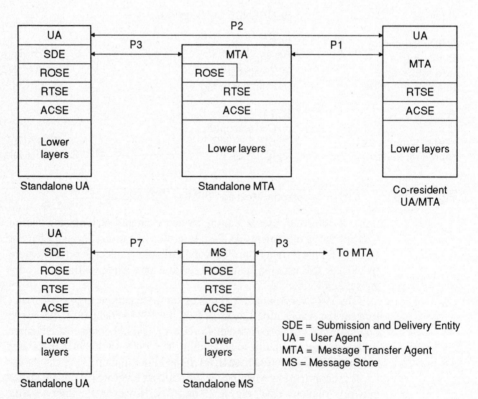

Figure 15.9   MHS protocol stacks

```
MTS-APDU ::= CHOICE {
            [0] Message,
            [1] Probe,
            [2] Report }
```

```
Message ::= SEQUENCE {
            MessageTransferEnvelope,           -- defined in Fig. 15.7
            content     OCTET STRING }
```

P2

The information objects that are conveyed as message contents between UAs are defined as the P2 protocol. It is carried as header information inside P1 or P3. There are only two types of elements, i.e. an Interpersonal Message (IPM) (the actual information) and an Interpersonal Notification (IPN) (containing receipt notification). These are illustrated below:

```
InformationObject ::= CHOICE {
interpersonalMessage                  [0] IPM, -- defined in Fig. 15.8
interpersonalNotification             [1] IPN }
```

P3

At the P3 (UA to MTA) level there are a greater number of protocol elements. Some elements are used as management services, i.e. change password, control and register, etc. The Probe element is used to test the operation of the MHS on a specific message (i.e. if the originator sends this, can the MTS deliver it?). The common P3 elements used for the exchange of messages are: Submit, Deliver and Notify. P3 is implemented as a set of Remote Operations using the ROSE protocol. The invoke operations defined by P3 are listed below:

- Message submission

- Probe submission

- Cancel deferred delivery

- Submission control

- Delivery control

- Message delivery

- Report delivery

- Register

- Change credentials.

P7

The P7 protocol supports the MS which resides between the UA and the MTA. The P7 protocol elements in conjunction with P3 protocol elements are used to perform operations on the MS. The standard submission and delivery functions of P3 are used on the MS to MTA interface, whereas facilities such as List, Fetch, Summarize, Delete, Register and Alert are used by the UA on the MS. Submission of messages by the UA via the

MS to the MTS is referred to as indirect submission. P7, like P3, is implemented as a set of Remote Operations:

- Summarize

- List

- Fetch

- Delete

- Register

- Alert

15.4 MHS ADDRESSING

15.4.1 MTA Domains

ADMD

In the total scheme of an international MHS, MTAs are interconnected and organized into domains. A collection of at least one MTA, zero or more UAs, zero or more MSs, and zero or more AUs operated by an organization constitutes a *Management Domain (MD)*. These domains exist at the highest level as an *ADMD (Administrative Management Domain)*. Below this, domains exist at the private level and are referred to as *PRMDs (Private Management Domains)*. ADMDs generally exist as a carrier or a national service providing messaging services to the public. They play a central role in the global MHS by interconnecting to one another internationally, and to PRMDs domestically, to provide an international backbone.

PRMD

PRMDs exist at the corporate level. PRMDs access the international backbone via the ADMDs. They may also connect to other domestic and international PRMDs independently of the ADMDs.

The names of the management domains form the top levels of the hierarchical O/R Address structure. Thus, a MHS user is addressed using the hierarchical address structure of Country – ADMD – PRMD – Organization Name – Personal name. This address must be globally unique. However, routing is not constrained by the hierarchy. Any ADMD and PRMD MTA systems can be interconnected, provided the routing tables of the MTAs are correctly configured; i.e. a domain is logical not physical.

Specific bilateral agreements are required between the management authorities of MTAs before they can exchange messages. This may be required for commercial and security reasons.

15.4.2 O/R Addresses

The hierarchical O/R Address, illustrated in Figure 15.10, is the basis by which the MHS system operates. Each user is allocated an unambiguous O/R Address that reflects the division of domains into countries, administration and private domains. An O/R Address typically consists of the following fields:

Country name — Either a 2 character code from ISO 3166 or an X.121 Data Country Code (3 digits).

ADMD name — A distinct name for an administrative domain selected by the carrier.

PRMD name — A distinct name for a private domain agreed between the carrier and the PRMD.

Organization name — The name of the user's company or organization.

Organizaional unit names — Possibly multiple names such as department, division and section — as required to unambiguously identify the user.

Personal name — Surname, initial, first name, etc.

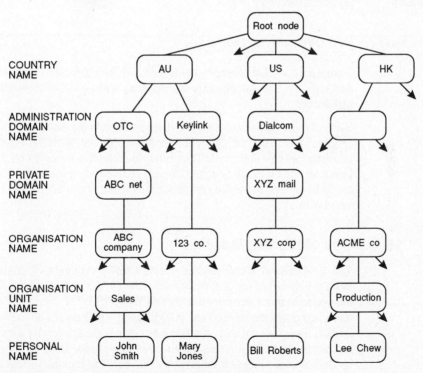

Figure 15.10   MHS hierarchical O/R Address structure

```
ORName ::=        [APPLICATION 0] SEQUENCE {
address           ORAddress,
directory-name    [0] Name                                        OPTIONAL }

ORAddress ::=     SEQUENCE {
                      StandardAttributes,
                      DomainDefinedAttributes,           -- for interworking
                      ExtensionAttributes }              -- 1988 extensions

StandardAttributes ::= SEQUENCE {
                      CountryName                               OPTIONAL,
admd-Name             AdministrationDomainName                  OPTIONAL,
x.121-address         [0] NetworkAddress                        OPTIONAL,
                      [1] TerminalIdentifier                    OPTIONAL,
prmd-Name             [2] PrivateDomainName                     OPTIONAL,
                      [3] OrganizationName                      OPTIONAL,
                      [4] NumericUserIdentifier                 OPTIONAL,
                      [5] PersonalName                          OPTIONAL,
                      [6] SEQUENCE OF OrganizationalUnitNames

                                                                OPTIONAL }

PersonalName ::= SET {
surname           [0] PrintableString
given-name        [1] PrintableString
initials          [2] PrintableString
generation        [3] PrintableString }
```

Figure 15.11   MHS O/R names and addresses

Domain   Other naming fields necessary for a particular domain may
defined   be required for interworking with non-X.400 systems.
attributes

Some of these fields are optional. It can be seen from the ASN.1 definition
(Figure 15.11) that an O/R Address has sufficient attribute types to
facilitate message delivery to Teletex terminals on data networks (X.121),
terminals and facsimile systems (Domain Defined Attributes). The Physical Delivery Service defines extensions to this for postal addresses (1988
version only).

15.4.3 Use of the Directory

The 1984 version of the standard operates solely with the O/R Address.
With the advent of the X.500 Directory, the 1988 X.400 standards have
the option to use a directory name (see Chapter 16). The directory name
has a less restricted format (e.g. ADMD and PRMD names are omitted)
and it is more user friendly. If a directory name is used to specify message
recipients, the MTAs present the directory name to the Directory to look
up the corresponding O/R Address for the user. The naming format used

in 1988 X.400 is an O/R Name that contains either a directory name, or an O/R Address or both.

Name resolution

The message contains O/R Names as originator and recipient information. The MTA and UA must resolve these O/R Names to real network and higher layer addresses to which a connection is made to forward the message, (i.e. a PSAP address of an adjacent MTA, MS or UA). The MHS systems may use local information (e.g. address translation tables) or access the Directory.

Typically, an interface to the Directory (i.e. the Directory User Agent, DUA) will be integrated into the connection services used by the MHS. This permits O/R Name resolution which needs to occur in the P3 and P1 protocols. Both the UA and the MTA can independently access the Directory.

Distribution lists

The Directory is also used for distribution list expansion. This feature permits an O/R Name to specify a group of recipients. This requires the MTA to access the Directory to expand the distribution list into a discrete list of O/R Addresses.

Security

Aspects of an asymmetric key management scheme to support X.400 security services are provided by the Directory Authentication Framework (X.509). The Directory stores certified copies of public keys for MHS users which can be used to provide authentication, and to facilitate key exchange in data confidentiality and data integrity mechanisms.

15.5 X.400 STANDARDS

15.5.1 Existing Standards

X.400 is in fact the generic name for a set of standards. Table 15.3 lists the current (1988) versions of the standards.

EDI

Although X.400 in its original form can be used to carry EDI messages, a new UA and protocol (X.435) was developed in 1990 to cater for the specific requirements of EDI.

The new standards will carry existing EDI messages with any of the EDI syntaxes (i.e. EDIFACT, X12, UN/TDI) in the message body. The message header contains a combination of fields similar to those in P2, and those found in an EDI message header, but encoded in ASN.1. EDI is covered separately in Chapter 23.

Table 15.3   MHS standards

CCITT	ISO	SUBJECT MATTER
X.400	10021-1	Service and System Overview
X.402	10021-2	Overall Architecture
X.403	—	Conformance Testing
X.407	10021-3	Abstract Service Definition Conventions
X.408	—	Encoded Information Type Conversion Rules
X.411	10021-4	MTS Service Definition
X.413	10021-5	Message Store Service Definition
X.419	10021-6	Protocol Specifications
X.420	10021-7	Interpersonal Messaging System
X.435	—	EDI Messaging

15.5.2 Future Work

As with all Application Layer standards, the initial scope of the X.400 committees was to cater for basic requirements in the initial release. In the case of X.400 MHS, this is the 1984 version. The 1988 version introduced a number of major concepts and functions such as the MS, support for physical delivery systems, security features and Directory interworking. Now that 1988 systems and products are entering the market, the X.400 standards development groups are looking toward the 1992 version. This section identifies the areas of work being reviewed and, depending on progress and acceptance, which may become part of the 1992 (or later) version of the X.400 standard.

Management model

The management aspects of MHS are being developed in conjunction with the OSI systems management model (X.700 — as described in Chapter 19). The OSI management model identifies accounting, configuration, performance, fault and security as five major functional areas.

As X.400 MHS services enter into the commercial world, accounting mechanisms are mandatory. The functions performed by MTAs that possibly can incur a charge or tariff are: size of message; class of service; number of copies performed; grade of delivery; use of the Directory; and general tariff parameters. Such information will be retrieved from the MTAs via the management mechanisms.

Configuration covers: creation, modification and deletion of MTA, MS and UA entities; management of MTA routing tables; management of user O/R names and addresses; control of directory access; setting of statistical and alarm thresholds; setting of configuration parameters; and setting of accounting tariff parameters.

Performance and statistics cover: collection of message rate (arrival and delivery) statistics; undelivered message statistics; and current MTA status (e.g. current active connections).

Fault management covers: alarm management; failure and recovery control; and testing and diagnostics.

Security covers: security key management; verification and authentication process control; encryption algorithm management; and audit trail control and management.

Although existing X.400 systems operate satisfactorily with proprietary management facilities, standardization of the management aspects of X.400 MHS is becoming an important factor in the realization of commercially operated X.400 MHS services. Standardized management facilitates the operation of global messaging services and enables a rapid response to changing user demands.

Routing

The optimization and dynamic configuration of message routes between networks of MTA is another work item. Routing must also consider security aspects for access from the administrative domains into a private domain.

Voice mail

Voice mail (VM) products originally stemmed from the telephone (PABX) markets. These products were based on storage and replay of the normal analogue voice message. As digitized voice systems became more widespread, the voice message became just another electronically encoded message. As X.400 MHS performs a generic messaging service, the requirement to interface it to voice oriented submission and delivery systems has been recognized. The current standards include a "voice" body part but there are no standardized procedures for its use.

Work is now progressing within the X.400 group with an aim to standardize the protocol and encoding of voice based messages for transfer by the generic X.400 protocols. The standard is called X.440. X440 is an alternative protocol to the IPM (P2) protocol as it specifies a heading and a body of the message. The heading of a voice mail message is similar in overall terms to the P2 heading (i.e. it contains the originator and recipients, the subject, the importance and the sensitivity, etc. of the message). In addition, the VM heading also contains language and voice encoding type. Also, the message recipient fields have an extension to include the "spoken name" and the notification types required for the voice message. The voice encoding type is defaulted to 32 kbit/s Adaptive Differential Pulse Code Modulation (ADPCM CCITT G.721). The body in a VM message has the following fields, that, at the top level, are defined as voice parameters and voice data:

- Voice parameters indicate the voice (message) duration in seconds, the encoding used and supplementary information. Supplementary information is optional and user specific.

- The voice data parameter is defined as an octet string and contains the encoded voice message.

With the exception of other minor changes in the types of notifications and the error codes in non-receipt notifications indicating unrecognized language, the voice mail service is similar to IPM.

File messages   The use of X.400 MHS to transfer files is a major requirement. To date, files have been transferred (and distributed) through the MHS as binary or IA5 type message body types. This in itself causes a number of problems if P2 IPM is used, namely — there is no parameter in either of these body types to supply the name of the file. If only one file is sent, then the subject field could be used to indicate to the recipient the name of the file (e.g. Subject: This is usr/mydir/myfile). However, where two or more files are sent in the same message as multiple body parts, the problem is open to all sorts of customized answers. Also the file at its source has attributes (such as creator, size, date written, owner, access controls, etc.) and these cannot be transferred as separate data items in the above scenario. To adopt a consistent approach to the problem, a body-part type of File Transfer is being defined that has the same definition as the FTAM specification (see Chapter 17). It is expected that the File Transfer body part will be included in the 1992 version of X.400.

MS extensions   The message store concept, which was introduced in the 1988 version of X.400 MHS is being reviewed and extensions will be added by 1992. Generally, these extensions are directed at the management and integrity of the stored messages and the provisioning of some audit mechanisms (inlog and outlog).

It is also worthy of note that the MS supports list and fetch functions based on message attributes. As new message types emerge (e.g. EDI, VM and message attributes relating to X.500 directory use) then the MS standard will be updated (with addenda or related documents) to reflect the support of such message attributes.

15.5.3 Group Communications

Group Communications (GC) and asynchronous computer conferencing is a major new concept of X.400 MHS. It is directed at multi-party manipulation of documents and messages. The overall concept of GC is that users of the service can become members of one or more "topics" which are directed at multi-party operations such as bulletin boards, co-authorship of documents, multi-party editing and computer conferencing. These functions are defined within the GC system as *activities*. An activity is defined as a named organization of a set of messages and a set of users. An activity may also contain activity policy and access control information. To support such group operations, the current X.400 MHS entities such as UAs, MS and MTAs can be used where appropriate. The GC model also has similar entities referred to as GCUA (Group Communications User Agents) and GCSAs (Group Communications Service Agents). There is also a GC Storage System Agent defined (and it is used in addition to the concept of the MS). The GC model interfaces to the X.400 MHS services for message distribution. It also interfaces to the X.500 Directory for activity definition storage and distribution list management. Perhaps the main feature of this service beyond that of

X.400 MHS is that messages (or part messages) can be searched and retrieved from a group of messages (subject to access policies). (Retrieval from the current version of the MS is limited to "locally" held specific user messages.) The elements of the GC service permit activity creation, deletion and membership, control of the distributed nature of the stored information (duplication), purging, listing members, members' role definition and message retrieval or purging based on filter specifications. Because of the number of discrete OSI system components involved, i.e X.400 MHS, X.500 Directory and possibly document storage systems, the GC concept will require good management and administration mechanisms to ensure integrity of the overall service. Although the 1988 X.400 MHS IPM (P2) protocol is being considered for GC communications initially, a CCITT X.gc protocol definition is being developed (to support the document retrieval requirements).

In conclusion, many features are being added to the X.400 MHS model. These include different body types such as FTAM files; new message protocols such as VM and PEDI; and they include two larger areas of work relating to systems management and group communications. This evolution will ensure that X.400 MHS will support a significant proportion of the world's messaging in the future. The system aspects of these technologies are also described in Chapter 24.

15.6 QUESTIONS

Question 15.1   Devise an X.400 O/R Address structure suitable for your organization.

Question 15.2   List the major differences between the 1984 and 1988 version of X.400.

Question 15.3   Name the protocols used between the major components of the MHS.

Question 15.4   What is an O/R Address and how does it affect the organization/configuration of the MHS?

Question 15.5   What are the components of an X.400 IPM message when being transferred within the MTS?

Question 15.6   List the basic functions of an MTA that can be applied to a message.

Question 15.7   How does a user of the MHS determine if the messages sent arrive at their destination correctly?

Question 15.8   What does the Message Store provide the MHS user with beyond that of direct access to the MTS?

Question 15.9   Why does the Message Store need to know about message attributes?

Question 15.10   How does the X.500 directory interface to the X.400 service and what X.400 components does it affect?

16 The Directory

16.1 OVERVIEW OF THE DIRECTORY

16.1.1 Directory Service

The utility of the telephone network would be severely limited without the familiar paper directories, and directory assistance services. Not only are public directories published, but every organization maintains its own internal corporate directory. However, paper based directories have some shortcomings:

- They are expensive to print and transport to the users.

- Typically, some information is invalidated by network changes before the directory even reaches the user.

- Paper directories are not amenable to automatic look-up by computer systems.

Purpose
The standards committees recognized early that an electronic directory service was central to the success of any modern global telecommunications service, and the X.500 series of standards are the outcome of their work on this topic. The objective is to provide a logical global database for public and private directory services. The driving force for the establishment of the directory service is the growth of X.400 Messaging Handling Systems (MHS), but the directory supports a variety of other OSI and non-OSI applications — e.g. an electronic white pages directory for the telephone system.

The Directory is a collection of distributed open systems that cooperate to hold a logical database of information about a set of objects in the real world. The users of the Directory, including people and computer programs, can read or modify the information, or parts of it, subject to having permission to do so. The access to the Directory is interactive — supporting both browsing by human users and automatic look up by application processes.

User friendly naming
In the OSI world, where logical names are used, the Directory performs a number of functions that resolve the logical names to physical OSI addresses. A logical name is intended to be easily derived and remem-

bered by human users, and independent of location; e.g. with MHS, the logical name of a recipient may be: Country, Organizational Names and Personal Name — yet this needs to be resolved to a presentation address that contains a string of digits dependent on location and network structure. The Directory is used by the MHS application to resolve this name when it wishes to pass the recipient the message. Also, many other OSI distributed applications require the use of a directory for name resolution, e.g. to translate a target application title to a presentation address.

Multiple names It is common for people and other objects to be known by multiple names. So the directory must support aliases, nicknames and alternate names. The Directory can also store distribution lists, i.e. lists of the names of people or objects that belong to certain identified groups.

Security In addition to security services that control access to the Directory information itself, the Directory can be used to support security functions for other applications. The Directory can hold a password for a specific user or certified public keys for cryptographic systems, suitably protected against tampering. Being in a directory, this information has one administration point and specific security information can be accessed only by those who have permission to retrieve it.

Aid to applications It is sometimes desirable to ascertain the capabilities of target applications before attempting communication with them. For instance, the Directory can store information about MHS user capabilities to determine any constraints applying to the delivery of messages and to arrange conversion if necessary. The Directory can support system management with information about the management capabilities of remote systems and the types of objects that are present.

Non-OSI uses The Directory is not limited to data networks. It is generalized in order to support a variety of telecommunications services and both white pages and yellow pages telephone directory services are expected to be commercially significant implementations of the Directory.

16.1.2 Standards

The Directory standards are CCITT Recommendations X.500 to X.521 that were published in 1988. ISO equivalents are ISO 9594 parts 1 to 8 that reached International Standard (IS) status in 1990. The initial standards provide a basic service that is the subject of the main body of this chapter. A large number of extensions are currently being developed and these are summarized at the end of the chapter to give an insight to future trends.

16.1.3 Directory Organization

A global Directory requires co-operation between a large number of network operators and service providers, each of which administers a range of names and addresses, and maintains its own separate database. To facilitate the uniform operation of a global directory, the standards provide for the interconnection of the databases and the procedures to access them by users' applications.

Functional organization

The X.500 standards identify two major functional components for the Directory. These are the Directory User Agent (DUA) and Directory System Agent (DSA). The DUA represents a user of the Directory and provides the access to the DSAs that process the actual Directory requests. The Directory information may be distributed amongst a set of co-operating DSAs to provide an integrated service called a *distributed Directory*. A DSA may also operate as a free standing single database, in which case it is referred to as a *centralized Directory*. The X.500 standards define the DSA and its abstract ports (interfaces) and services, and the protocols used to access the DSA. The DUA is an abstract component that represents the accessor of the DSA(s) and directory service. The standards do not define the functionality of a DUA which is customized to the user's needs. The DUA and DSA will be described in more detail in following sections after the Directory structure is described (see Section 16.3).

Domains

The Directory is organized into a number of interrelated administrative domains — this is similar to the domain concept in X.400. A domain is formed by one or more distributed database systems under the common management of a public or private organization. Each system holds a fragment of the global database.

Ownership

In practice, a carrier may own the national Directory (to permit a single point for international access to the national service), but private companies may own and administer their own corporate wide Directory. In principle, the private Directories will be linked as subordinates to the national Directory in a hierarchical structure. Access controls permitting, users may access the corporate Directory either directly or via the directory hierarchy. The service supplied to users is independent of whether the request for information was by direct access to a Directory or access initiated from a *superior* or *subordinate* Directory system.

Replication

Conceptually, the simplest configuration for the Directory information is for each DSA to have a separate fragment of the global Directory. However, because the accessors are generally dispersed, and some form of back-up redundancy is usually required for the information, part of the Directory information may be replicated and interlinked. Some DSAs hold copies of information belonging to others — this is referred to as *shadowed* or *replicated* Directories. Such replication would optimize the

Directory by locating copies of frequently accessed information close to
its users.

**Naming
authorities**

The Directory information itself is organized as a hierarchical structure
(see Figure 16.1). Naming authorities are responsible for ensuring that
distinct names are allocated at each level in the hierarchy. Such a structure
is required to facilitate the overall management of the Directory and to
ensure the allocation of unambiguous names. In order to participate in the
growing global open network, it is essential that each person and addres-
sable object in any company or other organization be allocated an unambiguous name. All organizations should apply to have their names
registered with the appropriate naming authorities in each country (the
registration authority is usually the ISO national member).

16.2 DIRECTORY STRUCTURE

In total, the information entries contained in the Directory are referred to
as the *Directory Information Base (DIB)* and are structured to form an
inverted tree, referred to as the *Directory Information Tree (DIT)* (see
Figure 16.1). The Directory standards are not intended to be a model for
a generalized distributed database. In particular, the design of the Directory has three simplifying assumptions that reflect the nature of the
telecommunications applications that will be using it:

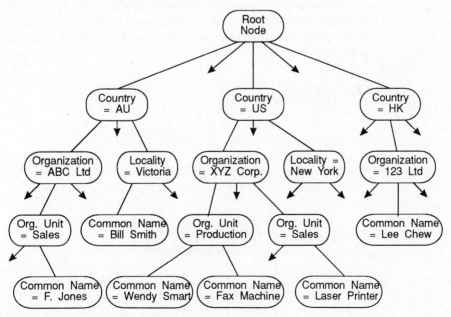

Figure 16.1   X.500 hierarchical name structure

- Queries (i.e. reads from the Directory) will be much more frequent than updates (i.e. writes to the Directory).

- Transient conditions, in which parts of the DIB are not entirely consistent, are tolerable (although short lived).

- A hierarchical architecture is used for the DIT.

16.2.1 Directory Information Base

Objects

The Directory is made up of information about *objects*. The term "object" is used to refer to the actual instance of something, e.g. a person, a plumber. Each object belongs to an *object class* — an identified family of objects that share common characteristics (e.g. organizational person, residential person).

Entries

The DIB is composed of (Directory) *entries*, each of which consists of a collection of information on one object. The term "entry" is used to refer to the information (held in the Directory) about a specific instance of an object, e.g. the plumber's name, telephone number and address. Each object has one *object entry* that is the primary collection of information about that object. In addition to the object entry, there may be one or more *alias entries* that provide alternate names for the object.

DIT

The entries of the DIB are arranged in the form of a tree, the DIT. The vertices of the DIT represent the entries (see Figure 16.2). Entries higher in the tree (nearer the root) represent objects such as countries or organizations, while entries lower in the tree represent people or application processes, etc.

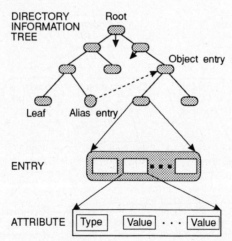

Figure 16.2   Structure of X.500 Directory Information Tree (DIT) and of entries

Attributes

Each entry is made up of *attributes.* Entries have a set of attributes defined by an attribute type and one or more values. The presence and type of attributes that make up a particular entry are dependent on the *class* of object that the entry describes. For example, an organization object class may include the following attributes:

- Organization Name;

- Description, Business Category;

- Location, Postal Address;

- Telephone, Facsimile and ISDN Numbers etc.

The organizational person object class may include the following attributes:

- Common Name (e.g. William Smith);

- Surname;

- Organizational Unit Name (e.g. department, division or section name);

- Title, Description;

- Location, Postal Address;

- Telephone, Facsimile and ISDN Numbers, etc.

The application entity class contains:

- Common Name (e.g. an application entity qualifier — see Section 14.1.1, page 247);

- Presentation address (i.e. Presentation Service Access Point, PSAP address);

- Description, Location;

- Organization and Organization Unit names;

- Supported application contexts (see page 248).

The Directory standards define a number of object classes of general use such as those above, and provide for the creation of new object classes by refinement of the standard classes. For instance, the 1988 X.400 MHS standards define additional attributes (e.g. O/RName) and object classes (e.g. User Agent) for message handling systems use.

Alternate values

Each attribute of an object may have multiple values stored under the object's entry in the Directory; e.g. there may be multiple telephone numbers listed for an organization or person.

Table 16.1   Example of distinguished names

RELATIVE DISTINGUISHED NAME		DISTINGUISHED NAME	REGISTRATION AUTHORITY
Root	{}	{}	–
Country	C = UK	C = UK	ISO
Organization	O = Telecom	C = UK, O = Telecom	National Registration Authority
Organization unit	OU = Sales	C = UK, O = Telecom, OU = Sales	Corporate

16.2.2 Directory Names

Every entry has a *distinguished name* that uniquely and unambiguously identifies the entry. The properties of the distinguished name are derived from the tree structure of the information i.e. a Directory name consists of an ordered sequence of the names of the entries from the root down the tree to a particular entry.

RDN

Within the DIT, each entry has a unique *Relative Distinguished Name (RDN)*. An RDN is a set of specially nominated attribute values (the distinguished values) of the entry. Frequently, only one attribute value will be nominated as the RDN of an entry. However, in some circumstances, more than one attribute (e.g. Common Name and Location attributes) may make up the RDN for a particular entry in order to differentiate between two objects with similar names.

As illustrated in Table 16.1, the RDNs of all the entries with a particular immediate superior are distinct. It is the responsibility of the relevant naming authority for that entry to ensure that this is so by appropriately assigning distinguished attribute values. The naming authority should never hand out the same name twice for entries with common immediate superiors.

The RDN for an entry is chosen when the entry is created. It may be altered by users with appropriate access rights.

Distinguished name

The *distinguished name* of a given object is defined as being the sequence of the RDNs of the entry that represents the object and those of all its superior entries (in descending order). Because of the one to one correspondence between objects and object entries, the distinguished name of an object can be considered to identify the object entry also.

The distinguished name starts at the root node and contains the RDNs of all the respective branch and leaf entries.

Alternate names

In addition to the RDN, the name attribute for each entry may have a number of alternate values to admit common abbreviations and variations in spelling. This accommodates *alternate names*; e.g. the Common Name attribute for a person may have William Smith as the distinguished value, and alternate names may be: Bill Smith and Mr W. Smith. Thus, William Smith must be used in the RDN in order to access the entry directly (in a read operation). If the correct distinguished name for an entry is not known, then the user may request the Directory to locate any entry that matches certain attributes. For example, a request to search for entries with a Common Name attribute that matched Bill Smith would also be effective to locate the entry for William Smith above. (Other attributes, e.g. Location, may also be supplied to narrow down the search.)

Alias names   Some of the entries at the leaves of the tree are *alias entries*, while other entries are object entries. Alias entries contain no information but point to object entries. An alias, or an alias name, for an object is a name at least one of whose RDNs is that of an alias entry. Alias names provide the basis for multiple name forms for the corresponding objects; i.e. alias entries are used to redefine objects. The Directory identifies and re-evaluates the alias to find the corresponding object entry. Alias names permit object entries to achieve the effect of having multiple immediate superiors. Just as the distinguished name of an object expresses its principal relationship to some hierarchy of objects, so an alias represents a different hierarchy of objects.

16.2.3 Directory Operations

The hierarchical structure is the basis by which users access the Directory information. Users may supply a complete distinguished name and access information for the corresponding entry. Alternatively, users may supply one or more attributes and request the Directory to search the database and supply information from any matching entries. The operations performed on the Directory fall into three major classifications, i.e. read, search and modify. Within these classifications are specific services:

Read   A read request is aimed at a particular entry, and causes the values of some or all the attributes of that entry to be returned. The user must specify a complete distinguished name in the request to identify a specific entry. Where only some attributes are to be returned, the user supplies the list of attribute types of interest.

Compare   A compare request is aimed at a particular attribute of a particular entry. The user supplies a distinguished name and a proposed value for an attribute. The operation causes the Directory to check whether the supplied value matches a value of that attribute. The Directory returns with a true or false response.

Abandon   An abandon request, as applied to an outstanding interrogation request, informs the Directory that the originator of the request is no longer interested in the request being carried out. The Directory may, for example, cease processing the request, and may discard any results so far achieved.

List   A list request causes the Directory to return the list of immediate subordinates of a particular entry in the DIT. The user must supply the distinguished name of a particular entry, and the Directory returns the names of the subordinates of that entry (if any exist).

Search   A search request causes the Directory to return information from all of the entries within a certain portion of the DIT that satisfy some condition(s). The user's request includes arguments to identify the scope of the search of the DIT and the conditions to filter matching entries. The information returned from each entry consists of some or all of the attributes of that entry, as with read.

Add/remove entry   An add entry request causes a new leaf entry (either an object entry, or an alias entry) to be added to the DIT. A remove entry request causes a leaf entry to be removed from the DIT.

Modify entry   This operation changes the attributes of a specified entry.

Modify RDN   This operation changes the RDN of a leaf entry.

Access control   Objects within the Directory can have discrete access control categories to protect entries from unauthorized access and modification. Access control can be applied to a group of entries (a subtree), a single entry, an attribute within an entry or a single value of an attribute. Where access control is applied to any of the above, the component being protected is referred to as the protected "item". The following categories of protection are identified in an appendix to ISO 9594 part 2/X.501:

Detect   Allows the protected item to be detected (i.e. it exists) by the accessor.

Compare   Allows the protected item to be compared by the accessor.

Read   Allows the protected item to be retrieved (read) by the accessor.

Modify   Allows the protected item to be updated by the accessor.

Add/delete   Allows the protected item to be created, deleted or updated by the accessor.

Naming   Allows the modification of the RDN of the subordinate of the protected entry by the accessor.

In general, the access control mechanism checks the categories prior to the operation on the protected item. The standards, however, do not specify how access control is implemented and leave it as a local matter for the DSA administrators. It is recognized that the administration of such features requires substantial effort.

16.2.4 Directory Schema

The Directory enforces a set of rules to ensure that the DIT remains well-formed in the face of modifications over time. These rules are known as the *directory schema*. The directory schema is a set of definitions and constraints concerning the fundamental structure of the DIT and the possible ways entries are named, the information that can be held in an entry, and attributes used to represent that information. These schema definitions are applied during directory access to prevent entries having the wrong types of attributes for their object class, attribute values being of the wrong form for the attribute types, and even entries having subordinate entries of the wrong class.

Formally, the directory schema is comprised of a set of:

Structure definitions   Rules that define the distinguished names that entries may have and the ways in which they may be related to one another through the DIT.

Object class definitions   Definitions for the set of mandatory and optional attributes that must be present, and may be present, respectively, in an entry of a given class. Object classes are defined by an Object Identifier (OID) and by a listing of attribute types identifying whether they are optional or mandatory.

Attribute type definitions   Rules that specify the object identifier by which the attribute is known, its syntax, and whether it is permitted to have multiple values.

Attribute syntax definitions   Definitions for each attribute of the underlying Abstract Syntax Notation One (ASN.1) data type and matching rules.

Figure 16.3 summarizes the relationships between the schema definitions on the one side, and the DIT, directory entries, attributes, and attribute values on the other.

The directory schema is distributed, like the DIB itself, and may vary between the directory systems. Each administrative authority establishes the schema that will apply for those portions of the DIB that it administers.

The schema enables the Directory system to, for example:

- prevent the creation of subordinate entries of the wrong object class (e.g. a country as a subordinate of a person);

- prevent the addition of an attribute types to an entry inappropriate to the object class (e.g. a serial number to a person's entry); or,

- prevent the addition of an attribute value of a syntax not matching that defined for the attribute type (e.g. a printable string to a bit string).

16.3 THE DISTRIBUTED DIRECTORY

The main functional components of the Directory are the Directory User Agent (DUA) and the Directory System Agent (DSA), as shown in Figure 16.4.

DUA

Each user is represented in accessing the Directory by a *Directory User Agent (DUA)*, which is an application process. There is a one to one relationship between a user and the corresponding DUA. The DUA is accessed by the Directory user and the requested operations are then passed by the DUA to the Directory.

The Directory can be accessed at a number of points by DUAs. To access the Directory, the DUA communicates with one or more DSAs. The DUA and DSA are logical components. In a physical configuration, the DSA and the DUA can be combined or distributed, and if distributed they are associated via underlying OSI protocols.

DSA

The DSA can be a single component (called a *centralized* Directory) or connected to other DSAs (a *distributed* Directory). When there are multiple interconnected DSAs, name resolution can be performed by one or many DSAs. A single DSA, or group of DSAs can be referred to as a DMD (Directory Management Domain).

Each DSA has a fragment of the DIB. Yet an important requirement of the Directory is that the answers it returns are independent of the identity and location of the enquiring user. Furthermore, the DUA should not need to know the internal structure of the DSAs and their interconnections.

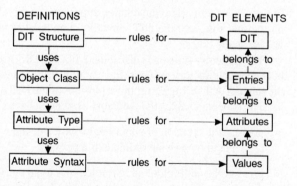

Figure 16.3   Directory schema

Naming context

A DSA is responsible for a part of the total DIB. This name space responsibility is referred to as the *naming context* of the DSA. In order to identify the position of the DIB at which a naming context starts, the DSA is given a context prefix. A context prefix is empty on the DSA containing the logical root node of the directory. The context prefix of subordinate DSAs corresponds to the RDN of the initial entry of the DSA.

Replication

The initial versions of the standards do not provide protocol support for replication of data, although this is the subject of proposed additions (see Section 16.6.1, page 305). Nevertheless, DSAs using the initial versions of the standards may use replication to speed access by keeping a copy of information which is actually owned by another DSA. In this case, management and updating of the copies is a local matter (e.g. by bilateral agreement with the owner).

16.3.1 DSA Interactions

The directory access process commences with the DUA establishing an association with a DSA and requesting an operation on the Directory. Depending on the location of the information, three modes of DSA interactions are defined, namely chaining, multi-casting and referral as shown in Figure 16.5. The DSAs make use of knowledge about the location of the components of the DIB — such knowledge is in the form of references to other DSAs.

Chaining

The chaining mode of communication may be used by one DSA to pass on a remote operation to only one other DSA when the former has specific knowledge about the naming contexts of the latter. Chaining may be used to contact a DSA up or down the naming hierarchy (i.e. in a superior reference or a subordinate reference), or a cross reference can optionally be used if additional information about other naming contexts is available to optimize name resolution. A number of DSAs may be chained together.

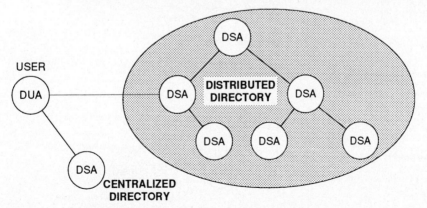

Figure 16.4   Functional components of the Directory standards – Directory User Agent (DUA) and Directory System Agent (DSA).

Referral   A referral is returned by a DSA in its response to a remote operation which it had been requested to perform, either by a DUA, or by another DSA. The referral may constitute the whole response, or just part of the response. The referral contains the Presentation address of another DSA that either has the desired information or can access it. The requesting DUA or DSA then establishes another association to the DSA identified by the referral.

The DSA or DUA receiving the referral may use the knowledge reference contained therein to subsequently chain or multi-cast (depending upon the type of reference) to other DSAs. Alternatively, a DSA receiving a referral may in turn pass the referral back in its response.

Multi-cast   The multi-cast mode of communication is used by one DSA to pass an identical remote operation, either in parallel or sequentially, to one or more other DSAs. Multi-casting is used when the originating DSA does not know the complete naming contexts held by the other DSAs. Multi-casting is used by a DSA only to contact other DSAs pointed to in a non-specific subordinate reference. Normally, only one of the DSAs will be able to continue processing the remote operation, all of the others returning the "unable to proceed" service error.

Parameters can be set by the user to inhibit chaining and referral on DSA operations.

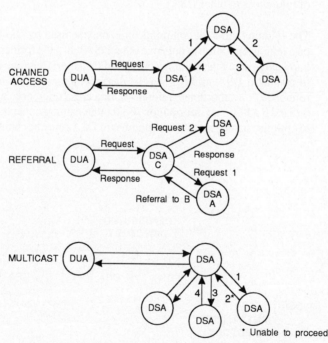

Figure 16.5   DSA interactions — chaining, referral and multi-cast

16.3.2 DAP and DSP Protocols

Figure 16.6 depicts the DUA and DSA as separate OSI entities. The *Directory Access Protocol (DAP)* operates between the DUA and a DSA. The *Directory System Protocol (DSP)* operates between distributed DSAs.

Both the DAP and the DSP are protocols that provide communication between a pair of application processes. In the OSI environment, this is represented as communication between a pair of application entities (AEs) using the presentation service. The function of an application entity is provided by a set of Application Service Elements (ASEs). The interaction between the application entities is described in terms of their use of the services provided by the ASEs. Two ASEs common to both of the Directory protocols are ROSE and ACSE.

Remote Operations Service Element (ROSE) supports the request/reply abstract operations that are used in DAP and DSP. The Directory ASEs provide the mapping function of the Directory abstract service onto the services provided by the ROSE. The Directory ASEs are specified using the Remote Operations notation (RO notation).

The Association Control Service Element (ACSE) supports the establishment and release of an application association between a pair of application entities. Associations between a DUA and a DSA may be established only by the DUA.

DAP The Directory Access Protocol (DAP) is used to realize the Directory abstract service. It comprises three directory specific ASEs in addition to ROSE and ACSE. These are: readASE, searchASE and modifyASE.

DSP The Directory System Protocol (DSP) is used to realize the functionality of distributed directory operations. It comprises three directory specific ASEs in addition to ROSE and ACSE. These are: chainedReadASE, chainedSearchASE and chainedModifyASE. It is similar to the DAP with the addition of chaining.

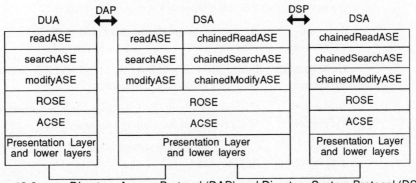

Figure 16.6 Directory Access Protocol (DAP) and Directory System Protocol (DSP)

16.3.3 Knowledge Trees

The DIB is potentially distributed across multiple DSAs with each DSA holding a DIB fragment. It is a requirement of the Directory that, for particular modes of user interaction, the distribution of the Directory is rendered transparent, thereby giving the effect that the whole of the DIB appears to be within each and every DSA.

In order to support the operational requirements described above, it is necessary that each DSA holding a fragment of the DIB be able to identify and optionally interact with other fragments of the DIB held by other DSAs.

Knowledge is defined as the basis for the mapping of a name to its location within a fragment of the DIT. Conceptually DSAs hold two types of information:

- directory information

- knowledge information.

Directory information is the collection of entries comprising the naming context(s) (i.e. a part of the DIB) for which the administrator of a particular DSA has administrative authority.

Knowledge information embodies the naming context(s) held by a particular DSA and denotes how these fit into the overall DIT hierarchy. Distributed name resolution, the process of locating the DSA that has administrative authority for a particular entry given that entry's name, is based on knowledge information.

References The Directory must ensure that each entry be accessed from every DUA. Therefore a reference path, which is a continuous sequence of references, must exist from each DSA to all naming contexts within the Directory. The knowledge possessed by a DSA is defined in terms of a set of one or more knowledge references.

To be able to fulfil the requirements to reach every DIB entry from any DSA, every DSA is required to have knowledge about the entries that it itself holds, and about subordinates and possibly superiors thereof. This gives rise to the following types of knowledge references:

Internal references An internal pointer to an entry held in the same DSA.

Subordinate references Information about DSAs that hold specific entries that are lower in the naming hierarchy.

Superior references Information about the DSA that contains entries at the next level up in the naming hierarchy.

Cross references Optional information about other DSAs and the entries that they hold.

Non-specific subordinate references   Optional information about other DSAs that hold unspecified entries at a lower level in the hierarchy.

Figure 16.7 indicates the structure of a number of DSAs that combine to form a hypothetical DIB. The lower diagram identifies the structure of the knowledge tree within DSA3. Thus, it identifies references as internal, superior and non-specific subordinate (i.e. refer to DSA4). (These references also appear in Table 16.3.)

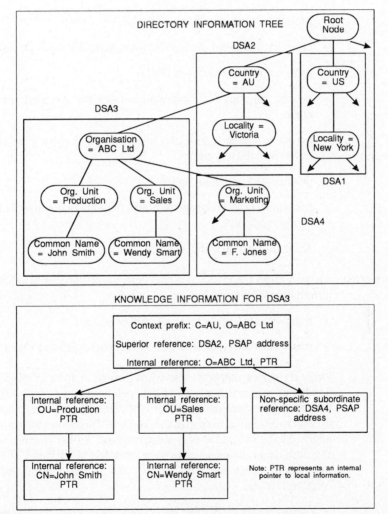

Figure 16.7   Knowledge information – the information a DSA has about the entries it holds and how to locate other entries in the Directory

16.3.4 Operation Arguments

Directory operations submitted by the user via a DUA may contain various arguments to control the access to the Directory. Directory reads, searches or other operations are subject to various constraints defined by the arguments listed below.

Service controls

A number of controls can be applied to the various service requests, primarily to allow the user to impose limits on the use of resources that the Directory must not surpass. Controls are provided on, among other things: the amount of time, the size of results, the scope of search, the interaction modes, and the priority of the request. The various optional arguments are listed below:

- prefer chaining (do not use referrals);

- chaining prohibited (do not distribute request to other DSAs);

- local scope (single DSA or DMD);

- do not use copy (use information from the specified entries, not copies);

- do not dereference alias (this allows the alias entry to be accessed, rather than the real entry);

- priority (high, medium, low);

- time limit (in seconds) and size limit (maximum number of objects to be returned); and,

- scope of referral (DMD, country).

Entry selection

An entry information selection parameter allows the user to indicate what information is being requested:

- return selected attributes or all attributes; and,

- return attribute types only, or both attribute types and values.

Filters

Requests whose outcome involves information from or concerning a number of entries (e.g. search or list operations) may carry with them a filter. A filter expresses one or more conditions that an entry must satisfy in order to be returned as part of the outcome. This allows the set of entries returned to be reduced to only those relevant. A filter is expressed as an assertion about the presence or value of selected attributes of an entry. The user specifies the attribute type, and asserts a value and a filter condition such as:

- equality (only entries that have a value that equals the asserted value are returned);

- substring (selects entries that have a value containing the asserted substring);

- less than, greater than (selects entries depending on relative ordering with respect to the asserted value); and,

- present (selects entries that include the named attribute).

The filters can be combined with logical operators such as AND, OR and NOT.

Security

Security parameters may also be included in the operation request in support of cryptographic techniques used to protect the information in the Directory from unauthorized access.

The above-mentioned arguments are used in conjunction to narrow down the amount of information to be returned.

16.4 DSA OPERATIONAL BEHAVIOR

Each DSA is equipped with procedures capable of completely fulfilling all Directory operations. In the case that a DSA is centralized, all operations are, in fact, completely carried out within that DSA. In the case that the DIB is distributed across multiple DSAs, the completion of a typical operation is fragmented, with just a portion of that operation carried out in each of potentially many co-operating DSAs.

Every Directory operation may be thought of as comprising three distinct phases:

- The Name Resolution phase in which the name of the object on whose entry a particular operation is to be performed is used to locate the DSA that holds the entry.

- The Evaluation phase in which the operation specified by a particular directory query (e.g. read) is actually performed.

- The Results Merging phase in which the results of a specified operation are returned to the requesting DUA. If the chaining mode of interaction was chosen, the Results Merging phase combines the information from a number of DSAs.

Name resolution

Name Resolution is the process of sequentially matching each RDN in a purported name to an arc (or vertex) of the DIT, beginning logically at the root and progressing downwards in the DIT. However, because the DIT is distributed between arbitrarily many DSAs, each DSA may be able to perform only a fraction of the Name Resolution process. A given DSA performs its part of the Name Resolution process by traversing its local knowledge. When a DSA reaches the border of its naming context, it will

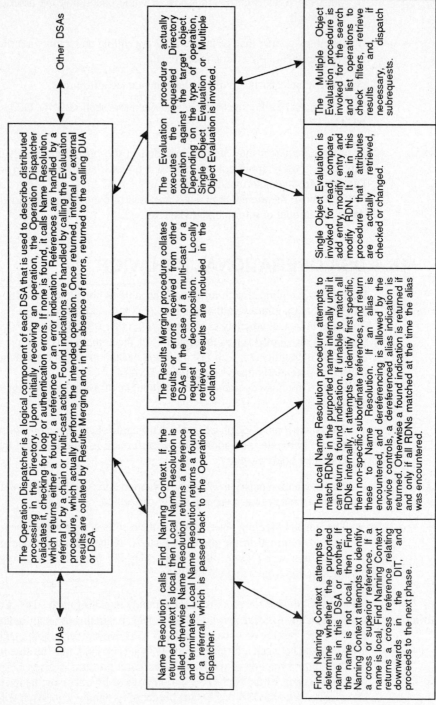

Figure 16.8   DSA operational behaviour

know whether resolution can be continued by another DSA, or whether the name is erroneous.

Evaluation
When the Name Resolution phase has been completed, the actual operation required (e.g. read or search) is performed.

Operations that involve a single entry (read, compare, add entry, remove entry, modify RDN and modify entry) can be carried out entirely within the DSA in which that entry has been located.

Operations that involve multiple entries (list and search) need to locate subordinates of the target, which may or may not reside in the same DSA. If they do not all reside in the same DSA, subordinate references are used to complete the evaluation process.

Results merging
The Result Merging phase is entered when the whole of the Evaluation process has been completed.

In those cases where the operation has affected only a single entry, the result of the operation can simply be returned to the requesting DSA. In those cases where the operation has affected multiple entries on multiple DSAs, results returned by the DSAs need to combined with those generated locally to form a consolidated set of results.

The permissible responses returned to a requester after Results Merging include:

- A complete result of the operation.

- A result that is not complete because some parts of the DIT remain unexplored (applies to list and search only). Such a partial result may include continuation references for those parts of the DIT not explored.

- An error (a referral being a special case).

Operation Dispatcher
The Operation Dispatcher is a logical component of each DSA that is used to describe distributed processing in the Directory. Figure 16.8 describes the behavior of the Operation Dispatcher.

16.5 SECURITY SERVICES

16.5.1 Password Authentication Procedure

A mechanism for implementation of a simple password check by MHS Message Transfer Agents (MTAs) using the Directory is illustrated in Figure 16.9.

❶ The originating user A sends its distinguished name and password to a recipient user B.

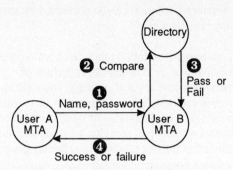

Figure 16.9   Authentication using simple password check

❷   B sends the purported distinguished name and password
                     of A to the Directory in a compare operation, where the
                     password is checked against that held as the User
                     Password attribute within the entry for A.

❸   The Directory confirms to B whether or not the creden-
                     tials of A are valid.

❹   The success or failure of authentication may be conveyed
                     to A.

The advantage of this scheme is that user A can be authenticated to use
many different applications without individual passwords being recorded
on each system. User A can frequently change the password at the
centralized Directory without needing to update many different systems.

16.5.2 Strong Authentication

X.509 provides support for an asymmetric public key management
scheme that can be used for a variety of security services. It is the basis
of the 1988 X.400 security services. The Directory stores certified copies
of user's public keys that can be used in cryptosystems to provide
authentication, and in data confidentiality (encryption) and data integrity
services.

16.6 X.500 STANDARDS

CCITT and ISO jointly developed the Directory standards listed in
Table 16.2. The CCITT version was approved in 1988 and the ISO version
in 1990.

    As with all standards, the initial effort aimed to stabilize the base level
and then progress the standard when the wider issues were recognized and
understood. For instance, the subject of replication and distribution of
information across two or more DSAs was omitted from the initial
standards.

Table 16.2   Directory standards

CCITT	ISO	TITLE
X.500	9594-1	Overview of Concepts, Models and Services
X.501	9594-2	Models
X.509	9594-8	Authentication Framework
X.511	9594-3	Abstract Service Definition
X.518	9594-4	Procedures for Distributed Operation
X.519	9594-5	Protocol Specifications
X.520	9594-6	Selected Attribute Types
X.521	9594-7	Selected Object Classes

16.6.1 Future Work

A set of draft amendments to the X.500 base standards have now been prepared. The thrust of these amendments is directed at distributed DSAs. Because distributed systems need mechanisms and knowledge (held in special attributes other than the directory entry itself) the amendments also introduce some "operational" attributes as extensions to the overall Directory schema. The other main concept introduced in this work on distributed DSAs is the "administration" of the DIB. As the DIB can be fragmented across many DSAs and can also be replicated across many DSAs, it is important to identify components of the total DIB (subtrees) with administrative knowledge (i.e. who owns it and what the rules are for access and modification, etc).

Fragmentation   DSAs can be distributed from a DIB perspective. The top level DSA is the "superior" DSA and ones that contain entries below the DIB fragment held in that DSA are "subordinates". A DUA can access the superior DSA that can chain the request to its subordinate DSA, or a DUA can access the subordinate directly. The "physical break" in the DIB must therefore have knowledge on both sides to indicate where its superior or subordinate DSA is. For example, if an operation on a subordinate DSA deletes an entry that has a direct superior entry in another DSA, the subordinate DSA must advise the superior DSA to delete its reference to the subordinate, before deleting the entry itself. It can be seen from this example, that special attributes which are coupled to the entry itself, are needed to act as containers for this "knowledge". Such attributes are defined in the extensions to the X.500 standards.

Replication   DSA information may also require "replication", e.g. for back-up purposes, for optimized access when concurrent requests are high and for cases where geographic distribution is required of the DSA data. For these reasons an additional protocol can exist between DSAs — it is referred to as the Directory Replication Protocol (DRP). The services of the DRP allow the DSA that owns the original entry to co-ordinate updates of replicated entries on shadow DSAs.

Systems entries   In the initial version of the X.500 standards, the Directory entry (user data) held in a DSA had a number of "associated attributes" to permit knowledge of other DSAs to be associated with the hierarchy of the actual DIB entry. Based on initial experience, and refinement of replication and fragmentation of DIB data, the definition of an entry has been broadened and reclassified as a DSA Systems Entry (DSE). A DSE can contain entry attributes (for the user data) and operational attributes to support the administration of the entry and the   replication and fragmentation management of distributed DSAs. The DSE operational attributes are split into two groups: DSA specific attributes (intra DSA entry management) and DSA shared attributes (inter DSA entry and DIB management). A DSE may have only the entry attributes, the operational attributes or both depending on its role within the total DIB. Therefore, to identify an entry with its role and DIB location and its effect in the scheme of the total (and possibly distributed and replicated) DIB, a number of DSE entry types have been defined as listed in Table 16.3. There are considerable "management" and DIB "location reference" entry types and only a few "user data" entry types. Also, entry types are not exclusive in a single entry e.g. an entry can be defined to be a "Shadow" and a "Cross Reference" entry type.

Attributes   Corresponding to the increased number of entry types, a number of new attributes are defined, considerably extending the attributes defined in the initial version of the standards.

16.6.2 Conclusion

The additions to the Directory standards provide extensive support for the various management, DIB administration and distributed aspects of the Directory. Developments in other standards will also continue to impact on the Directory. Because the Directory is potentially a knowledge and storage base for other OSI applications (e.g. X.400 MHS, X.700 Systems Management, EDI, etc.), as attributes and object classes are extended in these other services, the definitions of these items must be added to the scope of the Directory schema.

In the long term, reliable operation of the Directory will be central to the success of other applications. When operated in a distributed environment and integrated with other standards, the Directory will require sophisticated product administration and management tools to accommodate the inherent complexity of the above mechanisms and the burgeoning amount of information needed to support global OSI communications.

Table 16.3   Directory system entries

ENTRY TYPE	CLASS	DESCRIPTION
Root	DIB	A Root entry identifies the top of the total DIB.
Glue	DIB	A Glue entry provides a "null" entry to link DIB fragments. Only knowledge (operational) attributes are stored in a Glue entry.
Cp	DIB and Data	A Context Prefix entry holds the naming context of the subordinate DIB (fragment). The Cp entry may also contain entry information.
Entry	Data	This is a user's data entry.
Alias	Ref	An Alias entry references an alternate entry with a natural name.
Subr	Ref	A Subordinate entry provides a Cp reference to an entry in a subordinate DSA.
Nssr	Ref and Data	An Non-specific Subordinate Reference entry references an entry in another DSA by the DSA name (not its Cp). The Nssr entry may also contain entry information.
Supr	Ref	A Superior entry indicates that this entry is the Root entry within this DSA but it has a superior entry in another DSA.
Xr	Ref	A Cross Reference entry provides a Cp reference into another DSA.
Adm-point	DIB and Data	An Administration Point entry identifies the start of a DIB subtree for a specific DIB administration entity. The Admpoint may also contain entry information.
Sub-entry	Def	A Subentry entry is located under the Admpoint entry and defines the bounds of the subtree(s) associated with the administration point. Subentries can also define the schema rules(syntax) of the subtree specified.
Sha-dow	Data	A Shadow entry indicates that the entry is a complete or partial copy of the original entry. The entry may also contain additional knowledge information.
Cache	Data	A Cache entry indicates that the entry is a complete or partial copy of the original entry that the DSA has cached.
Imm-Supr	Ref	An Immediate Superior entry provides a Cp reference to an immediate superior entry in another DSA.

The entry types are classified in the table to indicate the nature of the entry. These classifications are not part of the standard and are provided to demonstrate how DIB DSE entry types are used. The classes are:

DIB — Types that perform a linkage within the DIB between or with entries, e.g. Root, Glue, etc.

Data — Types that contain actual DIB user data entries, e.g. Entry, Cache, etc.

Ref — Types that provide references to other entries, other DSAs via a naming context prefix or other DSAs by a DSA name, e.g. NSSR, Xref and Alias.

Def — Types that provide DIB component (e.g. subtree specifications) definitions, e.g. Subentry.

16.7 QUESTIONS

Question 16.1   What is the difference between the DIT and a DIB?

Question 16.2   What are the ASEs of the DAP and what service elements do they support?

Question 16.3   What is the relationship between a distinguished name and the DIB?

Question 16.4   What do the modifyRDN and remove operations do and why is there a restriction applied to them?

Question 16.5   What are a DSA naming context and context prefix and what purpose do they serve?

Question 16.6   Why are DSAs interconnected?

Question 16.7   How does a DSA know that it must access another DSA to resolve an operation?

Question 16.8   What are the three major areas of verification applied to data in the Directory?

Question 16.9   What is the mechanism that a Directory user can apply to limit the response of a DSA?

Question 16.10   What additional information is stored with a user's Directory entry and why?

17 File Transfer, Access and Management

17.1 OVERVIEW OF FTAM

The standard for *File Transfer, Access and Management (FTAM)* allows applications to access files on remote file systems. Files may be passed as a whole between communicating application processes, or remote files can be accessed for read and write operations. It allows access to an information storage facility in such a way that data can be added or removed and the description of the data maintained without there being a need for any vendor specific knowledge of how the filing system is being provided.

FTAM model Figure 17.1 illustrates the main logical components of FTAM in two communicating computer systems. FTAM is defined in terms of the dialogue over the association between an FTAM *initiator*, that supports the user's application, and a *responder* that supports the remote filestore. The initiator corresponds to the client and the responder to the server in proprietary file server architectures. Each activity on a remote file is started by the initiator. The responder reacts in a passive way to carry out the requested action. The *virtual filestore* is a generic model of a set of files. The remote files may be as simple as a floppy disk on a personal computer or the root of a large mainframe file system or database. To achieve vendor independence, the virtual filestore performs the mapping from the generic FTAM model of a filestore onto the real file system. The implementation details of the data source are not visible to the filestore user.

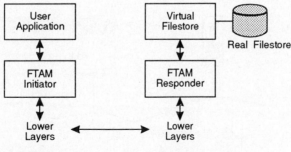

Figure 17.1   FTAM model

Applications on one computer use FTAM to access files on a remote computer. FTAM uses OSI application associations to create the appearance of a local resource. Features of FTAM include:

- support for both unstructured and structured (sequential and hierarchical) files;

- transfer of complete files (in either direction) between the application and the filestore;

- access to parts of files (i.e. read or write individual records on structured files);

- support for a variety of typical file attributes (e.g. file name, size, date of creation, etc.); and,

- management of the remote files (i.e. create or delete files).

Typical configurations for the use of FTAM are illustrated in Figure 17.2. In a Local Area Network (LAN) file sharing configuration, the workstations would be fitted with initiator capability and the file server would have the FTAM responder. Systems fitted with both initiator and responder capability would have full peer to peer access to each others' files.

Standards

The standard, ISO 8571 (there is no CCITT equivalent), is divided into four parts:

Part 1	General Description
Part 2	Virtual Filestore Definition
Part 3	File Service Definition
Part 4	File Protocol Specification.

Filestore management

The initial version of FTAM, finalized in mid-1988, did not include the concept of a file directory and provided only basic management actions on the file store. A series of amendments, which reached International Standard (IS) status in 1991, add the concepts of a file directory and can

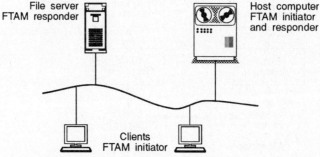

Figure 17.2   Examples for implementation of FTAM

work with structured file path names. New actions are also defined to create, delete and list directories, as well as move and copy files and directories on the virtual file store.

For an integrated treatment, this chapter is based on the new version of FTAM as amended in 1991. However, the emphasis of the main body of this chapter is the initial version that is generally available in a wide range of products. The new work on filestore management is covered briefly where appropriate, but at an overview level only. The concepts and terminology used in FTAM are defined first, and a simple example file is used to illustrate salient points.

17.2 VIRTUAL FILESTORE

The basic concepts in FTAM are introduced in the next section and some key terms are defined in Table 17.1. FTAM is based on the concept of a virtual filestore. The virtual filestore is an abstract description or model of real filestores that exist in real open systems. All of the FTAM definitions and protocol specifications are given in terms of the characteristics and data of the virtual filestore rather than any real local filestores. It is the responsibility of each open system to map the virtual filestore

Table 17.1 FTAM terminology

TERM	DEFINITION
DATA	Any representation to which meaning is or might be assigned
Information	The combination of data and the meaning it conveys
File	An unambiguously named collection of information having a common set of attributes
Filestore	An organized collection of files, including their attributes and names, residing at a particular open system
Virtual filestore	An abstract model for describing files and filestores
FILESTORE MANAGEMENT	The description and management of the organization of filed information (FTAM Amendment only)
Object	A file, file directory or reference
File directory	A mechanism for the grouping of files, references and file-directories in a logical tree structure
Reference	A reference points to one other object — either a file or file directory
Pathname	A series of object names identifying a target object
FILE ACTION	A type of action performed on the contents of the filestore
File transfer	A function that moves an entire file between open systems
File access	The inspection, modification, or replacement of part of a file's content
File management	The creation and deletion of files, and the inspection or manipulation of the attributes associated with a file as a whole
ATTRIBUTES	Identifiable properties of an object
File attributes	The name, size, date of creation, etc of an individual file
Activity attributes	The attributes describing the activity of using the file service

descriptions and operations into the files and operations of its local file management system.

17.2.1 Form of Virtual Filestore

The definition of the virtual filestore forms a framework for the description of filed information. A virtual filestore contains files and provides for remote actions defined on the filestore and the files it contains.

Filestore management

In the initial version of the standard, the filestore could only contain files. The addenda introduce the FTAM *object* that now encompasses normal files, file directories and reference objects (see Figure 17.3). These additional objects have been introduced into the filestore to permit the concept of file path management and linking filestore objects.

Directories

File directories provide a means of grouping objects to provide a structural order (the filestore tree) within the filestore. This is similar to the structure common on many real file systems. It allows objects to be identified by a pathname that consists of the series of file directory names from the filestore root to the object. The filestore can keep track of the user's location in the tree. The current default file directory is called the *current name prefix* in FTAM.

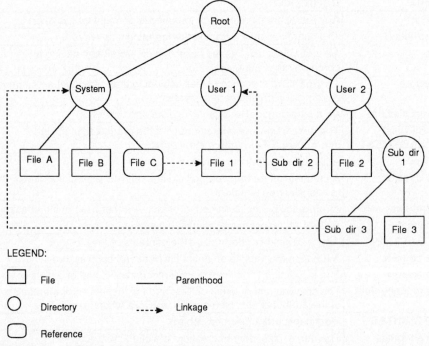

LEGEND:

☐ File   _____ Parenthood

◯ Directory   ----▶ Linkage

▢ Reference

Figure 17.3   Filestore objects

References

For convenience of access, a *reference object* provides a linkage to one other object; either a file or a file directory. References provide a simple means of allowing an object to appear in more than one place in the filestore tree without having to duplicate the object.

Files

File objects have specific properties. The properties of a file are described by the values of a set of file attributes. A file is either empty or has contents. Contents are described by a data structure. The data structure is identified by some of the file attributes. In this description, a file has the following aspects:

File name   Allows the file to be referenced without ambiguity. File name is replaced by pathname in the filestore management addenda.

Management properties   Express such attributes of the file as size, accounting information, history, etc.

Structural properties   Describe the logical organization and dimensions of the data stored in the file.

Data   Forming the contents of the file.

These file attributes are all aspects of the file that can be observed by any authorized initiator. If two observers make the same enquiry about these aspects, they will obtain the same information.

17.2.2 File Access Structure

Data Units

A file consists of an ordered set of named *Data Units (DUs)*. These DUs may be related in some logical fashion. In general, these relations may be sequential, hierarchical, network, or relational. In the FTAM standard, ISO has selected as its virtual filestore model a tree structure (i.e. hierarchical model) to represent the relationship between the DUs in the file for access and identification purposes.

Figure 17.4 (page 314) gives examples of hierarchical file access structures, including two cases that are widely used (unstructured and flat files). These are:

Unstructured   The access structure of the file consists only of the root node and one DU. For example, an unstructured binary file can be represented as just a root node and a single DU of type binary string.

Flat   The access structure of a flat file consists of two levels. There are DUs only on the leaf nodes. There is no DU on the root node. A special case of a flat file is a file where all the DUs are instances of the same typed data object. An ASCII (American Standard Code for Information Interchange) file can be represented as a flat file where all the DUs are instances of type character string (called ISO646String in Abstract Syntax Notation One, ASN.1).

Hierarchical   Examples of a more complex hierarchical file are a spreadsheet (organized with rows at one level and columns at the next level in the tree), a FORTRAN array, or a (hypothetical) airline seat reservation file. In the example, nodes in descending order contain DUs with information about airline details, departure city, destination, flight details and seat allocation.

File model   Figure 17.5 shows an example of the hierarchical file access structure.

FADU   Each *node* of the hierarchical access structure contains an *identifier*, zero or one DUs, and a *subtree* (zero or more ordered subordinate nodes with this same node structure). The entire collection is called a *File Access Data Unit (FADU)*. The FADU is the unit on which operations on the file content are performed. The FADU is a typed data object and must be representable by and maintained through the Presentation Layer.

Individual FADUs can be identified either by node name or an integer representing the FADU position in the so called *pre-order traversal sequence*. The node name is optional and it is omitted in some file types. FTAM defines a linear ordering of nodes in the tree. When applied to examples such as Figure 17.5, where the nodes appear in order from left to right, start at the root node at the top of the figure, include nodes going

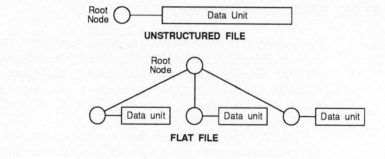

UNSTRUCTURED FILE

FLAT FILE

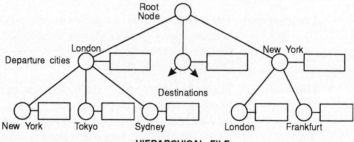

HIERARCHICAL FILE

Figure 17.4   FTAM file structures: examples of unstructured, flat (or sequential) and hierarchical file.

down and to the left, go to the right if you can't go further down, and up if you can't go right. The preorder traversal sequence for the example is nodes R, A, B, C, D, E, F.

The *level* of a node is the sum of the arc lengths from the root node to the node concerned. An arc is a directed line between two nodes from parent to child, and the arc length is a positive integer.

This access structure of the file is identified by the registered abstract syntax name ISO8571FSTR. ISO may develop other access structure standards in the future for access to and identification of DUs associated with other models such as a relational model. These future standards will be identified by different standard context names. The use of a hierarchical structure for the file access model does not prevent the application from representing non-hierarchical logical structures. Other structures can be represented by use of references within the file access data unit contents.

17.2.3 Constraint Sets and Document Types

The FTAM standards define a number of commonly used file structures to provide FTAM users and vendors a basis for specifying file interworking. The definition is done in two steps:

- document types; and,

- constraint sets.

Document type A document type defines a class of file structure; i.e. it defines the file type, its structure (flat or record oriented), and the syntax of the data contained in the DUs (string types, record lengths, etc). The document type also references a constraint set. The FTAM standard defines five document types:

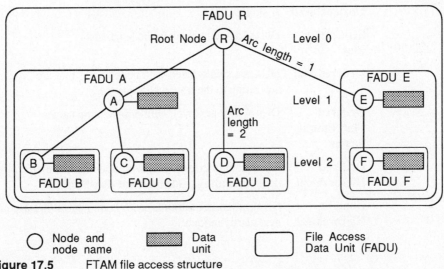

Figure 17.5   FTAM file access structure

FTAM-1	Unstructured Text (single ASCII DU).
FTAM-2	Sequential Text (ordered sequence of ASCII DUs).
FTAM-3	Unstructured Binary (single binary DU).
FTAM-4	Sequential Binary (ordered sequence of binary DUs).
FTAM-5	Simple Hierarchical File.

Each document type is assigned a registered Object Identifier (OID). A document type may have an ASN.1 parameter that describes the document and bounding conditions (e.g. record length etc). FTAM is intended to support a large range of document types and additional document types are defined in various functional standards and profiles (e.g. National Institute of Standards and Technology (NIST) document types are also implemented by some products). To facilitate interworking, the FTAM standards also identify file relaxation and simplification mechanisms that permit the FTAM responder to degenerate the file structure to suit the accessor; e.g. a structured file could be degenerated to an unstructured file by the responder for transfer to the initiator.

Constraint set   Constraint sets are directly related to the document type and define the available access contexts and allowed actions for that document type. Access contexts determine the data view of the file. Typically, an access context would enable just the DUs to be accessed on their own or the DUs and their node descriptors together. The available actions specify the possible actions permitted on the document type; e.g. if the file is structured, locate and insert actions are possible. These actions are obviously not permitted on an unstructured file.

FTAM defines the following constraint sets by specifying them as subsets of the general hierarchical access structure:

Unstructured	A single DU.
Sequential Flat	DUs at a single level, no node names.
Ordered Flat	DUs at a single level, with node names that are ordered according to the traversal sequence.
Ordered Flat, Unique names	DUs at a single level, with unique node names.
Ordered Hierarchical	No structural constraints, with node names that are ordered according to the traversal sequence.
General Hierarchical	No structural constraints, with node names that are not necessarily unique.

General   No structural constraints, with unique node names.
Hierarchical,
Unique
Names

17.2.4 FTAM Access Contexts

The user's view of file data within the FTAM access structure varies depending on the amount of detail needed. The user view in effect at any instant is called the *access context*. Seven different access contexts are defined in the FTAM standard and they are listed in Table 17.2. The access context in effect determines which structuring information and which DUs are included when reading the file for access or data transfer. These terms will be explained by example in a later section.

17.2.5 FTAM Abstract Syntaxes

For data transfer purposes, the file data consists of data values that are conveyed to the presentation service, which carries out the actual data transfer. A number of presentation contexts are used to convey the data and to carry out the transfer.

FTAM   The FTAM Protocol Control Information (PCI, i.e. the protocol header)
protocol syntax is conveyed to the presentation service according to the abstract syntax

Table 17.2   FTAM Access Context determines the user's view of the file

ACCESS CONTEXT	NAME	DESCRIPTION
HA	Hierarchical all DUs (i.e. entire FADU)	Access to all DUs within the addressed FADU, together with complete FADU description information (i.e. FADU structure)
HN	Hierarchical no DUs (i.e. FADU structure only)	Access to the complete FADU structure description within the addressed FADU, without any DUs
FA	Flat all DUs (i.e. nodes with data only)	Access to the name and DU of all nodes which have data. Nodes which do not contain data are omitted
FL	Flat one level DUs (i.e. given level nodes only)	Access to the name and DU of all the nodes in a given level of the addressed FADU. Only nodes which have data are included
FS	Flat single DU (i.e. root DU only)	Access only to the DU associated with the root of the addressed FADU, but without any FADU description information
UA	Unstructured all DUs (i.e. DUs only)	Access to all DUs within the addressed FADU, but without any FADU description information
US	Unstructured single DU	Access to the single DU belonging to the root node of the addressed FADU

defined in FTAM Part 4, The File Protocol Specification. This FTAM PCI abstract syntax is identified as ISO8571-FTAM.

FADU structure syntax

The file structuring information is conveyed to the presentation service according to the abstract syntax defined in FTAM Part 2, The Virtual Filestore Definition. This file structure abstract syntax, identified as ISO8571-FSTR, defines the data types that need to be transferred to describe the hierarchical tree structure of the file access.

User data syntax

The file user data is transferred by the presentation service according to the user data abstract syntax associated with each individual DU. In general, the DUs are considered as being made up of individual atomic data elements for which an individual abstract syntax is defined. The data elements are related within the DU according to some relationship that, in general, is considered to be a tree. The user data may be identified as some general ISO standard, or it may be some specialized user data syntax that is standardized by a user group and registered with ISO, or it may be a privately defined data syntax.

The presentation service is responsible for maintaining the order and context of data presented to it, and for conveying the data in that order and context to the other presentation user transparently. (The presentation service takes the responsibility for agreeing on and transferring the data in a concrete syntax.) The FTAM entities need be concerned only with the context identifiers and abstract syntax used to convey the data between the FTAM and the presentation service.

17.2.6 File Attributes

Each file is described by one set of file attribute values. The scope of the file attributes is the filestore, and if a file attribute value is changed by the actions of one initiator, the new value is seen by any other initiators that subsequently read that attribute. Examples of file attributes include:

- Filename

- Permitted Actions List

- Access Control List

- Account

- Date and Time of Creation

- Identity of Creator

- Context Requirements

- File Size.

These attributes are defined more fully in Section 17.4.3 (page 327) in conjunction with the example. Each attribute has exactly one of three possible attribute types, defined in Part 2 of the standard:

Scalar attribute   Has one value at a given time.

Vector attribute   Has a value that is a list of zero or more elements, each of which has a distinct value. The elements are uniquely ordered.

Set attribute   Has a value that is an unordered set of zero or more elements, each of which has a distinct value.

Each attribute value has exactly one of six possible attribute value types, i.e. for each attribute, the type of its value (or of the value of its elements for a vector or set attribute) is defined in the standard. The value type is one of the following:

- An a-string; i.e. a sequence of printing characters (called a-characters), as registered in ASN.1, from the character set defined by the international reference version of ISO 646, or from any character set defined under the procedure for the registration of escape sequences (ISO 2375).

- A sequence of octets.

- An integer.

- A file service access point address (this is a virtual filestore name, the syntax of which is not defined in the standard, but is considered a local matter, or perhaps a matter for other standards such as an application standard).

- A date and time, limited to those expressible in ISO 8601. The resolution and accuracy with which these values are maintained are determined by the responder. The responder may indicate precision by truncation of ISO 8601 from the right. Truncation from the left (e.g. year number) may not be used.

- An item from a named set of values defined by enumeration in the standard.

In all cases, an attempt to read the value of an attribute may result in an indication that the value cannot be determined or, in some cases, that the value is currently not set.

17.3 FILE SERVICE

Filestore activities

Each file activity is started by one file service user, the filestore accessor (the initiator), who has some established aim to achieve. The other file service user, the filestore provider (the responder), merely reacts to this initiative in a passive role. This relationship applies even when a file is being transferred from one filestore to another, because the protocols do not need to carry information about the filestore at the initiator, but only about the responder. The act of transfer can be considered as being performed by a copying application that has local access to one file and remote access to the other.

Activity attributes

Zero or more accessors may have an application association with a filestore at any one time. Such an association may be used to operate on zero or one file of the filestore at any one time. The operating relationships between an individual accessor, an application association and a filestore are described by the values of a set of activity attributes. The activity attributes are concerned with aspects such as authentication, progress of the activity, and accumulated cost. There is an independent set of these attributes for every activity in progress.

File actions

File activities are made up of individual operations called actions. Actions apply to DUs and the state of a filestore. The actions are invoked by FTAM service primitives issued by the filestore user. The real filestore performs its interpretations of the requested actions and provides the corresponding results as reflected in its local filestore implementation. The FTAM file service primitives defined in the initial version of the standard are listed in Table 17.3. Selected primitives and their application to files are described in more detail in following sections. The new primitives introduced in the FTAM addenda are shown in Table 17.4 (page 322). The description of the new primitives and their application to file directory and reference objects is omitted from the following text for brevity. The file service definition (FTAM standard Part 3) states which actions each primitive performs on which data elements. The sequence of service primitives must take place in a defined order as specified in the standard. In particular, the ability to perform certain actions is governed by the service regime; e.g. access to a file typically involves a series of stages to identify a file, open the file, transfer data and close the file, etc. Each of these stages is described as a regime. (FTAM regimes are defined in Section 17.5.1, page 331.)

Some actions are subject to access control; i.e. there is a component of the access control list that is used to either permit or deny access to the action on the file depending on whether there is a match between the access control conditions specified for the file and the values of activity attributes such as identity of initiator, password, and location of initiator. The applicability of each action is subject to concurrency control, governing the parallel activities allowed during and after that action. Release of concurrency controls is co-ordinated with commitment control mechanisms to avoid deadlock.

17.3.1 Filestore Actions on Complete Files

Some of the filestore actions refer to complete files viewed as single entities, and other actions refer to the internals of files as viewed through the defined file access structure. The filestore actions on complete files, as specified in ISO 8571 Part 2, include the following:

Table 17.3   FTAM file service primitives

PRIMITIVES	DESCRIPTION
Association Control	
F-Initialize	These services are used to establish and terminate the FTAM initiator/responder association
F-Terminate	
F-U-Abort	
F-P-Abort	
File creation & deletion	
F-Create	Creates a new file.
F-Delete	Deletes a file; i.e. removes it from the virtual filestore.
File selection and opening	
F-Select	Identifies an existing file and gains control of it
F-Deselect	End of activity on the file and relinquish control
F-Open	Allows actions on contents
F-Close	Ends actions on file
Attribute access	
F-Read Attribute	These services are used to manage the characteristics of the file
F-Change Attribute	
File services group control	
F-Begin Group	Identify the start of a sequence of file operations to be performed as a group
F-End Group	Identify the end of the sequence and initiate processing of the group
Miscellaneous operations	
F-Locate	Locate an FADU. Required for access to individual FADUs to operate on parts of files
F-Erase	Erase an FADU or file
File and data transfer operations	
F-Read	Initiate the read of a part of a file or a complete file
F-Write	Initiate the write of a part of a file or a complete file
F-Data	Transfer a part or a complete file
F-Data End	Signal the end of a data transfer
F-Transfer End	Signal the end of a read/write operation
F-Cancel	Cancel the FTAM data transfer operation
F-Recover	Recover the transfer/access activity after failure.

Create file Creates a new file and establishes its attributes. It establishes the file selection regime and selects the newly created file. Initially, a file contains only a root node with no DU.

Select file Establishes a relationship called the file selection regime between the initiator and a particular file and is a prerequisite for the remaining actions on complete files. An error is reported if the parameters do not specify exactly one file.

Read attribute Returns the values of the requested attribute. For a vector or set attribute, it returns the complete list of element values. This action is subject to access control.

Change attribute For a scalar attribute, the action modifies the existing value of the attribute, or deletes the existing value, or assigns a value if its value is currently null. For a vector attribute, the action replaces the complete list of elements with a given list. For a set attribute, the action adds a given element or elements to the attribute, or removes an

Table 17.4   New FTAM services provided by the addenda

PRIMITIVES	DESCRIPTION
Object creation & deletion	
F-Create	Creates a file, directory or reference
F-Delete	Deletes a file, directory or reference
File directory	
F-Copy	Copy a file/object to another location in the filestore
F-Move	Move a file/object to another location in the filestore
F-Change Prefix	Change the user's path attribute
F-List	List one or more FTAM objects/files (scope and attribute selectable)
Group operations	
F-Group Select	Select a group of FTAM objects by providing a list of path names to permit operations on a number of objects concurrently
F-Group Delete	Delete a group of FTAM objects
F-Group Copy	Copy a group of FTAM objects
F-Group Move	Move a group of FTAM objects
F-Group List	List a group of FTAM objects
F-Select Another	Select (add) an object to the currently selected group
Object linking and link management	
F-Link	Create a reference link on the current object to the specified target object in order to provide object relationship references
F-Unlink	Remove the reference link
F-Read-Link-Attributes	Read the object's link references
F-Change-Link-Attributes	Change the object's link references

element or elements equal to a given value from the attribute. This action is subject to access control.

Open file   Establishes a suitable regime for the performance of the actions for file access (see next section). It operates on a previously selected file.

Close file   Removes the open regime in an orderly manner.

Delete file   Deletes the selected file, and removes the file selection regime. This action is subject to access control.

Deselect file   Simply removes the file selection regime in an orderly manner, but does not delete the file. This action is not subject to access control.

17.3.2 Filestore Actions for File Access

The actions for file access operate in the open regime, and they use the specific hierarchical file access structure described earlier.

Each file access action operates on the currently located FADU. When the file is first opened, the currently located FADU is the root, and any file access action will therefore act on the file as a whole. If it is desired to operate on any other FADU, the locate action is invoked to locate a specified FADU explicitly, or a particular FADU may be specified in the request primitive of the other file access actions. The locate action is not subject to access control, but all other file access actions are subject to access control.

The initiator's view of the FADUs is determined by the value of the access context activity attribute. The responder generates this view from the local file format, suppressing any unwanted information. Similarly, when writing data to the file, the responder stores complete FADUs, mapping the data received into them on the basis of the current access context.

When a file is first opened, the access context in effect is set to access context HA (access to all DUs in the FADU together with complete FADU description information) until changed. File access actions include:

Locate   Attempts to locate the specified FADU. The FADU can be located in a number of ways: by relative position in the preorder traversal sequence (i.e. the first, last, next, or previous FADU, or beginning or end of file); by node number that indicates the position in the sequence; by node name that identifies a node within the current FADU; or, by a sequence of node names starting at the root. The identifier of the located FADU can be returned in the confirm primitive. After a FADU is located, the permitted actions file attribute determines which actions can be performed on the FADU.

Read	Accesses and reads the identified FADU. The location after the access will be unchanged. The DUs and structuring information to be transferred are determined by the access context requested in the read request primitive.
Insert as child	Creates a new FADU and inserts it into the appropriate position in the file. Insert as child creates an FADU whose parent is the root node of the currently located FADU, and that will be read before any other FADUs that were existing subtrees of the same parent. The current location is not changed.
Insert as sister	Creates a FADU that is placed after the currently located FADU and whose parent is the same as the parent of the currently located FADU. The current location becomes the root node of the inserted FADU.
Replace	Replaces the contents of the currently located FADU with the new contents provided.
Extend	Adds the data provided to the end of the DU associated with the root node of the currently located FADU. For both replace and extend actions, the current location does not change.
Erase	Deletes the entire FADU and locates the next FADU in sequence, or end of file if no FADUs remain.

17.3.3 File Access

The access to a file by a user is restricted and refined by many levels of control. Document types, constraint sets, access control, etc, all serve to define the overall access to the data in a file.

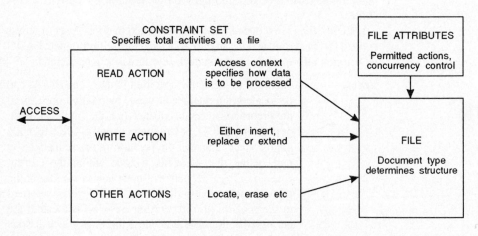

Figure 17.6   Access to a file is governed by a number of levels of control.

Some of these controls are identified in Figure 17.6. At the core is the file itself. The file structure is specified by the document type that determines the overall activities that can be performed on the data in the file. Associated with the file are the file attributes. One of these file attributes specifies permitted actions. Other attributes govern concurrent access to the file. The values of these attributes for example can inhibit read or insert (write) access to the file.

Above this level is the constraint set that specifies the legality of the requested FTAM action on the file (i.e. its allowed access context and the results of the available actions). The access context determines the result of an FTAM read action. The actual effect of a write operation depends on whether an insert, extend or replace is to be performed.

17.4 VIRTUAL FILE EXAMPLE

ASCII file

A virtual file is a collection of information. As the name implies, a virtual file is not a real object but a conceptual object. To give some reality to the FTAM concepts, a simple example of a file will be used.

The example is an ASCII file named by a character string "EX-AMPLE TXT". The contents of the file are defined as a FADU, which is shown in a graphical representation in Figure 17.7. The example is a sequential file (ordered flat constraint set with unique names) and its contents consist of an FADU that is identified as TEXT. The root node does not contain a DU. The FADU subtree consists of three branches (children), each of which is also an FADU.

Nodes may be identified either by the hierarchical order (the file root node is number 0) or by the node names. FADU number 1, that has a node name of 1, contains a DU consisting of the typed object a-string "ABC", and does not contain a subtree. FADU 2 contains the DU "DEFG" and does not contain a subtree. FADU 3 contains the DU "HI" and does not contain a subtree. There are no other FADUs.

The virtual file in our example can be represented in many ways. For example, the filename of a virtual file is defined in Part 2 of the FTAM standard as a vector of a-string (i.e. a list of components each of which is a character string as defined in ASN.1). FTAM does not define how a filename would be represented to a user. The filename of our example file could be represented in any of the following syntactic forms:

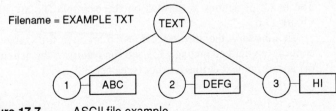

Filename = EXAMPLE TXT

Figure 17.7   ASCII file example

- ("EXAMPLE", "TXT")

- EXAMPLE.TXT

- EXAMPLE/TXT

or many other forms.

17.4.1 ASN.1 Definition of FADU

The structure of such a file could be represented in ASN.1 by the following abstract syntax (this is a simplification of the general definition of an FADU):

```
FADU ::=      SEQUENCE {
node          NodeName                              OPTIONAL,
data          [0]IMPLICIT DataUnit                  OPTIONAL,
children      [1]IMPLICIT {SEQUENCE OF FADU}

                                                    OPTIONAL }

DataUnit ::=  ISO646String                -- ASCII string
```

Expressed in English, this reads roughly as: "A FADU is a sequence consisting of a name, a data unit which is optional and an optional subtree that is a sequence of FADUs. A data unit is an ASCII string."

The undefined terms in this example are defined in either the ASN.1 standard, the FTAM standard or in other places. SEQUENCE and ISO646String are defined in ASN.1 (ISO646 is the ISO standard corresponding to ASCII.) NodeName is defined in FTAM Part 2, The Virtual Filestore, as follows:

```
NodeName ::= CHOICE {
            [0] IMPLICIT GraphicString,
userDefined  EXTERNAL }
```

The full definition of a FADU includes a number of other elements (such as arc length, subtree delimiters, etc) that are omitted from this example for clarity.

17.4.2 Actions on ASCII File Example

The result of actions performed on the example file are illustrated in Figure 17.8.

In summary, the allowed actions on an open file (subject to access control) are defined on page 323 and the results of the action depend on the access context defined earlier (see page 317).

17.4.3 File Attributes

The example ASCII file is used to describe the file attributes defined in the FTAM standard. The following paragraphs give the attribute name and a description. For the common attributes, an example of the attribute value is listed in Table 17.5 (page 329). Most of the attributes are initialized at the time the file is created. The following paragraphs also indicate whether a file attribute can be changed from its initial value by using the change-attribute action.

File name In the initial version of the FTAM standard, each file in a filestore has a *file name* that is unique within the scope of the filestore. File name is a vector attribute, the elements of which form a sequence of name components. Note that this abstract definition allows, but does not standardize,

Location Before	Action	Access Context	Location After	Result
TEXT	Read	HA (entire FADU)	TEXT	Diagram A
1	Read	HA (entire FADU)	1	Diagram B
TEXT	Read	UA (all DUs only)	TEXT	Diagram C
2	Insert as sister: FADU node name = 5, DU = XYZ	Not applicable	5	Diagram D

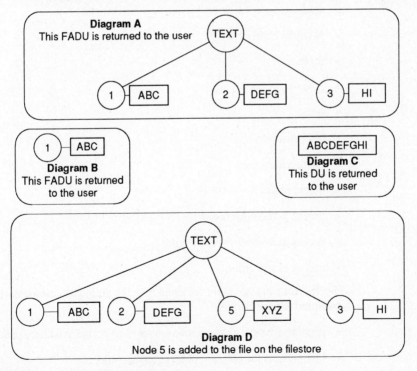

Diagram A
This FADU is returned to the user

Diagram B
This FADU is returned to the user

Diagram C
This DU is returned to the user

Diagram D
Node 5 is added to the file on the filestore

Figure 17.8 Actions on example file

any particular syntactic division of names, or interpretation of names, or any use of names to select access paths to the file. The naming mechanism is transparent to the initiator and the responder. In the filestore management addenda, file name is replaced by the pathname attribute. The file name can be changed by the change attribute action.

Pathname

The filestore management addenda introduces *pathnames*. The Primary pathname attribute is a vector attribute of type graphic string. It belongs to the object and identifies the single path in the file store tree from the root to the object. It consists of series of the object names from the root to the target.

Object name

The *object name* attribute provides the name of an object; i.e. its relative name within the file directory hierarchy.

Object type

The *object type* attribute determines the nature of the FTAM object; i.e. a file, a file directory or a reference object.

Permitted actions

The *permitted actions list* is a vector attribute that indicates the range of actions that are allowed to be performed on the file. The elements of the vector are boolean values, each of which indicates the availability or non-availability of an action or a situation in which actions can apply i.e.:

- read

- insert as child or sister

- replace

- extend

- erase

- read attribute

- change attribute

- delete object

- access in traversal order

- access in reverse traversal order

- access in any order.

The filestore management addenda add the following elements to the permitted actions list:

- passthrough permits the use of a reference object name within a pathname

- link permits the creation of links to this object.

The permitted actions list cannot be altered from its initial value.

Table 17.5   Typical attributes for ASCII file example

ATTRIBUTE	EXAMPLE ATTRIBUTE VALUE
File Name	EXAMPLE TXT
Permitted Actions	T, F, T, T, F, T, T ...
Access Control	T, T, T, T, T, T, T, T; Gary Dickson; XXX; Home (i.e. permitted access; identity; password; location)
Account	NPSC 007
Date & Time of Creation	1988-08-01 14:59:59
Identity of Creator	Gary Dickson
Object Availability	Immediate
Presentation Contexts	ISO8571-FSTR, ISO646String
Access Structure Type	Hierarchical, 1 — maximum depth
Current Size	116 Octets
Legal Qualifications	Copyright protected

Access control   The *access control list* is a set attribute. Each element of the set gives one condition under which access to the file is allowed. Access to the file is allowed if at least one of these conditions is satisfied. A condition is a statement of a permitted access together with up to three other terms. It is fulfilled if all the terms present are satisfied. The terms are the following:

- Permitted access: a boolean vector whose elements allow the actions read, insert, replace, erase, extend, read attribute, change attribute, delete and, with the addenda, passthrough and link. The term is satisfied if every element that is true in the value of the requested access activity attribute for the association is also true in the value of the permitted access term.

- Optionally, an identity of initiator attribute.

- Optionally, a password.

- Optionally, a location of initiator.

The access control list is set at the time the file is created but it may be changed.

Account   The *account* attribute is a scalar a-string that identifies the accountable authority responsible for the accumulated file storage charges. The account is set at file creation, but can be changed by the change attribute action.

Date and time of creation   This scalar date and time attribute is set by the responder to the responder's local date and time when the create action is performed. It cannot be changed.

Date and time of last modification
This is a scalar date and time attribute. It is set to the responder's local date and time when the close action is performed following a file open for modification or extension, and it cannot be changed.

Date and time of last read access
Another scalar data and time attribute set to the responder's local date and time when the close action is performed following a file open for reading. It cannot be changed.

Identity of creator
This scalar a-string attribute is set by the responder to the value of the identity of initiator activity attribute when the object is created. It cannot be changed by change attribute.

Identity of last modifier
This is set by the responder to the value of identity of initiator when the file is closed following a file open for modification or extension. It is a scalar a-string and cannot be changed by change attribute.

Identity of last reader
This is set by the responder to the value of identity of initiator when the file is closed following a file open for reading.

Object availability
This scalar enumeration item indicates whether delay should be expected before the object can be accessed. The value, that may be either immediate availability or deferred availability, is set at object creation, but can be altered by change attribute. The distinction between immediate and deferred is supposed to be meaningful to the responder, and is not intended to be a quantitative measure.

Presentation context
The presentation context requirements is a set attribute. Each member of the set names a presentation context that will be necessary to maintain the complete file structure and semantics during the transfer of the file. A context name may be the name of a single data type, a named union of data types, or an externally defined context that may imply a data structure. It may indicate any of the following:

- standard character sets used in the file;

- standard data types used in the file;

- registered or user defined (non-standard) contexts or sets of data types; or,

- registered names of data structures that specify the relation of FADUs and DUs in the file, used for Presentation context of FADUs and DUs during bulk data transfer (e.g. a FORTRAN ARRAY or a partitioned data set structure could be registered).

The value of the presentation context attribute is set when the file is created, and cannot be changed by the change attribute action.

Access structure type

This vector attribute indicates the category of access structure needed to access the file contents. For hierarchical files, a maximum depth for the hierarchy is stated. The first element of the vector is an enumeration item, either unstructured, flat or hierarchical. The vector has a second element only if the first element is hierarchical, and is an integer giving the maximum depth of the hierarchy. The value of this attribute is set when the file is created and cannot be changed.

Current size

Current object size is a scalar that indicates the nominal size of the complete object in octets. An object's size depends on the real filestore's particular representation. The **future size** is the nominal size to which the object may grow as a result of modification and extension.

Legal qualifications

This conveys information about the legal status of the file and its use.

Private use

This is a set that can take any form. Its meaning is not defined in the standard. Private use is strongly discouraged, because it leads to incompatibilities.

17.5 FILE SERVICE DEFINITION

FTAM provides communication between entities in the Application Layer. The application entities use the *file service* provided at File Service Access Points (FSAP) by file service elements. File service elements are specific Application Service Elements (ASEs) and reside within the application entity in the Application Layer. A file service user may be a user element or another ASE of the OSI application entity.

The file service elements use other ASEs and the service of the six lower layers as seen at the presentation service boundary. FTAM uses the Association Control Service Element (ACSE) and optionally Commitment, Concurrency and Recovery (CCR). The file service elements perform required functions and exchange data and control actions by means of the FTAM protocol to provide the Quality of Service (QOS) required by their users.

17.5.1 File Service Regimes

The file service and its supporting protocol are concerned with creating, in a series of stages, a working environment in which the user's desired activities can take place. The dialogue must, in turn:

- allow the initiator and the responder to establish each other's identity;

- identify the file that is needed;

- establish the attributes describing the file structure that is to be accessed on this occasion; and,

- engage in file management, access or bulk data transfer.

These steps build up various parts of an FTAM operational context. The period for which some part of the contextual information is valid is called a regime. As progressively more contextual detail is established, a nest of corresponding regimes is built up. This nesting is shown in Figure 17.9.

A period of time in which protocol exchanges have a particular purpose, such as establishing, using or releasing an operational context is called a phase. For each phase, a set of valid messages is defined in terms of state transitions. At any time, each application entity is in precisely one phase. Phases cannot be nested one within another. The phases are as follows:

- Application association establishment/termination phases commence or dissolve the application association regime. They also establish or dissolve any authorization and accounting information necessary for the filestore operations.

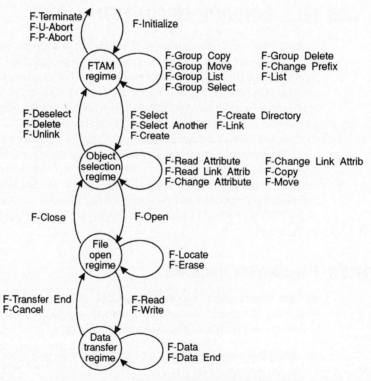

Figure 17.9   Regimes define the applicability of various FTAM services. The state diagram shows typical sequences of FTAM primitives.

- File selection/deselection phases establish or release the file selection regime and identify or create a unique file that operations in subsequent phases will apply to.

- File management phase enables the file service user to perform various management actions on the file as a whole, such as reading or updating file attributes.

- File open/close phases establish or release the open regime in which file data transfer can take place. This includes establishing the desired access context that gives an application oriented view of the file structure.

- Data access phase allows specified operations on specified FADUs. Each operation is either locate a specified FADU, bulk data transfer of a specified FADU, or erase a specified FADU.

17.5.2 FTAM Service Functional Units

The FTAM service as a whole contains many individually defined services. For ease of structuring, these services have been placed into useful sets; they are first grouped into functional units that are then further grouped into five service classes. The functional units are defined in Part 3 of the FTAM standard, The File Service Definition, as follows:

Kernel   Supports the basic file services for the establishment and release of file service regimes. Consists of application association establishment service; application association termination service (orderly release); application association abort service (abrupt release); file selection service; file deselection service; file open service; and, file close service.

Read   Supports the transfer of data from the responder to the initiator. Consists of read bulk data service; DU transfer service; end of data transfer service; end of transfer service; and, cancel data transfer service for non-recoverable errors.

Write   Supports the transfer of data from the initiator to the responder. Consists of write bulk data service; DU transfer service; end of data transfer service; end of transfer service; and, cancel data transfer service for non-recoverable errors.

File access   Allows any FADU in the file access structure to be identified for file access and allows any FADU to be removed from the file access structure. Consists of locate FADU service and erase FADU service.

Limited file management	Supports file management for the creation and deletion of files and the interrogation of the attributes of files. Consists of file creation service, file deletion service, and read attributes service.

Enhanced file management	Adds the capability to modify the attributes of files. Consists of change attributes service.

Grouping	Allows several regimes to be established in one exchange, by forming several independent primitives into a group for procedural purposes. Consists of beginning of grouping service and end of grouping service.

Recovery	Allows the initiator to recreate an open regime that has been destroyed by some failure. Consists of regime recovery service; checkpointing service; and, cancel data transfer service for recoverable errors.

Restart data transfer	Allows a data transfer to be interrupted and restarted at a negotiated point. Consists of restarting data transfer service, checkpointing service, and cancelling data transfer service for recoverable errors.

FADU locking	Allows the invocation of concurrency control locks on a FADU basis in addition to a file basis.

The filestore addenda add the following functional units and enhance the management functional units:

Object manipulation	Provides services to manage and position objects within the filestore and to duplicate files within the filestore (e.g. move and copy files).

Group manipulation	Provides services to manipulate and control grouping of objects within the filestore (e.g. group select, group list). This functional unit used in conjunction with the object manipulation functional unit permits moving and copying activities on multiple objects.

The limited management functional unit is supplemented by the addenda with interrogation of the file directory object attributes. It also supports management of the current name prefix attribute. The enhanced management functional unit is supplemented with modification to the object attributes. It also permits management of reference objects (thus the ability to link files and file directory objects within the filestore by references).

17.5.3 FTAM Service Classes

The functional units are grouped into five generally useful service classes: file transfer class, file access class, file management class, transfer and management class, and unconstrained class. In the application association establishment request primitive, that is called F-Initialize request, the initiator names the service class requested and also the set of functional units required. If the responder is unable to support the service class requested, it rejects the application association establishment attempt.

The functional units requested must be contained in the set of functional units associated with the service class requested. The service provider removes from this set any functional units it is unable to support and signals the remaining set to the responder on the F-Initialize indication primitive. The responder then removes from this set any functional units it is unable to support and signals the remaining set to the service provider on the F-Initialize response primitive. Next, the service provider signals the same set to the initiator on the F-Initialize confirm primitive. This final set of functional units is then available for use on the application association. An application association links an entity in the role of initiator to an entity in the role of responder. A particular entity plays the same role, either initiator or responder, in all the functional units negotiated on that application association.

File transfer class

An initiating application entity that wishes to perform a file transfer may request the responding application entity to support the file transfer service class, that consists of the following:

- Kernel functional unit

- One or both of the read or write functional units

- Grouping functional unit

- Optionally, the limited file management functional unit

- Optionally, but only if the limited file management functional unit is present, the enhanced file management functional unit

- Optionally, in the user correctable file service, the recovery functional unit

- Optionally, in the user correctable file service, the restart data transfer functional unit.

In the file transfer service class, the use of the functional units is constrained so that the sequence of events on an application association is as follows:

- a single concatenated sequence (defined in the standard) to establish a file open regime;

- a single bulk data transfer procedure (described later), for either a read transfer or a write transfer; and,

- a single concatenated sequence to release the file regimes.

File management class
An initiator that wishes to create or delete a file or to interrogate or change the attributes of an existing file might request the responder to support the file management service class, that consists of the following:

- Kernel functional unit
- Limited file management functional unit
- Enhanced file management functional unit
- Grouping functional unit.

Transfer and management
The transfer and management service class combines the two previously described classes.

File access
An initiator that wishes to examine or modify the contents of a file would request the responder to support the file access service class, that supports a rich variety of functional units. The file access class consists of the following:

- Kernel functional unit
- Both the read and write functional units
- File access functional unit
- Optionally, the grouping functional unit
- Optionally, the limited file management functional unit
- Optionally, but only if the limited file management functional unit is present, the enhanced file management functional unit
- Optionally, in the user correctable file service, one or both of the recovery and restart data transfer functional units
- Optionally, FADU locking functional unit, but only if read or write functional units and file access functional units are present.

Unconstrained class
The unconstrained service class leaves the selection of functional units to the designer of the distributed application giving full flexibility, but no guarantee of a common set of functional units.

17.6 FILE SERVICE PRIMITIVES

The FTAM file service primitives are categorized according to their use by the initiator or the responder, as indicated in Table 17.3 (page 321). In nearly every case, the initiator plays the active role and the responder plays the passive role.

Most of the services are confirmed dialogues, which means that the service action is completed only when a confirm primitive is received at the FSAP following the request primitive (the complete sequence is request, indication, response, confirm). For most of the primitives, a failure of the requested action is indicated by a diagnostic parameter accompanying the confirm primitive.

17.6.1 Common File Service Parameters

Each of the file service primitives has one or more parameters that convey information between the service user and the service provider. The following file service parameters are common to several primitives:

Diagnostic   The diagnostic parameter conveys information on the success or failure of a requested action, and the reason for any failure. The parameter is divided into a number of parts namely:

> **Error type**   Indicates whether the error is permanent, transient or informative.
>
> **Error iden-**   The actual error code.
> **tifier**
>
> **Entity type(s)**   This has two components: error observer and source. They indicate which FTAM entity received the error and which entity detected it. These are: no categorization possible; initiating file service user; initiating file protocol machine; service supporting the file protocol machines; the responding file protocol machine; and, the responding file service user (the filestore).
>
> **Suggested**   Indicates a possible time by which the error condition
> **delay**   should be cleared.
>
> **Further**   Provides an optional text description (or diagnostic in-
> **details**   formation) about the error.

Account   The current account parameter identifies the account to which costs incurred in the regime that is being established are to be charged.

Charging   The charging parameter conveys information on the costs incurred during the regime that is being released.

Attributes   The attributes parameter conveys a list of file attribute names and values associated with the file to be selected.

Access   The requested access parameter indicates the basis on which the file is being selected. The value gives as a vector the actions to be performed during the selection. The value of the parameter on request and indication primitives indicates the initiator's requirements. The value on response and confirm primitives conveys the access that will actually be allowed.

Passwords   The access passwords parameter provides passwords associated with the actions specified in the access control parameter.

Concurrency   The concurrency control parameter indicates the relation of the file selection regime to other activities on the same file. The value is a vector whose elements indicate, for each of the access control elements, whether the access is shared or exclusive.

Multiple ASEs   The shared ASE information parameter allows information of other ASEs to be associated with FTAM primitives. This is used where file transfer is used with commitment control (CCR).

File lock   The FADU lock parameter is used to set individual FADU locks from values "not required" to "no access" and from "shared" to " exclusive" at the time of select and/or open.

State   The state result parameter conveys information relating to service state machine. It is present only on primitives that cause state changes and only where this may or may not be successful.

Identifier   The activity identifier parameter is used only in the user correctable file service. A different activity identifier is allocated to each activity between a particular initiator and responder. This activity identifier is used in re-establishing the data transfer regime after errors.

17.6.2 Bulk Data Transfer Service Primitives

Bulk data transfer is a self contained procedure that beings with an F-Read or F-Write request by the initiator. This leads to the issue of a sequence of F-Data requests followed by an F-Data End request by the sender of the data. The procedure is completed by the initiator issuing an F-Transfer End request.

Upon receiving the F-Read or F-Write indication, the filestore provider performs the locate action and then initiates a read, insert as child, insert as sister, replace or extend action as appropriate.

The read primitive specifies a data transfer from the service responder to the service initiator. The F-Read primitive signals a transfer of control from the initiator to the sender for the duration of the data transfer, i.e. until the exchange of F-Transfer End primitives. When the read action is completed, the filestore provider issues an F-Data End request primitive.

The write primitive specifies a data transfer from the service initiator to the service provider. The established direction of data flow continues until the exchange of F-Transfer End primitives. The write action must be completed before the issue of the F-Transfer End response primitive by the filestore provider.

The F-Data primitives transfer data between the users of the service. The data is transferred as typed data elements, using the underlying Presentation Service mechanisms. The data transfer may be from either entity, depending on whether a read or write transfer has been requested by the initiator.

The completion of data transfer is indicated by the F-Data End primitives. The sender issues an F-Data End request primitive when all the necessary data has been sent.

The completion of a transfer is indicated by an exchange of F-Transfer End primitives. This exchange is initiated by the initiator after having issued or received an F-Data End primitive. Receipt of the F-Transfer End indication or confirm (as appropriate) informs the sender that no further error recovery actions will be requested.

The F-Cancel primitive is used for reliability control of the reliable bulk data transfer service. Either of the service users may cancel a data transfer activity by issuing an F-Cancel request primitive. The file remains open after a sequence of F-Cancel primitives, although the result of interrupted operations is not defined.

The F-Check and F-Restart primitives (checkpoint and restart) are used for reliability control of the user correctable bulk data transfer service.

Sequence diagrams
The sequence of events in successful read and write operations are defined in the time sequence diagrams given in Figure 17.10 and Figure 17.11. The F-Data primitives in the figures represent an unspecified number of F-Data primitives.

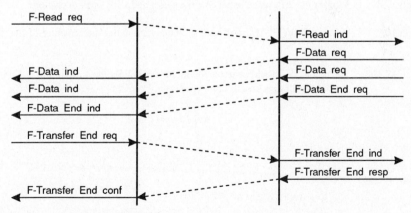

Figure 17.10   F-Read actions

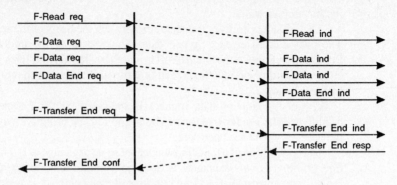

Figure 17.11   F-Write actions

17.7 QUESTIONS

Question 17.1   FTAM stands for File Transfer, Access and Management. What is the purpose of these three aspects?

Question 17.2   What is a service class?

Question 17.3   What is the virtual filestore?

Question 17.4   How are files represented in the virtual filestore?

Question 17.5   What are file attributes and how are they accessed by an FTAM user?

Question 17.6   What is a regime and how does affect the sequencing of FTAM operations?

Question 17.7   What is a group operation and why is it used?

Question 17.8   What is the difference between a file select and a file open operation?

Question 17.9   What does an FTAM user need to understand about the structure of the virtual filestore?

Question 17.10   What does an FTAM user need to understand about the structure of a file within the virtual filestore?

18 Virtual Terminal

18.1 TERMINAL SUPPORT

The standards for Virtual Terminal (VT) control the communications between Open Systems Interconnection (OSI) end systems in support of human interactions with application processes in remote systems. Such communications take the form of interactive character streams directed from some form of input device (e.g. keyboard, mouse) to the application, and an output stream from the application to some form of display (e.g. screen, printer). The VT standards provide a generic architecture for the interconnection of a variety of terminals to different applications independently of the type and make of the computer equipment.

Although the standards also support terminal to terminal, and application to application communications, the use of VT in these modes is expected to be minimal.

Originally, it was envisaged that standards would be devised to cover a wide variety of terminals, e.g. from basic class for simple text terminals to mixed class for advanced text processing and image terminals. However, difficulties were experienced with the complexity and magnitude of this range of terminals and, to date, the standards cover only the basic class. This chapter provides an overview of the basic class standard.

Standards   The VT standards were developed by ISO and there are no CCITT equivalents. They were finalized in 1990 after a protracted development. The VT standards are:

ISO 9040   Service Definition

ISO 9041   Protocol Specification

18.1.1 Applicability

X.400 Message Handling Systems (MHS), the X.500 Directory and File Transfer, Access and Management (FTAM) are expected to be commercially significant because of their broad utility. One would also expect VT to be important because a common problem in computer centers is the interconnection of a wide variety of terminals to different applications. However, the basic class provides only a limited functionality and stand-

341

ardization of the more advanced VT classes is not progressing. The reason is that VT standardisation has possibly been overtaken by:

- the rapid replacement of terminals by personal computers and work-stations; and,

- advances in proprietary graphical user interfaces (e.g. Presentation Manager, Windows, X-Window), and the possible adoption of these in the international standards arena.

These factors will probably see implementation of VT restricted to an interim measure in those environments where a number of existing "dumb" terminals in a network require the ability to interwork with a variety of new applications on different computers. VT is not seen as a replacement for existing proprietary terminal protocols for single vendor environments.

18.1.2 Terminal Support Methods

To put VT into perspective, Figure 18.1 illustrates a number of alternative methods for terminal communications. Traditionally, terminal support has been bound to proprietary communications architectures with little commonality between vendors in terms of terminal features, data stream support and communications protocols. Such diversity has made multi-vendor networking of terminals both difficult and expensive.

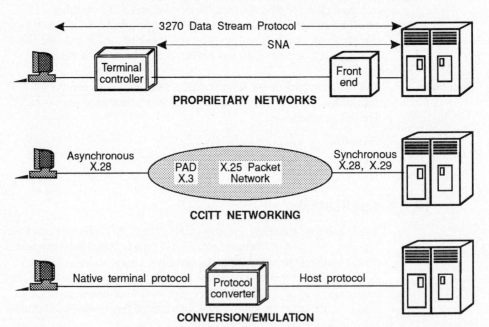

Figure 18.1   Traditional methods for terminal communications – proprietary, packet network PAD, and protocol converter.

PAD   CCITT introduced a series of standards in the mid-1970's to allow asynchronous terminals to access a packet switched data network. The standards are X.3, X.28 and X.29. They are specifically for terminal support and are not OSI standards. A logical component of the network, called a PAD (Packet Assembler/Disassembler), converts the character by character mode of operation of the terminal into packets for communication with the X.25 host computer. The operation of the PAD is controlled by a number of parameters that characterize the communications protocol used by the terminal and the conversions required to operate across the network. However, standard PADs do not perform data stream conversion, so applications are not independent of the terminal type.

Most proprietary terminal communications systems can also operate over X.25, making it suitable as a backbone network to support both OSI and non-OSI communications.

Another important concept is the protocol converter. This may be either a physically separate piece of equipment or integrated into the network. It supports two proprietary protocols, and maps character sequences to allow it to mimic a terminal supported by the application. Although many satisfactory products are available, a complex maze of conversions is required to allow communications with a mixture of different terminals and hosts. Another successful approach is the replacement of the terminal by a personal computer and the use of terminal emulation software to access various hosts.

OSI VT   The VT approach (Figure 18.2) differs from the above-mentioned traditional methods by describing the terminal operations in generic parameters exchanged between the terminal system and the application host. For instance, a series of characters generated by the terminal to say, move the cursor, is mapped into a generic command to the host that is independent of the type of terminal and host computer system. Both ends co-operate to achieve the desired mapping of terminal characteristics. The objective is to make the application as independent as possible from the terminal type.

X Windows   Whereas the above-mentioned methods are designed to accommodate the large population of existing text terminals, graphics applications need an entirely different approach. A graphics environment that has become popular in the industry is X Windows and its associated protocol. VT is

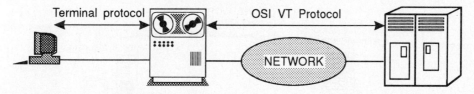

Figure 18.2   OSI Virtual Terminal model

based on dumb devices, whereas X protocols are based on graphics workstations closely coupled to applications on a host computer. X protocols have now been used as the basis for many applications and it is likely to supersede any further development of VT.

18.1.3 Implementation

Terminal subsystem

A variety of implementation scenarios are possible for the terminal subsystem and can accommodate existing terminals and new products such as a VT terminal server or a personal computer with specific VT support as shown in Figure 18.3. Such products are available from a limited number of vendors.

Applications

To benefit the most from VT, however, specific support is required in the host system and possibly the application. In existing proprietary terminal communications systems, it is common for terminals to be accessed from a specialized terminal driver or monitor.

One way of introducing VT would be to develop a special component in the host that interprets existing monitor commands and maps on to a VT environment. However, it may not always be possible to map specific proprietary terminal communications into VT. A potentially superior method is to replace the monitor with a system that included integrated VT functionality and the modification of the existing applications themselves to remove idiosyncratic features of the original monitor.

18.2 OPERATION OF VT

The VT standard applies to interactive applications requiring terminal oriented communication expressed in terms of graphical images. Terminal keyboards, screens, control functions, etc, are modeled by arrays of characters. The image structure is:

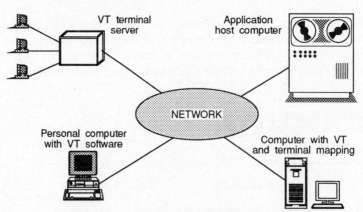

Figure 18.3   Scenario for the implementation of VT

- character box graphic symbols are used;

- either a one, two or three dimensional array;

- primary attribute is character value or null; and,

- secondary attribute describes foreground and background colour, emphasis (bold, underline, etc) and font.

For example, keyboard input may be represented as a linear string of characters — a one dimensional array. A screen display that allows up/down and left/right movement is modeled as a two dimensional array. A terminal that can store and switch between several pages of information is a three dimensional array.

Optional functional units in VT add the following capabilities to the above:

- Blocks are rectangular subdivisions of the array (typically used for partitioning a screen display). Blocks only affect addressing.

- Fields are rectangular subdivisions, although they cannot overlap. They are used for validation of data entry according to rules for data type and termination conditions.

Blocks and fields provide a simple forms mode of operation for structured enquiry response applications. (These capabilities were originally called the extended facility set and were described in addenda to the standard. They are now incorporated in the final version.)

18.2.1 VT Communication Model

CCA

The VT standards are based on a generic model of terminal communications — the *Conceptual Communication Area (CCA)*, illustrated in Figure 18.4. The CCA is a shared abstract data structure that represents the terminal environment. It forms the common virtual device that is mapped to the real terminal on one side and interacts with applications on the other side. The VT users, i.e. the application and the terminal subsystem, communicate with each other via the CCA. The CCA is, in effect, extended between the two distributed systems by the VT protocol between the VT application entities.

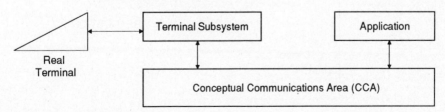

Figure 18.4   The CCA represents the terminal

The CCA contains a model representing the keyboard, screen and other I/O devices. The model is a collection of abstract data objects e.g. character arrays, control parameters. The applications operate on the model using OSI VT standard primitives instead of terminal specific commands.

A simplified representation of the CCA is shown in Figure 18.5. The CCA contains a number of data structures including:

- display objects

- control objects

- device objects.

Display objects

The CCA contains either one or two *display objects* (DO) on to which the real display and/or input device is mapped. The display object is parameterized for:

- number of dimensions and array size;

- capabilities for the definition of fields and entry rules; and,

- capabilities for the rendition of characters, e.g. highlight, font, etc.

All display data and input data is transferred via a display object. The display object is in fact distributed across the two systems and there is no direct communication between the application and terminal. For example, the display is not necessarily updated immediately.

Each display object can be assigned an access right that controls which end may at a given time write data into the object.

Control objects

Control objects reflect the allocation of tokens, access rights and other control data. There may be a number of control objects. For example, typical control objects include:

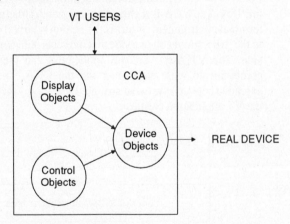

Figure 18.5   Abstract objects in the CCA

- Local echo control (controls the echo of characters at either end)

- Interrupt control, e.g. action on break signal

- Signal for termination of input and signal to update the other end

- Alarm bell or lamp indicator

- Printer on/off.

The optional functional units add:

- Control objects that define the placement of blocks and fields

- Data entry rules for fields, reactions to invalid data types, end of field, timeout waiting for entry.

Each control object may also be assigned access rights to govern which end may write data to the object. Control objects may be linked to device objects.

Device objects   In addition to the display objects and control objects, the CCA also contains device objects that represent the mapping function to real devices. Device objects and their mappings are not standardized, but are included in the model because their operation is affected by the VT parameters and is controlled by the control objects.

For example, there could be both a printer and screen for one display object requiring separate mapping functions. The device object is not updated directly by data transfers but may be influenced by the control objects.

The description of the CCA in the standard also includes the following elements:

ACS   The *Access Control store (ACS)* records the access rights of the user (represented by a parameter called the Write Access Variable - WAVAR).

CSS   The *Control, Signaling and Status store (CSS)* contains the VT control objects (the objects used for device control) and other objects, e.g. status objects.

DSD   The *Data Structure Definition store (DSD)* contains the data definitions of objects that reside in the CCA, e.g. control objects, display objects and device objects. The DSD is configured to define the Virtual Terminal Environment (VTE) from the VT parameters passed at association establishment time. The VTE may also be changed during an association by negotiation using the VT Switch Profile service.

CDS   The *Conceptual Data Store (CDS)* contains either one or two display objects, depending on the dialogue control mode (either A-Mode (two) or S-Mode (one), described in the next section).

**VT
environment**

Conceptually, the CCA could be viewed as a set of data paths and control paths. The data paths are the interfaces between the display object, the device object and the device. In this sense the device object assists in the mapping of data between the display object and the device itself. The display object's role is to provide a consistent (data) view of a terminal to the VT user (host). The characteristics of the data manipulation and transformation along these interfaces is controlled by the *Virtual Terminal Environment (VTE)*. The control aspects of the CCA set the environment in which the data is transferred between the display object and the device. Thus control objects are a critical aspect of the VT service. A description of the VT control objects and the way in which they are used is provided in Section 18.3.3.

18.2.2 Dialogue Control

VT supports two alternative communications modes that are common features of terminal communication (see Figure 18.6). They are known as:

A-mode   Asynchronous mode.

S-mode   Synchronous mode.

These have nothing to do with the underlying transmission technology used by the terminal. These modes distinguish between a two way alternate presentation service and a two way simultaneous presentation. A VT 100 terminal (with asynchronous character mode transmission) could be used in either S-mode or A-mode.

**Asynchronous
mode**

A-Mode provides two monologues in opposite directions, each manipulating its own display object. There are two independent data flows:

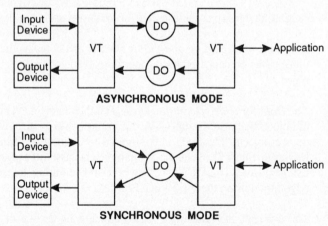

Figure 18.6   VT asynchronous and synchronous dialogue modes

- one flow from input device (keyboard to host); and,

- an independent flow from host to the screen.

There are two display objects and each end has non-reassignable access rights to one display object.

Synchronous mode

S-Mode uses two way alternate dialogue with a single display object. Each end takes turns to update the display:

- host sends a form to the screen;

- enquiry entered into screen from keyboard;

- then sent to host when input is terminated; and,

- host replies with information, and new form.

The VT standard defines a write access token that controls the right to access the display object. The token may be transferred between VT users to change the turn.

18.2.3 Display Object Operations

An overview of the display object operations is given below. The operations are subject to access right control and the capabilities of the terminal as defined in the VTE parameters.

Pointer location

Each display object has a display pointer that can be placed in the array of characters. Operations on the array contents take place relative to the pointer location. (It is not necessarily the same as the cursor.) The pointer provides an X, Y, Z addressing mode where:

X	Character position.
Y	Line number.
Z	Page number.

Addressing may be absolute or relative. The optional functional units add a block mode and forms mode. Block mode addressing uses X, Y, B, Z co-ordinates where:

B	Block number.
X, Y and Z	Position relative to the start of the block.

Forms mode uses N, F, Z addressing where:

N	Character number.
F	Field number.

Text   The text operation sets the primary attribute value; i.e. enters character values into the array at the display pointer. One or more characters may be set at a time. In the initial version of the standard, the text operation overwrites existing array values and there is no wrap around or line folding (this is the application's responsibility). The display pointer is left at the end of the inserted text.

A draft amendment to the standard includes an additional optional functional unit that provides insertion, deletion and copy operations for a display object. This will allow simple text editing with less communications overhead than the basic text operation.

The VT standard operates with any character set repertoire defined by ISO 646 (ISO 7-bit Coded Character Set) and ISO 2022 (ISO 7-bit and 8-bit Coded Character Sets — Code extension techniques). In the usual case, the character set used in display objects will consist of graphic characters only as the VT model is oriented toward operation with "displayable" characters. Typically, this will be the graphic characters of ISO 646 (the ISO version of American Standard Code for Information Interchange, ASCII).

Attribute   The attribute operation sets a secondary attribute, i.e. colour, emphasis, font, etc. Secondary attributes are set separately from text.

Erase   The erase operation sets primary and secondary attributes to null. It operates on single character positions or arrays.

Additional operations are defined for handling blocks and fields.

18.3 VT SERVICE AND PROTOCOL DEFINITION

The VT service definition includes:

- The means to establish, control and terminate the association between two peer VT users.

- Negotiation of the service subset and a consistent set of parameters for the CCA model. Negotiation takes place at association establishment and parameters may also be renegotiated during data transfer if the appropriate optional functional units are selected.

- A way of transferring data independently of the local representation and characteristics of the real terminal.

- Control integrity of the data transfer by management of the dialogue.

- An interrupt facility allows users to exchange priority information or resynchronize their activities.

Because of the complexity of the VT service, the service is divided into functional units. The functional units to be used during an association are selected during association establishment.

18.3.1 Profiles

The operation of VT is determined by a large number of parameters that characterize such aspects as:

- size of the array of characters in the display objects;

- addressing capabilities of the pointer; and,

- terminal rendition capabilities, etc.

The host application and terminal subsystem may negotiate these parameters individually or specify predefined profiles for the more common parameter sets. A profile is a consistent set of parameters for a typical terminal and application. Defaults are specified in the standard if profiles or parameters are not selected at association establishment.

VT specifies two default profiles — one for A-Mode and one S-Mode. Other profiles are defined by various groups and a register of VTE Profiles is administered by registration authorities. Such VTE Profiles can be selected by VT users by name, i.e. using an ASN.1 object identifier (OID). The VTE parameters and profiles can be negotiated at association establishment and renegotiated during the association. A number of profiles have been defined ranging from simple asynchronous terminal support (Telnet, PAD, etc) to forms mode terminals (GOSIP VT).

18.3.2 VT Protocol Specification

The CCA is replicated at both ends by the VT entities in the Application Layer as illustrated in Figure 18.7 (page 352). The purpose of the protocol is to keep both versions of the CCA synchronized and to transfer updates as a result of operations by users. Note that the mapping to the real terminal and the interface to applications is not standardized by VT.

The VT protocol uses the Association Control Service Element (ACSE) but otherwise makes specialized use of presentation layer directly and uses no other common application service elements. Particular use is made of normal, typed and expedited data, token control and resynchronize presentation services.

18.3.3 Control Objects

Control Objects (COs) form the heart of the VT concept. There are many types of COs and, in principal, they each perform discrete functions. A brief description of the VT COs and the way in which they are used follows:

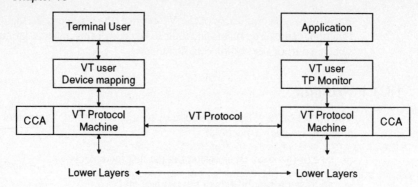

Figure 18.7   VT protocol model

CCO   *Context Control Objects (CCOs)* are optional and, if used, a CCO indi-
                  cates the starting point for data entry. The CCO can also indicate the point
                  at which the data entry terminated and the reason for termination.

ECO   The *Echo Control Object (ECO)* controls whether VT is in local echo
                  mode or not.

FDCOs   *Field Definition Control Objects (FDCOs)* contain an array of Field
                  Definition Records (FDRs). These records define the display fields (e.g.
                  length, screen position); display field attributes (colour, font, etc); pointers
                  to the previous and next field; transmission policy; and optionally,
                  FEICOs. The FDCOs define what is permitted to be entered and processed
                  within the field.

FEICO   *Field Entry Instruction Control Objects (FEICOs)* contain the parameters
                  that dictate the processing of a display or input field, i.e. the field size; the
                  character range; how to display; the time to wait for input, etc. FEICOs
                  contain the following parameters:

Number of entries	Controls the number of characters (entries) taken from the field size, e.g 10 from 15.
Allowed characters	Characters allowed from the terminal or host.
Forbidden characters	Characters forbidden from the terminal or host.
Allowed attributes	Foreground and background colour, emphasis and font.

FEPCO   *Field Entry Pilot Control Objects (FEPCOs)* are the most complex of the
                  control objects. FEPCOs contain an array of three types of elements:

                  • Field Entry Events (FEEs);

- Field Entry Conditions (FECs); and,

- Field Entry Reactions (FERs).

These three elements are grouped together to form an event/condition/reaction triplet. Sets of these triplets are used in the processing of input characters. For example, a FEPCO defines the processing to take place when specific function keys are input, or when information is entered into a field. Such events may result in local processing by the terminal subsystem and updated information being sent to the host application. A typical FEPCO entry set could be:

FEE = End of field	Input event is an entry at the end of a field
FEC = Not at last field	Current condition is not at the last field of the display
FER = Position at next field	Reaction (action to be taken) e.g. move cursor to next field

The above mentioned processing would take place in the local terminal subsystem and the application is only updated when the information entry is complete. The total FEPCO would contain any number of these sets to enable the processing of all terminal (keyboard) events for all the permitted terminal and display conditions.

TCCO The *Termination Condition Control Objects (TCCOs)* contain attributes that determine termination of input. These attributes are: data length; time out value; and termination event.

TPCO *Transmission Policy Control Objects (TPCOs)* contain attributes that determine what is delivered from the display object. These attributes are boolean values and they control:

Protected fields Either send all protected fields or do not send them.

Unprotected fields Send all the unprotected fields or those that have been updated.

Full content fields Send those fields that are full or send net effect of changes.

CCO update Allow or prohibit update of the CCO.

This control object is a replacement for those commands currently used in terminal protocols such as: read all, read modified data, etc.

RIO The *Reference Information Object (RIO)* is used to hold object update information (COs and DOs) for reference within the VTE. RIOs can be called (activated) during the session by direct protocol reference or by a FEPCO. RIOs can contain canned commands and strings for terminal responses, e.g. error messages such as "Only numeric characters are permitted in this field". RIOs can also be used to set up screen templates for data entry. These messages would be displayed via the FEPCO processing.

CO processing   The control objects listed above may seem complex, but placed within a processing sequence, their role within the VT architecture is clarified. An example (as guidance) of VT control object processing is depicted in Figure 18.8.

18.3.4 Functional Units

The VT standards define a number of functional units that identify the optional capability of the overall VT service. The functional units available to the VTE and the VT users are selected during the association establishment.

   The VT service provides negotiation services to enable the creation and modification of a single VTE in a manner acceptable to the service

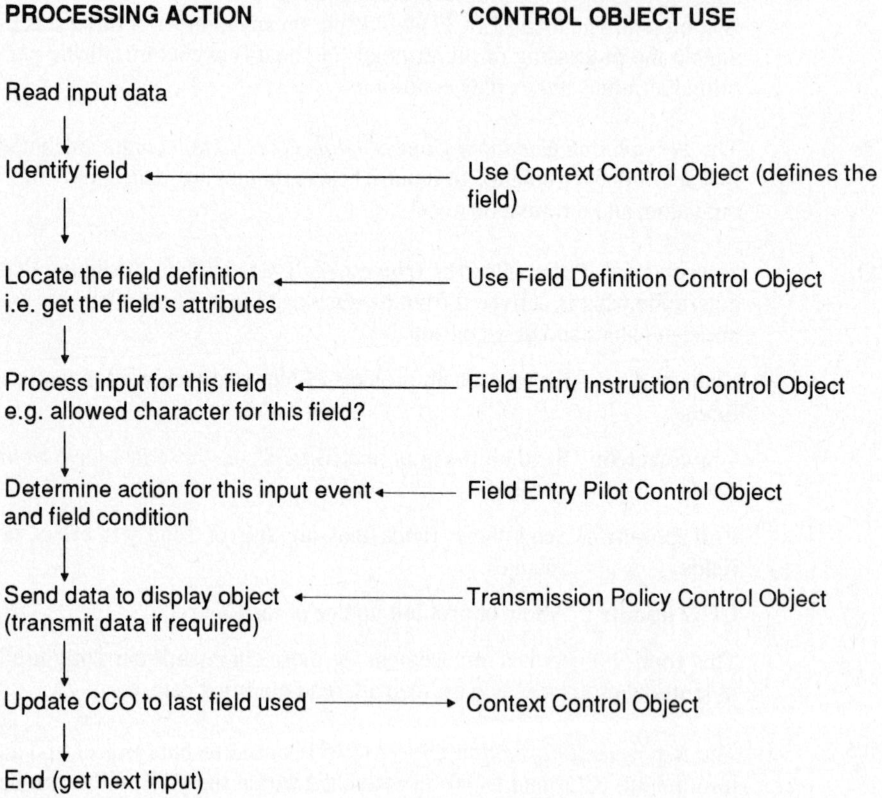

PROCESSING ACTION   **CONTROL OBJECT USE**

Read input data
   ↓
Identify field ←————————————————— Use Context Control Object (defines the
                                    field)
   ↓

Locate the field definition ←—————— Use Field Definition Control Object
i.e. get the field's attributes

   ↓

Process input for this field ←————— Field Entry Instruction Control Object
e.g. allowed character for this field?

   ↓

Determine action for this input event ←——— Field Entry Pilot Control Object
and field condition

   ↓

Send data to display object ←——————— Transmission Policy Control Object
(transmit data if required)

   ↓

Update CCO to last field used ————————→ Context Control Object

   ↓

End (get next input)

Figure 18.8   VT CO use and associated processing

provider and both VT users. VTE negotiation is a part of the association establishment facility. Additionally, VTE negotiation services are optionally available (depending on the functional units selected during the association process) that provide either a single switch profile negotiation or a multiple interaction negotiation. The functional units are listed below:

Kernel   Provides a basic set of facilities.

Switch profile negotiation   Alter the VTE parameters within the scope of the VTE profile. This service is a single confirmed service.

Multiple interaction negotiation   Negotiate (invite and offer and accept or reject) new parameter values of a full VTE in a series of steps. When this action is terminated the "draft" VTE replaces the current VTE.

Negotiated release   Accept or reject the release request. If this functional unit is not selected the release request must be honoured and the association terminated.

Urgent data   Transfer a small amount of data, possibly by-passing data already in transit. The VT urgent data facility is generally supported by the expedited data services of the lower layers.

Break   Pass the "Break" condition between VT users. The Break condition is a destructive interrupt.

Enhanced access rules   Additional access rules for control objects. In A-Mode the "no access" rule is added. In S-Mode an extensive set of access rules are added.

Structured control objects   Allows control objects to have more than one category of data element. This functional unit also permits the updating of these data elements individually, i.e. the control object can be partially updated.

Blocks   Structuring capability for a display object within the VTE. Updates to be written to a specific address (i.e. block) within the display object.

Fields   Structuring capability for a display object within the VTE. A field is a control mechanism that permits data in the display object to be classified.

RIO   Allows this particular form of control object to be used.

18.4 QUESTIONS

Question 18.1   What is the CCA and what are the three main components contained within it?

Question 18.2   Describe the two modes of VT.

Question 18.3   What are the three main characteristics of display objects?

Question 18.4   What does the FEPCO do in the processing of terminal data?

19 Systems Management

19.1 INTEGRATED SYSTEMS MANAGEMENT

19.1.1 Introduction

Multi-vendor networks

Few large information systems have the luxury of a single vendor. As computer networks grow, and voice and data systems coalesce, organizations now have a bewildering range of products and services to choose from. The emergence of open systems products will give users greater freedom to choose products from different vendors that best suit their needs. But to maximize the benefits of such diverse networks, users and vendors must also invest in improved network management systems to control, co-ordinate and monitor the behavior of the separate components (illustrated in Figure 19.1). Without integrated management systems, the networks may degenerate into an ineffective tangle.

Increasingly, business activities are information based and information technology has assumed a critical role in the fulfilment of the corporate mission. In this context, the ability to manage effectively large networks — whether to rectify problems, or to adapt a system to changing corporate goals, is crucial to network administrators. However, the available proprietary network management tools are frustratingly ineffective in the looming complexity of multi-vendor, distributed networks.

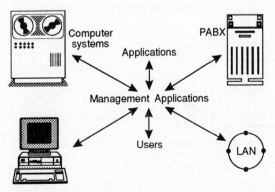

Figure 19.1   OSI Systems Management – distributed, multi-vendor management

Proprietary management

The current environment in the computer and telecommunications industries has evolved around proprietary network management systems, developed specifically by each manufacturer. All too often, the management of multi-vendor networks requires a room full of different network management consoles, and operators to watch them — one for each vendor specific portion of the network. The incompatibilities between different systems deprives end users of an efficient method for management of diverse heterogeneous networks.

Standard management

Hope is on the horizon in the form of the OSI Systems Management standards. The standards act as a common management language for networks. They provide a uniform way to exchange management information and control remote systems based on standardized models of the managed equipment. Although much work remains to complete the standards, there has already been strong vendor support for widespread adoption of the OSI management standards as the only way out of the present maze of incompatibilities.

Users and vendors now face a difficult balancing act. The only long term solution for multi-vendor network management is the development and implementation of open international standards. In the interim, however, existing requirements must be met by proprietary network management tools. The dilemma facing the industry is how to meet existing needs without distracting from the urgent task of standardization, and without over investment in obsolete solutions.

19.1.2 Models for Systems Management

Systems management can be defined as the set of activities that control, co-ordinate or monitor the use of resources in information technology systems. For the purpose of comparison between proprietary and standard systems, the automated network management tools used to support such activities can be modeled as shown in Figure 19.2. Management application software, running on a host computer, allows an authorized user to perform such management functions as controlling operating parameters in remote equipment, or receiving and interpreting alarms.

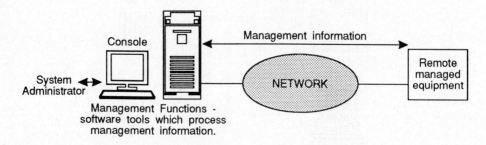

Figure 19.2   System Management model

The OSI standards for Systems Management govern the definition of the management functions, the protocols and syntax for information flow, and the models for managed objects. These are the essential elements for compatible interworking between different systems. The standards provide a generic, vendor independent model of the network management system as illustrated in Table 19.1. Provision of the user interface, and the mapping from the managed object models to the real equipment are not standardized and are left to the implementor. The user interface will be the subject of competition and innovation among vendors to provide automatic support and intelligent interpretation of events for network administrators.

The standards are a comprehensive framework for distributed network and application management, and they support a multitude of management applications, protocols, and equipment. Potentially, they will let network administrators consolidate their management tools on one console and maintain complex heterogeneous networks.

19.1.3 Impact on Today's Networks

The Systems Management standards are a very comprehensive and generalized solution for the future, but, in the interim, proprietary systems must be used to meet existing needs. The standards will need to co-exist with existing proprietary and purpose built management systems for some time to come.

Products implementing the OSI standards for the management protocol are already available from some vendors and product availability will grow during the early 1990's. Until the standards for the management functions and the managed objects are finalized, however, such products must operate with drafts of the standards and vendor specific models, and are therefore subject to alteration as the standards are progressed.

In the interim, existing equipment will continue to be supported using proprietary network management products. Even when the OSI management standards are introduced into a network, it may not be appropriate for the standards to take over management of the entire network. Existing systems should be upgraded only where the additional benefits are desired. For practical purposes however, it will be desirable to get away

Table 19.1 Comparison of proprietary and OSI Systems Management

MODEL ELEMENT	PROPRIETARY SYSTEMS	OSI MANAGEMENT STANDARDS
Management functions	Specific to product and vendor	Standardized and uniform. Vendor and product independent
Management application software	Constrained to one host environment	Open to any system which supports the necessary protocols
Information flow	Based on proprietary protocols and data encoding (syntax)	Uses OSI protocols and generalized syntax

from the multiple network console syndrome. Products that support both the OSI standards and individual proprietary requirements from one console are a pragmatic solution.

SNMP

A popular management protocol is the Simple Network Management Protocol (SNMP) that uses the TCP/IP (Transmission Control Protocol/Internet Protocol) communications technology. The management protocols and services of SNMP are limited. (Hence the simple part of SNMP.) SNMP is directed at Local Area Network (LAN) and TCP/IP network management although by extensions, it can apply to the UNIX server and workstation management entities as well. So in the short term, SNMP is seen as a very useful management system where previously none existed for LANs and TCP/IP.

In comparison with OSI management, two main compatibility issues arise. Although the semantics of SNMP are considered to be subset of CMIP, the protocols are incompatible. Furthermore, the management information model used in OSI management is far more sophisticated than SNMP. OSI management is directed at distributed systems management, not just LANs and TCP/IP. The managed objects used by SNMP products will have to be redefined (and reclassified) to be brought into line with OSI object definition rules. If OSI is eventually required, this means that SNMP based products will have to be re-engineered (e.g. with new software) to support OSI addressing, protocols and managed objects.

19.2 DISTRIBUTED MANAGEMENT

19.2.1 Concepts and Terminology

The Systems Management standards define the architecture, protocols, functions and data models used for management activities. These stand-

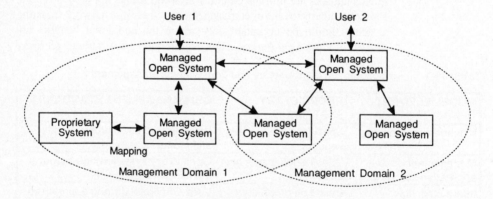

Figure 19.3   Distributed management architecture

ards do not actually define a complete management product. The standards provide the infrastructure guidelines and a tool box of features on which a management system can be implemented and used across OSI systems.

The network management standards are built on a distributed model that is depicted in Figure 19.3. A managed system, as shown in the figure, may be a part of the equipment being managed, or it may itself be a management system using either OSI or proprietary communications to manage others.

The central concept for management interaction between open systems is that of managers and agents. Typically, open systems will have both manager and agent roles for decentralized management. For a particular management action between two systems, one end takes the role of manager and the other the agent as illustrated in Figure 19.4.

MIS User   An OSI management process is called a *Management Information Service User (MIS User)*. An MIS User can provide both the manager and agent capability.

Agents   *Agents* are employed by one or more managers to achieve management activities. They are information gathering services, or functions that translate management commands into action at a remote site. For example, they maintain and regularly update data that can include timers, counters, statistics, flags and operational parameters. Some systems may have just the bare functions to act as an agent in order to communicate with the managers and translate commands to the real equipment. Communication with the real equipment, may in turn, require the agent to use proprietary protocols to control the real equipment e.g. a modem rack.

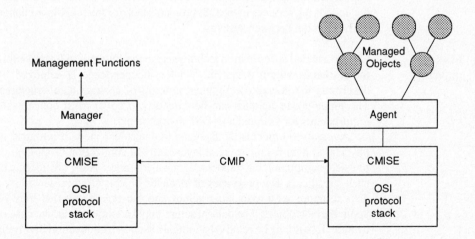

Figure 19.4   Model for definition of management standards

Managers

The *manager*, on the other hand, possesses the ability to process and interpret, on behalf of the network administrator, the information provided by multiple agents. The manager can also request such actions as setting the values of data, or the provision or removal of a resource at a remote location.

Management functions

The five broad areas supported by Systems Management are listed below.

- Fault management encompasses fault detection, isolation and the correction of abnormal operation. Conversely, it can provide reassurance that the system is functioning properly.

- Configuration management provides information about and control over the logical and physical resources of the system. It includes initialization and termination of resources, determination and setting of states, parameters and names.

- Accounting management allows monitoring the use of resources and the allocation of costs for such use.

- Performance management gathers statistics to evaluate network effectiveness and allows corrective actions to be taken.

- Security management supports the application and enforcement of security policies for systems.

CMISE and CMIP

In order to realize the management functions, the manager communicates with its respective agents using the *Common Management Information Service Element (CMISE)* and the associated *Common Management Information Protocol (CMIP)*. These act as the common management language and syntax across the distributed network. CMIP, in turn, uses the underlying services of the OSI protocol stack for the reliable exchange of information between systems.

Managed objects

Object oriented specification techniques are the foundation for modeling the resources within a system. Vendor independence is achieved by describing the managed equipment in terms of abstract data structures. The modeling techniques can be extended to cover most conceivable requirements for OSI and non-OSI environments.

A *managed object* is the Systems Management view of a logical or physical system resource viz: a layer entity, a connection or an item of physical equipment, e.g. modem. A managed object is the abstraction of such a resource. The properties of managed objects are represented by a data structure with associated values and the operations that may be applied to the object. The data structure may be simple, as in the case of a modem, or it may be relatively complex such as a connection involving multiple systems.

Managed objects can be specific to an individual OSI layer – known as (N)-layer managed objects, or relevant to multiple layers or the system as a whole – known as system managed objects. The translation between abstract managed objects and the real resources they represent is not defined by OSI. This is a matter for product developers to design and implement.

19.3 MANAGEMENT STANDARDS

Status

Following the successful development of the OSI standards, the focus of the international standards committees has now moved to Systems Management. CCITT and ISO are collaborating in this work and they publish equivalent standards that are listed in Table 19.2. (The number of management standards is growing continually so Table 19.2 is only a partial list.) A convenient way to refer to the standards is as the X.700 series.

Table 19.2   Standards for Systems Management

ISO	CCITT	TITLE
ISO 7498-4	X.700	Management Framework
DIS 10040	X.701	Systems Management Overview
ISO 9595	X.710	CMISE
ISO 9596	X.711	CMIP
ISO 10165-1	X.720	Management Information Model
ISO 10165-2	X.721	Definitions of Management Information
ISO 10165-4	X.722	Guidelines for Definition of Managed Objects
ISO 10165-5	X.723	Generic Management Information
ISO 10164-1	X.730	Object Management Function
ISO 10164-2	X.731	State Management Function
ISO 10164-3	X.732	Attributes for Representing Relationships
ISO 10164-4	X.733	Alarm Reporting Management Function
ISO 10164-5	X.734	Event Report Management Function
ISO 10164-6	X.735	Log Management Function
ISO 10164-7	X.736	Security Alarm Management Function
DIS 10164-8	X.740	Security Audit Trail Function
DIS 10164-9	X.741	Objects and Attributes for Access Control
DIS 10164-10	X.742	Accounting Meter Function
DIS 10164-11	X.737	Workload Monitoring Function
DIS 10164-12	X.745	Test Measurement Function
DIS 10164-13	X.738	Measurement Summarization Function
–	M.20	Maintenance Philosophy for Transmission Networks
–	M.30	Principles for a Telecommunications Management Network

ISO specifically sets out the standards for management of those systems that provide interconnection services, i.e. for management of the OSI layers, routers, etc. However, the standards are designed to be open ended and are intended also to support the management of applications and non-OSI systems. To fill in the some of the gaps for non-OSI systems, a group called the Network Management Forum has been formed by the major vendors. The aims of the Forum are to promote the development and implementation of the OSI Systems Management standards and to develop additional proposals for management of telecommunications equipment and services.

In addition, the CCITT is developing a set of Telecommunication Management Network (TMN) Recommendations. These are known as the M series and they provide models for the management of public networks such as ISDN and packet switching networks in accordance with the X.700 Recommendations.

Scope

The management standards have been formulated for the four main areas of distributed management; i.e.:

Architecture   The management architecture provides the concepts and overall model of distributed management. It defines the conceptual management interfaces of an open system and the distributed management processes that interact to control managed objects.

Management information model   These standards provide the guidelines for the definition of managed objects — their class, behaviour, relationships and their attributes — and form the Information Model for management. These standards are classified as the SMI (Structure of Management Information) documents.

Management communications   The definition of management services and protocols used by distributed management processed are contained in the CMISE and CMIP standards. These management services use the underlying services of the Remote Operations Service Element (ROSE), Association Control Service Element (ACSE) and the lower layers.

Management functions   The management functions are classified into a number of major areas, i.e. Configuration, Fault, Accounting, Performance and Security. These overall functional areas are further refined into discrete management function standards for Systems Management Application Service Elements (SMASEs). These standards define the services and data syntaxes for management functions such as log control, software distribution, object management, accounting and alarm reporting control. Generally the services defined in these documents are mapped on to the CMISE services.

19.3.1 Architecture

MIB

The managed objects in a managed open system are contained in a *Management Information Base (MIB)*. The MIB is a conceptual view of the data, control parameters and events that reflect the management properties of each system. Figure 19.5 illustrates the MIB and the associated architecture for the management of OSI protocol entities.

LME

Within each layer, *Layer Management Entities (LME)* put into effect the management actions by mapping between the abstract managed objects and the real data and events in the corresponding layer. The LMEs interact with the management entities via the MIB. In order to manage the protocol machines of a layer, LMEs directly access the management data associated with the local layer entity, and may further communicate with peer entities using a management protocol. The X.25 Registration and Diagnostic packets, and the Spanning Tree protocol used in LANs are examples of management protocols that are defined for specific layers.

19.3.2 Management Information Model

Systems Management uses the concept of managed objects to represent the real managed resource. The coupling between the managed object and the real resource is implementation dependent and outside the scope of OSI. However, the coupling provided by implementations of Systerms Management should be realistic.

Managed objects

The object oriented design paradigm, that is used in the Systems Management standards, provides four major characteristics:

- data abstraction;

- information hiding;

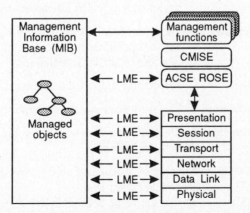

Figure 19.5   Architecture for management of OSI layers in a managed open system

- encapsulation; and,

- inheritance.

These characteristics require a separation between object type and instance. Managed objects represent a real managed resource and the behaviour of a managed object is defined in terms of a managed object class. The managed object class definition is an abstracted view of the *type* of resource. Object class definitions specify the structure and characteristics of an object. The actual object being managed within a system is an *instance* of the class. A managed object class is defined in terms of the following:

Object class   An ISO/CCITT object identifier (OID) is assigned to each managed object; i.e. each object class is allocated a registered, globally unique number.

Inheritance   Inheritance identifies the superior object to the one being defined, thus defining the properties inherited, i.e. what this object is derived from. All objects are ultimately derived from a root object that is referred to as the "Top". Inheritance means that the object inherits the properties of its superior. The object has additional properties to those of its superior. Inheritance is a "class" linkage and is used to derive (add properties to) a more complex object definition from a base object type.

Containment   Containment on the other hand is an ownership property — the managed object is linked to other managed objects by name. (For example, a house is linked to a street. The street being the superior object.) With containment if the superior ceases to exist, then all objects contained by it also cease to exist. (No street equals no houses!)

Behavior   The object's general behavior and, optionally, its behavior under specific operations and events is defined.

Attributes   The types of attributes within the object, their value range and the operations that can be applied to these attributes (e.g. Get or Set, etc) are defined.

Actions   The actions supported by the object.

Notification   The event notifications generated by the object.

Parameters   The data and syntax used in specific actions and notifications are defined.

A simplified example of a managed object class definition (a network level circuit) is given in Figure 19.6.

Managed objects are being defined by the respective protocol committees for each OSI layer, so that a consistent approach can be adopted

```
MANAGED OBJECT CLASS                    -- The definition of a managed object class

DERIVED FROM "ISO/IEC 10165/2" :Network Layer Entity   -- Defines the superior object
CHARACTERIZED BY circuitpackage PACKAGE                -- The start of the definition

BEHAVIOR        e.g. controls the operation of a communications circuit
ATTRIBUTES      e.g. virtual circuit number   -- permited values and permitted operations
                statistics                    -- permited values and permitted operations
                circuit state   values (active, inactive), actions (Get)
ACTIONS         activate,deactivate
NOTIFICATIONS circuit disconnect, protocol error, reset
PARAMETERS      parameter name                              -- parameter value

REGISTERED AS {ISO xxxx.moi circuit}                        -- the object identifier
```

Figure 19.6   Simplified example of the definition of a managed object indicating the main components

to create integrated management systems. Examples of such standards for managed objects are ISO 10737 for the Transport Layer and ISO 10733 for the Network Layer.

Naming   Within a system, instances of objects are derived from the class definitions. Object instances are referenced by their object name. Managed objects must be unambiguously named. Typically, the X.500 Directory scheme is used. The hierarchy of managed objects is known as the *Management Information Tree (MIT)*. The upper level of the MIT is populated by entries for countries, carriers, etc. Progressing down the tree are entries for nodes (systems), OSI layer entity, circuits, etc.

19.3.3 Management Communications

Management of an open system is performed by management entities in the Application Layer. A combination of different management entities supports one or more management functions, e.g. configuration, accounting, etc. Peer management entities communicate using CMISE/P (subject to access control). Other ASEs may also be present and used in conjunction with CMISE, e.g. FTAM to distribute software.

Operations   CMISE/P is a set of remote operations used for communication between the distributed manager and agent processes. The operations are summarized below.

Set-Modify   Used by the manager to establish, replace or remove attribute values of one or more managed objects.

Get   Reads the attribute values of one or more managed objects.

Cancel Get   Cancels a previously issued Get operation (i.e. suspend the Get results) on one or more managed objects.

Action   Performs an action on one or more managed objects.

Create   Requests the agent entity to make a new instance of a managed object.

Delete   Requests the agent entity to destroy a managed object.

Event Report   Forwards from an agent to the manager process an event notification about a managed object.

Parameters   Associated with the above operations are a number of parameters that convey information between the MIS users. Examples of some of the parameters are listed in Table 19.3.

19.3.4 Operations on multiple objects

Another capability within CMIS/P is to perform operations on one or more objects by the use of the scope (and optionally the filter) parameters. Managed objects are organized into an inverted Management Information Tree (MIT). The management process may wish to, for example, retrieve the state attribute values from a set of managed objects. The Get operation commences at the point of the managed object tree as specified by the Base Managed Object Instance parameter. The scope and filter parameters are then used to restrict the level of the object tree to which the operation applies and the data returned from the objects selected. For each of the objects that pass the selection criteria, a distinct CMIP response is sent back to the requestor in the form of "Linked replies". The scope and filtering mechanism for multiple managed object selection is similar to the Search and List mechanism used in the X.500 Directory.

19.3.5 Functional Units

The Kernel functional unit includes all of the CMISE services except for the Cancel Get service. Other optional functional units are:

- Cancel Get which adds the Cancel Get service;

- Multiple Object Selection which permits the use of the scope parameter;

- Filter functional unit which permits the use of the filter parameter;

- Multiple Replies functional unit which permits linked responses and the use of the Link Identifier parameter;

- Extended Service functional unit which permits direct use of the Presentation Layer services (e.g. P-Alter Context, P-Typed Data, etc) by the CMISE user.

Table 19.3   CMIP parameters

PARAMETER	PURPOSE
Invoke Id	A sequence number for the operation. It is used to uniquely identify the different instances of management operations.
Link Id	Used to group two or more management operations when there are multiple responses to a single request e.g. send statistics every five minutes
Mode	Either confirmed or unconfirmed
Scope	Used to limit the depth of objects to which an operation is applied
Synchronization	Used to request that operations on two or more managed objects be atomic
Filter	Selects the type and values of attribute data returned on a Get or the attributes and objects used on Set or Action operation etc
Access Control	Provides protection to managed objects. It is optional and externally defined to CMISE/P (user specific).
Base Managed Object Class	The Base Managed Object Class parameter is used to specify the class of the object instance being accessed.
Base Managed Object Instance	Specifies the object instance to which the operation applies. Where multiple objects are selected (via the scope parameter), this parameter indicates the highest object on the object tree at which the operation commences. This parameter is generally a Distinguished Name (or an RDN), similar to that used in the X.500 Directory.
Attribute Id List	This parameter is used in a Get request service to request the agent to select specific attributes (their types and values) from one or more managed objects.
Attribute List	Used in a Get response or a Set service to transfer specific attributes (their types and values) between the manager and agent processes
Action Id	Used in a Action service to identify the type of action and to specify the syntax and semantics of the Action Information parameter
Action Info	Used to convey the information (parameters) relating to the specific action.
Event Id	Used in an Event service to identify the type of notification and to specify the syntax and semantics of the Event Information parameter
Event Info	Conveys the information (parameters) relating to the specific event
Errors	Indicates whether the CMISE service or the responding CMISE user failed the operation

19.3.6 Management Functions

The management functions are defined by the ISO 10164/CCITT X.73x and X.74x series of standards. These standards define the models and concepts for the management function services; the specific services and the syntax of the elements of that service; and the mapping to CMISE. For example the Alarm Reporting function (ISO 10164-4/CCITT X.733) defines the following types of alarms:

- communications failure;

- Quality of Service (QOS) failure;

- processing failure;

- equipment failure; and,

- environmental failure.

It also defines the syntax for the associated alarm parameters (alarm information) such as: probable cause, severity levels, backed up status, threshold parameters, trend indication, correlation information, problem data, proposed repair action, and the managed object status. When these alarms are generated by the Alarm Reporting function (on behalf of a managed object) they are transferred between the management entities via the CMISE/P protocol as an Event Report. The alarm type and information are mapped on to CMISE according to the definitions in the Alarm Reporting function standard. For example, the Alarm Type parameter is mapped on to the CMISE Event Type parameter and the Alarm Information attributes are mapped on to the CMISE Event Information field.

19.4 QUESTIONS

Question 19.1   What are the five functional areas of management?

Question 19.2   What is the MIB?

Question 19.3   What is a managed object?

Question 19.4   What is a LME?

Question 19.5   What are the four areas of scope covered by the Systems Management standards?

Question 19.6   How does SNMP relate to Systems Management standards?

Question 19.7   How does TMN relate to Systems Management standards?

Question 19.8   What are the main characteristics of a managed object?

Question 19.9   The manager and agent role are common definitions within management. What is the scope of these terms?

Question 19.10   In what way are managed objects similar to X.500 Directory entries?

20 Distributed Transaction Processing

20.1 LINKING TRANSACTION PROCESSING SYSTEMS

The Open Systems Interconnection (OSI) standards for linking online transaction processing systems have recently stabilized. OSI Distributed Transaction Processing (DTP) is specifically designed to support the synchronization and co-ordination of distributed applications to ensure that a unit of work (a transaction) is reliably completed on multiple systems (e.g. updating multiple data-bases). Providing functionality equivalent to, and in some areas exceeding, a strategic IBM communications service known as LU 6.2, OSI DTP is seen as vital for widespread acceptance of OSI in the commercial data processing arena.

20.1.1 What is a Transaction?

The definition of this term varies, so its meaning is illustrated by some simple examples.

TP monitor The main users of online transaction processing have been in the financial, banking, booking, and travel industries. Figure 20.1 illustrates a centralized transaction processing system. To cope with such transactions as flight reservations and funds transfers, special mainframe software is used to co-ordinate terminal access, database updates and output to peripherals, such as a printer. The objective was to make transactions atomic:

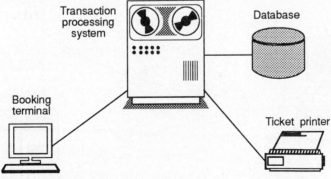

Figure 20.1   Centralized transaction processing

- if a withdrawal was valid or a booking succeeded, the ticket or cheque was printed, and the database updated without delay; but,

- if the transaction failed, any partially complete actions are rolled back so that effectively no actions would take place.

Distributed transactions

Originally, transaction processing systems were centralized, but there is increasing need to interconnect such systems. For example, to allow a travel agent to make bookings on multiple airlines, hotels and car rental services for an individual trip requires the co-ordination of several systems. Possibly, different systems will be involved for different bookings. Figure 20.2 illustrates a scenario for distributed transaction processing. The standards allow all parties to come to an agreement on whether to complete the booking, or, if there is no agreement, then no unwanted change takes place on any system.

Such co-ordination is achieved by a two phase commitment procedure which is supported by the DTP standard.

20.2 DISTRIBUTED TRANSACTION PROCESSING CONCEPTS

Transaction

In the DTP model, a *transaction* is identified as a unit of work performed by the transaction partners. A unit of work is characterized by four attributes:

Atomicity   The unit of work is either performed or not, i.e. no partial results.

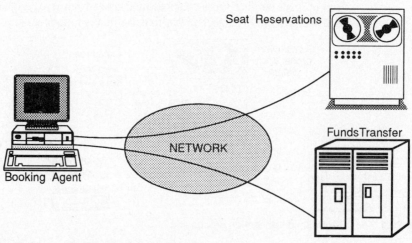

Figure 20.2   Distributed Transaction Processing

Consistency	The unit of work is performed accurately, correctly and with validity.
Isolation	Partial results of the unit of work are not accessible.
Durability	All effects of the unit of work are not affected by any sort of failure.

ACID   The term ACID is used throughout the standard as an acronym for these characteristics. DTP alone does not give these properties. Overall, the transaction is dependent on the applications to enforce atomic results — DTP ensures that applications can maintain the ACID properties over the communications link in a distributed system. As with other OSI standards, interfaces to local resources or applications are not defined by DTP.

20.2.1 DTP Service

DTP is an OSI Application Layer standard. It provides the Transaction Processing (TP) service. The TP service user is provided with a defined abstract interface and a set of services that support transaction processing across **two or more** DTP systems. The other standards covered in this book provide communication between one pair of end systems at a time. DTP introduces the concept of a dialogue as a way to structure and control multiple associations between end systems.

The TP service itself uses the underlying OSI lower layer services, and the following Application Service Elements (ASEs): Association Control Service Element (ACSE); and, Commitment, Concurrency and Recovery (CCR). In effect, it extends CCR to provide synchronized support of transactions across multiple systems.

Associations   The various computer systems that wish to participate in distributed processing first set up a pool of associations between them. Not all the associations will necessarily be used for each transaction. In the seat reservation example, the seat reservation system may set up associations with various agents and hotels at the start of the business day.

Dialogue   A *dialogue* is peer to peer relationship set up over the associations for the duration of a series of transactions. The dialogue identifies the type of transactions that will take place. A dialogue tree identifies which systems will be involved in the series of transactions. For example, the booking agent may establish a dialogue involving the seat reservation and fund transfer systems. The seat reservation system will propagate the dialogue to other systems if required. The dialogue tree is supported by the associations but is durable over association failures — if a communications failure disrupts an association, a new association can be established to allow the dialogue to proceed.

Transaction tree

A dialogue may support a series of transactions. Each transaction is modeled as an inverted tree with the root node as the initiator of the transaction.

The root node is referred to as the Superior, and nodes on the transaction branch are either intermediate nodes, or leaf nodes if they terminate the branch of the tree (see Figure 20.3). If subordinate nodes are unable to fulfil the root's requests on their own, they may initiate dialogues with other nodes in the tree, becoming superiors to the new subordinate nodes. All of these nodes are then partners in the transaction, and synchronized by the TP service provider.

A distributed transaction is initiated by the Superior node. This transaction is then propagated and synchronized through the TP service to the underlying nodes. The TP service then synchronizes the responses from the underlying nodes and provides a single response to the TP user.

Service elements are available within the TP service to grant control to an intermediate or leaf node, thus the transaction tree is logical and can change in physical terms from transaction to transaction. It is not necessarily the same as the dialogue tree. The root of the dialogue tree and the transaction tree may be different, and the same dialogue may support a sequence of distinct transactions. Also, the TP service permits individual nodes to be isolated from the transaction tree on a per transaction basis.

20.3 PROTOCOL FLOW

DTP ensures the integrity of data associated with the transaction — the *bound data*. The basic transaction flow for a transaction supported by the TP service provider is illustrated in Figure 20.4:

- When the transaction commences, the initial value of any bound data that is being updated, and a transaction identifier, is recorded in stable store (e.g. disk) by all parties.

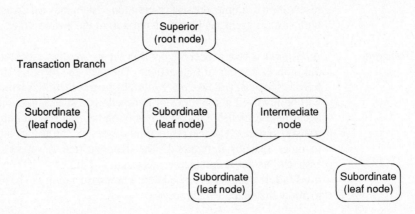

Figure 20.3   Transaction tree

- The transaction data is exchanged/passed between the respective TP service users. This data forms a new value for the bound data object. The new value will ultimately replace the old value if (and only if) the transaction is successful.

- To complete the transaction, the root node issues a TP-Commit request to the provider. The provider propagates this to all subordinates. If the subordinates are able to proceed, they ensure that both the initial value and the new value are recorded in stable store, record a ready log and reply with TP-Commit Continue. The subordinate nodes respond with TP-Rollback if unable to proceed. Rollback results in the initial value being restored in all nodes.

- If all subordinates are ready, the provider records a commit log, updates its own data, and issues the TP-Commit Result to the users in all nodes. Alternatively, if an error had occurred, the Superior would order rollback.

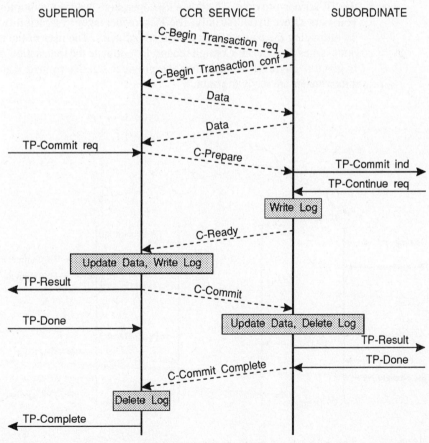

Figure 20.4   Transaction protocol

- The subordinates commit the new value of the bound data, discard the old and issue a TP-Done request to the Superior.

- On receipt of confirmations from all subordinates, the superior deletes its own commit log, and the transaction has completed.

The transaction machine must therefore retain old value data, create new value data and, during the commitment process, update the old value data with the new data. Figure 20.4 shows how the TP service between two systems is realized using the two phase commitment of the CCR ASE (see also Section 14.5, page 258).

20.3.1 Multiple System Transaction Process

Figure 20.5 shows a complete sequence for a successful transaction using the provider supported commit level of co-ordination. The root has two subordinate nodes, one of which has a further subordinate.

The figure shows the primitives between the TP user in each node and the TP service provider. The down tree operations between subordinate nodes are shown in outline only. The TP provider takes responsibility for co-ordinating the commitment for all subordinates. The user in the root node issues a single TP-Commit request to terminate the transaction, and is given a single TP-Result when the provider has determined that all subordinates are ready to commit.

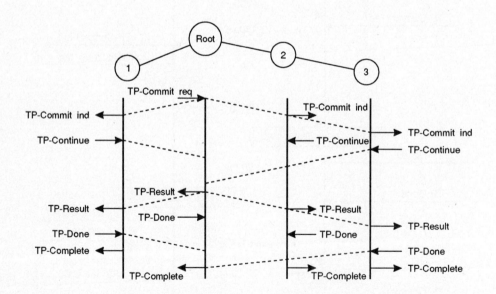

Figure 20.5   Commitment of a distributed transaction

The TP-Done is issued to the TP provider by the TP service user when the bound data has been secured by the TP user. The TP provider acknowledges this event to the user in the root node with a TP-Commit Complete when all subordinates have secured their data.

20.4 OVERVIEW OF THE DTP STANDARDS

The DTP standard progressed to second DIS (Draft International Standard) ballot in mid-1991. Although reasonably stable, it is still subject to change. The standard is ISO DIS 10026 and there is no CCITT equivalent.

The TP service and its supporting protocol are concerned with creating an environment in which two or more users can interact to:

- Begin a dialogue to establish each other's identity and mode of operation

- Exchange data with semantics chosen by the user and/or the user application service element

- Co-ordinate work with different levels of synchronization and commitment

- Delimit provider supported transaction units

- Prepare for commitment, and commit or rollback a transaction

- Report errors

- End a dialogue abnormally when necessary

- Have provider supported transactions either chained together or separated from one another

- Co-ordinate processing by hand-shaking.

In addition, features to resynchronize transactions after failures or a system crash are offered but are not necessarily visible to the user.

20.4.1 Functional Units

The following functional units are defined:

Kernel	Supports the basic TP services required to begin a dialogue, initiate a transaction, send data, signal a user or provider initiated error and end the dialogue. User or provider abort may signal abnormal termination.
Shared control	Both TP partners can issue request primitives subject only to the normal sequence constraints of the primitives.

For example, data can be transferred by both TP users at the same time.

Polarized control   One TP user has control of the dialogue at any time. Many request primitives can be issued only by the TP user that controls the dialogue. This restriction is in addition to the normal sequence constraints for the primitives. For example, data can only be transferred by the partner that has control of the dialogue.

Commit   Supports reliable commitment and rollback of provider supported transactions. There are two forms of the commit functional unit (level A and level B). They both give the same capabilities for interworking between open systems, but level B is designed to support TP users that have direct control over bound data, while level A is designed to support users that do not have such control.

Unchained transactions   Allows a superior to exclude one of its subordinates from a sequence of provider supported transactions, and to re-include it in later provider supported transactions.

Handshake   Allows a pair of TP users to co-ordinate their processing with one other.

20.4.2 Comparison with LU 6.2

IBM has a proprietary protocol under the SNA architecture known as Logical Unit 6.2 (LU 6.2) that can be used to interlink distributed systems. DTP is LU 6.2's OSI equivalent. There is a one to one correspondence between many aspects of DTP and the service provided by IBM's LU 6.2 protocol which is known as Advanced Program to Program Communications (APPC). The semantics are deliberately designed to be identical, although OSI protocols are used instead of SNA. Some of the equivalent concepts are illustrated in Figure 20.6.

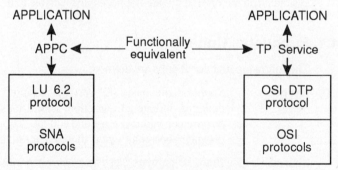

Figure 20.6   Comparison of IBM LU 6.2 and OSI DTP

While such correspondence between LU 6.2 and DTP facilitates the use of gateways for interworking between them, the interface to DTP is likely to be different from LU 6.2 because of differences in syntax, naming and methods of access to resources in the SNA and OSI environments.

20.5 QUESTIONS

Question 20.1   What are the four attributes associated with a transaction?

Question 20.2   What ASEs support DTP?

Question 20.3   What is the transaction tree?

Question 20.4   Does the DTP standard define the actual transaction?

Question 20.5   How does a node on the transaction tree inform the initiator that it is unable to complete the transaction?

Part 5 – Document Handling Standards

21 Open Document Architecture

21.1 DOCUMENT TRANSMISSION

Open Document Architecture (ODA) and Open Document Interchange Format (ODIF) are international standards for the use and transfer of documents by electronic information systems. The standards are now finalized as the ISO 8613/CCITT T.410 series. The purpose of the standards is to facilitate the electronic interchange of documents, or parts of documents, in a manner such that:

- different types of content, including text, image, graphic and sound, can co-exist within a document; and,

- the intentions of the document originator with respect to editing, formatting and presentation can be communicated most effectively between different processing systems.

Traditional word processing

The full potential of office automation cannot be realized unless documents can be exchanged and imaged as the originator intended. Yet the increasing diversity and complexity of proprietary text editors, word processors and desktop publishing systems has exacerbated incompatibility. Typically, to exchange such documents electronically, software packages to convert from one word processor format to another are necessary. However, as more proprietary formats become involved, the number of conversions required becomes unmanageable, and many imperfections and limitations in the conversion are evident.

ODA

The demand for common document interchange format has lead to the creation of the international standards for ODA, although this has not yet been adequately reflected in products. ODA defines a rich document interchange format. Initially, ODA will not replace proprietary products, although it has the potential to serve as the internal architecture for word processors. Typically, ODA will be implemented as a conversion gateway and ODIF will used as the common medium for interchange between different proprietary systems.

21.1.1 Origins of the Standards

Although these standards are fairly new to the international scene, they are in fact the result of progression of the more familiar document interchange standards known as the Telematic Services. The common standards for document interchange include Telex, Facsimile, Teletex and, recently, Message Handling Systems (MHS, X.400).

Group 1, 2 and 3 facsimile are the older generation of machines that are designed to work on the analogue public switched telephone network and have a unique control protocol. Group 4 facsimile provides the same document characteristics of Group 3, but is designed to operate on data networks and uses Open Systems Interconnection (OSI) Transport and Session layer protocols, defined by CCITT (International Telegraph and Telephone Consultative Committee) T.70 and T.62 respectively. Facsimile transmission represents an image as an array of picture elements (abbreviated as either "pels" or "pixels"). Teletex is designed for communicating word processors as an advanced electronic replacement for Telex. It uses OSI communication standards. Although popular in Europe and a service is available in Australia, Teletex is not widely used elsewhere.

In the past, each mode of document interchange had its own characteristics and it was difficult for documents to be exchanged between services. In the early 1980's, the International Organization for Standardization (ISO) commenced work on an architecture for interchanging the sorts of documents found in a typical office environment. The CCITT recognized that this work could form the basis for a mixed mode service that combined facsimile and Teletex, and the two groups began intense collaboration. At the 1984 CCITT plenary meeting, Recommendation T.73, "Document Interchange Protocol for Telematic Services" was the first outcome of this work. The continuation of the work saw the publication of the Open Document Architecture and Interchange Format standards by CCITT and ISO in 1988 and 1989 respectively. Note that the ISO version was originally called Office Document Architecture, but they have now changed to the common title.

21.1.2 Telematic Document Characteristics

The Telematic standards describe a document in terms of a number of defined characteristics. To permit the exchange and reproduction of a document electronically, these characteristics must be represented as a series of attributes within the exchange protocol.

The major characteristics of a document interchange are:

Physical presentation   Size, margins, fonts and rendition.

Terminal   Facsimile, Teletex, mixed mode.

Communica-	Group 1, 2, 3 facsimile or OSI transport, session
tions	protocols.

The above characteristics are the subject of the various Telematic standards that were the starting point for the evolution of ODA/ODIF. T.60 and T.61 are the standards that cover Teletex and these specify document and text characteristics. T.5 and T.6 provide the specifications for document and content of Group 4 facsimile messages.

Initially, Teletex and facsimile devices were independent. However, with Teletex devices being incapable of providing facsimile information, and the need for a single device to provide both types of document transmission, a mixed mode device has evolved. A mixed mode device can handle facsimile (Pixel) information and Teletex (character based) information in separate messages or combined in a single message.

Two types of document formats have been developed in the T series Recommendations to accommodate this: TIF0 that is pixel information only and TIF1 that combines both the pixel and character graphics information. Mixed mode physical document layout is specified in CCITT T.72, and the actual document content is encoded in the format specified by T.73. Facsimile and Teletex documents formatted in T.73 protocol are exchanged over Session (T.62) and Transport layer (T.70) services. T.73 is the CCITT Telematics Document Interchange protocol that is a subset of the ODA/ODIF standards.

21.2 DOCUMENT SPECIFICATION

In the office environment, documents can have very complex structures. Many of the existing word processing systems were developed when character text was the only form of content. Formatting and presentation requirements were embedded in the text as special character strings and other content types, such as image, were added as exceptions.

ODA	ODA was designed from the beginning to make a clear separation
documents	between:

- document structure or architecture;

- content type; and,

- styles.

Document	Document architecture specifies the **structure** of the document as a whole
architecture	without regard to the content types used in the document. In ODA/ODIF,
	a document consists of:

Logical view	The logical relationships between the components of a complete document; i.e. a letter has a heading, a body that consists of several paragraphs, and a signature.

Layout view   The physical placement of the components of the letter on pages described in terms of page set, page and block.

Both of these views describe different (but related) aspects of the complete document structure as illustrated in Figure 21.1. Documents in the ODA environment can exist in a number of forms, i.e.

Processable form   Suitable for editing and containing the logical view and contents (also called a revisable form).

Formatted form   Suitable for printing and containing the layout view and contents (also called final form). ODA does **not** define the imaging or printing process which is a local matter.

Processable formatted form   Suitable for both editing and printing. It contains both the logical and layout views as well as contents.

Content architecture   The specification of the document architecture is general enough to be used for any content type — including those not yet envisaged. There are three content architectures standardized:

- character content architecture, i.e. text;

- geometric graphics content architecture, i.e. business graphics or computer drawing graphics; and,

- raster graphics content architecture, i.e. pixel based image encoding.

Some structuring information within the content portions is necessary, for example, to specify certain text to be underlined or the number of picture elements per line in a raster graphics picture. The content architectures include such rules for the structuring information embedded in the contents.

Styles   Whereas the above mentioned architectures describe the document structure and content, the information necessary to control layout and imaging processes is contained in a separate set of constituents called *styles*. The attributes necessary to lay out a processable form document or to image

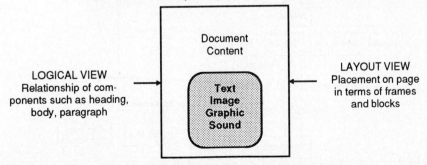

Figure 21.1   ODA separates the specification of document structure from its contents.

a formatted form document would be contained in styles referenced from the components in the structures. Styles form the link between the logical view and the layout view. A layout style specifies the rules for locating the position of an object such as a paragraph or heading on a page.

21.2.1 Logical Structure

The logical structure of a document is the way in which the originator wishes to organize the document text in relation to the heading and content, etc. In the logical structure, the document is divided and sub-divided on the basis of the meaning of its components.

A generic logical structure is like a template that is used at the beginning of an editing session to create a particular type of document, e.g. a report or letter. The generic logical structure for a letter is used in Figure 21.2 as an illustration of a logical structure.

The logical components of a document start at the root node which, in this example, is the Letter. Below this, other nodes exist such as Header and Body, and the document is further defined by subordinate logical nodes, i.e. Date, Address, Subject, Paragraph, Drawing, Caption, Ending and Signature. The logical structure has no connection with paper size, content type, fonts and rendition.

Logical objects The various components of the structure mentioned above are called *logical objects*. An object that is not subdivided into smaller objects is called a basic object. All other objects are called composite objects. For logical objects, no other classification is defined in the document architecture. Classifications such as chapter, section, and paragraph are application dependent and can be defined by applications using mechanisms provided in the standards. Logical objects such as running headers and footers may also be defined and bound to their respective parts of the logical structure. Each logical object is described by a set of attributes

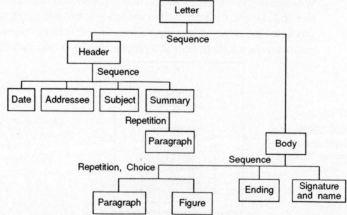

Figure 21.2   The logical structure of a document describes a document in terms of objects and their relationships.

describing its properties; e.g. certain objects may have attributes that automatically generate section numbering.

21.2.2 Layout Structure

The layout structure provides the physical position and presentation information that is applied to the document logical structure. It divides and subdivides the document on the basis of its physical form. The generic layout structure, in the example in Figure 21.3, again is comprised of a root node, Letter, to which subordinate nodes provide the positional information for the logical subordinate nodes.

Layout objects Layout structures consist of Letter, Page Set, Page, Block and Frame. These *layout objects* are defined in the document architecture as:

Block	Basic layout object corresponding to a rectangular area on the presentation medium.
Frame	Composite layout object corresponding to a rectangular area on the presentation medium and containing one or more frames or blocks.
Page	Basic or composite layout object corresponding to a rectangular *unit* on the presentation medium and, if it is a composite object, containing one or more frames or blocks.
Page Set	Set of one or more pages.

21.2.3 Styles

The collection of attributes that characterize the detailed layout or rendition of a document are called *styles*. References to styles may be made from both logical and layout objects.

Layout styles Layout styles are a constituent of a document that is used in the document layout process. The layout style attributes specify the appropriate layout

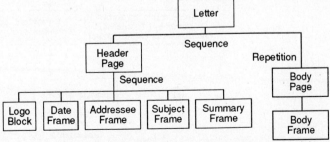

Figure 21.3   The layout structure describes a document in terms of the placement of contents in relation to pages and position on the page.

object for each logical object and express any constraints that may apply; e.g. that the content is to start at a certain offset from the edge of the layout object.

Presentation styles

The layout process itself is controlled by information supplied in presentation attributes contained in the presentation styles, that are particular to the content type. Examples of presentation attributes are:

- line spacing or indentation in a character content;

- clipping in raster graphics; and,

- line rendition in geometric graphics.

21.3 DOCUMENT PROCESSING MODEL

A document during its construction and exchange can have two basic forms. The first, in processable form, where the document is created and edited into its logical state. The logical information can be supplemented with layout information to produce the formatted form. Formatted form then makes the document complete for the imaging process which then produces the document in its real form.

Documents can exist in the ODA environment in either the processable form, the formatted form or a combined processable formatted form as illustrated in Figure 21.4. A particular document may pass through several editing iterations involving various combinations of these processes and forms. Note that only the interchange data structures are standardized, not the editing or imaging process which remain proprietary.

A more detailed model of the components and processes that make a document into a form where it can be reproduced are illustrated in

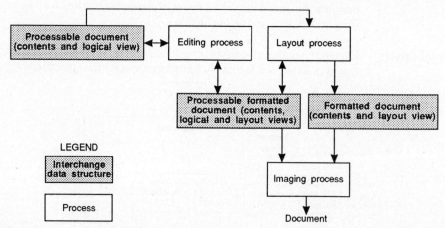

Figure 21.4   ODA defines documents in three forms and standardizes the data structures for their interchange.

Figure 21.5 (the editing loops are omitted for clarity). Starting with a template (generic logical structure), the specific content is generated and edited to produce the processable form. The resulting specific logical structure is combined with the generic layout structure and layout styles to produce the specific layout structure. The presentation styles provide further attributes for laying out the document (formatted form). The total formulation results in the generation of the information that is used to represent the document image.

21.3.1 Document and Object Classes

In many documents, the logical objects and the layout objects may have similarities related to logical features such as chapter/section/paragraph hierarchy, or to physical features such as size or style, or to content such as page headers/footers. Even an entire document may be a member of a group of similar documents, e.g. a letter, a memorandum or a company report format. Documents or objects that have a common set of characteristics can be described in terms of a document class, i.e. a collection of attributes, components and styles that typically make up a letter or a company standard report format.

Document classes

Document classes are defined by means of generic layout and/or logical structures, which have two main uses:

- to predefine the structures for consistency; and,

- to reduce the amount of information required to represent a document by holding common information.

The generic structures are like templates that determine what objects a document (of a certain document class) can or must have and the characteristics of those objects.

Object classes

The characteristics of related objects are defined in terms of object classes. For example, two object classes may be used for **page** to distinguish

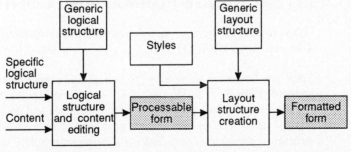

Figure 21.5 ODA document processing model showing role of generic structures and styles

between the different layout requirements for left and right sides. Each actual page would then be an instance of one or the other of these object classes. The set of logical object classes and layout object classes associated with a document class, and their relationships, are called the generic logical structure and generic layout structure. (Generic logical and layout structures were used in the examples in Figure 21.2 and Figure 21.3.)

21.3.2 Descriptive Model of a Document

The above-mentioned processing model of a document introduces several of the components of a document. The components of a document are applied to discrete processes to formulate the document image. These document components are identified in ODA as a document model. A more complete description of the components of a document as interchanged between two systems includes:

Document profile	Describes what is going to follow in the bit stream in terms of selections of attributes, document class, character set used, etc, and management information such as author, date of creation. The profile allows the recipient to evaluate the complexity of the document before attempting to process or image it.
Generic structure	List of any standard logical and layout object classes that are used.
Styles	Definition of layout and presentation attributes that apply.
Specific structure	Specific logical and layout object descriptors, and contents for this document.

Each of these components has to be encoded in some way for transfer between two systems.

21.4 INTERCHANGE FORMAT AND CONTENTS

ODA provides for the use of two alternative ways to represent and encode a document viz: ODIF and SDIF.

ODIF   The *Open Document Interchange Format (ODIF)* is defined in the ODA series of standards. It is a superset of T.73, and it uses the Abstract Syntax Notation One (ASN.1 see Chapter 13) to represent and encode a document. During transfer, the document is represented as a set of data structures called *interchange data units*. In summary, ODIF is a definition of interchange data units that represent the constituents of a document, i.e. profile, class, object identifiers, logical and layout descriptors, styles, document content, etc using ASN.1. Since it is a data format standard rather than a communications protocol, a more complete description of ODIF is beyond the scope of this book.

SDIF

An alternative to the use of ASN.1 based ODIF encoding is a clear text representation using the Standard Generalized Markup Language (SGML) of ISO 8879. This is known as the *SGML Document Interchange Format (SDIF)* (ISO 9069). This option is incorporated in the ISO version by reference and there is a one to one mapping between ODIF and SDIF (although non-character content is handled transparently).

Since ODIF uses ASN.1 type, length, value binary encoding, it is the most efficient interchange format for OSI communications, and for direct processing and conversion to local forms of document representation. It can be used to represent all forms of ODA documents and content types. SDIF uses human readable character "tags" (e.g. <para>) to identify document constituents. SDIF is particularly appropriate for systems that share information through marked-up text files, especially where human users can access the markup directly, e.g. publishing systems.

21.4.1 Document Content

There are a number of document content types, each specified by a particular ODA/ODIF series standard:

Character content	Character strings are represented by ISO 2022 and related character set standards. The character string may include text, graphic characters, control functions and space characters. The standard defines presentation attributes that may be embedded in the text, e.g. to specify certain text to be underlined.
Geometric graphics	Documents with images consisting of geometric information such as angles, aspect ratios and orientation, and elements such as lines, arcs, areas, etc, are represented using the Computer Graphics Metafile (GCM) binary encoding defined in ISO 8632.
Raster graphics	Pictorial images represented by an array of pixels use coding specified in CCITT Recommendations T.4 and T.6 (i.e. facsimile image encoding) or a bitmap encoding.

Other content architectures are possible and future extensions may include digital encoded sound information, spreadsheets, etc.

21.5 STANDARDS

Table 21.1 lists the ODA standards. T.411 to T.416 are the CCITT equivalents of the ISO 8613 standards. In addition to defining ODIF, ISO 8613 part 5 defines SDIF by reference to ISO 9069.

The CCITT T.500 series (T.501 to T.504 and T.521 to T.541) are document application profile standards. They specify a subset of the ODA features to support the interchange of different forms of documents.

21.5.1 Document Transfer

The T.400 and T.500 series of recommendations are related to the other document, messaging and OSI recommendations. The X.400 series for MHS, the X.500 Directory, Teletex and facsimile services are related to the total picture of document structure, message handling and document distribution in accordance with the OSI model. The CCITT also has a specific set of standards for Document Transfer and Manipulation (DTAM) T.431 to T.433.

ODA/ODIF is independent of the vehicle used to transfer documents. Documents can be constructed and encoded using the T.400 series recommendations and submitted to the MHS system as defined by X.400 series recommendations for forwarding to the recipients. X.400 MHS uses the underlying services of an OSI stack.

Alternatively, FTAM could be used as the transport mechanism, or documents could be transported by non-OSI protocols, or even physical transfer on magnetic media.

Table 21.1　　ODA/ODIF document standards

CCITT	ISO	TITLE
T.411	8613-1	Introduction and General Principles
T.412	8613-2	Document Structures
T.414	8613-4	Document Profile
T.415	8613-5	Open Document Interchange Format (ODIF)
T.416	8613-6	Character Content Architectures
T.417	8613-7	Raster Graphics Content Architecture
T.418	8613-8	Geometric Graphics Content Architecture

21.6 QUESTIONS

Question 21.1　　What is the purpose of ODA?

Question 21.2　　What are the predecessors of the ODA standard?

Question 21.3　　What are the three major aspects of an ODA document specification?

Question 21.4   What is the difference between a logical view and a layout view?

Question 21.5   What is the difference between a document in processable form and formatted form?

Question 21.6   How is the OSI object class mechanism applied to ODA?

Question 21.7   What is the syntax notation used to specify the components of an ODA document?

Question 21.8   What is the difference between ODIF and SGML?

Question 21.9   What is the relationship between ODA and X.400 MHS?

Question 21.10   What is the business benefit of ODA?

22 Document Transfer and Manipulation

22.1 OVERVIEW

This chapter provides a brief overview of Document Transfer and Manipulation (DTAM), and Document Filing and Retrieval (DFR). DTAM is the generic name for a group of standards for document handling services, i.e. for office automation. In fact Open Document Architecture and Interchange Format (ODA/ODIF, described in the previous Chapter) fall under the DTAM umbrella. Whereas ODA and ODIF provided the encoding and interchange standards for electronic documents, the other standards provide the necessary protocols for (remotely) accessing and manipulating documents through OSI services. DFR is a related area of standardization. The various standards (listed in Figure 22.1) allow:

- the transfer of complete documents between systems;

- the remote access to and modification of parts of documents (document manipulation); and,

- document filing and retrieval.

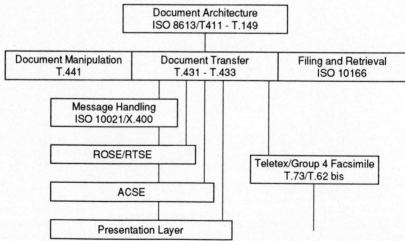

Figure 22.1   DTAM in the OSI environment – a comprehensive set of standards for office automation

In common with all OSI application services, DTAM uses the underlying services of other Application Service Elements (ASEs, e.g. X.400 Message Handling Services, Association Control Service Element, ACSE, etc) and the lower layer services. In other words, documents can be transferred using X.400 or via other DTAM defined protocols. The DTAM application entities are distributed between two OSI systems with a communicating protocol and an initiator/responder service user interface. A direct link from DTAM to the Teletex service is provided solely to allow interworking in transparent mode using T.73 (a restricted DTAM service). To complete the picture, the X.500 Directory should also be mentioned to illustrate the comprehensive support for office automation provided by the integrated use of OSI standards.

The operational functional units provided in DTAM are:

- Bulk Transfer functional unit, i.e. create, delete and modify for transferring documents.

- Manipulation functional unit.

22.2 DOCUMENT FILING AND RETRIEVAL

The DTAM services manipulate single documents. Document standards are also available for filing and retrieval of groups of documents. These standards are fairly new. The DFR abstract service is modeled as a service providing user client interfaces for the filing of documents on and the administration of a remote document store (the DFR server).

The main concepts of this standard provide organizational guidance (architecture) to the way in which documents are stored and retrieved. In addition to this, the standard defines the DFR object and document attributes (which are used to organize, manage and classify the documents) and the relationships that can exist between the storage objects.

DFR services   The services provide an electronic document storage system. In the following sections, the term *object* is used to refer generically to an DFR object which is either a document, reference, etc. The DFR services are defined as:

Create   Create an object in a DFR group. Other objects can be referenced to provide initial values for the new object/document.

Delete   Remove an object/document.

Copy   Copy an object from one group to another group.

Move   Move an object from one group to another group.

Read   Read some or all of the attributes and/or content of a object/document.

Modify	Modify some or all of the attributes and/or content of a object/document.
List	List returns the attributes for the members of a specified group or the elements as specified by a Search Result List. Only members are listed — not their descendants.
Search	Search for objects within a domain that satisfy a search criteria. A search domain is specified as one or more groups or search result lists. Thus recursive searching can be performed on such aspects as document languages, authors and dates.
Reserve	Reserve indicates the intention to modify an object/document and is used as an object interlock. Two levels are defined, exclusive write (others can read) or exclusive access.
Unreserve	Unreserve removes the object interlock.
Abandon	Abandon a previously requested DFR service.

Information model   The DFR server offers its users (via the DFR services above) operations on objects in the document store. The DFR object classes are Documents, Groups, References and Search Result Lists. These objects are arranged in a hierarchy as depicted in Figure 22.0.

- The Root Group object is the top of the hierarchy and is used as the anchor for all other objects.

- The Group object is used to contain a list of objects (as a group).

- The Reference object contains references to other objects (documents, groups) to avoid the replication of objects within the storage system; e.g. a document can belong to more than one group.

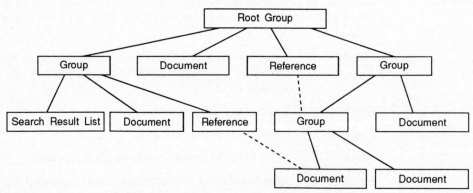

Figure 22.2   Document Filing and Retrieval information model

- The Search Result List object is used to hold the results of a search operation (as an object list). This can be read by the user or used as the "domain" on which to do additional searches.

- The Document object is the user document itself.

Object definition

The Object definition specified by DFR is as follows:

Attributes   A description of the object and references.

Content   The document itself.

Object attributes

Numerous Object attributes are used by DFR. For the sake of brevity they are simply listed as follows:

- Object Identifier (OID) for use by the DFR system.

- Object references for relationships with other objects or for groups or lists, etc.

- Document organizers, owners, authors, preparers, version(s) and title.

- Access control information and status.

- Creation, modification and purge date and time.

- Document languages, page quantity, profile and architecture.

The majority of the document related attributes (not the internal DFR reference attributes) are equivalent to the ODA standard.

Object content   The content of the object is one of the following:

Document content   A real document.

Root group   The top of the DFR object tree contains a list of objects.

Proper group   Contains a list of objects.

Internal reference   Object reference with no application entity reference, i.e. DFR owned.

External reference   Object reference with owning application entity reference.

Search result   List of objects, date/time, search criteria, etc.

As with all other OSI Application Layer standards, the DFR standard is quite comprehensive. DFR in its own right has a narrow application. However, DFR is coupled to the ODA standards and is now being considered as an adjunct to the X.400 Message Store (as a back end generic storage system). This will probably mean that DFR can be used as an archive for facsimile, voice mail and file data types as documents. Also note that any application that uses the DFR standard has also be aware of the document management requirements of storing documents within a storage system.

22.3 QUESTIONS

Question 22.1   What is the relationship between ODA and DTAM?

Question 22.2   What type of services does DTAM offer?

Question 22.3   What is the main purpose of DFR?

Question 22.4   How does DFR impact the DFR user with respect to the organization and management of documents?

Question 22.5   Is there any similarity between the DFR service elements and those provided by the X.500 Directories?

Question 22.6   What is the difference in user services offered by these two standards?

Question 22.7   What is a DFR Group?

Question 22.8   What is a search result list and how is it used?

Question 22.9   What is a DFR reference?

Question 22.10   What is the relationship between DFR, DTAM, ODA and X.400?

23 Electronic Data Interchange

23.1 ELECTRONIC TRADING

Electronic Data Interchange (EDI) has developed to improve the interchange of information between different companies and departments. Typically, the transactions within and between company groups are founded on paper documentation with manual processing resulting in transit (postal) delays, transcription errors, verification problems, and high paper and administration costs. EDI avoids these costly overheads through the use of data communications between interlinked computers. Figure 23.1 illustrates the trading environment that is the target of EDI applications (the diagram is not intended to exclude other applications of EDI). Electronic interchange of trading documents such as orders, invoices, delivery notes, etc, improves the accuracy, speed, reliability and security of intercompany transactions. The advantages of EDI are both qualitative and quantitative. Techniques such as just in time manufactur-

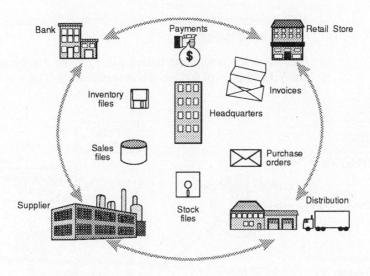

Figure 23.1   Example of the trading environment for EDI

ing and efficient stock control systems benefit from the use of EDI because of the speed and reduced manual overheads. Administrative organizations benefit from improved office efficiency, faster handling of financial transactions and improved service to clients. In summary, the benefits are the result of:

- Faster transmission of documents between trading partners.

- Elimination of the manual re-entry of data at the receiving organization, leading to reduced errors and cost savings.

- Rapid dispatch and processing of documents reducing lead times for final deliveries.

- Improved integration of corporate information systems.

- Standardization of documents facilitates international trade.

- Standardization increases competition between suppliers of information systems leading to lower prices and improved products.

Standards   Because EDI is a multi-party distributed application, it is a prime candidate for international standardization. The unfortunate aspect of EDI is that its inception was during the evolution of Open Systems Interconnection (OSI) and so a number of different national EDI standards emerged. The mid-1980's saw the advent of two major regional standards for EDI viz:

- X12, standardized by the American National Standards Institute (ANSI) in North America.

- Guidelines for Trade Data Interchange (TDI) in Europe developed under the auspices of the United Nations (also abbreviated as UNTDI).

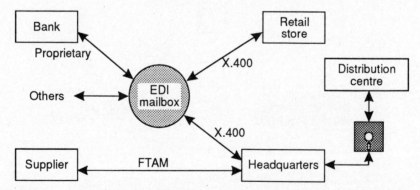

Figure 23.2   EDI transactions may take place over OSI communications, either directly between trading partners or via a third party mail box. Non-OSI exchanges are also common.

These different standards, however, have been harmonized through working groups and international committees. The international community
agreed to merge these two to become EDIFACT (Electronic Data Interchange For Administration, Commerce and Transport). It is published as
ISO 9735, (1988). Although EDIFACT is agreed as the long term common standard for EDI, it will be some time before established systems
change over from X12 or TDI.

Also, in its initial phase, EDI messages by necessity were communicated over proprietary protocols, so in a sense much of the early EDI use
was by bilateral arrangements and not open in the true sense of the word.
Now that generic messaging functions and infrastructures are available in
OSI standards and products, the availability and connectivity of an EDI
network is now potentially much higher. As shown in Figure 23.2, EDI
transactions are independent of the data communications service and they
may be transported over a mixture of OSI and non-OSI services.

This chapter gives a brief outline of the business aspects of EDI, the
EDI standards and the underlying OSI protocols being evolved specifically for EDI use. Because X.400 Message Handling Systems (MHS) is
seen as the prime OSI vehicle for EDI, it is assumed that the reader has
read Chapter 15 on MHS.

23.1.1 Business Interactions

Figure 23.3 demonstrates the use of EDI for a typical ordering process
between one company and another. The process is then followed through
to product delivery and final payment. The example highlights the quantity and timing of the interactions. In this simple process, ten actions have
to occur, each relying on internal processing and internal and external
communications. Also because of non-efficiency or various credit, payment and stock holding policies, the timing of any process could be

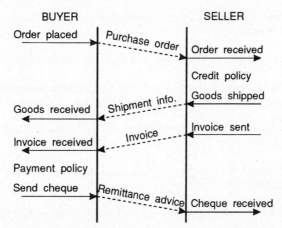

Figure 23.3   Typical sequence of actions and exchange of trading documents to
process an order

extended to the detriment of either party. Studies of the total costs of such processes have been quoted at $30 to $50 per order when performed manually. Once this set of interactions is committed to pure electronic mechanisms, the costs associated with this typical process drop to approximately 10% to 20% of the manual cost.

Evaluating EDI

Before entering into the use of EDI, a number of points should be reviewed. Also the scope of EDI standards and the impact on the user should be understood. EDI standards define the data formats (syntax) and the meaning (semantics) of what is transferred (interchanged) between trading partners. The user of EDI still needs to design the specific application process (or processes) for the business that handles these EDI transactions and controls the nature of the interchanges. Typically, this application may spawn other electronic data transfers within the organization to partition the process; e.g. an order is passed to accounts, warehousing and transport management concurrently. Verification by an external audit company is also often a requirement. This EDI application design area requires a sound and thorough business analysis, as it will define the operating procedures and policies between the business trading partners. Such analysis should consider the lifetimes of the business types, trading changes, takeovers, etc, to ensure the viability and maintenance levels required of the total EDI process. It may be more efficient in some cases to use manual trading methods in some areas, electronic trading by the exchange of media and direct electronic trading in others. To address and evaluate the benefits EDI in a basic way, Table 23.1 lists a number of

Table 23.1   Checklist for evaluating the benefits of EDI.

List partner company names, locations, service profile, and computer and communications equipment.
List your own equipment, applications and business needs.
List principal business interactions and document exchange requirements, and the monthly and annual volumes of trading documents.
Identify and prioritize the major trading partners with regard to volumes of business.
Identify stationery, postal, facsimile and telex costs, and associated processing costs, e.g. equipment, data entry, filing, space and disposal. Identify costs in re-tracking, verifying and correction.
Identify time and money costs incurred in trading, e.g. for late payments. Identify effects on stock holding and distribution functions.
Identify business effects (e.g. competitive advantage, supplier locking, customer relationships), and the effects on computer and communications hardware, software and operating costs.
Plan the implementation. Start with a pilot phase and implement more advanced applications later on.
Plan the neccessary organizational and supporting structure changes to cater for the new methods of operation.

issues and activities that can serve as a starting point for cost benefit analysis. This list is not considered exhaustive and is given for guidance only.

23.2 EDI STANDARDS

23.2.1 Terminology

The EDI standards define the structure, syntax and encoding for the interchange of trading documents. The standards mimic the familiar paper documents. The paper trading documents are used as a metaphor in the following paragraphs to explain the terminology used in the standards. EDI standards define the interchange formats and the protocol information at a number of levels as illustrated in Figure 23.4.

Connection At the highest level, documents are interchanged over a *connection* between two end systems. One or more interchanges may take place over the connection which is like the document delivery mailbag. (The communications protocols to establish and maintain the connection are not defined by the EDI standards.)

Transaction A *transaction* or *interchange* is a complete information package that is transferred between one EDI user and another. This is like an envelope containing a collection of trading documents to be exchanged between two business partners. Typical transaction types are: orders, manifests, invoices, customs forms, receipts, etc. A *functional group* is a set of messages of the same type, e.g. invoices.

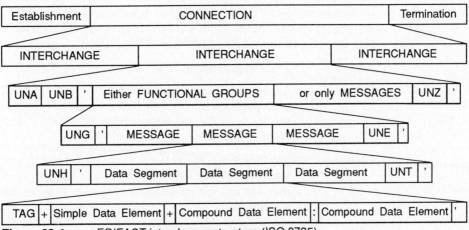

Figure 23.4   EDIFACT interchange structure (ISO 9735)

Message	One or more *messages* can exist within a transaction. A message corresponds to a single form or document, i.e. a separate purchase order or invoice.
Segment	Data *segments* correspond to the sections or lines on a form (which may consist of multiple items). Segments perform an organizational role in the definition of different transaction sets; i.e. a specific segment type can exist in many different types of transaction definition or can be repeated within a single transaction. For example, a list of product details can exist in an order or an invoice. Typical segment types are: identification, currency details, consignee information, product details, payment information and references.
Data elements	At the lowest level of information definition are the *data elements* (attributes). Examples of attributes are: reference number, name and address, account number, currency code, etc. Specific sets of attribute types form a message. The specific attribute type can also be used in one or many of the messages within a single transaction, e.g. a date and time reference.

EDIFACT terminology is used for the above definitions and other terms in this book. Unfortunately, the terms used in the three major EDI standards (ANSI X12, UNTDI, and EDIFACT) are similar but not identical! To highlight the sheer number of EDI definitions, the ANSI X12 standard has approximately 130 transaction types, 360 segment types and 800 data elements.

23.2.2 EDIFACT Syntax

EDIFACT (ISO 9735) provides a concrete syntax that allows trading partners to format and encode trading documents. The various levels of an interchange described above are separated by interchange headers and field separators, e.g. apostrophe ('), plus sign (+), colon (:), etc. ASCII (American Standard Code for Information Interchange) text characters are used for the headers, separators and the data elements. The purpose of each is briefly described below (see Figure 23.4 also):

TXT	Text character string.
UNA	The Service String Advice interchange is optional, but if used, it must precede all other interchanges. It is used to specify separator and other service characters if non-standard ones are applied during the session.
UNB	The Interchange header starts, identifies and specifies an interchange. This level contains sender and recipient, date and time of preparation, references, priority and identification.
UNE	Terminates a Functional Group.

UNG   The Functional Group header commences and identifies a functional group (a group of messages of the same type). This level is optional and if present contains functional group identification, application identification, date and time of preparation, reference number, controlling agency, message version and password.

UNH   The Message Header introduces a message. This level can exist one or more times within an Interchange and contains message reference number, message identifier, common access reference and status of the transfer.

UNS   Section Control is used to separate header, detail and summary sections of a message.

UNT   Terminates a message.

UNZ   Terminates an interchange.

A brief example of an EDIFACT Invoice message is shown in Figure 23.5. ISO 9735 does not specify the content of the EDIFACT message. This must be previously agreed by all trading partners. Other EDIFACT

SEGMENTS	DATA ELEMENTS
Message Header	UNH
Message Reference	Message type, version and agency
Beginning of Message	Document details and references
References	Reference and line number
Name and Address	Name and address, party name, street and number, country and postal code
Contact Segment	Contact name and number, communications channel identification
Financial Institution	Finacial institution identification, account name and number
Tax Related Information	Duty/tax/fee type, category, rate and amount
Currencies	Currency code, qualifier, rate of exchange, date
Payment Terms	Identification, basis, type, date, number of periods, penalties
Transport Details	Conveyance reference, mode, identification, carrier code, transit limits
Section Control	UNS – for invoiced items
Line Item	Item number, product identification, unit price
Allowances and Charges	Allowance or charge number, rates, special services
Tax Related Information	Duty/tax type code, tax amount, tax identification number
Section Control	UNS
Total Amounts	Monetary amount, discounts, tax and totals
Free text	As required
Message Trailer	UNT

Figure 23.5   An example of typical components of an EDIFACT invoice message

standards define the structure and content of various types of messages; e.g. Invoice message, Purchase Order message. There are now 30 documented message types with others under development. The Standards associated with EDIFACT are listed in Table 23.2.

23.2.3 EDI and X.400 MHS

ANSI X12, UNTDI and EDIFACT define the high level business protocol of EDI and as previously mentioned, this protocol can be carried over any agreed communications protocol (even Telex). With the development of X.400 MHS, EDI is seen as a typical messaging application that can be exchanged over the X.400 Message Transfer Service (MTS).

IPM

However, there are differences between the distribution characteristics and profiles of EDI messaging and interpersonal messaging (IPM). (As X.400 is defined in Chapter 15, only the major differences between IPM and EDI are explained below.) EDI is used for computer to computer communication as opposed to IPM which is oriented for human user communication. Within the MHS environment, the support of EDI is viable using the EDI message as a body part over the IPM protocol (i.e. P2). Thus today, some EDI users are operating their businesses with EDI over X.400 MHS, but the EDI message is essentially a distinct part of an IPM message. Also, the body type can be ANSI X12, UNTDI or EDIFACT, so message compatibility problems may occur between potential EDI partners. The use of X.400 MHS services is considered a reasonable solution in the interim.

PEDI

However, there are many features and characteristics of EDI interchange that are not readily supported by IPM and so an X.400 *PEDI* service and protocol has been developed. This service and protocol is defined in CCITT F.435 and X.435 respectively which were finalized in 1990.

Table 23.2   EDIFACT and associated standards

STANDARD	TITLE	DESCRIPTION
EDIFACT (ISO 9735)	EDIFACT Application Syntax	Character set, interchange structure, header encoding, etc
UNTED (ISO 7372)	United Nations Trade Data Elements Directory	Defines the attributes and definitions for data used in EDIFACT messages
EDSD	EDIFACT Data Segments Directory	Description of all data segments used in standard messages
EDMD	EDIFACT Data Message Directory	Description of all standard messages
PEDI (X.435)	Protocol for EDI Messaging	Definition of X.400 content type for EDI

EDI application program

PEDI only standardizes the communications aspect of an EDI system. The user's application program has to be developed to meet the business needs of the enterprise. Typically, this would be layered as follows:

- business application;

- EDI syntax; and,

- communication protocol processing.

Business

At the top level is the actual business application that schedules the information and resources within the organization. This area is not subject to standardization, but typically it will include: interchange sequencing, access to databases, other processes, printing and backup storage media, information distribution (to PCs, etc) and query tools. This level will also submit messages to the EDI protocol processing using an EDI abstract syntax.

EDI

The EDI processing layer is responsible for the encoding and decoding of the EDI messages (as per the ANSI X12, UNTDI or EDIFACT standards), providing EDI message acknowledgements and EDI message error responses (if appropriate). The EDI processing layer is also responsible for interfacing to the communications system (preferably via a standardized API).

Communications

The communications system consists of PEDI and the X.400 MTS. The X.400 PEDI layer (or IPM layer, if P2 is used) is the EDI User Agent (UA) and it maps the EDI messages onto the X.400 protocol. Where IPM is used, the EDI message is carried as a body part. Where PEDI is used, some of the EDI interchange protocol fields are mapped directly on to the PEDI header. Typically these would be the fields from the interchange header. The other fields in the PEDI header are of X.400 origin. At the lowest level is the X.400 Message Transfer Services that provide the message distribution services (i.e. the MTAs).

PEDI model

The model of PEDI messaging is similar to that of X.400 MHS in so far as there is an EDI UA, Message Transfer Agents (MTAs), Message Store (MS), etc. (The term EDIMG is used to refer to EDI messaging.) The main differences between EDI interchange and IPM are in the forwarding and notification areas. In EDI interchanges, a message may be sent to one party, who modifies it and forwards it on to another party. A typical example is a payment advice (cheque) sent by the purchaser to the seller and then forwarded with additional information to the bank for clearance.

Notifications

The sender of the message may require notification that the seller has forwarded it and may also require that the bank informs the sender of its acceptance. These business related concepts are provided for within the PEDI protocol and are used by setting the notification control fields in the message. In the scenario above, the buyer requires a forwarding notification from the seller and a responsibility (accepted) notification from the bank. As notifications arrive at the buyer's office, he is made aware of the position of the transaction. The PEDI protocol permits the nature of notifications and expected responsibilities of each of the recipients to be defined. The protocol also permits the specification of an independent notification receiver (e.g. an Audit department) if required. Beyond this, the PEDI protocol essentially provides the normal features of IPM plus the encoding for the EDI protocol itself.

An overview of the PEDI message Heading and Body is described in Figure 23.6. Many of the fields are optional. It can be seen from the figure that PEDI is a mixture of the EDIFACT (or other similar protocols) and X.400. The heading supports the UNA and UNB fields and the body carries the UNG and UNH, etc, fields.

23.2.4 Other Related Standards

The work on EDI and PEDI and its introduction into the X.400 MHS environment has placed dependencies on other standards. In the main; these are X.413 (the Message Store, MS) and the X.500 Directory.

Message store The user of the MS can List and Fetch messages based on message attribute types. Any new message attributes, such as those introduced by PEDI, must be added to the MS to provide the desired services. Therefore the PEDI standard provides a list of EDI message attributes that should be recognized by the MS if EDI messages are to be fully processed. The majority of these attributes have been identified in the section above on PEDI.

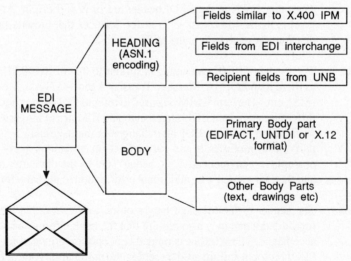

Figure 23.6　The PEDI message Heading and Body

Directory   EDI object classes and attributes have to be defined within the Directory so that it can support   verification and Directory operations on such objects and attributes. Working papers on the issue have identified EDI object classes such as: EDI User and EDI UA. They have also identified EDI attributes such as EDI capabilities and EDI processable documents. The inclusion of these items into the Directory is a matter of agreement, registration and some form of implementation mechanism (e.g. by configuration). The EDI group also require the use of a new name form of EDI User to be introduced. Again the issue is one of agreement, registration of the EDI name form and getting the Directory to support such forms.

23.3 QUESTIONS

Question 23.1   What are the three major EDI format standards and which one is now emerging as the universal EDI standard?

Question 23.2   What are the five levels of information used to form an EDI exchange?

Question 23.3   What are the component parts of the EDIFACT message syntax?

Question 23.4   How is EDI supported by X.400 MHS and what are the differences between the alternatives?

Question 23.5   How does one identify whether EDI is valuable to your company?

Question 23.6   How does EDI affect your application design?

Question 23.7   How does EDI affect your trading partners and your operations?

Part 6 – OSI Distributed Systems

24 OSI Systems Integration

24.1 APPLICATION INTEGRATION

For the description of Application Layer standards in the previous chapters, the focus was on the capabilities and behaviour of each individual standard. In reality, the standards don't exist for their own sake — they are there to serve business needs. Furthermore, an enterprise will use multiple standards in an integrated fashion to meet corporate goals.

Using the standards to merely replace existing proprietary systems does not achieve their full potential — the challenge for the future is to adjust the applications and indeed the enterprise itself to synthesize new distributed systems that are enabled by the standards. The purpose of this chapter is to propose changes in attitude necessary to maximize the benefits of the combined use of the standards.

Don't reinvent the wheel

Application design and maintenance in the large corporate organizations is an on-going investment in the business. In fact some companies have built their core business around a computer application, e.g. banking, software product suppliers. The time and resources taken to generate such applications in traditional systems have always been seen as a normal aspect of the business. As development costs escalate and technology and business change marches on, constant reviews are required to maintain and enhance the developed applications. Applications development and maintenance accounts for millions of dollars. The major design criteria for such applications has generally been to accommodate the architecture of the incumbent mainframe supplier. Thus most of the current applications are strongly tied to a proprietary system and are not readily transferred to new technology (a locked-in, ageing asset). This position indicates skill profile and supplier lock-in, which is undesirable and increasingly expensive.

Assuming that hardware and software products based on OSI standards and other open systems platforms become the mainstream in the information technology marketplace, then the focus of software developers will move away from proprietary to "portable" software. There are now available comprehensive standards covering many aspects of information technology (not just communications as is covered in this book). The use of these standards instead of proprietary systems gives a tool box approach to application development, allowing the developer to focus on the customized parts of the application. The broad range of standards is not well recognized by applications developers in commerce and industry because they are so used to being tied to proprietary solutions — they have become reliant on a vendor. Continuing to ignore the wealth of the standards will cost a considerable amount in re-inventing the wheel and future redevelopment.

24.1.1 Application Program Interface

To facilitate software portability, application developers require common interfaces to OSI products supplied by vendors on their various hardware and software platforms. However, the CCITT (International Telegraph and Telephone Consultative Committee) and ISO (International Organization for Standardization) expressly avoided the definition of such interfaces. The standards specify the semantics and abstract syntax for the OSI application services but not the concrete interface syntax. The standards committees are focussed on the essential aspects for interoperability. To fill in this gap, a number of industry initiatives have reached agreement on more precise syntactic specifications and associated C programming language bindings for Application Program Interfaces (APIs) for a number of key OSI products.

API   APIs provide an application developer with a set of OSI services via program function interfaces — similar to that of standard functions provided in common programming languages. The objective is to give the developer access to a uniform set of OSI services so that the development work is directed at the application itself, and the developer is relieved from the work to design, write and test the underlying protocol stack and application services. APIs are developed in alignment with the specific OSI standards, e.g. X.400 Message Handling Systems (MHS) and the X.500 Directory.

For example, a developer writing an Electronic Data Interchange (EDI) application would incorporate an interface to the X.400 API. To realize the product, the developer would purchase the X.400 messaging components and the API libraries from a software supplier. The API interface supports the sending and receiving of messages to the X.400 service on defined interfaces. The application programmer relies on the X.400 package to perform all of the protocol and functional processing of X.400 in conformance with the standards. The developer would then design and write the EDI application only and link in the API libraries.

API association   For the X.400 standard, an API association has been formed to develop common agreements on interface specifications. The association members also participate in the formulation of the respective CCITT and ISO standards. The Manufacturing Automation Protocol and Technical Office Protocol (MAP/TOP) Foundation and the X/Open group of companies also specify APIs. API specifications are not standards in their own right as they are "implementation rules" providing a specific set of functions that use a particular set of data structures and data types. Thus the groups that formulate and maintain the API specifications are industry based product suppliers who wish to provide tools for this style of development or have portable applications based on these API specifications. API specifications (and products) are already available for a number of the more mature OSI application standards.

API products   The API products are described by their information characteristics and functional interfaces. Object oriented programming principles are used for the definition of the APIs. The API products use this object principle to model message and items exchanged over the interface. In the X.400 API product, for example, objects are the major components in an X.400 message or the message itself, e.g. O/R descriptors, a message, message content, a probe, etc. Although they are yet to be realized widely in products, API specifications are available for the following:

X.400   APIs are defined to support access to an Interpersonal Message (IPM) User Agent (UA) for the exchange of electronic memos and to the underlying transfer service of the Message Transfer Agents (MTAs).

X.500   The X/Open Directory Services API offers services consistent with (but not limited to) the X.500/ISO 9594 standards. It is designed for operational interactions with a Directory rather than management or administration of the Directory database.

Object Management   The Object Management API defines a general purpose interface for the creation, examination and modification of specific information objects. These objects are derived from the ASN.1 definitions of their respective standard (e.g. some X.400 objects are identified above.) Accompanying these defined objects are their attributes which are also derived from their ASN.1 (Abstract Syntax Notation One) definition counterpart. In order to use an underlying OSI service (e.g. X.400), the programmer uses the Object Management API to: create an object; add to it the attributes required; and then send the object to the X.400 API for transfer to the MHS. In essence, the APIs (the Object Management and the X.400 and X.500 APIs together) provide the programmer with a consistent set of interfaces and data structures for those standards and also shield the programmer from the complexities of ASN.1 used within the standard. Therefore, an API product is really just a programming language dependent definition of the standard.

FTAM UI & **MMS-I**	The MAP/TOP user groups specify these APIs for file transfer and factory floor integration.
Transport	The X/TI API is defined by X/Open for access to the OSI Transport Layer. (It also supports the Transmission Control Protocol/Internet Protocol, TCP/IP.)

24.2 BEYOND ELECTRONIC MAIL

In its initial realization as products and as a public service, X.400 MHS has necessarily been confined to interpersonal mail. While important, this is almost trivial compared to its future potential. Chapter 15 described the general purpose message transfer service as a vehicle for the transport of a variety of different types of information. Although it is some years away yet, a fully fledged implementation of the 1988 version of X.400 with security, message store and integrated with other OSI applications provides a comprehensive global information delivery service far beyond the scope and capabilities of any current system. When combined with the Directory and document handling standards, X.400 allows the integration of many functions that are performed by a variety of present day systems, many of which are still manual operations:

- X.400 IPM is the natural replacement for office memos, but MHS can also potentially be used to transfer facsimile messages, files, voice mail to replace answering machines, etc.

- EDI via PEDI (Chapter 23) for the exchange of trading documents between companies to replace paper orders, invoices, etc.

- Office correspondence can be exchanged electronically via X.400 as formatted, multimedia documents using Open Document Architecture (Chapter 21), and held on computer filing systems using Document Filing and Retrieval (Chapter 22).

- X.400 will also play a role in the emerging area of group communications.

- In the long term, X.400 will be closely integrated with X.500 for Directory services (Chapter 16). The Directory will substitute for the paper corporate telephone directories and eventually become a global Directory service.

- The Directory will underpin many other distributed systems to locate communications partners and for security services.

- To efficiently control and monitor all of the above, the OSI System Management standards (X.700 Chapter 19) will need to be integrated with the other components mentioned.

Although the implementation of the level of integration described above is somewhat in the future, it highlights the expanding potential of X.400 based multi-vendor information exchange. X.400 MHS is destined to become an essential adjunct to the personal and corporate communications infrastructure for all organizations.

24.3 GLOBAL INTERCONNECTION

An examination of an organization's major information flows (paper correspondence, telephone, facsimile, etc.) reveals a mixture of internal (within the organization) and external communications. We take for granted the ability to dial a number for virtually instant voice or image communication. Corporate telephone systems are designed to be outward looking to provide global interconnection. In stark contrast, existing corporate data networks are typically inward looking and almost isolated from external communications.

Improved external communications for multi-vendor distributed applications will stimulate a change in the design of private data networks. One of the objectives of an open network is for it to be able to interwork across a chain of international and national interlinked networks and subnetworks. The network will need to support multiple connections to other networks, both public and other private networks. This is required so that customers and other agreed entities can co-operate in a common business enterprise. Some points on this interconnection issue are raised in the following paragraphs.

Technology The availability and affordability of transmission capacity will continue to improve for some time. Future network technologies will integrate video, data and voice services and use internationally defined standards to provide these services to the market place. Because these standards universally follow the OSI model, there is potential for integration between the voice services and information systems.

Seamless connectivity As is done with the telephone network, design data networks to facilitate connectivity to all other systems that agree to communicate. Corporate networks should conform to the standards in order to achieve uniform international, domestic and internal interconnection without recourse to the expense and complexity of using specialized gateway devices. Gateways are high cost, short life network components and generally, with OSI standards, there is little or no reason to have them.

Security Although the goals of providing open systems and keeping them secure against unauthorized access may seem inconsistent, the problems of providing security in an OSI environment are no different from the security concerns in any proprietary system. Much of the protection must be embedded in the application and operating system and OSI does little to change this. Security is a large subject in its own right and it is outside the scope of this book. However, security is an important topic of the OSI committees and a brief description of their work is given in the following paragraphs.

Many OSI Application Layer standards have security features built into them, and, while this covers essential needs, it is far from comprehensive. The ISO committees are working to improve security, and the primary documents are:

X.800/   Basic Reference Model - Part 2, Security Architecture.
ISO 7498-2

ISO 10181-1 Security Framework for Open Systems - Part 1, Overview.

ISO 10181-2 Security Framework for Open Systems - Part 2, Authentication Framework.

X.509/   The Directory, Part 8, Authentication Framework.
ISO 9594 - 8

In addition to the above, other working drafts have recently been produced to refine the security framework. These are:

- Integrity Framework

- Confidentiality Framework

- Non-Repudiation Framework.

In general, secure communications are achieved by the generation, exchange and processing of security information using cryptographic techniques. The OSI standards do not, however, specify the use of a particular cryptographic or other security algorithm. In practice, security conscious applications will use a number of different algorithms. It should also be noted that ISO in fact does not standardize cryptographic algorithms. Security functions defined in the model fall into two categories:

- generalized functions that provide security for all distributed applications; and,

- functions to protect specific security applications (e.g. key management) as a part of the overall system's security infrastructure.

As the upper layers security model progresses, more advanced security functions can be incorporated in the Application Layer standards and eventually in OSI products.

Who and where

The first action when designing a distributed system is to determine its naming and addressing scheme. The subject of naming and addressing in OSI has been described where it arose in previous chapters. Despite the dispersed treatment of the subject, it is crucial for organizations to conform to the OSI standards in this area if they wish to participate in open communications. The key issues and references to their detailed explanation are covered in the following paragraphs.

A Service Access Point (SAP) address was defined in Section 2.3 (page 35), as the key way to locate distributed applications and communications resources in OSI. In particular, unambiguous numeric NSAP addresses are allocated globally to identify each computer participating in OSI communications. The NSAP numbering plan and its relation to the addresses used in real subnetworks was described in Section 4.4, page 62 and Section 8.4.1, page 144. In the long term, all OSI end systems, routers and private packet switching networks will need to perform routing on the NSAP address and map it on to real subnetwork addresses.

Names

In the upper layers, many objects are referred to by a name:

* Application entity title, Section 14.1.1, page 247 and Section 14.2.3, page 252.

* X.400 O/R Address, Section 15.4.2, page 277.

* Directory names, Section 16.2.2, page 290.

* Object identifiers, Table 1, page 228.

Mapping from name to address to provide communications between systems is performed in the Application Layer which may use local translation tables or access an X.500 Directory database (Chapter 16). This OSI naming and address structure must be used by OSI systems to **identify** each other.

Naming and addressing permeates all OSI standards and in fact dictates the system architecture. OSI addressing can only be approximated by proprietary system architectures. Naming authorities have been established to ensure unambiguous names are allocated to all objects in OSI. Each organization or company that wishes to participate in OSI communications will need to establish its own naming and addressing committees to get its own naming scheme in order, and will need to manage and control the implementation of directory and routing functions in its network. As with all naming and addressing schemes, any network that does not accommodate such internationally defined schemes is isolated. This situation would be comparable to not being known by the postman in a postal service or a having totally private telephone number. It is hardly a position to be in when doing business. In OSI terms, a network that uses these schemes will be a subnetwork of the global communications network.

OSI conformance

Global, multi-vendor networking requires care and effort on the part of the vendors and users alike for assured compatibility. This is the subject of the next two chapters.

25 Functional Standards and GOSIP

25.1 FROM STANDARD TO PRODUCT

The ultimate goal of Open Systems Interconnection (OSI) is to allow the exchange of information, trade documents and business transactions with an indefinite number of partners in multi-vendor networks. The global interoperability of distributed applications demands unprecedented uniformity and compatibility of products from competing vendors. To achieve this, the vendors need the following things:

- Motivation to develop conformant products. In other words, purchasers.

- Unambiguous specifications of the products to be supplied. In other words, purchasers have a responsibility to correctly express their requirements for OSI conformance.

- A way of testing and certifying products.

The standards for OSI are a very comprehensive set of protocol definitions covering almost all conceivable application and networking environments. They are intended as generic specifications and they allow considerable latitude in terms of options and parameter ranges to allow flexibility for implementors.

However, the base OSI standards are not precise enough to guarantee compatible implementations of OSI. For instance, if there is no technical reason to define the length of a particular parameter, the standard will leave it undefined. However, for practical reasons, implementors must put constraints on the range of parameter lengths and values, and select options from the standards appropriate to their application and network requirements. If implementors took arbitrary choices, there would be little chance that similar choices would be made by all, and so a low probability that different systems would interwork.

Profile   So a further step of functional standardization is necessary to achieve compatibility. The role of functional standardization is illustrated in Figure 25.1. A functional standard, also called a *profile*, is an agreement between implementors, or a specification by purchasers, of the details chosen for compatibility of different products.

419

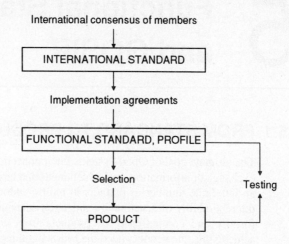

Figure 25.1   The role of functional standardization and conformance testing in OSI product implementation

Testing   Conformance testing, then, is a way of measuring the degree of conformance of a product to a specific profile. Indeed, it is not possible to test for conformance to the base standard because that is too open ended. The subject of conformance testing is covered in more detail in Chapter 26.

In effect, a profile is a selection of subsets of the OSI standards chosen on the basis of network and application needs and taking product availability into account. A profile can be described as a narrow stack selection from the base OSI standards, corresponding to a fourth level of specification detail as illustrated by the shaded areas in Figure 25.2. A profile defines a consistent combination of the subsets, functional units, options, parameter value ranges and lengths for a collection of standards to be used for a particular service.

Objectives   The objectives of functional standardization are to:

- Accelerate the availability of products by forming agreement in the information technology community about needed functionality and the priorities for the implementation of OSI products.

- Provide a focus for developers because the full set of OSI standards has a very broad scope. Starting with a limited number of key profiles narrows the size of the software development task and the number of products to a practical and manageable project.

- Aid implementors by removing indefinite choices.

- Ensure interworking by providing greater compatibility between different systems.

- Aid testing by ensuring that only the functionality in the profile is tested and un-implemented options are ignored by the tester.

The profiles do not alter the base OSI standards. The international standards remain as the definitive statement of the constitution of OSI — only changing gradually to incorporate additional services. Implementation of products conforming to the standards, however, will begin with small subsets as reflected in initial profiles and work towards more comprehensive implementations as the market demands.

Profiles reflect product availability and facilitate purchasing by providing a uniform specification for use by different departments and organizations in separate procurement activities. For assured compatibility of OSI products, users should explicitly state the profiles and standards required in their procurement specifications and these should be aligned with internationally recognized profiles.

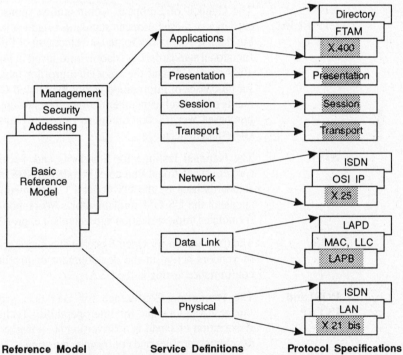

Reference Model   Service Definitions   Protocol Specifications

Figure 25.2   A profile defines subsets of the OSI standards (shaded areas in the diagram) to meet particular application and network requirements.

25.2 PROFILES

A number of regional and industry initiatives have created their own functional standards giving rise to the acronyms listed below:

MAP/TOP   The Manufacturing Automation Protocol (MAP) was instigated by General Motors for factory floor integration of process controllers using MMS (Manufacturing Message Specification) and FTAM (File Transfer, Access and Management) over Token Passing bus LANs. The Technical Office Protocol was instigated by Boeing using FTAM and X.400 MHS (Message Handling Systems) for the exchange of engineering design information over LANs. The MAP/TOP functional specifications are now developed and maintained by the World Federation of MAP/TOP Users groups.

SPAG

The Standards Promotion and Application Group is a European grouping of vendors that developed a "Guide to the Use of OSI Standards" and is active in the formulation of profiles and conformance testing.

CEN/ CENELEC/ CEPT

The Council of European Communities sponsors the activities of these European standards organizations that build on SPAG's work for the development of European functional standards. Legislation introduced in February 1988 made OSI and the associated profiles mandatory for purchases of information technology by all Governments of the twelve member nations. The law applies to purchases over 100,000 European Currency Units by all Government agencies.

NIST

The National Institute for Standards and Technology (previously National Bureau of Standards, NBS) sets the standards used by the US Federal Government. NIST sponsors the US OSI Implementor's Workshop which formulates implementation agreements, i.e. profiles.

COS

The Corporation for Open Systems is a major grouping of vendors active in the development of profiles and conformance testing in the USA.

POSI and INTAP

The Promoting Conference for OSI is a group of Japanese vendors, and the Interoperability Technology Association of Japan is a Government sponsored body developing profiles and conformance testing.

GOSIP

Government OSI Profiles have been developed by a number of countries. The UK Government GOSIP is mandatory by dint of the European legislation. The US GOSIP became mandatory in August 1990. Other Governments have followed suit, with a European Procurement Handbook for Open Systems (EPHOS) being developed under the auspices of the European Community, Canadian OSI Application Criteria (COSAC), Swedish Government OSI Profile (SOSIP), the Australian and New Zealand GOSIPs (derived from the UK document) and GOSIP-K in Korea to mention a few.

ISP

To prevent divergences between these organizations, three regional Workshops (covering Europe, North America and Asia/Oceania) have been established for joint development of the profiles. The Workshops operate under the umbrella of the **Feeders Forum** which co-ordinates the projects to avoid unnecessary regional differences between European, North American and Asian OSI products. The ISO (International Organization for Standardization) and IEC (International Electrotechnical Commission) have formed a special group under Joint Technical Committee 1 (JTC1) to accept proposed draft profiles from the Feeders Forum (and others) for ballot to process them as *International Standardized Profiles (ISP)*. The first ISPs became available in 1991. Most initial products from vendors were designed to comply with one or more of the Government profiles or profiles from the above-mentioned groups. These are expected to be replaced with the ISPs as they progressively become available.

The Governments now committed to GOSIP implementation have a combined annual information technology budget in the order of US$20 billion. The spending power of the large and influential Government market has now set the future direction for networking. For maximum benefit, the private sector should develop purchasing policies in line with these international trends. For this reason, the UK and US GOSIP profiles are summarized in the following sections. The Australian GOSIP is also mentioned for parochial reasons.

25.2.1 United Kingdom GOSIP

The various GOSIPs go beyond the specification of profiles. GOSIP is like a template developed by Government for purchases of OSI products to ensure at least a minimum level of compatibility is achieved between various departments. The UK GOSIP splits the OSI stack at the transport service boundary and defines a number of subprofiles in the following categories:

- T-subprofiles specify consistent subsets of the lower four layers (Transport, Network, Data Link, Physical) for LANs (Local Area Networks) and WANs (Wide Area Networks).

- A-subprofiles specify the subsets of Application Layer standards and the corresponding requirements for the Session and Presentation layers.

- F-subprofiles extend the specification outside the basic communications protocols into the area of data interchange, i.e. ODA (Open Document Architecture) and EDI (Electronic Document Interchange).

- C-subprofiles deal with regional character sets to correspond to the various languages that have to be supported.

Version 3.1 (1990) of the UK GOSIP is depicted in Figure 25.3. (GOSIP is updated regularly, so the details may have changed since publication.) Salient points are summarized below:

- X.25 connection oriented is the strategic mode for both LANs and wide area networking — connectionless is permitted when both end systems are on same LAN.

- FTAM support covers the basic transfer class (unstructured and sequential text files) and optionally management and access service class (sequential files).

- Support of MHS 1984 version is mandatory and the 1988 version is a provisional specification.

- A simple forms mode terminal profile is defined for enquiry response applications using OSI Virtual Terminal (VT).

- A provisional specification is given for the X.500 Directory.

- ODA is specified for exchange of formatted documents according to the Government Document Application Profile (GDAP).

- EDIFACT is specified for EDI.

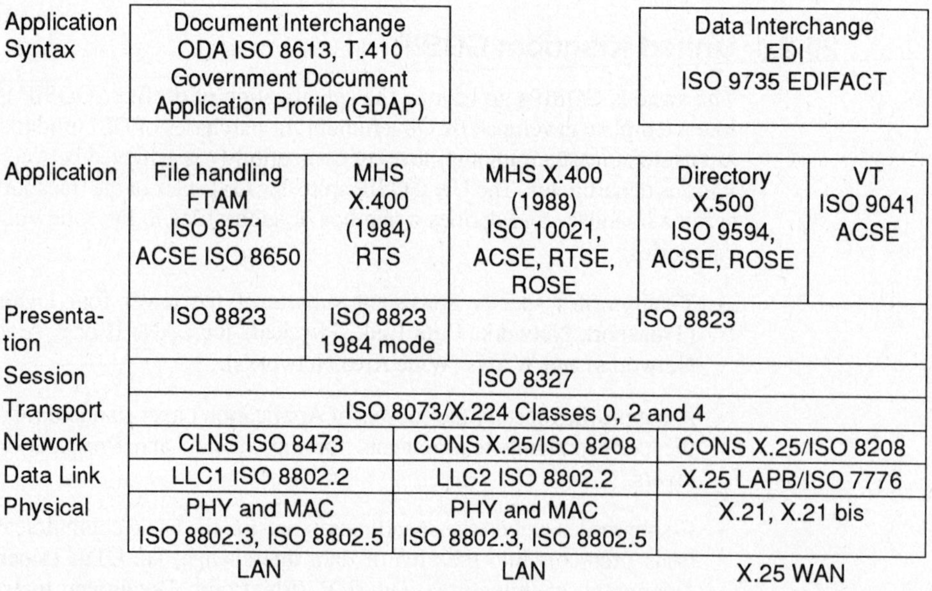

Application Syntax	Document Interchange ODA ISO 8613, T.410 Government Document Application Profile (GDAP)			Data Interchange EDI ISO 9735 EDIFACT	
Application	File handling FTAM ISO 8571 ACSE ISO 8650	MHS X.400 (1984) RTS	MHS X.400 (1988) ISO 10021, ACSE, RTSE, ROSE	Directory X.500 ISO 9594, ACSE, ROSE	VT ISO 9041 ACSE
Presenta-tion	ISO 8823	ISO 8823 1984 mode	ISO 8823		
Session	ISO 8327				
Transport	ISO 8073/X.224 Classes 0, 2 and 4				
Network	CLNS ISO 8473		CONS X.25/ISO 8208	CONS X.25/ISO 8208	
Data Link	LLC1 ISO 8802.2		LLC2 ISO 8802.2	X.25 LAPB/ISO 7776	
Physical	PHY and MAC ISO 8802.3, ISO 8802.5		PHY and MAC ISO 8802.3, ISO 8802.5	X.21, X.21 bis	
	LAN		LAN	X.25 WAN	

Figure 25.3   The United Kingdom GOSIP uses connection oriented networking.

25.2.2 Australian GOSIP

The Australian GOSIP, which became mandatory in August 1991, is based on the UK GOSIP version 3.1 with amendments to the T-sub-profiles. It is shown in Figure 25.4 and the key changes from the UK are:

- The connection oriented LAN profile has been removed.

- Connectionless networking is used for LANs and for interworking between concatenated networks, i.e. LAN to WAN interworking.

- Connection oriented or connectionless mode may be used for wide area networking.

- The Australian GOSIP application profiles are the same as the UK GOSIP except that VT has been moved to the supplement.

Application Syntax	Document Interchange ODA ISO 8613, T.410 Government Document Application Profile (GDAP)			Data Interchange EDI ISO 9735 EDIFACT	
Application	File handling FTAM ISO 8571 ACSE ISO 8650	MHS X.400 (1984) RTS	MHS X.400 (1988) ISO 10021, ACSE, RTSE, ROSE	Directory X.500 ISO 9594, ACSE, ROSE	VT ISO 9041 ACSE
Presenta-tion	ISO 8823	ISO 8823 1984 mode	ISO 8823		
Session	ISO 8327				
Transport	ISO 8073/X.224 Classes 0, 2 and 4				
Network	CLNS ISO 8473	CLNS ISO 8473	CLNS ISO 8473 over X.25	CONS X.25 ISO 8208	
Data Link	LLC1 ISO 8802.2	LAPB/ISO 7776	X.25 LAPB ISO 7776	X.25 LAPB ISO 7776	
Physical	PHY and MAC ISO 8802.3, ISO 8802.5	X.21, X.21 bis	X.21, X.21 bis	X.21, X.21 bis	
	LAN	Point to point WAN	X.25 WAN	X.25 WAN	

Figure 25.4 The Australian GOSIP is based on the UK GOSIP with the addition of connectionless wide area network profiles from the US GOSIP.

25.2.3 US GOSIP

Version 1 of the US GOSIP is depicted in Figure 25.5. It is based on the NIST OSI implementation agreements. Salient points are:

- All systems must implement connectionless networking, i.e. ISO 8473 and Transport class 4.

- Additionally, systems on X.25 networks may implement connection oriented.

- The X.400 and FTAM application profiles are similar to the UK GOSIP.

A draft of the next version has been distributed for comment. (The new version will probably be in place by the time this book is published.) Proposed additions to the US GOSIP include:

- VT for simple terminal and forms mode terminal applications.

- ODA for the exchange of formatted documents.

- ISDN, Integrated Services Digital Networks.

Application	File handling FTAM ISO 8571 ACSE ISO 8650		MHS X.400 (1984) RTS
Presenta- tion	ISO 8823		ISO 8823 1984 mode
Session	ISO 8327		
Transport	ISO 8073/X.224 class 4		ISO 8073/X.224 class 0
Network	CLNS ISO 8473	CLNS ISO 8473 over X.25	CONS X.25/ISO 8208
Data Link	LLC1 ISO 8802.2	X.25 LAPB/ISO 7776	X.25 LAPB/ISO 7776
Physical	PHY and MAC ISO 8802.3, 4, & 5	X.21, X.21 bis	X.21, X.21 bis
	LAN	X.25 WAN	X.25 WAN

Figure 25.5   The US GOSIP uses connectionless networking.

25.2.4 Taxonomy of Profiles

The ISP procedure provides a way in which harmonized profiles can be developed. In fact, it is intended that, in the future, the GOSIP documents will not contain their own profile definitions but will reference the ISPs when suitable ones are available. Because ISPs are being produced for the majority of the OSI standards, some form of common and agreed ISP document organization and numbering (identification) system is required.

This organizational aspect is defined in two ISO Technical Reports, namely:

TR 10000-1   Framework and taxonomy of international standardized profiles (Part 1 Framework).

TR 10000-2   Framework and taxonomy of international standardized profiles (Part 2 Taxonomy of Profiles).

TR 10000-1 groups the profiles into categories and allocates prefix letters for groups of ISPs:

F   Interchange format and representation profiles, e.g. ODA.

A   Application profiles using connection mode transport service (T profiles).

B   Application profiles using connectionless mode transport service (U profiles).

T   Connection mode transport service.

U   Connectionless mode transport service.

R   Relay functions between T profiles or between U profiles.

TR 10000-2 identifies the specific OSI standards (e.g. Network, FTAM, X.400 MHS, etc) to which ISP apply. It then subsets these standards (by topic or function) and provides a numbering scheme e.g. FTAM is divided into two main groups called File Transfer Service and File Access Service. These two main groups are further subdivided (refined) with each part given a next level number, i.e. 1, 11, 12, 13, etc.

Table 25.1 (page 428) provides a list of ISPs. Over time this list will be expanded, therefore the list should be seen as indicative of the ISPs available at the time of writing and the way in which the taxonomy documents are used to allocate ISP numbers.

Table 25.1   List of International Standardised Profiles

STANDARD	ITEM	PROFILE ID
Directory	Directory Access Protocol	ADI1
FTAM	Positional File Transfer	AFT12
FTAM	Positional File Access	AFT22
FTAM	File Management	AFT3
FTAM	Filestore Management	AFT4
MHS	Common Transfer Facilities MTA to MTA (P1)	AMH11
MHS	Common Transfer Facilities UA to MS (P7)	AMH12
OSI Management	Taxonomy of CMIP profiles	AOM1
Management	Basic CMIP for managing and managed systems	AOM11
Management	Full CMIP for managing and managed systems	AOM12
Management	Taxonomy of system management function profiles	AOM2
Virtual Terminal	Basic class, A-Mode, Telnet	AVT12
Virtual Terminal	Basic class, S-Mode, Forms	AVT22
ODA	Simple Document structure (character content)	FOD11
ODA	Enhanced Document structure (character & graphics)	FOD26
ODA	Extended Document structure (character & graphics)	FOD36
TP	Transaction Processing	ATP
RDA	Remote Database Access	ARD
LAN	Token Bus: CLNS	TA52
LAN	Token Ring: CLNS	TA53
LAN	FDDI part, SMT/MAC/PHY	TA54
LAN	FDDI part, SMT/MAC/PHY	RA or RD 54
WAN	ISDN: CLNS	TA 1x or 4x
WAN	ISDN: CS services	TC or TD1 and 41 or 42
WAN	ISDN: PS services	TC or TD and 431,2,3
WAN	PSDN: access	TC or TD and 1131 or 1231
Relay	Mac Layer Relay CSMA/CD to CSMA/CD	RD51.51
Relay	Mac Layer Relay CSMA/CD to Token Ring	RD 51.53
Relay	Mac Layer Relay Token Ring to Token Ring	RD53.53

26 Conformance Testing

26.1 AN INTRODUCTION TO TESTING

Independent conformance testing was not so important in the past, because computer communications were concerned mainly with the local problem of interfacing between two pieces of equipment, usually from the same supplier. In multi-vendor networks, however, internationally recognized conformance testing facilities are essential to provide a common reference for product developers and to give confidence that different products will interwork.

There are a number of ways in which variations in the implementation of a standard can lead to incompatibilities between different products:

- The standards describe the required behavior of each protocol layer, but not how to achieve such behavior. Implementors must devise their own ways to realize the standard on various systems.

- In some areas, the standards may be unclear, ambiguous or ill-defined because the standards are written in natural language (i.e. English) or because it may not have been possible to achieve consensus on more precise wording. This can lead to different interpretations or misinterpretation by implementors.

- The standards allow many options and subsets.

- Errors may be introduced during the development process.

Users cannot take for granted vendor's claims that products conform to the standards. Testing is necessary to give confidence that vendor's products correctly implement the standard and associated profile.

However, conformance and compatibility are not conferred to a product by one test. As with any large software system, it is impossible for any test to guarantee conformance to the standard or the absence of errors. There may be an infinite number of pathways through the protocol software of any one product. It is only possible to test a representative portion of them. Testing reveals the presence of errors, it cannot prove the absence of errors. Instead, testing should be seen as a vital part of the quality assurance process for the entire product development life cycle. Quality is achieved by the progressive refinement of OSI products by correcting the errors revealed by testing.

429

The vendors realize that they cannot achieve the goals of OSI by working alone. If two products from different vendors claiming conformance to the standards failed to interwork for whatever reason, then the reputation of both vendors would be tarnished, regardless of which one is at fault. To reduce the possibility of incompatibility, the standards committees have developed standards for testing and the vendors have co-operatively developed test equipment and they participate in joint testing of products. Purchasers should expect that OSI products offered to them have been through several extensive phases of testing before reaching the market. These testing phases are described in the following sections.

26.1.1 OSI Product Testing

Products typically pass through three forms of tests:

- developmental testing;

- formal conformance testing; and,

- interoperability testing.

Test systems are available now for most of the stable OSI standards and they should be used from the earliest stages of implementation. Test systems may be purchased for in-house use, which is usually the most desirable approach for the developer. A number of test houses have also been established to provide testing as a bureau service.

Developmental Since there is no product reference for reverse engineering of OSI products, the test system itself becomes the embodiment of the standard as a development tool. From the time that a developer starts to write software, the prototype product is subjected to iterative trial and error testing against the test tool (Figure 26.1).

Conformance When product development has reached the final stages, but (ideally) prior to marketing, it is time for a rigorous and controlled assessment of conformance (Figure 26.2). The tester is regarded as a reference implementation of the standard that is traceable to an internationally recognized source. The product is then put through an agreed standardized series of tests with the objective of producing a test report. This should be a formality if the same test system has been used as a development tool.

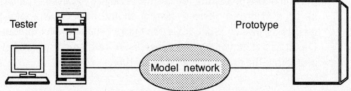

Figure 26.1   Developmental testing is used to reverse engineer a product and to debug software.

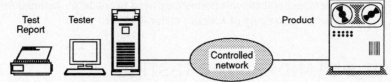

Figure 26.2   Conformance testing is conducted to international standards to produce a formal test report.

Conformance testing is only meaningful for protocol standards. It involves testing of an implementation's capabilities and behavior against the requirements in the relevant standard(s) and against those stated by the supplier in a profile statement. Conformance testing increases the probability that different implementations can interwork but it is not a guarantee. A successful conformance test means that:

- the part of the system that was tested behaves according to the standard; and,

- the product might interwork with other conforming systems.

Conformance testing is a functional test. It is not:

- an assessment of performance; or,

- a measure of the quality of the implementation.

Inter-operability   Interoperability testing is conducted between two or more products in an operational mode with a normal application and network environment, rather than the artificial laboratory conditions of conformance testing (Figure 26.3). The vendors typically conduct interoperability tests in a co-operative fashion. The leading interoperability testing organization is OSINET in North America and the results of tests between various vendors are publicly available. EUROSINET in Europe and OSIcom in Australia also participate in interoperability testing. A successful interoperability test means that the systems involved will interwork satisfactorily within a defined environment.

However, such testing by vendors does not necessarily cover all aspects relevant to a particular user. The testing does not cover user interface issues or integration with other application or system software.

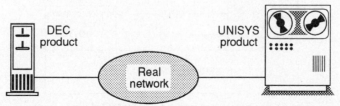

Figure 26.3   Interoperability testing is conducted between different vendors.

Users and systems integrators may need to conduct additional testing to check the integrity of a multi-vendor network.

26.2 STANDARDIZED TESTING

The ISO Conformance Testing Methodology and Framework standard (ISO 9646) is an internationally accepted definition of a common testing methodology and appropriate practices for test houses. Its contents cover:

- general concepts and the meaning of conformance;

- abstract test suite specifications;

- executable test derivation;

- the test language specification;

- requirements on suppliers and clients of test laboratories;

- test laboratory operations; and,

- interpretation of test results.

26.2.1 Test Method

Figure 26.4 illustrates the general principles used in conformance testing. The terms used in the figure are described below:

IUT	Implementation Under Test. The IUT is the software for one (or more) OSI layers in a product undergoing testing. It is regarded as a "black box". Only the external behaviour is observable, not the internal mechanisms.
ASPs	Abstract Service Primitives. Tests are based on the observation and control of ASPs at upper and lower interfaces.

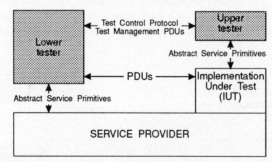

Figure 26.4   The co-ordinated test method (ISO 9646) defines the general principles used by OSI test houses.

Upper tester   A test responder acts as a known and controllable user at the upper interface. (Typically the responder software is supplied by the test house and has to be integrated with the IUT by the vendor.)

Lower tester   The reference implementation of the standard. It controls the testing process and records test results for analysis.

Service provider   It is assumed that the service provider is a conformant implementation of the lower layers and that the lower interface of the IUT is reflected by the provider.

TCP   Test Control Procedure. The Test Management Protocol (TMP) is used to co-ordinate upper and lower testers. This may be an active communications protocol that requires at least basic functionality in the IUT, or it may, in part, be a dialogue between two human operators at each end.

26.2.2 Single Layer Test System

The test system architecture, defined in the ISO conformance testing standards, can be realized with the components shown in Figure 26.5.

The test responder behaves as a controlled user of the implementation that is being tested. In some cases, e.g. X.400 testing, it may be an interface to a human user following an agreed series of actions. For the lower layers, the responder is a special piece of code that must be interfaced to the IUT by the implementor before testing can commence. Typically, the supplier

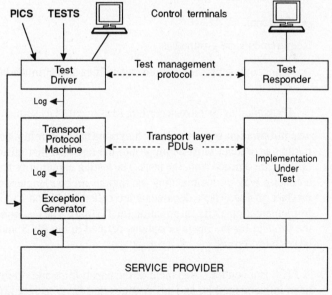

Figure 26.5   An example of a single layer tester for the Transport Layer

of the test equipment or service provides the specification, source code and check-out exercises for the test responder.

The lower tester consists of a special reference protocol machine, an exception generator and various controlling and data logging facilities. This is the core of the test equipment supplied by the test house and it is a very complex system.

The exception generator is used to produce invalid protocol behavior in order to test the response to abnormal situations.

For flexibility, the test driver is table driven and its behavior is determined by a large number of parameters that must be individually set up for specific tests. It must be supplied with extensive details of the tests to be performed, i.e. the test suites, and with details about the system under test. Standard test suites may be used, or test suites can be tailored to explore parts of the implementation not covered by the standard tests. Information about the system under test is supplied from a document known as the Protocol Implementation Conformance Statement (PICS).

26.2.3 PICS and PIXIT

A supplier would normally develop a product to conform to an internationally recognized profile. Products may also be developed to suit particular customer requirements or applications. So the test system may need to be configured differently for each product that is tested. Conformance requirements of the OSI standards and profiles may be:

- Mandatory

- Conditional

- Optional.

Requirements are grouped as:

- Static; e.g. support of certain capabilities and/or multi-layer dependencies.

- Dynamic; e.g. behave according to allowed PDU sequences.

The information specifying which options have been implemented for a particular product must be input into the tester so that un-implemented options are omitted from the tests. The testing community has developed a concise way of documenting the options and parameters chosen for a product profile. These documents are called PICS and PIXIT (Protocol Implementation eXtra Information for Testing). The test house then tests the product for the range of options defined in the PICS and PIXIT and issues a test report.

PICS

A PICS is a vendor's statement of the capabilities and options that have been implemented in, and any features that have been omitted from, an OSI system. It is a standardized proforma that provides information about a particular implementation, and it typically takes the form of a detailed table that specifies the capabilities supported, options implemented and parameter ranges to be tested. The preparation of the proforma that lists the items that make up a PICS have been added to the responsibility of the subcommittees that write the base OSI standards, and standardized PICS are now becoming available.

In addition, the PICS are used by some purchasers to specify the profiles required for procurement activities. In particular, the UK (and the Australian) GOSIP contain PICS for the main profiles that have been marked up to specify the options required for Government purchasing.

PIXIT   The PIXIT provides additional information to assist testing. It is a proforma that defines the testing environment, network addresses, timer values and other administrative matters.

26.2.4 Test Suites

A test suite is an agreed list of individual test cases to be executed on the test system. To generate test suites, protocol experts go through a laborious process of defining, in increasing detail, possible sequences of events for the protocol. (The test cases for X.25 amount to over 750 pages!) This is a task for the committees that write the protocol standards. The objective of the standards committees is to define abstract test cases that are independent of the test system and product. The abstract test cases can then be converted by the test house into executable test cases that are loaded into the test system for automated testing.

A test suite typically consists of thousands of tests and their description is broken down into a hierarchical structure to provide a logical ordering for the testing. Typically, a test case is specified in three steps:

- preamble from a chosen stable state (or idle state) to prepare for the test;

- test body; and,

- postamble to chosen stable state or idle state, ready for the next test.

TTCN   A notation called *Tree and Tabular Combined Notation (TTCN)* is used by the standards bodies and test houses to specify the tests. TTCN is not a formal language. Defined in ISO 9646, it is a mixture of notations such as:

- Tables that list static information, e.g. lists of primitives.

- Data declarations, including the use of ASN.1 (Abstract Syntax Notation One).

- Behavior trees.

An example of a TTCN description of two behavior trees is shown in Figure 26.6. Each behavior tree is prefixed by a tree name unique within the test suite specification; e.g. "Testcase" and "Data Transfer" in the example. The following notation is used:

- The names of events to be initiated by the tester are prefixed by an exclamation mark (!).

- Events that are possible for the tester to receive are prefixed by a question mark (?).

- Trees may be attached to other trees by substituting the name of the tree prefixed by a plus sign (+).

During a test, the tester automatically executes the test suite and generates one of three outcomes for each test, i.e.:

Passed   Conforms to the standard for the test case.

Failed   Does not conform.

Inconclusive   Not possible to resolve whether the IUT, or the network or the tester is responsible for not successfully completing the test.

Inconclusive results may require repetition of the test, or the manual examination of detailed test logs to resolve. The test report consists of a listing of the result for each of the potentially thousands of tests and it requires the skills of a protocol expert to interpret. It is not suitable for user evaluation of a product.

```
!CONreq
              ?CONcnf
                            +Data Transfer
                                          [result = 'F'] Failed
                                          [result = 'P'] Passed
                                          [result = 'I'] Inconclusive
              ?DISind




Data Transfer
              !DATreq
                            ?DATind (result:= 'P')
                            ?DISind (result:= 'I')
                            ?otherwise (result:= 'F')
              ?DISind (result:= 'I')
              ?otherwise (result:= 'F')
```

Figure 26.6   An example of the use of the Tree and Tabular Combined Notation (TTCN) to define a test case

26.3 ROLE OF VENDORS AND USERS IN TESTING

Vendors

Conformance testing is usually regarded as the responsibility of the vendor who may use either in-house facilities or an independent test house. A number of test houses offer access to test systems over public X.25 networks as a bureau service.

The tester should be used as a part of the development process to reverse engineer the product. In other words, a prototype is connected to the tester as soon as possible to allow an iterative trial and error process using the tester as a development tool. This ensures that errors are reduced prior to formal conformance testing and speeds the development cycle.

For this reason, and because the vendors require confidentiality about product development, self testing is the preferred mode of operation. The developer needs to have full control of its own testing environment.

An international community of testing agencies has been established in the last couple of years to develop conformance test equipment and procedures for the various profiles. Because self testing is preferred, these bodies are also setting up a system to accredit test labs and certify products to ensure uniformity of test results.

Users

Purchasers of OSI products should ask for evidence that products have been formally conformance and interoperability tested. However, a test report or certificate should not be accepted as **proof** of conformance. Ultimately, conformance can only be interpreted as the absence of errors during the lifetime of the product. No product is perfect, and the correction of OSI protocol errors should be included in maintenance provisions.

The software code for the OSI protocol component of a product is only of the order of 10% of the total product — the remainder being the customized application, user interfaces and interfaces to system resources. So conformance testing only covers a small portion of a product. Although the remainder of a distributed system would be useless if the OSI component did not conform to the standard, a conformance test is not the only basis for acceptance of a product.

By consistently insisting on proven conformance to the standards, users and purchasers will require the vendors to compete in terms of their compatibility, instead of their incompatibility. The vendors will focus on improved performance, price or service instead of vendor lock-in for market share.

27 Buying OSI

27.1 OSI — FROM PROMISE TO MARKET LEADER

The introduction of new standards into the market has always been a sluggish process. Earlier standards, such as X.25 and facsimile, have taken ten years to become widespread and OSI can be expected to take even longer because it is more ambitious. Only when large scale commercial OSI networks are in place in the mid-1990's will the promise of open networking be fully realized.

The more innovative companies and users are implementing OSI networks now in order to achieve strategic advantages or cost savings. However, while the initial penetration of OSI is low, it will be difficult for conservative organizations to justify OSI when there are few others to communicate with. At some point in time in the next couple of years, however, the penetration of OSI will necessitate the implementation of the standards to remain accessible to customers and trading partners.

Organizations with a particular requirement for OSI now can purchase products from an increasing number of vendors. Many companies already have done so, and public X.400 services are available from the carriers in most countries. In a 1990 study of user acceptance of OSI, it was found that in Europe, one company in three has implemented OSI and almost the same number again are committed to implementation in the near future. In the USA, however, only one in ten had implemented OSI although twice that number have a future commitment to do so. Now that the standards and products are increasingly available, the remaining barrier to improved electronic communications is corporate resistance to change.

A time of change
The market penetration of OSI is expected to grow rapidly over the next five years, so organizations must prepare for a long period of change. OSI will not necessarily replace the need for other protocols. OSI will serve as the mainstream for general use, but other protocols will serve niche applications. The changeover from the present day mix of proprietary communications protocols to the OSI standards demands a great deal of planning and control to achieve global compatibility. The extent of the change wrought by this technology should not be underestimated — OSI,

EDI (Electronic Data Interchange) and the related standards have the potential to change the way business is done.

27.2 COMMITMENT

Top level corporate commitment is necessary to overcome resistance to change and possible short-term cost penalties for the sake of long-term benefits. Cost effectiveness and accountability are keywords for business success. Now that corporate life is dominated by information processing and transfer, the expenditures, cost savings and strategic benefits of the enterprise's communications systems needs to be re-evaluated in the light of the international trend to standards. Any such analysis of the business case for OSI should identify strategic concerns such as:

- Insufficient communications between computers constrains the organization.

- Competitive advantages through the provision of new services.

Such benefits are difficult to quantify and many organizations accept as an act of faith that conformance to the standards will reap long-term strategic gains. Easier to quantify are the savings that are identified below:

- Improved productivity by using electronic instead of paper correspondence.

- Reduction in overlap and duplication of networks by improved sharing of resources.

- Many people and resources occupied in solving incompatibilities between existing systems can be used more productively with standard systems.

- Increased competition between vendors leading to lower equipment costs (and lower margins).

However, these savings are often offset by increased (sometimes unexpected) levels of use of the network as it becomes easier to apply to business needs.

Commitment to OSI now is vital to prepare an organization for transition to OSI. A corporate policy for the implementation of OSI, endorsed by senior management is essential to:

- Capitalize on competitive advantage of improved communications.

- Commence education and training of all staff concerned.

- Ensure a smooth transition with minimum disruption to the network.

- Control purchases of non-OSI products to minimize obsolescence.

- Alert suppliers to your needs.

OSI will only come about through co-operation. By definition, the sender and receiver of any communication must co-operate for effective information transfer. The equipment suppliers and communications partners must also co-operate to resolve any incompatibilities that impede or corrupt the communications. It is important, therefore, to align the corporate policy with international trends to be assured of the availability of products and to implement the network in step with trading partners.

27.2.1 OSI Policy

An organization's OSI purchasing policy should be spelt out in a document that becomes the foundation for all procurement specifications. This ensures uniformity for interworking between separately procured systems. The document should encompass:

- A policy statement that covers things like the extent of commitment to OSI, the time scales for mandatory compliance, the policy with regard to non-OSI systems and the attitude to conformance testing.

- The specification of the selection of standards and profiles to suit particular application and network requirements. The strategies here depend on particular business needs and requirements.

- Finally, a procurement specification should define the technical details of the OSI standards that have been selected, i.e. the profiles. Although some large organizations have developed their own profiles, most purchasers would be best served by referring to existing internationally recognized profiles to ensure on-going availability of suitable products.

Staff education and training should not be overlooked in the formulation of corporate policies and plans. New skills and knowledge will be required to support OSI and to implement the corporate OSI procurement policy. OSI could be perceived as a threat to established network empires in an organization if open networking is incorrectly introduced.

27.3 IMPLEMENTATION PLAN

Given a corporate policy and set of business or organizational requirements, the next step is to develop a transition plan. For example:

- Use of OSI for new applications only, leaving existing systems in place.

- For some applications, it may be possible to provide a gateway between proprietary systems and OSI.

- For an enterprise wide requirement to support a range of applications, a change over to a common subnetwork is recommended (X.25 is a good backbone for a mix of proprietary and OSI communication).

- The OSI upper layer protocols can then be progressively introduced in the computer systems. The alternatives would be to build up OSI conformance in all end systems layer by layer or introduce complete application protocol stacks one by one, e.g. corporate wide X.400 Message Handling Systems (MHS) followed by File Transfer, Access and Management (FTAM).

- For individual requirements for the interconnection of only two specific computers, OSI should be considered as it will facilitate future integration.

- In some cases, it may be necessary to use a non-OSI solution as an interim — but ensure that an upgrade path is available and get commitment to migrate to OSI when appropriate products are available.

Model for transition

During the transition, a small but increasing number of systems that implement the OSI standards will need to co-exist with a large number of different proprietary systems. In such an environment (illustrated in Figure 27.1), the following categories of computers may exist:

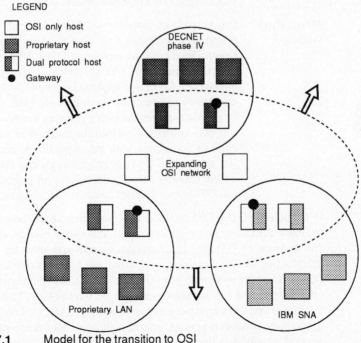

LEGEND

☐ OSI only host
▨ Proprietary host
▧ Dual protocol host
● Gateway

DECNET phase IV

Expanding OSI network

Proprietary LAN

IBM SNA

Figure 27.1   Model for the transition to OSI

OSI only hosts	Computer systems that implement only an OSI protocol stack and no other. Initially, these will be in the minority.
Proprietary only hosts	These do not implement OSI, and will be isolated from full open networking until they are replaced or upgraded. Proprietary only hosts dominate existing networks and will continue to exist for some time.
Dual protocol hosts	Systems that implement both an OSI protocol stack and a proprietary stack. Applications on such hosts will have the best of both worlds; i.e. they may use OSI for communication with systems from different (or the same) vendors and use the proprietary protocol with like systems. The applications will have to take into account the differences in functionality between the OSI and proprietary protocols.
Gateways	Specialized applications on dual protocol hosts may perform a best effort mapping to provide limited exchange of information between OSI systems and proprietary only systems. Such exchanges will take place hop-by-hop, e.g. transfer a file using OSI standards to the gateway, translation by the gateway to proprietary format and subsequent transfer of the file to the proprietary host. Gateways should be used only as an interim solution because of the inevitable incompatibilities between proprietary and OSI protocols and services.
Mixed stack systems	Products that implement a mixture of OSI and proprietary protocols (e.g. X.400 over Transmission Control Protocol/Internet Protocol, TCP/IP; and, Netbios over OSI Transport Class 4, connectionless Local Area Network, LAN) have appeared, apparently to appease mandatory requirements to implement OSI. They must be used in conjunction with a gateway to interwork with full OSI systems. To avoid the creation of yet another class of equipment with incompatible protocol stacks (i.e. neither full OSI nor proprietary), it is necessary to ensure that any such products have an upgrade path to full OSI before they are considered for any network.

In the initial stages, OSI products may not have all of the capabilities available in existing proprietary networks. It is essential to provide for the co-existence of OSI and proprietary networks and plan for a phased introduction of OSI capabilities. The time lag between publication of a standard and the availability of initial products that typically implement only a subset of the standard must not be overlooked. There will be inevitable upgrades as more capable versions are released. When using proprietary networking as an interim solution, only those proprietary network capabilities that are similar to the OSI services should be used.

Idiosyncratic features that will make it difficult to convert to OSI in the future should be avoided.

27.4 CONFORMANCE

What purchasing policies are needed to ensure that competing vendors will co-operate to supply compatible products?

In order to acquire products that will successfully interoperate, it is not sufficient to specify that the product shall interwork with some other vendor's system using an OSI standard. For instance, both parties may implement some obscure profile or there may be some errors that are not revealed by that particular combination of products. This of course would make it difficult to communicate with other parties. The crucial point is that purchasers must put the onus on vendors to achieve conformance with the standard, and also with a defined profile. Evidence of conformance testing and interoperability testing should be requested. Despite prior conformance testing and interoperability testing at other sites, there may still be a need to conduct further interoperability testing to check the integrity of a multi-vendor network with any particular combination of products and applications.

It is also vital to ensure that there is an upgrade path for the OSI network. New standards will become available over time and existing standards will be enhanced. Hard won compatibility may decline if everyone else moves on to a new version of a standard.

27.5 CONCLUSION

The things that need to be done to make OSI a reality are:

- obtain top level corporate commitment;

- prepare an OSI procurement policy;

- develop an implementation plan and act on it;

- communicate your intentions to your vendors;

- educate and train staff; and,

- ensure that products are adequately tested.

A commitment to achieve and demonstrate global interoperability and improved performance through standards will prepare any organization for the challenges ahead and give the business an advantage in the market.

In the opening chapters of this book, it was stated that the OSI model in its infancy was all about seven layers. However, if one takes a global view of the amount of money, effort and resource that is being dedicated to the OSI standards and OSI product development, then OSI takes on a new meaning. For those involved in the standards process, OSI has now become a multi-billion dollar global development project directed at the total scope of distributed systems. Although this sounds like blue sky, consider that the public telephone system, facsimile services, international data services, electronic mail systems, EDI, teleconferencing, fibre optics and video are based on international standards. All of these technologies emerged over the last few decades, and most of them are now seen as essential to business operation. With this in mind, it is very obvious that those today who do not have phones, facsimile machines and data networks do not do well in business. Tomorrow, those businesses who do not have OSI networks will have the same dilemma. OSI is not an option — from a global perspective, the information technology industry considers OSI as the way of life and its future. The global village is being created.

Appendices

A Glossary of Terms

ABM	Asynchronous Balanced Mode — one of the variants of the HDLC protocol.
ACSE	Association Control Service Element — an Application Layer standard.
ADMD	Administration Management Domain — a domain within the X.400 MHS environment under the control of a PTT, i.e. a telecommunications carrier.
AE	Application Entity
AFNOR	Association Francaise de Normalisation — French standards association.
ANSI	American National Standards Institute.
API	Application Program Interface. When used in OSI, usually referring to an interface to the software implementing a particular OSI layer and accessible to application programs (frequently specified in terms of OSI service primitives for the layer).
ARPANET	Advanced Research Projects Agency Network.
ASCII	American Standard Code for Information Interchange. Equivalent to CCITT IA5.
ASE	Application Service Element.
ASN.1	Abstract Syntax Notation One — standards used in the Application and Presentation layers for representing data types and their encoding (ISO 8824 and 8825).
Asynchronous terminal	A simple terminal connected via asynchronous communications that typically depends on a host computer for screen formatting, etc.
ATM	Asynchronous Transfer Mode.
AUSTEL	The Australian telecommunications regulatory organization.
AUSTPAC	Telecom Australia's public X.25 packet switching network.
BAS	Basic Activity Subset — one of the subsets defined in Version 1 of the Session Layer (ISO 8326 and 8327).
BCS	Basic Combined Subset — one of the subsets defined in Version 1 of the Session Layer (ISO 8326 and 8327).
BER	Basic Encoding Rules for ASN.1.
BRA	Basic Rate Access interface for ISDN.

BSI   British Standards Institute.

BSS   Basic Synchronized Subset — one of the subsets defined in Version 1 of the Session Layer (ISO 8326 and 8327).

CASE   Common Application Service Elements — name not used any more — a set of Application Layer standards that provide common functions for application programs and other Application Layer standards. See ACSE as an example.

CCA   Conceptual Communications Area in VT standards.

CCITT   International Telegraph and Telephone Consultative Committee — (part of the International Telecommunications Union) one of the principal international standards making organizations, comprising mainly PTTs.

CCR   Commitment, Concurrency and Recovery — one of the Application Layer standards.

CCTA   Central Computer and Telecommunications Agency. UK Government body responsible for UK GOSIP.

CD   Committee Draft — an ISO standard at the first stage of development. Previously called Draft Proposal (DP). It reflects the current state of agreement within the committee but it is subject to substantial editorial and technical alteration.

CEN   European Committee for Standardization — the European counterpart of ISO.

CENELEC   European Committee for Electrotechnical Standardization — the European counterpart of IEC.

CEPT   European Conference of Posts and Telecommunications — the European counterpart of CCITT.

CIM   Computer Integrated Manufacture.

CLNS/CLNP   Connectionless Network Service/Protocol (ISO 8473).

CMISE/P   Common Management Information Service Element/Protocol. Protocol for the exchange of network management information between OSI end systems.

CO   Control Object in VT.

CONS   Connection Oriented Network Service.

COS   The US based Corporation for Open Systems.

COTP   Connection Oriented Transport Protocol.

CPU   Central Processing unit.

CSMA/CD   Carrier Sense, Multiple Access/Collision Detection — one of the major classes of low level network technology, and a method of preventing data corruption used mainly for LANs. Ethernet is an example of this. The OSI standard version is specified in ISO 8802/3 and IEEE 802.3.

DAD   Draft Addendum (ISO status).

DCC   Data Country Code — three digit code used to identify countries in NSAP addresses.

DCE   Data Circuit terminating Equipment.

DCS   Defined Context Set — a set of Presentation Layer contexts.

DDS   Digital Data Service

DFR   Document Filing and Retrieval

DIB   Directory Information Base

Directory   A joint CCITT (X.500) — ISO (ISO 9594) Application layer standard.

DIS   Draft International Standard — an International Standard from ISO at its final stage prior to becoming an agreed standard.

DIT   Directory Information Tree

DP   Draft Proposal — a proposed ISO International Standard at the first stage of development. Now called Committee Draft (CD).

DQDB   Distributed Queue, Dual Bus — a MAN standard (IEEE 802.6).

DSA   Directory System Agent (CCITT X.500/ISO 9594).

DTAM   Document Transfer, Access and Manipulation.

DTE   Data Terminal Equipment.

DTP   Distributed Transaction Processing (ISO DIS 10026).

DUA   Directory User Agent (CCITT X.500/ISO 9594).

Duplex   In the Session Layer standards, the name given to one of the functional units that allows simultaneous messages in both directions in the session connection.

ECMA   European Computer Manufacturers' Association — a trade organization active in generation of common standards.

EDI   Electronic Data Interchange — The exchange of such trading documents as orders and invoices electronically between trading partners. Applicable standards for the syntax and format of the data are ANSI X.12 and ISO EDIFACT.

EDIFACT   Electronic Data Interchange for Administration, Commerce and Transport (ISO 9735 and ISO 7372).

EFT   Electronic Funds Transfer.

EN   European Norm — a standard within the European Community.

ENV   European pre-standards from CEN/CENELEC/CEPT.

ES   End System.

ES–IS	End System – Intermediate System — routing exchange protocol.
ETHERNET	A type of LAN based n CSMA/CD technology, originally developed by Digital Equipment Corporation (DEC), Intel and Xerox, now the subject of OSI standards (ISO 8802/3 and IEEE 802.3).
EUROSINET	A European version of OSINET. A supplier co-operative organization that demonstrates OSI products and systems.
FADU	File Access Data Unit — the part of a file accessed by FTAM.
FDDI	Fibre Distributed Data Interface for fibre optic backbone LANs.
Front end processor	A computer that typically has the task of communications processing for the lower layers, and is considered logically to sit between a main processor and a communications line, i.e. at the front end of the mainframe.
FTAM	File Transfer, Access and Management — an Application Layer standard for remote file handling (ISO 8571).
Gateway	See OSI gateway.
GDAP	Government Document Application Profile.
GKS	Graphical Kernel System (ISO).
GOSIP	Government OSI Profile. Both UK and US variants exist although they are similar. The Australian GOSIP is based on the UK version.
HDLC	High level Data Link Control — a Data Link Layer protocol.
I frame	Numbered Information frame in HDLC and LAPB.
IA5	International Alphabet No. 5 — CCITT equivalent of ASCII character set.
ICD	International Code Designator — a numeric code used to identifiy organizations in NSAP addresses.
IEC	International Electrotechnical Commission — a standards body.
IEEE	Institute of Electrical and Electronics Engineers (USA) — another organization highly active in standards making, mainly relevant for LANs.
Intercept	The use of draft OSI specifications, prior to final agreement as international standards, following achievement of technical stability.
Interconnection	A lesser level than full interworking such that two systems can communicate and exchange data but without consideration of how the dialogue between application programs is controlled or how the data is presented or recognized,e.g. the service provided by X.25 alone.
Interoperate, Interwork	Ultimately, the achievement of proper and effective communication or linking between different application programs and data despite the fact that these may be on different systems from different manufacturers, connected remotely by some transmission medium or network, e.g. as achieved by use of the OSI standards.

IP   In OSI: Connectionless Internetworking Protocol (ISO 8473). In US Department of Defense: Internet Protocol — precursor to OSI protocols, still widely used, particularly in USA. Used with TCP and referred to as TCP/IP.

IPDU   Connectionless Internetwork Protocol Data Unit (ISO 8473).

IPM   Interpersonal Message — one form of message in X.400 MHS.

IPSIT   International Public Sector Information Technology group.

IS   In Network Layer: Intermediate System. In reference to a standard: International Standard, as agreed and published by ISO.

ISDN   Integrated Services Digital Network.

ISO   International Organization for Standardization — major body responsible for the development of OSI standards; also used as prefix to an International Standard number.

ISP   International Standardized Profile.

IT   Information Technology

IWU   Interworking Unit — Network Layer component for network interconnection.

JTC1   Joint Technical Committee 1 — the joint ISO/IEC standards committee responsible for OSI.

JTM   Job Transfer and Manipulation — Application Layer standard for activating and controlling remote processing (ISO 8831 and 8832).

LAN   Local Area Network — facilities for interconnection between two or more systems located within a single site. Ethernet is a class of LAN.

LAPB   Link Access Procedure Balanced — one of the variants of the HDLC Data Link protocol used primarily between peer systems, and is the standard on which level 2 of X.25 is based.

LAPD   Link Access Procedure for D-Channel — the Data Link protocol for the ISDN signaling channel.

LLC1/LLC2   Logical Link Control type 1 and 2 — Data Link Layer protocols defined for use over LANs (ISO 8802/2 and IEEE 802.2). Type 1 provides a connectionless link and type 2 a connection oriented link.

LU   Logical Unit — a component in an IBM SNA network.

MAC   Medium Access Control used in LANs.

MAN   Metropolitan Area Network.

MAP   Manufacturing Automation Protocol — a set of functional standards developed under the auspices of General Motors in the USA.

MHS   Message Handling Systems — a general term for the Application Layer standards defined by X.400 and MOTIS for electronic mail.

MIB   Management Information Base.

MIS	Management Information Services.
MMS	Manufacturing Message Specification for MAP systems (ISO 9506).
MOTIS	Message Oriented Text Interchange Systems — a set of text handling standards developed by ISO in conjunction with CCITT, with a more comprehensive scope than X.400 (1984) — now encompassed within X.400 (1988)/ISO 10021.
MS	Message Store in MHS.
MTA	Message Transfer Agent — within MHS, the system responsible for storing and delivering messages.
MTS	Message Transfer Service — the service provided by MTAs.
Multiplexing	The carrying of more than one data stream over the same connection (apparently) simultaneously.
NBS	The US National Bureau of Standards — now called NIST.
NCC	National Computing Centre. UK organization that developed OSI conformance testing technology.
NCMS	Network Connection Management Subprotocol — an optional protocol in the Transport Layer.
NIST	A US agency that sets standards for the US Federal Government and that organizes workshops on OSI and OSINET. Also the originator of the US GOSIP.
NSAP	Network Service Access Point.
Object	An abstract representation of a real system resource in Application Layer standards.
ODA	Open Document Architecture (ISO 8613/CCITT T.400 series).
ODIF	Open Document Interchange Format.
ODP	Open Distributed Processing — area of work leading to future ISO standards.
OID	Object Identifier — used in ASN.1.
O/R name, O/R address	Originator/Recipient name or address as used to identify users in X.400 MHS.
OSI	Open Systems Interconnection.
OSIcom	An Australian OSI demonstration organization.
OSI^{one}	A co-operative grouping of the OSI demonstration and interoperability testing organizations.
OSI Gateway	A method of providing access to OSI systems from a network of non-OSI systems. The gateway maps between OSI and non-OSI protocols.

OSINET   An OSI demonstration network in the USA organized by NBS (now NIST).

OSITOP   European TOP Users Group.

P1,P2,P3,P7   The different classes of protocol specified within the CCITT X.400 (MHS) standards.

PABX   Private Automatic Branch Exchange.

Packet switch One of the computer systems involved in providing the services of a packet switching network.

PAD   Packet Assembler/Disassembler — converts data at a terminal into packets (discrete quantities) for transmission over a communications line and sets up and addresses calls to another PAD (or system with equivalent functionality). It permits terminals that cannot otherwise connect directly to a packet switched network to access such networks.

PCI   Protocol Control Information — the header of a PDU.

PDAD   Proposed Draft Addendum (ISO status), equivalent to DP.

PDU   Protocol Data Unit — data element exchanged between peer protocol entities in a layer.

PDV   Presentation Data Value.

PEDI   Protocol for EDI messaging in MHS.

PICS   Protocol Implementation Conformance Statement.

PLP   Packet Level Protocol of X.25.

PRA   Primary Rate Access — interface to ISDN.

PRMD   Private Management Domain — a domain within the X.400 MHS environment under the control of a private organization.

Protocol stack The set of OSI protocols at all seven layers required for a particular function or implemented in a particular system.

PSAP   Presentation Service Access Point.

PSDN   Public Switched Data Network — CCITT term for public packet switched network.

PSE   Packet Switching Exchange.

PSTN   Public Switched Telephone Network.

PTT   National postal, telephone and telegraphy organizations.

PVC   Permanent Virtual Circuit in X.25.

QOS   Quality of Service.

RDA	Remote Database Access — ISO DIS 9579 draft standards for transaction mode access to database systems using standard SQL commands between OSI end systems.
RDN	Relative Distinguished Name — part of a Directory name.
RNR	Receive Not Ready — frame and packet type in X.25.
ROS, ROSE	Remote Operations Service (Element) — ASE used by X.400 MHS, the X.500 Directory, and Systems Management (CCITT X.219 and X.229/ISO 9072).
RR	Receive Ready — frame and packet type in X.25.
RTS, RTSE	Reliable Transfer Service (Element) — ASE used by X.400 MHS (CCITT X.218 and X.228/ISO 9066).
SAP	Service Access Point — an addressable point at the boundary between two layers in the OSI model.
SC	Sub-committee. Within ISO, SC 21 has responsibility for development of standards for OSI layers 5 to 7, SC 6 for layers 1 to 4, SC 18 for text and MHS.
SDH	Synchronous Digital Hierarchy.
SDU	Service Data Unit — the unit of data exchanged between layers in a service primitive.
Service primitive	The elements defined in OSI standards that specify in a precise manner the services provided by a particular layer.
SFD	Simple Formatable Document in MHS.
SGML	Standard Generalized Markup Language (ISO).
SNA	Systems Network Architecture — proprietary communications architecture and a set of protocols for use between IBM computer systems.
SNDCP	Subnetwork Dependent Convergence Protocol.
SNMP	Simple Network Management Protocol — for TCP/IP networks.
SPAG	Standards Promotion and Application Group — a consortium of European suppliers developing functional standards.
SQL	Structured Query Language.
SVC	Switched Virtual Circuit in X.25.
TA	Terminal Adapter (in ISDN).
TC	Technical Committee. Within ISO, TC 97 has responsibility for SC 6, SC 18 and SC 21, which are the primary subcommittees developing OSI standards.
TCP	Transmission Control Protocol — US Defense Department precursor to OSI protocols, still widely used together with IP as TCP/IP.

TE	Terminal Equipment (in ISDN).
Token bus	One of the types of LAN, specified in ISO 8802/4 and IEEE 802.4. The primary LAN for MAP systems.
Token ring	One of the types of LAN, specified in ISO 8802/5 and IEEE 802.5. The type of LAN given primary support by IBM.
TOP	Technical and Office Protocols — a set of functional standards designed for the office environment, initiated by Boeing in the USA.
TP	Transaction Processing (ISO DIS 10026).
Transport classes	The method by which the options of the Transport Layer are grouped into five subsets.
Triple X	The CCITT Recommendations X.3, X.28 and X.29 which jointly define standards for asynchronous terminals to access a mainframe (or X.25 packet terminal) via a PAD.
UA	User Agent — within MHS, the system responsible for originating and receiving messages.
UI	Un-numbered Information frame in HDLC and LLC.
VAN(S)	Value Added Network (Services)
Virtual circuit	A logical connection between two parties across one or more physical circuits that may be shared or multiplexed with other virtual circuits.
VT	Virtual Terminal — one of the Applications Layer protocols developed to allow standard terminal access to computer systems (ISO 9040 and 9041).
VTE	Virtual Terminal Environment.
WAN	Wide Area Network.
X.3,X.28,X.29	The set of Triple-X protocols for asynchronous terminal access to X.25 data networks.
X.25	The CCITT Recommendation defining interfaces to packet mode terminals on packet switched networks, as used by Telecom Australia's AUSTPAC and many other national and private networks.
X.25 (1988, 1984, 1980)	The variants of X.25 agreed by CCITT at plenary meetings in 1988, 1984 and 1980 respectively. The 1980 version is a subset of the 1984 and 1988 versions.
X.400	The CCITT series of MHS Recommendations for message interchange. The 1988 version is equivalent to the final ISO standard (MOTIS ISO 10021) for message handling and document interchange.
X.500	CCITT series of Directory Recommendations (equivalent to ISO 9594) agreed in 1988.

B List of Standards

The following table lists the OSI and associated standards in numerical order. The second column of the table refers to standards that are technically aligned with the listed standard, i.e. equivalent or supplementary or otherwise related. CCITT standards are listed first, followed by the ISO standards.

STANDARD NUMBER	RELATED STANDARD	TITLE
E.164		International numbering for ISDN networks
I.411		ISDN user-network interface - Reference configurations
I.430		Basic user-network interface - Layer 1 specification
I.431		Primary rate user-network interface - Layer 1 specification
I.440	Q.920	ISDN user-network interface data link specification - General aspects
I.441	Q.921	ISDN user-network interface data link specification
I.451	Q.931	ISDN user-network interface layer 3 specification
I.461	X.30	Support of X.21, X.21 bis and X.20 bis based DTEs by an ISDN
I.462	X.31	Support of packet mode terminal equipment by an ISDN
M.10 - M.782		Maintenance of International Transmission Systems and Telephone Circuits
Q.920	I.440	ISDN user-network interface data link layer - General aspects
Q.921	I.441	ISDN user-network interface data link specification
Q.931	I.451	ISDN user-network interface layer 3 specification
T.6		Group 4 facsimile
T.50	ISO 646	International Alphabet No. 5 (IA5)
T.411	ISO 8613.1	Document Transfer, Access and Manipulation (DTAM) - Document Architecture (ODA) and Interchange Format - Application Rules
T.412	ISO 8613.2	Document Transfer, Access and Manipulation (DTAM) - Document Structures
T.414	ISO 8613.4	Document Transfer, Access and Manipulation (DTAM) - Document Profile
T.415	ISO 8613.5	Document Transfer, Access and Manipulation (DTAM) - Document Interchange Format
T.416	ISO 8613.6	Document Transfer, Access and Manipulation (DTAM) - Character Content Architectures
T.417	ISO 8613.7	Document Transfer, Access and Manipulation (DTAM) - Raster Graphics Content Architectures

STANDARD NUMBER	RELATED STANDARD	TITLE
T.418	ISO 8613.8	Document Transfer, Access and Manipulation (DTAM) - Geometric Graphics Content Architectures
T.419		Document Transfer, Access and Manipulation (DTAM) - Composite Graphics Content Architectures
T.431		Document Transfer, Access and Manipulation (DTAM) - Services and Protocols - Introduction and General Principles
T.432		Document Transfer, Access and Manipulation (DTAM) - Services and Protocols - Service Definition
T.433		Document Transfer, Access and Manipulation (DTAM) - Services and Protocols - Protocol Specification
T.441		Document Transfer, Access and Manipulation (DTAM) - Operational Structure
T.500 series		Application profiles for DTAM
V.10	X.26	Electrical characteristics for unbalanced double-current interchange circuits for general use with integrated circuit equipment in the field of data communications
V.11	X.27	Electrical characteristics for balanced double-current interchange circuits for general use with integrated circuit equipment in the field of data communications
V.24		List of definitions for interchange circuits between data terminal equipment and data circuit-terminating equipment
V.28		Electrical characteristics for unbalanced double-current interchange circuits
V.35		Data transmission at 48 kbit/s using 60-108 kHz group band circuits
X.3		Packet assembly/disassembly (PAD) facility in a public data network
X.21		Interface between data terminal equipment (DTE) and data circuit-terminating equipment (DCE) for synchronous operation on public data networks
X.21 bis		Use on public data networks of data terminal equipment (DTE) which is designed for interfacing to synchronous V-series modems
X.25		Interface between data terminal equipment (DTE) and data circuit-terminating equipment (DCE) for terminals operating in the packet mode and connected to public data networks by dedicated circuit
X.28		DTE/DCE interface for a start-stop mode data terminal equipment accessing the packet assembly/disassembly facility (PAD) in a public data network
X.29		Procedures for the exchange of control information and user data between a packet assembly/disassembly (PAD) facility and a packet mode DTE or another PAD
X.31	I.462	Support of packet mode terminal equipment by an ISDN

STANDARD NUMBER	RELATED STANDARD	TITLE
X.32		DTE/DCE interface for terminals operating in the packet mode and accessing a packet switched public data network through a public switched telephone network or an ISDN or a circuit switched public data network
X.121		International numbering plan for public data networks
X.200	ISO 7498	Reference model of Open Systems Interconnection for CCITT Applications
X.208	ISO 8824	Specification of Abstract Syntax Notation One (ASN.1)
X.209	ISO 8825	Specification of basic encoding rules for Abstract Syntax Notation One (ASN.1)
X.210	ISO TR 8509	OSI Layer Service Definition Conventions
X.211	ISO 10022	Physical service definition
X.212	ISO 8886	Data link service definition
X.213	ISO 8348	Network service definition
X.214	ISO 8072	Transport service definition
X.215	ISO 8326	Session service definition
X.216	ISO 8822	Presentation service definition
X.217	ISO 8649	Association control service definition
X.218	ISO 9066.1	Reliable transfer: model and service definition
X.219	ISO 9072.1	Remote operations: model, notation and service definition
X.223	ISO 8878	Use of X.25 to provide the OSI connection-mode Network service
X.224	ISO 8073	Transport protocol specification
X.225	ISO 8327	Session protocol specification
X.226	ISO 8823	Presentation protocol specification
X.227	ISO 8650	Association control protocol specification
X.228	ISO 9066.2	Reliable transfer: protocol specification
X.229	ISO 9072.2	Remote operations: protocol specification
X.244	ISO TR 9577	Protocol identification in the Network layer
X.26	V.10	Electrical characteristics for unbalanced double-current interchange circuits for general use with integrated circuit equipment in the field of data communications
X.27	V.11	Electrical characteristics for balanced double-current interchange circuits for general use with integrated circuit equipment in the field of data communications
X.290	ISO 9646	OSI conformance testing methodology and framework for protocol Recommendations
X.300		General principles for interworking between public networks, and between public networks and other networks for the provision of data services
X.305		Functionalities of subnetworks relating to the support of the OSI connection mode network service
X.400	ISO 10021.1	Message handling systems: System and service overview
X.402	ISO 10021.2	Message handling systems: Overall architecture
X.403		Message handling systems: Conformance testing

STANDARD NUMBER	RELATED STANDARD	TITLE
X.407	ISO 10021.3	Message handling systems: Abstract service definition conventions
X.408		Message handling systems: Encoded information type conversion rules
X.411	ISO 10021.4	Message handling systems: Message transfer service definition
X.413	ISO 10021.5	Message handling systems: Message store service definition
X.419	ISO 10021.6	Message handling systems: Protocol specifications
X.420	ISO 10021.7	Message handling systems: Interpersonal messaging system
X.435		EDI Messaging
X.500	ISO 9594.1	The Directory - Overview of concepts, models and service
X.501	ISO 9594.2	The Directory - Models
X.509	ISO 9594.8	The Directory - Authentication framework
X.511	ISO 9594.3	The Directory - Abstract service definition
X.518	ISO 9594.4	The Directory - Procedures for distributed operations
X.519	ISO 9594.5	The Directory - Protocol specifications
X.520	ISO 9594.6	The Directory - Selected attribute types
X.521	ISO 9594.7	The Directory - Selected object classes
X.700	ISO 7498.4	Reference Model of Open Systems Interconnection - Management Framework
X.701	ISO 10040	Systems Management Overview
X.710	ISO 9595	Common Management Information Service (CMIS)
X.711	ISO 9596	Common Management Information Protocol (CMIP)
X.720	ISO 10065.1	Management Information Model
X.721	ISO 10165.2	Definition of Management Information
X.722	ISO 10165.4	Guide-lines for Definition of Managed Objects
X.723	ISO 10165.5	Generic Management Information
X.730	ISO 10164.1	Object Management Function
X.731	ISO 10164.2	State Management Function
X.732	ISO 10164.3	Attributes for Representing Relationships
X.733	ISO 10164.4	Alarm Reporting Management Function
X.734	ISO 10164.5	Event Report Management Function
X.735	ISO 10164.6	Log Control Function
X.736	ISO 10164.7	Security Alarm Reporting Function
X.737	DIS 10164.11	Workload Monitoring Function
X.738	DIS 10164.12	Test Management Function
X.740	DIS 10164.8	Security Audit Trail Function
X.741	DIS 10164.9	Objects and Attributes for Access Control
X.742	DIS 10164.10	Accounting Meter Function
X.745	DIS 10164.13	Measurement Summarization Function

STANDARD NUMBER	RELATED STANDARD	TITLE
ISO 646	T.50	ISO 7 bit Coded Character Set for Information Interchange (ASCII)
ISO 2022		ISO 7-bit and 8-bit Coded Character Sets - Code Extension Techniques
ISO 2110		25-pole DTE/DCE Interface Connector and Contact Number Assignments
ISO 2375		Procedure for Registration of Escape Sequences
ISO 2593		34-pole DTE/DCE Interface Connector and Contact Number Assignments
ISO 3166		Specification of Codes for the Representation of Names of Countries
ISO 3309		High-level Data Link Control (HDLC) procedures - Frame Structure
ISO 4335		High-level Data Link Control (HDLC) procedures - Elements of Procedure
ISO 4873		8-bit Coded Character Set for Information Interchange - Structure and Rules for Implementation
ISO 4902		37-pole DTE/DCE Interface Connector and Contact Number Assignments
ISO 4903		15-pole DTE/DCE Interface Connector and Contact Number Assignments
ISO 6429		ISO 7-bit and 8-bit Coded Character Sets - Additional Control Functions for Character Imaging Devices
ISO 6523		Structure for the Identification of Organisations
ISO 6937.1		Coded Character Sets for Text Communication, Part 1: General Introduction
ISO 6937.2		Coded Character Sets for Text Communication, Part 2: Latin Alphabetic and Non-alphabetic Graphic Characters
ISO 6937.3		Coded Character Sets for Text Communication, Part 3: Control Functions for Page Image Format
ISO 7350		Registration of Graphic Character Subrepertoires
ISO 7372		United Nations Trade Data Elements Directory (UNTDED)
ISO 7478		High-level Data Link Control (HDLC) procedures - Multilink Procedures
ISO 7492		Graphics Kernel System (GKS) - Functional Description
ISO 7498	X.200	Basic Reference Model for OSI
ISO 7498.1		Basic Reference Model for OSI - Addendum 1: Connectionless Mode Transmission
ISO 7498.2		Basic Reference Model for OSI, Part 2: Security Architecture
ISO 7498.3		Basic Reference Model for OSI, Part 3: Naming and Addressing
ISO 7498.4	X.700	Basic Reference Model for OSI, Part 4: Management Framework

STANDARD NUMBER	RELATED STANDARD	TITLE
ISO 7776		High-level Data Link Control (HDLC) procedures: X.25 Compatible DTE Data Link Procedures
ISO 7809		High-level Data Link Control (HDLC) procedures: Classes of Procedure
ISO 8072	X.214	Connection Oriented Transport Protocol Specification
ISO 8072		Addendum 1: Network Connection Management Subprotocol
ISO 8072		Addendum 2: Class 4 Operation over Connectionless-mode Network Service
ISO 8073	X.224	Connection-Oriented Transport Protocol Specification
ISO 8073		Addendum 1: Network Connection Management Subprotocol
ISO 8073		Addendum 2: Class 4 Operation over Connectionless-mode Network Service
ISO 8208		X.25 Packet Level Protocol for Data Terminal Equipment
ISO 8326	X.215	Basic Connection Oriented Session Service Definition
ISO 8326	X.215	Addendum 1: session Symmetric Synchronize
ISO 8326	X.215	Addendum 2: Unlimited User Data
ISO 8327	X.225	Basic Connection-Oriented Session Protocol Specification
ISO 8327	X.225	Addendum 1: Session Symmetric Synchronize
ISO 8327	X.225	Addendum 2: Unlimited User Data
ISO 8348	X.213	Network Service Definition
ISO 8348	X.213	Addendum 1: Connectionless-mode Transmission
ISO 8348	X.213	Addendum 2: Network Layer Addressing
ISO 8348	X.213	Addendum 3: Additional Features of the Network Service
ISO 8473		Protocol Providing the Connectionless-mode Network Service
ISO 8473		Addendum 1: Provision of the Underlying Service Assumed by ISO 8473
TR 8509	X.210	Service Definition Conventions
ISO 8571.1		File Transfer, Access & Management, Part 1: General Introduction
ISO 8571.2		File Transfer, Access & Management, Part 2: Virtual File Store
ISO 8571.3		File Transfer, Access & Management, Part 3: File Service Definition
ISO 8571.4		File Transfer, Access & Management, Part 4: File Protocol Specification
ISO 8571.5		File Transfer, Access & Management, Part 5: PICS Proforma
ISO 8613.1	T.411	Office Document Architecture (ODA) & Interchange Format, Part 1: Introduction and General Principles
ISO 8613.2	T.412	Office Document Architecture (ODA) & Interchange Format, Part 2: Document Structures

STANDARD NUMBER	RELATED STANDARD	TITLE
ISO 8613.4	T.414	Office Document Architecture (ODA) & Interchange Format, Part 4: Document Profile
ISO 8613.5	T.415	Office Document Architecture (ODA) & Interchange Format, Part 5: Open Document Interchange Format
ISO 8613.6	T.416	Office Document Architecture (ODA) & Interchange Format, Part 6: Character Content Architectures
ISO 8613.7	T.417	Office Document Architecture (ODA) & Interchange Format, Part 7: Raster Graphics Content Architectures
ISO 8613.8	T.418	Office Document Architecture (ODA) & Interchange Format, Part 8: Geometric Graphics Content Architectures
ISO 8632		Computer Graphics - Metafile for Transfer & Storage of Picture Description Information
ISO 8648		Internal Organisation of the Network Layer
ISO 8649	X.217	Service Definition for the Association Control Service Element
ISO 8650	X.227	Protocol Specification for the Association Control Service Element
ISO 8802.2	IEEE 802.2	Local Area Networks, Part 2: Logical Link Control
ISO 8802.3	IEEE 802.3	Local Area Networks, Part 3: CSMA/CD Access Method & Physical Layer Specification
ISO 8802.4	IEEE 802.4	Local Area Networks, Part 4: Token Passing Bus Access Method & Physical Layer Specifications
ISO 8802.5	IEEE 802.5	Local Area Networks, Part 5: Token Ring Access Method & Physical Layer Specifications
ISO 8802.6	IEEE 802.6	Local Area Networks, Part 6: Distributed Queue, Dual Bus Access Method
ISO 8822	X.216	Connection Oriented Presentation Service Definition
ISO 8823	X.226	Connection-Oriented Presentation Protocol Specification
ISO 8824	X.208	Specification of Abstract Syntax Notation One (ASN.1)
ISO 8825	X.209	Specification of Basic Encoding Rules for ASN.1
ISO 8831		Job Transfer and Manipulation (JTM): Concepts and Services
ISO 8832		Job Transfer & Manipulation (JTM): Basic Class Protocol Specification
ISO 8859		8-bit Single-byte Coded Graphic Character Sets, Parts 1-9
ISO 8877		Interface Connector and Contact Assignments for ISDN Basic Access Interface Located at Reference Points S and T.
ISO 8878	X.223	Use of X.25 to provide the Connection-mode Network Service
ISO 8879		Standard Generalised Markup Language (SGML)
ISO 8880.1		Protocol Combinations to Provide and Support the OSI Network Service, Part 1: General Principles

STANDARD NUMBER	RELATED STANDARD	TITLE
ISO 8880.2		Protocol Combinations to Provide and Support the OSI Network Service, Part 2: Connection-mode Network Service
ISO 8880.3		Protocol Combinations to Provide and Support the OSI Network Service, Part 3: Connectionless-mode Network Service
ISO 8881		Use of X.25 Packet Level Protocol in Local Area Networks
DIS 8886	X.212	Data Link Service Definition
ISO 9040		Virtual Terminal Service
ISO 9041		Virtual Terminal Protocol
ISO 9066.1	X.218	Reliable Transfer (RTSE), Part 1: Model & Service Definition
ISO 9066.2	X.228	Reliable Transfer, Part 2: Protocol Specification
ISO 9069		SGML Document Interchange Format (SDIF)
ISO 9072.1	X.219	Remote Operations (ROSE), Part 1: Model, Notation & Service Definition
ISO 9072.2	X.229	Remote Operations, Part 2: Protocol Specification
ISO 9314		Fibre Distributed Data Interface (FDDI) Token Ring
ISO 9542		End System to Intermediate System (ES-IS) Routing Exchange Protocol for Use in Conjunction with ISO 8473
ISO 9545		Application Layer Structure
ISO 9574		Provision of the OSI Network Service by Packet Mode Terminal Equipment Connected to an Integrated services Digital Network (ISDN)
DIS 9576		Connectionless Presentation Protocol
DIS 9576		Connectionless Presentation Layer Protocol
DTR 9577	X.244	Protocol identification in the Network layer
TR 9578		Communication Interface Connectors used in Local Area Networks
DIS 9579.1		Remote Database Access - Part 1: Generic Model, Service and Protocol
DIS 9579.2		Remote Database Access - Part 2: SQL Specialization
ISO 9594.1	X.500	The Directory, Part 1: Overview of Concepts, Models & Services
ISO 9594.2	X.501	The Directory, Part 2: Models
ISO 9594.3	X.511	The Directory, Part 3: Abstract Service Definition
ISO 9594.4	X.518	The Directory, Part 4: Procedures for Distributed Operations
ISO 9594.5	X.519	The Directory, Part 5: Protocol Specifications
ISO 9594.6	X.520	The Directory, Part 6: Selected Attribute Types
ISO 9594.7	X.521	The Directory, Part 7: Selected Object Classes
ISO 9594.8	X.509	The Directory, Part 8: Authentication Framework
ISO 9595	X.710	Common Management Information Service (CMIS)
ISO 9596	X.711	Common Management Information Protocol (CMIP)

STANDARD NUMBER	RELATED STANDARD	TITLE
DIS 9646.1	X.290	OSI Conformance Testing Methodology and Framework, Part 1: General Concepts
DIS 9646.2	X.290	OSI Conformance Testing Methodology and Framework, Part 2: Abstract Test Suite Specification
DIS 9646.3		OSI Conformance Testing Methodology and Framework, Part 3: The Tree and Tabular Combined Notation (TTCN)
DIS 9646.4		OSI Conformance Testing Methodology and Framework, Part 4: Test Realization
DIS 9646.5		OSI Conformance Testing Methodology and Framework, Part 5: Requirements on Test Laboratories and Clients for the Conformance Assessment Process
ISO 9735		Electronic Data Interchange for Administration, Commerce and Transport (EDIFACT) - Application Level Syntax Rules
ISO 9804		Commitment, Concurrency and Recovery (CCR) Service Element
ISO 9805		Commitment, Concurrency and Recovery Protocol
ISO 10021.1	X.400	Message Oriented Text Interchange Systems (MOTIS), Part 1: Service and System Overview
ISO 10021.2	X.402	Message Oriented Text Interchange Systems (MOTIS), Part 2: Overall Architecture
ISO 10021.3	X.407	Message Oriented Text Interchange Systems (MOTIS), Part 3: Abstract Service Definition Conventions
ISO 10021.4	X.411	Message Oriented Text Interchange Systems (MOTIS), Part 4: Message Transfer System: Abstract Service Definition and Procedures
ISO 10021.5	X.413	Message Oriented Text Interchange Systems (MOTIS), Part 5: Message Store: Abstract Service Definition
ISO 10021.6	X.419	Message Oriented Text Interchange Systems (MOTIS), Part 6: Protocol Specifications
ISO 10021.7	X.420	Message Oriented Text Interchange Systems (MOTIS), Part 7: Interpersonal Messaging System
ISO 10022	X.211	Physical Service Definition
DIS 10026.1		Distributed Transaction Processing - Part 1: Model
DIS 10026.2		Distributed Transaction Processing - Part 2: Service Definition
DIS 10026.3		Distributed Transaction Processing - Part 3: Protocol Specification
CD 10028		Definition of the Relaying Functions of a Network Layer Intermediate System
DIS 10030		End System Routeing Information Exchange Protocol for Use in Conjunction with ISO 8878
ISO 10040	X.701	Systems Management Overview
ISO 10164.1	X.730	Object Management Function
ISO 10164.2	X.731	State Management Function
ISO 10164.3	X.732	Attributes for Representing Relationships

STANDARD NUMBER	RELATED STANDARD	TITLE
ISO 10164.4	X.733	Alarm Reporting Management Function
ISO 10164.5	X.734	Event Report Management Function
ISO 10164.6	X.735	Log Management Function
ISO 10164.7	X.736	Security Alarm Management Function
DIS 10164.8	X.740	Security Audit Trail Function
DIS 10164.9	X.741	Objects and Attributes for Access Control
DIS 10164.10	X.742	Accounting Meter Function
DIS 10164.11	X.737	Workload Monitoring Function
DIS 10164.12	X.745	Test Management Function
DIS 10164.13	X.738	Management Summarization Function
ISO 10165.1	X.720	Management Information Model
ISO 10165.2	X.721	Definition of Management Information
ISO 10165.4	X.722	Guide-lines for Definition of Managed Objects
ISO 10165.5	X.723	Generic Management Information
ISO 10166		Document Filing and Retrieval (DFR) Service definition and Protocol specification
DIS 10173		Integrated Services Digital Network (ISDN) Primary Access Connector at Reference points S and T
DTR 10178		The Structure and Coding of Link Service Access Point Addresses in Local Area Networks
DIS 10589		Intermediate System to Intermediate System Intra-domain Routeing Exchange Protocol for use with the Protocol for the Connectionless Network Service (ISO 8473)
CD 10737		Transport Layer Management
CD 10733		Elements of Management Information related to OSI Network Layer Standards

C Answers to Questions

1 WHY OSI?

2 THE OSI REFERENCE MODEL

2.1 The Network Layer uses NSAP addresses for global addressing.

2.2 The Presentation Layer transforms the user's data for a common interpretation at both ends.

2.3 A connection oriented service can support:
- unconfirmed dialogues;
- confirmed dialogues; and,
- partially confirmed dialogues.

A connectionless service can only support unconfirmed dialogues.

2.4 Example A is incorrect because the two (N+1)-entities cannot be distinguished by an (N)-SAP. Example B is correct.

2.5 PDU is Protocol Data Unit and SDU is Service Data Unit. A PDU is created by a layer and passed to the layer below as an SDU.

2.6 See Figure 2.8, page 33 for guidance.

2.7 See Figure 2.8, page 33 for guidance.

3 OBJECT ORIENTED SPECIFICATIONS

4 THE LOWER FOUR LAYERS

5 PHYSICAL LAYER

5.1 The four main aspects of the Physical Layer are:

Mechanical	The specification of the pins, plugs and sockets.
Electrical	The signaling voltages/currents associated with the interface.
Functional	The meaning of the signals (e.g. DTR is Data Terminal Ready).
Procedural	The combinations and sequences of signals (e.g. CTS follows RTS).

5.2 The four services provided by the Physical Layer are:

Physical connections	Modelled as a connection activation/deactivation between two or more physical entities.
Data transfer	The Physical Layer SDU is modeled as 1 bit.
Sequencing	The bits given to the Physical Layer must be kept in order.

Layer management   Fault conditions may be notified.

5.3   The two main groups of Physical Layer interfaces are the WAN group and the LAN group. The main difference between them is that the WAN group generally requires the interchange signals (e.g. DSR, DTR and RTS, CTS) to be active before data transmission. LAN interfaces have no interchange signals at the physical level. Instead, LAN interfaces rely on the MAC level to provide similar mechanisms; e.g. a frame already on the LAN indicates to other stations a Not Clear to Send condition.

5.4   DSR and DTR are the two signals indicating online operation of the DCE and DTE respectively.

5.5   The R, I, T,C interchange signals belong to the X.21 interface. The C and I signals are used to distinguish between control or data transfer use of the R and T signals.

5.6   The transmission speed of Basic Rate is 144 kbit/s (2B+D) and Primary Rate is 1,544 kbit/s (23B+D) in North America and Japan or 2,048 kbit/s (30B+D) in Europe and Australia.

5.7   The B channels are Bearer channels and are for user specified transmission (data or voice). The D channel is used as the call management channel. B channel assignment (and call destination selection) is performed by signaling on this D channel.

5.8   The Reference points defined for ISDN are the R, S, T and U points. These points define the boundaries of ISDN functions and thus the lines of demarcation between the user (premises) equipment and the transmission and exchange equipment.

5.9   The S reference point identifies the user interface between the ISDN service (e.g. via a PABX) and the ISDN user equipment. The T reference point is the pre-multiplexed or single equipment attachment point.

5.10   The two distinct Physical Layer standards for ISDN provide cost effective access on existing two wire cable (BRA), or higher speed access for larger users (PRA). BRA is a multi-point service and access to the D channel is controlled by a level 1 protocol contention mechanism (via echo bits on the D channel). The PRA is a fixed point to point service.

5.11   ATM is Asynchronous Transfer Mode (also referred to as Broadband ISDN). It is a packet type technology based on fixed length cells.

5.12   The characteristics of 10base5, 10base2 and 10baseT are Thick, Thin and Unshielded Twisted Pair ethernet interfaces respectively.

5.13   The MAC protocols belong to the Data Link Layer because they define the format of frames. (The Physical Layer operates with 1 bit at a time).

6   DATA LINK LAYER

6.1   The purpose of the Data Link Layer is to organize the Physical Layer bits into frames for orderly transmission and error control. These frames perform the lowest level dialogue between two physical devices. Data Link functions include:

Addressing   To distinguish between different devices (terminals or stations) on the physical circuit.

Access   For sharing the physical circuit between different devices.

Error checking   To detect corruption of data by transmission noise.

Control   To manage the data link using commands and responses and in some cases acknowledgement and flow control.

6.2 The three modes of HDLC are Normal Response Mode (NRM), Asynchronous Response Mode (ARM), and Asynchronous Balanced Mode (ABM) that, in X.25, is referred to as LAPB.

6.3 Bit stuffing is used in HDLC for transparency of the data within the frames. The start and end flags of a frame are a zero bit and six contiguous ones followed by a zero bit (#7E). Any data between these two flags must not be transmitted as #7E. Therefore, all data within the frame is bit stuffed. After 5 contiguous ones are detected in the user data, the transmitter inserts a zero. The receiver performs the reverse action.

6.4 The Poll/Final bit is used to indicate that the sending station wants an explicit response to this frame (a poll). The responding station sets the bit (as the final bit) to indicate the response is matched to the poll. The poll bit is also used on multi-dropped lines (HDLC NRM) by the primary station to give the addressed secondary station the right to transmit.

6.5 The LAPB address is used to indicate a command or response. In LAPB a DCE has an address of 01 and a DCE an address of 03. If the DCE sends a frame to a DTE with an address of 03, the DTE sees it as a command; e.g. a Receive Ready with the Poll/Final bit set for a Poll. If, on the other hand, the DCE sends the same frame with an address of 01, the DTE sees this as a response (to a previous DTE command sent to the DCE) and sees the poll/final bit as a Final.

6.6 Link level flow control is achieved in HDLC explicitly or implicitly. Explicit flow control is exerted by issuing RNR (Receive Not Ready) frames to the other party. Implicit flow control is achieved by not responding immediately to polls or data (but keeping within the poll time out period T1). In this case, the receiver is not permitting the frame sequence number window to progress.

6.7 LAPB is a point to point protocol because it has discrete addresses for the DTE and DCE. LAPD is a multipoint protocol because its Link level addresses are numerous, dynamic and assignable.

6.8 The SAPI and a TEI are access points and addresses for management entities used within the ISDN connection management processes. Because the D channel uses LAPD which is a multiplexed protocol, the HDLC frame addresses need to be assigned on a dynamic basis. These are the TEIs.

6.9 MAC protocols control access to a LAN and provide the physical address of the device in which Data Link Layer entities reside. MAC protocols support the LLC protocols. LLC controls the communication between entities and distinguishes between different entities within a device.

6.10 There are three types of Logical Link Control:
- LLC1 is an unacknowledged connectionless service;
- LLC2 is a connection oriented service similar to LAPB; and,
- LLC3 is an acknowledged connectionless mode.

6.11 The spanning tree protocol is used by LAN bridges to enable and disable the use of back-up paths between LAN segments. In effect, parallel routes are weighted for the optimum path to the target LAN. The spanning tree protocol is then broadcast periodically by each bridge and where a bridge detects that it has higher priority path to the target LAN, then it functions as the bridge while all other bridges enter the standby mode.

7   NETWORK LAYER

7.1   The term subnetwork is used to refer to a collection of intermediate systems of the same type of network technology such as X.25, ISDN or LANs. Subnetworks can be interconnected via interworking units (routers).

7.2   The terms CONS and CLNS refer to the two communications modes offered by networks. CONS being the Connection Oriented Network Service and CLNS the Connectionless Network Service.

7.3   The network service is an abstract interface within the end system and is network independent. The network protocol is visible outside the system and is generally technology dependent, e.g. X.25, ISDN or LANs. The exception to this technology dependence is the Internet Protocol (OSI IP) which is carried over the top of the network dependent protocols and is used to provide a uniform interface to the network service user.

7.4   Virtual circuits multiplex network connections. Each X.25 virtual circuit is identified within the X.25 protocol by a distinct Logical Channel Number.

7.5   ISO 8473 is referred to as IP because it is an Internet Protocol. Its use is primarily to provide a generalized end to end network service over different interconnected subnetworks. A major facility provided by this protocol is the carriage of called and calling NSAP addresses. As NSAPs can (and should) be network protocol independent and since some network dependent protocols do not offer explicit fields to carry this necessary information, IP must be used.

7.6   Connectionless network nodes are designed to discard packets in the event of severe congestion. This is because there is no explicit connection reference held by interconnected nodes to signal flow control procedures in a connectionless environment.

7.7   ES–IS and IS–IS are classified as routing protocols. Routing protocols are used by these network nodes to publish their existence and their ability to route protocol elements to other ESs and ISs.

8   INTERNETWORKING

8.1   The answer is organization dependent.

8.2   An NSAP should be network protocol independent and constructed in such a way that it is globally unique and of a common universal format. Subnetwork addresses on the other hand are generally confined to the technology they operate on, e.g. X.25 uses X.121, ISDN uses E.164, etc. Although public subnetwork addresses can be allocated from a global address numbering scheme, they are not explicitly mandated to do this and they don't accommodate addressing within private subnetworks. Subnetwork addresses can be in fact just an arbitary range of numbers used within the confines of the subnetwork.

8.3   The E.163, E.164 and X.121 are network specific addressing schemes. Traditionally, these are used for the PSTN, X.25 packet switching and ISDN networks respectively. Recent extensions to these standards permit the use of X.121 addresses for packet mode services over ISDN and the use of E.164 addresses in X.25 via the use of the A bit and Type Of Address (TOA) indicator (defined in 1988 version of X.25 and the X.300 series of Recommendations).

8.4   See Figure C.1.

8.5   No answer supplied.

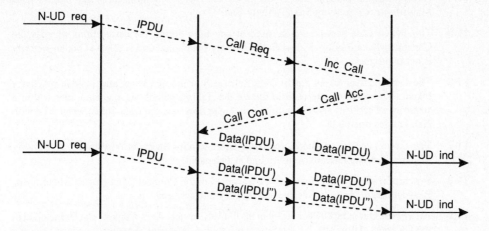

Figure C.1   Answer to internetworking tutorial.

9   TRANSPORT LAYER

9.1   There are five classes of Transport protocol (classes 0–4). Class 0 and 1 are the non-multiplexed classes and classes 2, 3 and 4 are the multiplexed classes.

9.2   The credit mechanism is used in classes 2, 3 and 4 transport connections to provide flow control of the data transfer. Credit values are conveyed in the Connection and Data Acknowledge TPDUs.

9.3   The Expedited service and protocol is used to convey control information between the Transport service users. The main reason for the expedited service is that it bypasses the flow control mechanisms of the normal data. Therefore, the Expedited service can be used to signal congestion or buffer shortage problems occurring in one end system to the peer entity in another.

9.4   Combine Figure 9.3, page 165, and Figure 7.7, page 113.

10   UPPER LAYERS

11   SESSION LAYER

11.1   The Session Layer provides a uniform set of dialogue control and synchronization services for communicating applications. It provides the mechanism for the session user (the application) to insert a standardized set of "punctuation marks" into the data stream of the application dialogue.

11.2   The Application Layer entities must define their rules for the use of the session services i.e. align their processing to use the session dialogue services (activities, etc) and synchronization point reference numbers, and the control and processing of tokens.

11.3   The session functional units are; Kernel, Negotiated Release, Half Duplex, Duplex, Expedited Data, Typed Data, Capability Data Exchange, Minor Synchronize, Symmetric Synchronize, Major Synchronize, Exceptions and Activity. The use of these functional units and the session services that they represent is negotiated at connection establishment.

11.4   An application dialogue unit is bound by the major synchronization services such as Major-Sync and Activity-Start, Activity-End.

11.5   The Typed Data service can be used at any time during the association, whereas the Capability Data is only valid when the Activity Functional unit is selected but an Activity is not in progress.

11.6   The Session Layer tokens are the Data, Release, Synchronize Minor and the Major/Activity tokens. These tokens are used to dictate the rights available to a session user within a sequence of services and to control the dialogue flow, e.g. the Data Token when used with Half Duplex operation.

11.7   The session services related to activities are: Activity Start, Activity Interrupt, Activity Resume, Activity Discard, Activity End and Capability Data.

11.8   Synchronization point references are conveyed in the Connect, Minor Sync, Major Sync, Resynchronize, Activity Resume and Activity End services.

11.9   All SPDUs can in fact be conveyed in the T-Data service. An S-Connect can be included in the T-Connect User Data, but this is implementation dependent. Session Expedited Data and Prepare PDUs may be conveyed in the T-Expedited service if it is available.

12   PRESENTATION LAYER

12.1   The Presentation Layer transforms between the application's local syntax (e.g. C structures representing the ASN.1 notation of the application protocol) to the transfer syntax (e.g. the ASN.1 Basic Encoding Rules). In other words, the conversion of syntax between that transferred between the application peers and the syntax that is used by the application.

12.2   The Presentation Context is the relationship formed between a specific abstract syntax definition and a transfer syntax definition for a presentation connection.

12.3   The parameters that are passed from the Application Layer when requesting a presentation connection are the called and calling PSAPs, the presentation context lists, presentation requirements (functional units), and the session service requirements.

12.4   A Presentation Service Access Point locates an application entity within an OSI end system. A presentation address is a concatenation of PSAP/SSAP/TSAP/NSAP selectors.

12.5   The Presentation Layer's functional units are the kernel functional unit, the context management functional unit and the context restoration functional unit.

12.6   The Presentation Layer restores the presentation context to that which was in use at the time of the synchronization point number specified in the resynchonize service request.

12.7   The Context Definition List is a list of context identifiers that is passed in the P-Connect and used by the presentation service users to negotiate the presentation contexts for use during the association.

12.8   Generally there is a one to one mapping between sesion and presentation, e.g. a presentation connection maps only onto a session connection. Thus little or no presentation PCI is required to determine what is the type of presentation protocol unit. Thus a PPDU is implicitly "typed" by its mapping between the presentation services to the session services.

12.9   If new attributes and services are added to an application, the presentation context (referencing the formatters and parsers) must be upgraded to suit the added abstract syntax. This should mean a new abstract syntax and presentation context identifiers.

13 ABSTRACT SYNTAX NOTATION ONE

13.1 ASN.1 is a notation tool for defining protocols. It is specifically used for OSI Application and Presentation layer protocols. ASN.1 standards also define Basic Encoding Rules that dictate how the abstract syntax is coded for transmission.

13.2 The majority (if not all) of the Application Layer standards use ASN.1.

13.3 The presentation protocol itself is defined in ASN.1 and, the Presentation Layer takes the derived structures of the abstract syntax and converts them to Basic Encoding Rules (the transfer syntax).

13.4 ASN.1 notation is used to define the Application Layer protocol in terms of application specific types (e.g. "Name"). BER is a set of rules that govern its encoding, e.g. a PrintableString.

13.5 A context specific tag is used uniquely to identify the protocol elements within a nested group of elements. This is used where some elements are of the same syntax type and/or are optional within the group. The term context specific means that the tag value itself is meaningful only within the bounds of its group.

13.6 The constructor bit in the tag field indicates whether to interpret the contents as a primitive encoding or as a constructed encoding. It is also used to permit implementations of ASN.1 to segment application level protocol fields, i.e. an implementation dependent application protocol segmentation mechanism, e.g. an Octet string could be encoded as a concatenated series of shorter strings.

13.7 The options that can be used in encoding the length of a value field are;
- Explicit length; i.e. the length field is set to the actual length (single octet and multi-octet forms are permitted.
- Indefinite length indicator (hex 80) and terminating the value field with End of Contents indicator (EOC hex 0000). Indefinite length form can only be used with constructed encoding.

13.8 ANY indicates the encoded data can be any of the defined types within the current context. EXTERNAL specifes that the encoded data belongs to another context.

13.9 The purpose of an ASN.1 compiler is to take the abstract syntax as defined by a specific standard and convert it into program structures, data and value definitions and also produce the source code for formatting and parsing these data structure elements into Basic Encoding Rules.

14 APPLICATION LAYER

14.1 An application context is the set of rules for combining various Application Service Elements (ASEs) and abstract syntaxes that together define an application protocol used for communication between application entities.

14.2 ACSE is a standard way for applications to establish and terminate communications. RTSE transfers bulk data on behalf of applications. ROSE is a basic form of procedure call between applications in different open systems. CCR allows applications to implement a two phase commit procedure.

15 MESSAGE HANDLING SYSTEMS

15.1 The answer is organization dependent.

15.2   The major differences between the 1984 and 1988 version of X.400 are the inclusion of, and support for, the Message Store, security features, physical delivery systems, X.500 Directory interworking and distribution list expansion. In addition, the 1988 version makes full use of the Presentation Layer and standardized ASEs.

15.3   The protocols used between the major components of the MHS are P2 and P7 between the UA and MS; P3 between the UA or MS and the MTA; and P1 between the MTAs.

15.4   An O/R address is the Originator/Recipient address used to identify the entities associated with a message. As the O/R address is used by the MTAs to route and deliver messages, each MTA must be configured to identify which path the message (or copies of the message) should take. The O/R addressing hierarchy determines the MTS configuration.

15.5   The components of a message when being transferred within the MTS are the P1 envelope and the P2 IPM (Heading and Body). The majority of the P1 fields are derived from the P2.

15.6   The basic functions of an MTA are delivery, conversion, copying, routing and transfer.

15.7   The delivery report (MTS) and receipt notification mechanisms can be used to determine whether messages arrive at their destination.

15.8   The Message Store provides the MHS users with the ability to sort, list and administer their messages based on the message attributes and a message selection criteria.

15.9   The Message Store needs to know about message attributes in order to process messages with user supplied selection criteria (e.g List, Fetch, etc).

15.10   The X.500 directory is used for Distribution List expansion, to resolve Directory names and for security services. The changes to the X.400 permit a Directory name to be used in place of an O/R address. Also additional attributes are added to P1 to control DL expansion and provide information about the DL expansion points (DL history).

16   X.500 DIRECTORY

16.1   The DIT defines the Directory structure (a tree) and has structure rules applied. The DIB is the instance of the Directory entries within one or more DSAs that are organized as per the DIT.

16.2   The ASEs of the DAP are Read, Search and Modify. The services these ASEs support are:

Read   Read, Compare, Abandon.

Search   Search, List.

Modify   Add/Remove Entry, Modify Entry, Modify RDN.

16.3   A Distinguished Name is used to navigate the DIB to access a DIB entry.

16.4   The Remove service destroys an entry in the DIB, the Modify RDN changes the name of the entry. These services can only be applied to leaf entries, otherwise they would fragment or possibly corrupt the DIB.

16.5   The naming context indicates the portion of the DIB that a DSA is responsible for. A context prefix is null on the DSA containg the ultimate ROOT node of the Directory. The context prefix of the subordinate DSA is the sequence of RDNs from the root of the DIT to the initial entry of a naming context.

16.6   DSAs are interconnected to allow geographic distribution or back-up of the data (replication) or to allow fragmentation of the DIB for administration or organizational purposes.

16.7 A DSA knows that it must access another DSA when it reaches a reference to another DSA during Name Resolution. If the entry type is an NSSR or Cross reference (another DSA), the DSA uses this reference to chain the active request to it.

16.8 The three major areas of data verification applied with the Directory are:

Name binding rules	This ensures that name form attribute types (of the Distinguished Name) are consistent with the class hierarchy of the DIB; e.g an entry named by a Country Name is not placed under a entry type named by Person. These naming rules are referred to as DIT structure rules.
Object class rules	This ensures that entries defined by an object class maintain the valid attribute types for that class, e.g a Person's Name attribute is not added to a Street Address.
Attribute syntax rules	These ensure that the attribute types declared for a given object class maintain their defined syntax, e.g. a numeric string is not stored into a Person's Name.

16.9 To limit the scope of the response from a DSA the user can specify size and time limits in the Service Controls parameter.

16.10 The additional information stored with the users data is referred to as the operational attributes of that entry. These attributes hold administrative information about the entry, e.g. entry type, DSA references, access information, master/copy flags, etc.

17 FILE TRANSFER, ACCESS AND MANAGEMENT

17.1 The FTAM standard has the following services:

Transfer	The ability to read and write whole files and transfer them between FTAM peers.
Access	The ability to locate and modify records within the file (and erase the file).
Management	Create and delete files and change the file attributes, e.g. change the file name or modify the access control attributes of the file.

17.2 A service class is an organizational aspect of the FTAM service. The service classes are: File Transfer, File Access, File Management, File Transfer and Management and an Unconstrained class. Service classes provide a logical grouping of the FTAM functional units. (The Unconstrained class permits customized grouping of the FTAM functional units.)

17.3 The virtual file store is an abstracted view of the real file system. It is defined so that independent implementations can share a common view of a real resource. The virtual file store defines the organizational and structure aspects of the file store (e.g. Directory and File hierarchy, File types, access constraints, file structure and file attributes, etc). It also implicitly, by the definition of certain file attributes, defines mechanisms to deal with file access control and file access concurrency.

17.4 Files are represented as a set of data units organized in a hierarchical structure.

17.5 The file attributes provide information about the file, e.g. the file's creator, the file name, its access controls, its size, etc. These attributes are explicitly accessed by the FTAM Read and Change Attribute operations.

17.6 The regime concept is a nested state machine mechanism for FTAM. This (regime) state machine indicates what overall stage the file operations have reached and what are the operations that are permitted next. In basic terms, it is an "operations progress" indicator (i.e. the file is selected, opened, etc.) and a sequencing validation mechanism (what operation(s) are valid next).

17.7   Group operations permit a set of FTAM operations to be sent to an FTAM responder and actioned in a compact sequence. The Begin group and End Group services encapsulate a set of FTAM services, e.g. Begin Group, Select, Open, Write, Close, Deselect, End Group. When used in this way the responder attempts all the services in one action and responds (with a sequence of responses) when the action in full is complete.

17.8   The difference between a Select and an Open operation is that file selection must be performed before any other action can be performed on the file. But selection on its own only permits action on the file attributes or an Open to be performed. An Open (peformed after a Selection) permits the reading and writing of a file and the locating components of the file.

17.9   An FTAM user needs to understand the structure of the virtual file store. Specifically, the FTAM user needs to understand the directory and file hierarchy, and the structure of the files. An FTAM user may also manage the virtual file store by changing file attributes and adding files and directories. So the FTAM user is no different to any file store user or manager, except the terminology and access procedures are those as defined by FTAM.

17.10   The FTAM user needs to understand the structure of a file within the virtual file store because the file structure (and file type) will have to be declared as a basis for communication in the FTAM association. Files within the FTAM environment have a Document type (e.g. FTAM 1, 2, 3) indicating the file structure; a constraint set (that defines what operations can be performed on that file type); a set of file parameters (indicating string length of records, etc) and a universal class indicating the string type used within the file (e.g. Visible string, IA5 string, etc). Therefore, an FTAM user is required to understand fully the file being accessed.

18   VIRTUAL TERMINAL

18.1   The CCA is the Conceptual Communications Area that provides "the common view" of a terminal device to both the application and the terminal driver mechanisms. The three main components of the CCA are Display Objects, Control Objects and Device Objects.

18.2   The two modes of VT are the S (Synchronous) mode and the A (Asynchronous) mode. The S mode provides the environment where the host sends a form to the terminal, the terminal (via the keyboard) modifies the display (form) in the local environment and once completed, sends the updates to the host. There is one display object (for the keyboard and screen). In the A mode, the terminal keyboard data is sent via its own display object to the host. The data from the host is sent independently to the screen (via its own display object).

18.3   The three main characteristics of the display object are:
- The number of dimensions and bound of the array (x, y, z capability and maximum).
- The field capabilities, e.g. field definitions within the array dimensions.
- The capabilities of character rendition, e.g. repetoire, colour, font, etc.

18.4   The FEPCO is used to determine the action from a specific input event (e.g. of a specific character) within a certain context.

19 SYSTEMS MANAGEMENT

19.1 The five functional areas of management are Configuration, Fault, Accounting, Performance and Security. These functional areas are for organizational purposes only to classify the standards. They are not functional standards themselves.

19.2 The MIB is the Management Information Base used by management as a repository for managed objects. The MIB is abstract in so far as it does not physically exist or reside in one specific end system. (Similar concepts to the Conceptual Communication Area in VT and the Virtual File Store in FTAM.)

19.3 A Managed Object is a management view of an object representing an OSI resource.

19.4 An LME is a Layer Management Entity. This entity is an abstract component of an OSI layer that has management functions and interfaces (at the side of the layer) to the systems mangement function. LMEs are accessed as part of the MIB via "internal means" and not by specific (N)-Layer defined services.

19.5 The four areas of scope covered by the management standards are the Architecture, the Management Information Model, Management Communications and the Management Functions. These areas are covered by the Management Framework and Overview documents (ISO 7498/4, ISO 10040), the Structure of Management Information documents (ISO 10165/x), the CMISE/P documents (ISO 9595 and ISO 9596) and the Systems Management function documents (ISO 10164/x).

19.6 SNMP has a subset of similar operations to that of CMIP, e.g. GET and SET (TRAP in SNMP = CMIP EVENT). Also, the data transferred between the "Manager" and the "Agent" is encoded in ASN.1 BER. Beyond this, inconsistencies occur mainly due to the unrestricted fields and sophistication of CMIP. SNMP was designed for simple networks; CMIP has been designed for distributed systems management.

19.7 TMN models the functional management requirements of specific telecommunications technologies (e.g. ISDN) using the OSI reference model and OSI systems management standards. TMN uses managed objects and CMISE/P to underpin such telecommunications management functions.

19.8 The main characteristics of a managed object are Naming, its Object Class and its attributes, its Behaviour, its Operations, its parameters, its Actions and Notifications.

19.9 The Manager and Agent role historically were tied to fixed processes or products, as in SNMP Managers and Agents. Within a fully distributed OSI environment, the manager and agent role are determined for the instance of communication. Thus two peer management processes can perform either or both manager or agent roles depending on the nature of the interactions and their capability.

19.10 Managed objects are similar to X.500 directory entries in so far as they have Object Classes (therefore structure rules) and can be addressed using the same naming syntax, i.e. Distinguished Names. So from a broad perspective, a tree of managed objects directly resembles a tree of directory entries. However, the application protocols applied to them are CMIP and DAP respectively.

20 DISTRIBUTED TRANSACTION PROCESSING

20.1 The four attributes associated with a unit of work are: Atomicity, Consistency, Isolation and Durability.

20.2 The common application services that support DTP are ACSE, ROSE and CCR, CCR being the primary service actually supporting the distributed two phase commit procedure.

20.3 The transaction tree is a set of interlinked nodes all of which attempt to participate in a concurrent transaction under control of the Superior node. Other nodes are referred to as subordinates.

20.4 The DTP standard does not in fact define the actual transaction. DTP only defines the boundary actions necessary to encapsulate the transaction.

20.5 A node that cannot perform (commit to) the completion of a transaction issues a Rollback response to its Superior. This is propogated to all other TP nodes which then restore all initial values.

21   OPEN DOCUMENT ARCHITECTURE

21.1 The purpose of ODA is to define a consistent, universal encoding scheme for the representation of documents for electronic transfer and storage.

21.2 The predecessor of the ODA standard is the Teletex recommendation CCITT T.73.

21.3 The three major aspects of an ODA document specification are the document architecture and structure, the contents (characters, graphics, etc) and the document style(s) (which control the layout).

21.4 The difference between a logical view and a layout view is that a logical view dictates the document's structure (e.g. a Chapter has a Heading and Paragraphs) and the layout view dictates placement of the logical components.

21.5 In processable form, the document can be edited. In the formatted form, the layout information has been added and the document can be printed.

21.6 In ODA, the components of the document have object classes. Thus, objects defined by an object class have structure rules defining their relationships with other objects, and attributes that they can contain; e.g. Object classes indicate Layout Descriptors, Logical Descriptors, Text Units and Profile Descriptors, etc.

21.7 The syntax notation used to specify the components of an ODA document is ASN.1.

21.8 ODIF is a machine readable notation (ASN.1) for the definition of a documents construction and SGML is a human readable markup language, e.g. used for publishing.

21.9 Both ODA and X.400 MHS are ISO standards directed at messaging. ODA is document construction. X.400 is message transfer.

21.10 ODA unifies the document structures within an organization. In the past (and still today) many parts of an organization have different, incompatible software and machines for document handling. This duplication and inefficiency would be improved if a consistent document storage format was used, i.e. ODA.

22   DOCUMENT TRANSFER AND MANIPULATION

22.1 ODA defines the document construction and DTAM provides the service environment for document transfer.

22.2 DTAM services provide document transfer and manipulation facilities, e.g. create, modify and delete, etc.

22.3   The main purpose of DFR is to provide a consistent way by which documents can be referenced and organized. It also permits the document storage to be searched for specific document references.

22.4   The DFR standard only specifies attributes and modeling concepts. The DFR user is totally responsible for the organization and management of documents.

22.5   There is a similarity between the majority of the DFR and X.500 service elements, because they both deal with object storage and the oganizational aspects of storing objects. However, there are major differences between the respective services they deliver.

22.6   DFR is a document storage system and X.500 is a knowledge base. DFR has no knowledge or mechanisms to deal with the document content. X.500 has to know explicitly every object class, attribute (the content) and name form used by the X.500 entry.

22.7   A DFR Group is a collection point that can be referenced for other DFR objects.

22.8   A Search Result List is an object that represents a list of DFR objects that is fomulated by the DFR service as the result of a search. This list can be either read by the DFR User or, used as a subsequent specification with an operation (e.g a List).

22.9   A DFR reference points to another object (a reference or document or group). It is used in the DFR system to avoid duplication and replication of DFR objects.

22.10   DFR is used to store and organize documents, DTAM is used to transfer and manipulate documents, ODA is used to define the construction syntax of documents and, X.400 can be used to provide the transfer system for documents (as messages).

23   ELECTRONIC DATA INTERCHANGE

23.1   The three major EDI standards are EDIFACT, ANSI X12 and UNTDI. EDIFACT is now emerging as the unversal EDI standard.

23.2   The five levels of information used to form an EDI exchange are the transaction (or interchange), the function group (optional), the message, the segment and the data items (attributes).

23.3   The component parts of the EDI (EDIFACT) message syntax are:

UNA	The Service String Advice.
UNB	The Interchange header.
UNG	The Functional Group.
UNH	The Message header.

The trailers are UNZ, UNE and UNT for interchange, functional group and message respectively.

23.4   EDI is supported by X.400 MHS either by using the P2 IPM and placing the EDI message as a body part of a IPM message or, by the use of PEDI protocol that maps EDIFACT fields into the PEDI heading. The normal IPM does not support the specialized message forwarding and message notification mechanisms offered by PEDI.

23.5   One identifies the value of EDI in general terms by:
- evaluating the paper processing methods and mechanisms within your organization;
- identify the value of the stock holding caused by this; and,
- identify the trading partners that would mutually benefit by reducing the abovementioned costs.

23.6   If IPM is used as the transfer service, the notification processing will have to be customized within the application. If PEDI is used, the application can use the notification mechanisms supported by the PEDI protocol.

23.7   EDI affects your trading partners and you because of the level of investment in a mechanism that ties (commits) a trading relationship for a reasonable period. Because EDI primarily customizes a set of interchanges for a specific need between trading partners, then a longer term view of the relationship is required. Such joint relationships may extend to the management of the system that supports the EDI service.

D Bibliography

T. Knowles, J. Larmouth, K. G. Knightson, *Standards for Open Systems Interconnection*, BSP Professional Books, 1987.

Fred Halsall, *Data Communications, Computer Networks and OSI*, 2nd Edition, Addison Wesley Publications, Wokingham, England, 1988.

J. Henshall, S. Shaw, *OSI Explained*, Ellis Horwood, Chichester, 1988.

Andrew Tanenbaum, *Computer Networks*, 2nd Edition, Prentice Hall, New Jersey, 1989.

Douglas Steedman, *Abstract Syntax Notation One (ASN.1) — The Tutorial and Reference*, Technology Appraisals Ltd, Isleworth, Middlesex, 1990.

Marshall Rose, *The Open Book — A Practical Perspective on OSI*, Prentice Hall, New Jersey, 1990.

William Stallings, *Handbook of Computer Communications Standards*, Volume 2, Howard W. Sams and Company, Carmel, 1990.

Uyless Black, *OSI, a Model for Computer Communications Standards*, Prentice Hall, New Jersey, 1991.

UK Government, Central Computer and Communications Agency, *UK Government OSI Profile*, Version 3.1, Her Majesty's Stationery Office, London, 1990.

Australian Government, Information Exchange Steering Committee, *Australian Government Open Systems Interconnection Profile*, Version 2, Australian Government Publishing Service, Canberra, 1990.

National Institute for Standards and Technology, F. Boland, Editor, *Stable Implementation Agreements for Open Systems Interconnection Protocols*, Version 3 Edition 1, IEEE Computer Society Press, Los Alamitos, 1990.

E   Index